april 2004

Ships of the Great Lakes Cookbook

Discover Their
Culinary Legends

Creative Characters Publishing Group

Ships of the Great Lakes Cookbook

Discover Their Culinary Legends

Researched and written by PK McKenna
Cover design by J. Bodis

Published by
Creative Characters Publishing Group
P.O. Box 217
Eastport, Michigan 49627
www.cookbookpublishing.com

Library of Congress Catalog Card Number: 2001091480

ISBN: 0-9711148-0-3

On the cover: *T.S. Playfair, S.S. Courtney Burton,* and *S.S. Keewatin* Dining Room. Back cover from top: *U.S. Brig Niagara* used with permission of *U.S. Brig Niagara*, photo by Lowry Photography, Erie, PA; *S.S. Keewatin, S.S. Badger* and *Lightship Huron* used with permission (see acknowledgements); *USCGC Mackinaw* used with permission of www.boatnerd.com.

Cover photo:
S.S. Courtney Burton - Sea Smoke
©Todd L. Davidson
Great Lakes Maritime Collections, Ltd. 2001
No reproductions of the photograph without the expressed written consent of the photographer.

Printed and bound in the United States of America

Acknowledgements

Never have the words "thank you" seemed as inadequate as they do when it comes to expressing gratitude for the help received in compiling information for this book. The individuals and organizations acknowledged here gave generously of their time, memories, archives and patience, often answering the same question several times as we sought a clear understanding of life on the Great Lakes. Knowing the importance of the Great Lakes in each of their lives, hopefully extending a "Great Lakes Thank You" to each of them more clearly conveys our gratitude.

We extend a Great Lakes Thank You to… John Polacsek, Director at the Dossin Great Lakes Museum in Detroit, Michigan for his initial guidance and help in putting this project in perspective; Philip J. Leier at The J.W. Westcott Company in Detroit, Michigan for his help in selecting ships and his time in delivering all the mail we continuously sent through the Detroit Marine Post Office; Frank Cornacchi for his friendship, for sharing his many years on the Great Lakes and for performing special photo assignments; Charles H. Truscott, Historian, for answering numerous emails containing hundreds of questions, for allowing us use of his own writings, for generously opening his archives to us and professionally reproducing even our slightest request, and for the many hours it took him to do it all; Donald J. Thurow for his invaluable knowledge on the history of the United States Coast Guard and for a lengthy and informative tour of the *Huron Lightship*; Thomas Hawley, Director of Public Relations on the Lake Michigan Car Ferry for use of his extensive historical writings and an in-depth tour of the S.S. *Badger*; Jim and Louise Plant for their time in conducting a personal tour through the S.S. *Milwaukee Clipper* and answering hundreds of questions along the way; Bob and Cindy Zimmerman for sharing excerpts from their upcoming book <u>Ninety Years Young: The Story of the S.S. Keewatin 1907-1997</u>, before its publication; Arlene and Dick Earl for openly sharing their personal family history and their hospitality, lakeside, with freighters passing within 200 feet; Julie Hayes Moe and Gert Hayes for opening their personal family photo albums and painting a vivid picture of life on the Great Lakes during the 1950s and 1960s; and George Yaworski, Retired Steward, for sharing his memories and writings, and answering countless questions on the day-to-day operation of a freighter's galley.

In addition, we thank the following individuals and organizations associated with each featured ship for their time in supplying us with historical information, photographs and recipes, and for generously allowing us to reproduce their information in illustrating life on the Great Lakes:

TALL SHIPS

Wisconsin's Flagship *Denis Sullivan*: Carrie M. O'Malley, Director of Operations, Wisconsin Lake Schooner Education Association; Kelly, WLSEA; Laurie Deely, WLSEA.
Photos Courtesy of Wisconsin Lake Schooner Education Association.

Schooner *Madeline*: Joni Robb and Bev Denyas, Maritime Heritage Alliance of Traverse City, Michigan. Edwin P. Brown, Founding Member, MHA.
Photos Courtesy of Maritime Heritage Alliance of Traverse City.

Tall Ship *Malabar* and Tall Ship *Manitou*: Kathy McAndrews, Stacie Kohler and Joni Pennington, Traverse Tall Ship Company, Traverse City, Michigan.
Photos Courtesy of Traverse Tall Ship Company.

U.S. Brig *Niagara*: Mary Jo Yonkers, Flagship Niagara League; Richard E. Liebel, Jr., Public Relations and Marketing, U.S. Brig Niagara. "Resapee for Bred" recipe courtesy of the Naval Academy Women's Club.
Photos Courtesy of U.S. Brig Niagara.

Tall Ship *Pathfinder* and Tall Ship *Playfair*: Lesley McLean and Kathy, Tall Ship Adventures, Toronto, Ontario, Canada.
Photos Courtesy of Tall Ship Adventures.

Tall Ship *Windy*: Captain Robert Marthai and Janine Marthai, *Tall Ship Windy*.
Photos Courtesy of Tall Ship Windy.

FREIGHTERS

M.V. *Algosoo:* Lois Sutch, Chief Cook. *Photos Courtesy of Lois Sutch.*

M.T. *Anglian Lady:* Frank A. Cornacchi, Steward; Purvis Marine, Ltd.
Photos Courtesy of Frank A. Cornacchi and Purvis Marine, Ltd.

M.T. *Atlantic Hickory:* Jeffrey Wilcox, Steward. *Photos Courtesy of Jeffrey Wilcox.*

M.V. *Canadian Enterprise:* Nikki Caldwell, Steward. *Photos Courtesy of Nikki Caldwell.*

M.V. *Canadian Miner:* Bernice Piercey, Chief Cook. *Photos Courtesy of Bernice Piercey.*

M.V. *Canadian Progress:* Tony Carter, Steward. *Photos Courtesy of Tony Carter.*

S.S. *Courtney Burton:* Todd Stewart, Steward. *Photos Courtesy of Todd Stewart.*

M.V. *English River:* Roderick Sandiford, Steward. *Photos Courtesy of Roderick Sandiford.*

M.V. *George Stinson:* Cornelius J. Gleason, Steward. *Photos Courtesy of Cornelius J. Gleason.*

M.V. *Indiana Harbor:* Dawn W. Weymouth, Steward. *Photos Courtesy of Dawn W. Weymouth.*

M.V. *Oglebay Norton:* Calvin Statham, Sr., Steward *Photos Courtesy of Calvin Statham, Sr.*

M.V. *Paul R. Tregurtha:* John R. Duning, Chief Cook. *Photos Courtesy of John R. Duning.*

M.V. *Sauniere:* Linda Orr, Steward. *Photos Courtesy of Linda Orr.*

M.V. *Steven B. Roman:* Frank A. Cornacchi, Steward. *Photos Courtesy of Frank A. Cornacchi.*

U.S. COAST GUARD

Dr. Robert Browning, U.S. Coast Guard Historian's Office, Washington, D.C.; Gerald B. Smith, Executive Director, Grand Haven Coast Guard Festival, Inc.; Lt. Mike Putlock, Operations Officer, USCGC Bristol.
Photos Courtesy of United States Coast Guard.

USCGC *Bramble:* Food Service Specialist 1st Class Brian P. Jackman, U.S. Coast Guard.
Photos Courtesy of Food Service Specialist 1st Class Brian P. Jackman.

USCGC *Mackinaw:* FSC Richard Reynolds, Food Service Officer, U.S. Coast Guard
Photos Courtesy of FSC Richard Reynolds.

PASSENGER VESSELS

MTS *Arcadia:* Ralph Diehl, Great Lakes Cruises, Inc. Waukesha, Wisconsin.
Photos Courtesy of Ralph Diehl.

S.S. *Badger:* Thomas Hawley, Director of Public Relations, Lake Michigan Car Ferry, Ludington, Michigan; Laura Fulker, 1st Cook; Jerry and Sally Cole, Cole's Antique Villa, Ludington, Michigan.
Photos Courtesy of Thomas Hawley; Menus Courtesy of Jerry and Sally Cole.

M.V. *Columbus:* Meike Holland, Hapag-Lloyd, AG, Hamburg, Germany. Lisa Marciniak, Seaway Port Authority of Duluth; Mitch Veldkamp, Instructor of the German Language, Creston High School, Grand Rapids, Michigan (recipe translations). *Photos Courtesy of Hapag-Lloyd, Hamburg, Germany.*

RETIRED SHIPS

Museum Ship *Alexander Henry:* Jo-Anne Lachapelle-Beyak, Public Services Manager, Marine Museum of the Great Lakes at Kingston. *Photos Courtesy of Marine Museum of the Great Lakes at Kingston.*

Huron Lightship Museum: Donald S. Thurow, *Huron Lightship* Museum, Port Huron, Michigan. Neil C. Hamilton, for use of poem "The *Huron Lightship.*" *Photos Courtesy of Donald J. Thurow and Creative Characters Publishing Group.*

S.S. *Keewatin:* Diane Peterson and Kathy Murphy, *Keewatin* Marine Museum, Douglas, Michigan; Bob and Cindy Zimmerman, *S.S. Keewatin* Researchers (and authors of Ninety Years Young; The Story of the S.S. *Keewatin* 1907-1997; Helen Seppala, recipe research.
Photos Courtesy of S.S. Keewatin Research; John Borkowski, Borkowski Advertising, Inc., Southbend, Indiana.

Michigan State Car Ferries: Mark Howell, Mark Howell Productions, Muskegon, Michigan; Frank J. Kelley; Richard Therrian, Steward; Charles H. Truscott, Historian; Marion Y. Gorton. *Photos Courtesy of Richard Therrian and Charles H. Truscott, Historian. 1951 Car Ferry Schedule Courtesy of Charles H. Truscott Collection.*

S.S. Milwaukee Clipper: Charles H. Truscott, Historian; Captain Robert Priefer; Jim and Mary Louise Plant, Sue Wiegers; Mark Howell. *Photos Courtesy of S.S. Milwaukee Clipper Preservation, Inc., Charles H. Truscott Collection.*

S.S. Valley Camp: Charlotte Hendrickson and Phyllis Weaver, Historic Museum Ship *Valley Camp*, Sault Ste. Marie Historical Sites, Sault Ste. Marie, Michigan. *Photos Courtesy of Sault Ste. Marie Historical Sites.*

Steamer William A. Irvin: Dennis Medgo, Director, The *Steamer William A. Irvin*; Jody Aho, (author of The Steam *William A. Irvin*, Queen of the Silver Stackers) *Photos Courtesy of Jody Aho.*

Steamship William G. Mather: Kristy Nolan, Assistant Director, *Steamship William G. Mather* Museum; George Yaworski, Retired Steward and current tour guide, *Steamship William G. Mather* Museum. *Photos Courtesy of Steamship William G. Mather Museum; Photos of Mather China Courtesy of Daniel C. Krummes (author of Dining on the Inland Seas.)*

SPECIAL INTEREST

Arlene Earl, "Flower Lady of the Great Lakes": Dick and Arlene Earl.
Photos Courtesy of Dick and Arlene Earl.

Lawrence Hayes, Steward: Julie Hayes Moe and Gert Hayes.
Photos Courtesy of Julie Hayes Moe and Gert Hayes.

George Yaworski, Steward: George Yaworski.
Photos Courtesy of George Yaworski.

General Information:

Christine Highsmith, American Sail Training Association, Newport, Rhode Island; Michigan History Magazine, Lansing, Michigan; Martha Long, The Great Lakes Historical Society, Vermilion, Ohio; Jan M. Holt, Great Lakes Shipwreck Historical Society; Sault Ste. Marie, Michigan.

Publications Referenced:

Ninety Years Young: The Story of the *S.S. Keewatin* 1907-1997, Bob and Cindy Zimmerman; News Release, International Marine Engineering, June 1920; The Steamer *William A. Irvin*, "Queen of the Silver Stackers", Jody Aho; U.S. Coast Guard Publication, *USCGC Mackinaw* (WAGB 83), 20874 (5-83) GL; U.S. Coast Guard Publication, Welcome Aboard the United States Coast Guard Cutter *Bramble* (WAB 392); U.S. Coast Guard Publication One Day, CG 7690-01-R01-1940 (7-94); Guardians of the Eighth Sea – A History of the U.S. Coat Guard on the Great Lakes, T. Michael O'Brien, Photojournalist First Class, United States Coast Guard; Steamboat Bills, Number 114 and Number 166, Steamship Historical Society of America, Providence, Rhode Island; St. Ignace News, September 23, 1982; Charlevoix County Press, December 23, 1987; Know Your Ships 1997 & 1998, Rogert LeLievre, Marine Publishing Co., Inc., Sault Ste. Marie, Michigan; Greenwood's and Dills' Lake Boats 97, Freshwater Press, Inc., Cleveland, Ohio. Before the Bridge – The Story of the Mackinac Straits Ferries, The *Milwaukee Clipper* – A Legend Saved, video documentaries produced by Mark Howell Productions, Muskegon, Michigan; The Ludington Car Ferry, *S.S. Badger* – Flagship for a Dream, video documentaries produced by Leben Productions, Saugatuck, Michigan; Lake Erie, Lake Superior, Lake Michigan, Lake Huron, Lake Ontario, by Ann Armbruster, Children's Press, New York, New York; MSN Encarta Learning Zone (www.encarta.msn.com); The Great Lakes Information Network (GLIN website); Microsoft Bookshelf Basics – Dictionary (website); Schooner Vocabulary (www.student.muskegon.cc.mi.us).

Each ship featured in *Ships of the Great Lakes…Discover Their Culinary Legends* was thoroughly researched to the best of our ability; spellings, dates, facts and photo credits were checked for accuracy. Recipes featured were also checked for accuracy, though admittedly not all tested in our kitchens. However, we did occasionally find two different answers to one question. If you discover an error or omission in our research, we welcome your input and corrections. Thank you.

Discover Their
Culinary Legends

WELCOME ABOARD...the voyage presented on these pages carries passengers on a culinary and historical cruise across the five Great Lakes of North America. Tall ships, passenger ships, Coast Guard vessels and magnificent steel freighters combine with beloved retired ships from days gone by in offering a glimpse into culinary secrets that have become legendary. Sailors from yesterday and today vividly bring to life an average day on board, from decks of ships that are anything but average, and talented cooks generously share their menus and recipes, bringing to life meals fit for kings and Great Lakes sailors!

Table of Contents

Legends of the Lakes

What is it about Great Lakes ships that we find so captivating? These vessels are fondly named, christened, bid bon voyage from docks filled with excited onlookers and welcomed home with equal fanfare. They are photographed, sketched, painted, written about and their passage faithfully followed from shore by millions of loyal ship watchers. They become "ours." When our magnificent ships are retired, we go to great lengths in preserving their memories and their well-earned place in the region's rich maritime history. And rightfully so, as most of the midwest section of North America owes its beginning, growth and continued prosperity to the dependable grand ships that sail the unpredictable waters of the Great Lakes.

Equally captivating are the sailors of the Great Lakes…a rare breed indeed, and as legendary in their own right as the ships they sail. We marvel at their courage, worry for their safety and pray for their quick return. Their loyalty and devotion to their ships and each other form a bond seldom seen between co-workers today. Shipmates become family for over nine months a year, depending on each other for friendship, encouragement, safety and even their lives.

One of the favorite members of every ship's crew has always been the steward. Seven days a week, from sun up to sundown, the steward can be found in the ship's galley preparing meals also legendary in their own right. Fantastic homemade meals, each prepared from scratch and each offering a feast to satisfy even the heartiest of appetites are common fare aboard ships that sail the Great Lakes. The aroma of freshly baked breads and rolls fills the galley early each morning, followed shortly thereafter by the bustle of chickens, steaks and seafood being prepared for the noon meal. Fresh salads and homemade desserts round out the day, and a never ending supply of cookies, snacks and other crew favorites stand ready for the asking. As you will soon discover, Great Lakes sailors eat well!

So again, we welcome you aboard some of the grandest ships ever to sail the Great Lakes. Your generous hosts are the sailors themselves. They've personally tested each recipe and wholeheartedly stand behind the meals they serve. You are welcomed into their galleys and dining rooms, invited to pull up a chair and proudly offered the culinary cruise of a Great Lakes lifetime!

Bon Appétit From the Sailors of the Great Lakes!

The Legendary Great Lakes

The magnificent ships, sailors and food presented on these pages would be nothing more than tales from far off seas if not for the legendary Great Lakes themselves. The natural beauty and wonder of Lake Ontario, Lake Erie, Lake Huron, Lake Michigan and Lake Superior combine to create the largest body of freshwater in the world. Together they hold approximately 20 percent of the fresh surface water on earth. As a group the area of their surface waters exceeds 94,000 square miles. When joined by rivers, canals and locks creating the St. Lawrence Seaway they present over 10,000 miles of natural shoreline and 6,000 miles of nautical highway connecting the Atlantic Ocean with the middle of North America. Numerous Native American groups originally fished and operated trade on the lakes including the Ojibwa, Ottawa, Algonquin, Erie, Iroquois, Huron, Fox, Winnebago, Kickapoo and Potawatomi. The importance of the Great Lakes in the development and growth of the region can be documented back centuries as the main route for exploration, raw materials, manufactured goods and even our ancestors. Today the waterway transports millions of dollars in commerce annually to the thriving ports scattered along U.S. and Canadian coastlines and out into the world beyond. Except for Lake Michigan, the lakes provide a natural border between Canada and the United States. It has long been a source of pride for both countries that the boundary requires no military supervision or protection.

Each of the five Great Lakes is legendary in its own right, holding records and playing host to numerous historical events responsible for making the region what it is today. Early French exploration, British-American naval battles, westward expansion and industrial revolutions have all taken place on the lakes. And the waters of each lake have tragically become the final resting place of many ships thought too sturdy and state-of-the-art to ever lose sight of the surface. Though sometimes called by different names — lakes, freshwater seas, sweet seas, inland oceans and the fifth coast of North America — they are always called unpredictable and more difficult to navigate than oceans. The statistics of each lake illustrate the size and magnitude of the waterway called home by the ships featured in this book and are the basis for many legends they have gathered over the centuries.

Lake Ontario

Smallest and most easterly of the Great Lakes, Lake Ontario is ranked the 14th largest lake in the world by surface area. Lake Ontario lies at the base of Niagara Falls. The oldest lighthouse on the U.S. side of the Great Lakes was set up at Fort Niagara in 1818.

Length:	193 Miles
Breadth:	53 Miles
Average Depth:	283 Feet
Maximum Depth:	802 Feet
Water Surface Area:	7,340 Sq. Miles
Shoreline Length:	712 Miles
Elevation:	243 Feet
Outlet:	St. Lawrence River to the Atlantic Ocean

Name: Champlain first called this body of water Lake St. Louis in 1632. In 1660 Creuxius gave it the name "Lacus Ontarius." Ontara in Iroquois means "lake," and "Ontario" means "beautiful lake."

Lake Erie

Fourth largest and southernmost of the Great Lakes, Lake Erie is ranked the 11th largest lake in the world by surface area. Lake Erie is the warmest and most biologically productive of the Great Lakes, providing walleye fishing widely considered the best in the world.

Length:	241 Miles
Breadth:	57 Miles
Average Depth:	62 Feet
Maximum Depth:	210 Feet
Water Surface Area:	9,910 Sq. Miles
Shoreline Length:	871 Miles
Elevation:	591 Feet
Outlet:	Niagara River and Welland Canal

Name: Most of the southern shore of this lake was at one time occupied by the Eries, a tribe of Indians from which the lake derived its name. This name is always mentioned by early French writers as meaning "cat." "Lac du Chat" means "Lake of the Cat." Many attribute this reference to the wild cat or panther.

Lake Huron

Second largest of the Great Lakes, Lake Huron is ranked the 5th largest freshwater lake in the world. Manitoulin Island, in Lake Huron, is the largest freshwater island in the world.

Length:	206 Miles
Breadth:	183 Miles
Average Depth:	195 Feet
Maximum Depth:	750 Feet
Water Surface Area:	23,000 Sq. Miles
Shoreline Length:	3,827 Miles
Elevation:	577 Feet
Outlet:	St. Clair River to Lake Erie

Name: Since its French discoverers knew nothing as yet of the other lakes, they originally called this body of water "La Mer Douce," the "sweet or freshwater sea." In 1656 the lake was referred to as "Karegnondi." Later French explorers met Indians in the area and call them "Huron." In French the word means "rough" and "untidy."

Lake Michigan

Third largest of the Great Lakes and the only one lying completely within the United States, Lake Michigan is ranked the sixth largest freshwater lake in the world. The world's largest freshwater dunes line the lakeshore.

Length:	307 Miles
Breadth:	118 Miles
Average Depth:	279 Feet
Maximum Depth:	925 Feet
Water Surface Area:	22,300 Sq. Miles
Shoreline Length:	1,638 Miles
Elevation:	577 Feet
Outlet:	Straits of Mackinac to Lake Huron

Name: Champlain originally called this body of water the "Grand Lac." In 1679 the lake became known as "Lac des Illinois" because it gave access to the country of Indians by that name. Through further exploration by Jolliet and Marquette, the lake received its final name of Michigan. Chippewa Indians called the lake "Michi-Guma," which means "big water." Over time Michi-guma became Michigan.

Lake Superior

Largest, deepest and most northwesterly of the Great Lakes, Lake Superior is one of the world's largest bodies of freshwater. Lake Superior could contain all the other Great Lakes plus three more lakes the size of Lake Erie.

Length:	350 Miles
Breadth:	160 Miles
Average Depth:	483 Feet
Maximum Depth:	1,332 Feet
Water Surface Area:	31,700 Sq. Miles
Shoreline Length:	2,726 Miles
Elevation:	600 Feet
Outlet:	St. Marys River to Lake Huron

Name: *The first French explorers approaching this great body of water referred to their discovery as "le lac Superieur." Translated, the expression means "Upper Lake," that is, the lake above Lake Huron. "Kitchi-gummi," a Chippewa Indian translation signifies Great-Water or Great-Lake.*

Language of the Lakes

Working with the men and women that sail and cook aboard Great Lakes vessels has been a wonderful experience. They graciously shared their favorite menus, recipes, culinary secrets and stories from across the region. The only problem was they shared their secrets in "their own language." We initially thought: *"The steward prepares food in the galley below deck, then serves it in the mess room where all hands eat in shifts and then share the latest scuttlebutt"* sounded a little primitive, if not downright barbaric! After quickly becoming bilingual, by learning the centuries-old language of the lakes, we returned and found the translation very appealing, if not downright mouth-watering: *"The talented cook creates a variety of homemade breads, rolls and entrées from scratch every day in the shiny modern kitchen located just below the main level of the ship. Crewmembers gather in their own fully appointed dining room and enjoy as much of everything as they want. Officers and guests dine on china at tables covered with white linen. Full menus, offering homemade soups, at least two entrées and an array of fresh desserts are common fare. After dinner, they linger over freshly brewed coffee, sharing the latest gossip."*

To aid in your navigation through the wonderful legends and recipes from the Great Lakes shared in this book, we offer the following definitions to nautical terms you will encounter:

Aboard: on board a vessel
Aft: near the stern (rear of a ship)
Aids to Navigation: buoys, beacons, electronic devices, lighthouses and other markers used by sailors to avoid danger
All Hands: the entire crew of a ship
Anchor: heavy metal weight created to dig into bottom of water to hold vessel in place
At the Helm: at the controls of a ship

Barge: large flat-bottom vessel, normally towed, used to transport goods
Beacon: lighthouse, or buoy secured over shallow water, to aid in navigation
Beam: greatest width of a ship
Bearing: direction of a ship
Below: below the deck
Berth: place to sleep on board, or place ship is docked
Bosun: officer in charge of deck operations on a ship
Bow: front end of a ship
Breadth: greatest width
Brig: two-masted vessel, with both masts square rigged
Brigantine: two-masted vessel, with fore mast square rigged
Bristol-Fashion: clean and neat
Bulk: cargo of a vessel, in its proper place on board
Bum Boats: small boats that bring supplies to vessel while in port
Buoy: floating aids to navigation

Cabin: living or sleeping area on board a vessel
Captain: officer in charge of a vessel
Cast Off: free vessel from dock for departure

Christen: ceremony when vessel is formally named
Clipper: sailing vessel
Coast: land along shore
Crew and Crewmembers: group of people working on a ship

Deck Hand: crewmember responsible for manual labor
Dinghy: small boat carried on larger vessel
Displacement: weight of water displaced by a vessel to achieve buoyancy
Dockhand: crewmember who works on docks
Draft: depth of water required to float a vessel
Even Keel: a vessel sitting evenly in the water
Eye of the Wind: direction wind is coming from

Fair Wind: wind that allows easy sailing
Fathom: measurement of six feet
Ferry: vessel that carries passengers and vehicles
Fog Horn: horn used to warn vessels of fog
Fore: forward section of vessel

Gale: strong wind
Galley: kitchen on a vessel

Heavy Sea: water's surface covered with numerous large waves
Helm: steering apparatus of a vessel
Hold: space or compartments below deck for cargo
Hull: main body of a vessel

Jib: triangular foresail in front of foremast

Keel: main component of vessel at bottom of hull, to which frames are attached
Knot: unit of nautical speed

Laid Up: decommissioned vessel
Launch: put a vessel in water
League: measurement of distance equivalent to three nautical miles
Liberty: crewmember's approved time off ship
Lightship: vessel with bright light and foghorn, anchored for navigational aid
List: vessel leaning to one side

Mainmast: tallest, principal mast of a ship
Mast: vertical pole that supports sails
Mate: crewmember
M.T.: motor tug
M.V.: motor vessel

Nautical Mile: distance of 6,076 feet, (land mile is 5,280 feet)
Naval Architect: designer of plans and specifications of vessel
Navigation: art of guiding vessel from one port to another
Ocean Going: vessel designed to sail on ocean
Offshore: a distance from the shore

Pilot House: cabin on deck enclosing helmsman and navigation equipment
Pitching: movement of a ship, rising and falling, while traveling through waves
Port: left side of a vessel when facing forward
Porthole: window on a vessel

Rigging: lines that control sails and masts
Roll: movement of a vessel from side to side
Rudder: blade shaped surface attached to hull under stern, used to control direction of vessel

Sail: piece of cloth that catches wind and thereby powers vessel; or to travel across water on a vessel
Sailor: crewmember or person traveling on board a ship
Saloon or Salon: lounging or main social area on board vessel
Salty: person accustomed to being around water
Schooner: sailing vessel with at least two masts, mainmast being the tallest
Scuttlebutt: rumors or gossip
Seadog: experienced sailor
Set Sail: leaving a harbor; also to raise a sail
Shipmate: a fellow crewmember or sailor
Shoal: a shallow place in a body of water; a sandy elevation of the bottom of a body of
   water, as a sandbar, constituting a hazard to navigation
Sloop: single-masted vessel
Spar: a mast or pole
Squall: sudden and violent blast of wind
S.S.: steamship
Starboard: right side of vessel when facing forward
Stem: vertical post at front of bow
Stern: rear end of vessel

Topsail Schooner: schooner with square sails on foremast
Tug Boat: sturdy boat built for towing and pushing barges and other vessels

Underway: vessel in motion, not anchored

Watch: a unit of time on a ship
Wheel: steering device on a vessel

Tall Ships
of the
Great
Lakes

What is a Tall Ship?..

"Tall Ship" is not a strictly defined type of sailing vessel. Most of us use the term when referring to a large, traditionally rigged sailing vessel, whether or not it is technically a "ship." The United States Coast Guard's flagship Eagle, *for example, is technically a barque. Tall ships can also be schooners, brigantines, barquentines, brigs, or sloops, depending on the number of masts and cut of the sail.*

– American Sail Training Association

Tall ships have been sailing the Great Lakes for over two centuries. They number in the thousands and have played a major role in America's struggle for independence, carried eager immigrants to their new home in the midwest and transported goods from port to port as the region quickly grew. They were the vessels of hopes and dreams as Americans moved ever westward.

The rustic accommodations and primitive navigational tools aboard yesterday's sailing ships are fondly recalled today as charming and romantic. And no wonder…today's quick one-hour trip on an airline from Detroit to Chicago replaced a leisurely week-long voyage across the vast waters of the Great Lakes. This progress did cut at least 120 hours off the trip, but it also substituted a bag of dry roasted peanuts for quiet walks on deck, stopping at bustling ports and dining on food freshly prepared on board.

Historians, concerned civic groups and dedicated individuals have gone to great lengths, and costs, to preserve and protect this era of shipping on the Great Lakes. Its historical significance has been painstakingly recreated for us in the form of reconstructed vessels and modern sailing ships built on designs used over a century ago. Actual timbers from 200-year-old ships, authentic designs and tools, and shipbuilding techniques from the past have all been used to construct replicas of yesterday's tall ships. U.S. Coast Guard regulations and personal safety concerns have required some changes in equipment and material use, all much appreciated by today's passengers, but sailing on a tall ship remains the same. The wind dictates your course and the waves control your appetite.

All of the ships featured in this section currently sail the Great Lakes, proud of the history they carry with them. Guests are welcomed aboard for tours, daily sailings, overnight stays, week-long adventures…and yes, even dining. Admittedly, today's recipes are much improved, as is the quality of food. The meals prepared on board by chefs today are downright delicious, and amazing, considering the conveniences they work without.

Wisconsin's Flagship Denis Sullivan

Wisconsin Lake Schooner Education Association

Built:	1996-2000, Milwaukee, WI Wisconsin Lake Schooner Education Association
Sparred Length:	137'
Overall Length:	103'
Waterline Length:	90'
Beam:	23' 6"
Draft:	8' 9"
Rig:	Three Masted Schooner
Mast Height:	95'
Passengers:	200 Dockside, 146 Daily Sail 42 Overnight
Crew:	5 to 7
Home Port:	Milwaukee, Wisonsin

Nicknamed "the ship built by a thousand hands and a thousand hearts," *Wisconsin's Flagship* takes shape along Milwaukee's lakefront with the help of hundreds of volunteers.

For three centuries the primary method of travel throughout the Great Lakes region was by water. Many of the area's settlers arrived on wooden schooners. Wisconsin became a major shipbuilding center during the nineteenth century, receiving hundreds of sailing ships a day at its ports. The City of Milwaukee was founded on shipping and produced 212 schooners in the late 1800s. Sadly, none of these vessels remain today.

Hand chiseled mortice joints will insure a strong and authentic ship.

In 1990 a group of Wisconsin citizens, (educators, business people and sailing enthusiasts) began their search for a project that would honor Wisconsin's rich maritime history as well as increase awareness of ecological issues concerning the Great Lakes. In 1991 they founded the Wisconsin Lake Schooner Education Association and unanimously agreed on the building of a tall ship. The dream took off from there.

The famous three-masted schooner *Moonlight*, built in Milwaukee in 1874, inspired their vessel. Its contemporary design is based on four Great Lakes schooners built between 1852 and 1868 – the *Challenger*, *Clipper City*, *Lucia A. Simpson* and the legendary "Christmas Tree Ship," *Rouse Simmons*.

Building *Wisconsin's Flagship Denis Sullivan* officially began in May of 1996 at Milwaukee's Municipal Pier. Construction was lead by a crew of shipwrights who taught shipbuilding skills to hundreds of enthusiastic volunteers from every walk of life. The dedicated crew worked side-by-side putting in over 900,000 volunteer hours to complete the vessel. Donations came from individuals and organizations, all deeply concerned with enriching Wisconsin's future by preserving it's past. One of the most unusual gifts came from the people of the Menominee Nation, who donated 150-year-old white pines to be used for the masts. The timbers were blessed in a tribal ceremony and children from Milwaukee's Indian School community planted six small white pines in a ceremonial replenishment of the earth's resources. *Wisconsin's Flagship* became known as "the ship built by a thousand hands and a thousand hearts." It is the first tall ship built in Wisconsin in over 100 years!

As *Wisconsin's Flagship Denis Sullivan* sets sail she will embody the sweat, souls and spirit of the community that worked side-by-side to see their dream come true. She will carry with her the hopes and dreams of the WLSEA, and all involved, of forging a link between their proud past and the present. Preservation of the area's rich maritime history, a floating traveling classroom used to teach trade vessel skills and ecosystem concerns, and a Goodwill Ambassador for the State of Wisconsin throughout the world are among the responsibilities carried on the majestic shoulders of *Wisconsin's Flagship*.

The galley of *Wisconsin's Flagship* has been given equal attention. What food to serve on board and how to prepare it has been on the minds of several volunteers who brought years of experience in the trade with them. Two of the volunteers, Laurie and John Deely, met in the town of Northport, Michigan where they both worked on the *Schooner Manitou*. John signed on as chief-mate and Laurie took the position of fulltime cook. Laurie's memories of working on the Great Lakes bring to life the hectic schedule on a schooner and the deep bond so easily formed with the region.

"When I was first approached in the spring about helping a cook on board the *Manitou* I declined, thinking I couldn't handle living so closely with shipmates and passengers without much space for privacy. Midsummer, John asked if I would fill in temporarily for a crewmember that needed some time off. This time I agreed, thinking okay, how hard could it be? After a few days aboard the cook became ill and I was suddenly thrust into the duty of preparing three meals a day for 26 people, on a wood burning stove, with provisions I was unfamiliar with. I must have done a good job because upon arrival back at the dock I was offered the position of permanent fulltime cook. I accepted, knowing all of the conditions.

The cook's day begins before dawn, starting with building a fire in the wood stove. You work until dusk (until everyone is finished with the evening meal) without much privacy and nowhere to ride a bicycle, a previous daily activity of mine. However, I was hooked. The long hours became enjoyable. I was working for the good of my shipmates who became my family. It must be similar to the old farm wives who cooked all day for the farm hands; it was a labor of love.

Volunteers John and Laurie Deely looking "salty" on the Great Lakes. Laurie brought her experience as a sailing cook, and her recipes, to the galley of *Wisconsin's Flagship*.

There were other rewards too. We got to explore deserted islands in the Great Lakes with rich and varied histories. The best part of everyday was coming out of the galley after sweating like crazy over a wood stove and jumping into the crisp clean fresh water of Lake Michigan.

When I began cooking on a schooner my family thought it curious that I would be following in my ancestor's footsteps. Pearl May Soule (June 28, 1888-December 11, 1929) a cousin of my grandfather George A. Soule, had been a cook on board Great Lakes ships during her lifetime. Her father had built her a house on the shore of Lake Huron, near Port Sanilac, for her to live in when she stopped working on the ships. He purchased a 50-foot lot for $15 a foot! She never lived there, but the house still stands.

Scaffolds were necessary to reach the deck of the Flagship.

Today, after cooking on board different traditional sailing ships and a private sailing yacht, the Great Lakes have called my husband John, our son John-Paul and myself back. John contributed to the building of *Wisconsin's Flagship*. The Great Lakes have brought us a lot of joy and we hope our contribution to *Wisconsin's Flagship* will help preserve this natural resource for future generation's health and well being."

Laurie's recipes became favorites of crewmembers and passengers alike.

BUCKWHEAT PANCAKES

These are an excellent "do ahead" breakfast item. In the morning, add the last few ingredients, put on some world renowned Wisconsin sausage, make a pot of coffee and heat up some of the outstanding Maple Syrup from the Great Lakes region.

1 Tbsp.	active dry yeast
1/4 c.	warm water
1 c.	whole wheat pastry flour
1/2 c.	buckwheat flour
3/4 tsp.	salt
1 c.	cold water
1 Tbsp.	brown sugar
2 Tbsp.	butter, melted
1/2 tsp.	baking soda
1/4 c.	hot water

Dissolve yeast in warm water. Combine whole wheat flour, buckwheat flour and salt. Stir dry ingredients and cold water into yeast mixture. Cover and refrigerate overnight. In the morning add brown sugar, melted butter, baking soda and hot water; let stand 30 minutes. Fry on hot griddle.

Yield: 4 Servings

MARINATED FOCACCIA BREAD SANDWICHES

This is an excellent recipe because you can make it ahead of time. If today is smooth sailing on the Great Lakes, tomorrow may very well not be and you don't want to be in the galley while beating to weather.

2 (14-inch)	Focaccia flat breads, homemade *or* purchased at Italian bakery (Bobbi also works)

Marinade

1/4 c.	extra virgin olive oil
2 Tbsp.	fresh basil
1 tsp.	dried oregano
2 Tbsp.	onion, finely minced
2 Tbsp.	garlic, finely minced
2 Tbsp.	green olives, finely minced
	Salt and pepper, to taste

Filling

1/2 lb.	salami, sliced
1/2 lb.	proscuitto, thinly sliced
1/2 lb.	Provolone cheese, sliced

Combine ingredients for marinade and set aside. Cut a very thin top layer off each bread to expose bread and allow marinade to soak in. Spread 1/2 marinade on the cut side of 1 of the flat breads. Layer cheese, proscuitto and salami on marinated side of bread. Spread remaining marinade on cut side of second flat bread; place on top of layered filling ingredients. Wrap in plastic wrap and refrigerate overnight. Unwrap, cut into squares and serve.

TOMATO BASIL SOUP

This soup is an excellent accompaniment to Marinated Focaccia Sandwiches. This is best when made while the tomatoes are ripe and fresh basil is available.

1/4 lb.	butter
1 c.	onion, finely minced
1/8 c.	garlic, minced
1 Tbsp.	flour
2 c.	heavy cream
8 c.	fresh tomatoes, chopped
1 c.	fresh basil, cut
	Salt and pepper, to taste
	Tabasco sauce, to taste, (optional)

Melt butter and sauté onions until translucent. Add garlic and flour; stir continuously until thick roux is present. Slowly add heavy cream, stirring constantly. Reduce heat to low and let heat through. Add tomatoes, basil and seasonings. Simmer 30 minutes and serve.

BLACKENED WHITEFISH

This is a very spicy way to perk up the mellow flavor of whitefish, or any other fresh water fish. This works best when using a cast iron skillet or grill. However, make sure you clean your surface really well after this dish or you are apt to have "spicy" pancakes tomorrow morning.

1 Tbsp.	paprika
1 tsp.	salt
1 tsp.	onion powder
1 tsp.	cayenne pepper
1 tsp.	white pepper
1 tsp.	black pepper
1 tsp.	garlic powder
1 tsp.	ginger
1 tsp.	chilies, crushed
1/2 tsp.	thyme
1/2 tsp.	oregano
4	whitefish filets

Combine all ingredients except fish. Heat and lightly oil cast iron surface to sizzling hot temperature. Lay flesh side of fish in spice mixture and slide around to coat. Move flesh side of fish right onto hot surface. Sneeze from all of the pepper! Cook until done, approximately 8 minutes. Serve with Mango Chutney (see next recipe).

Yield: 4 Servings

MANGO CHUTNEY

1	mango, chopped
1	jalapeno pepper, chopped
1 Tbsp.	red onion, chopped
1	garlic clove, chopped
2 Tbsp.	fresh cilantro, chopped
	Juice of 1/2 lime
	Dash of sugar
	Sour cream

Combine all ingredients except sour cream; stir together to mix. Finish with a dollop of sour cream.

WALNUT BREAD

I was once told that there are two things passengers will remember about their trip. One is a really good loaf of bread and the other is dessert. This is the really good loaf of bread. It works very well for an afternoon snack with some cheese and a bottle of Chardonnay.

1/2 c.	butter *or* walnut oil
3/4 c.	onion, finely chopped
2 c.	warm milk
2 Tbsp.	sugar
2 env.	dry yeast
2 tsp.	salt
5 c.	unbleached flour
3/4 c.	walnuts, (black if available), toasted, coarsely chopped

Melt butter in skillet; add onion and sauté until tender. Set aside. Combine milk and sugar in large bowl. Sprinkle yeast over milk mixture and stir to blend; let stand until foamy, approximately 10 minutes. Mix in onion mixture, salt, and 1 cup flour. Blend in enough remaining flour, 1 cup at a time, to form a smooth ball. Transfer dough to floured work surface and knead until smooth and elastic. Shape dough into ball. Butter a large bowl; place dough in bowl, turning to coat. Cover and let rise until doubled. Butter large baking sheet. Punch down dough. Place dough onto floured work surface and knead in walnuts. Form dough into 2 round loaves and place on baking sheet. Cover and let rise until doubled. Bake at 400 degrees until golden brown. If you are baking on a schooner, baking time will depend on which tack you are on and how warm the weather is. However, if you have an oven with a temperature control, it should take approximately 25 to 30 minutes.

Note: Use black walnuts if they are available, they will make this incredibly good bread into something you will never forget.

CURE-ALL GINGER SNAPS

There is a theory that ginger is a remedy for seasickness. I am not sure if it is scientifically proven or not, but I have seen a whole group of teenagers feel much better after eating these cookies.

1-3/4 c.	unbleached flour
1 tsp.	ground cinnamon
1 tsp.	ground ginger
1/2 tsp.	baking soda
1/4 tsp.	salt
1/4 tsp.	ground cloves
1/2 c.	butter, at room temperature
2/3 c.	brown sugar, packed
1	egg
2 Tbsp.	molasses
	Sugar

In small bowl mix together flour, cinnamon, ginger, baking soda, salt and ground cloves; set aside. In separate bowl beat together butter and brown sugar until fluffy. Beat egg and molasses into butter mixture. Beat in dry ingredients. Cover and refrigerate overnight. Preheat oven to 325 degrees and lightly butter 2 large cookie sheets. Form dough into small balls, roll each ball in sugar and place on cookie sheet; press top with a glass to flatten. Bake approximately 12 minutes.

LAYERED MOCHA CREAM TORTE

This is the dessert that will stay on everyone's mind, long after they have left.

Crust

2-1/2 c.	chocolate wafer cookies, ground approx. 1-1/3 (9-oz.) packages
1-1/2 Tbsp.	instant coffee powder
6 Tbsp.	unsalted butter, melted

Fillings

12 oz.	bittersweet (not unsweetened) *or* semi-sweet chocolate, chopped
6 Tbsp.	unsalted butter, cut into pieces
6 tsp.	instant coffee powder
1/2 c.	sugar
3 Tbsp.	water
5 lg.	egg whites
2-3/4 c.	whipping cream, chilled
1/4 c.	powdered sugar
1/4 tsp.	ground cinnamon

Preheat oven to 350 degrees. To prepare crust blend ground cookies with coffee powder in processor. Set aside 3/4-cup cookie crumb mixture. Add butter to remaining crumb mixture and process until crumbs are moist. Press mixture onto bottom and up sides of 9-inch diameter springform with 2-3/4-inch high sides. Bake crust until just firm to touch, approximately 10 minutes. Cool completely.

To prepare fillings stir chocolate pieces together with butter and 1 teaspoon coffee powder in heavy saucepan over medium-low heat until melted and smooth. Transfer to large bowl. Set chocolate mixture aside while preparing meringue. To prepare meringue stir 1/2 cup sugar and 3 tablespoons water together in small saucepan over low heat until sugar dissolves. Increase heat and boil syrup without stirring until candy thermometer registers 240 degrees, tilting pan to submerge bulb, approximately 4 minutes. Meanwhile, using electric mixer, beat egg whites in large bowl to soft peaks. Gradually beat hot syrup into whites. Continue beating until medium-stiff peaks form, approximately 3 minutes. Fold 1/3 of meringue into lukewarm chocolate mixture to lighten. Fold in remaining meringue. Set chocolate meringue aside.

Combine 1/4 cup cream with 5 teaspoons coffee powder in large bowl; stir to dissolve. Add 1/2 cup cream, powdered sugar and cinnamon; beat until firm peaks form. Fold 1-1/2 cups coffee whipped cream into chocolate meringue, forming mocha mousse. Spoon 1/2 mocha mousse over bottom of crust. Sprinkle 3 tablespoons reserved crumb mixture over mousse. Spoon 1/2 coffee whipped cream over crumbs; sprinkle with 3 tablespoons crumbs. Repeat layers with remaining mocha mousse, crumbs, coffee whipped cream and crumbs. Cover and refrigerate until set, approximately 4 hours. This torte can be made 2 days ahead; keep refrigerated. Run knife around pan sides to loosen torte. Remove pan sides and serve.

Wisconsin Lake Schooner Education Association

Wisconsin's Flagship Denis Sullivan sets sail with the sweat, soul and spirit of the community that worked side-by-side to see their dream come true. When at her home port along Milwaukee's waterfront, visitors are welcomed aboard the schooner for tours, dockside receptions, day sails, and adult and youth overnight discovery expeditions. During the winter months, *Wisconsin's Flagship Denis Sullivan* offers 3 to 5 day sailing adventures off the waters of Florida and the Bahamas.

Come visit the first tall ship built in Wisconsin in over 100 years! To find out about tours, membership, youth programs, sponsorship, or volunteer opportunities call Wisconsin Lake Education Association and become part of Wisconsin's future by helping to recapture a part of our past.

A Sesquicentennial Project for our State's 150th Anniversary!

WISCONSIN'S FLAGSHIP DENIS SULLIVAN
Wisconsin Lake Schooner Education Association
500 N. Harbor Drive, Milwaukee, Wisconsin 53202
Phone: (414) 276-7700 · Fax: (414) 276-8838
Website: www.wis-schooner.org

Schooner Madeline

Maritime Heritage Alliance

Original Built:	1845 – Fairport, OH
Reproduction Built:	1985 to 1990 by the Maritime Heritage Alliance, Traverse City, MI
Launched:	1990
Sparred Length:	92'
Length on Deck:	55'
Beam:	16'
Draft:	7'
Rig:	Gaff Topsail Schooner, 2 Masts
Mast Height:	68' and 71'
Sail Area:	2,200 sq. ft.
Crew:	Up to 21 (usually includes 7 to 9 instructors and 12 to 14 trainees or passengers)
Home Port:	Clinch Park Marina Traverse City, Michigan

The Schooner Madeline, all sails unfurled, gracefully sails the Great Lakes as Official Goodwill Ambassador of Traverse City and the Great Lakes Region.

*T*he *Schooner Madeline*, replica of a nineteenth century merchant schooner, brings back an era gone-by but not forgotten on the Great Lakes. A time when sailing ships ruled the waters carrying cargo and passengers from Chicago to Detroit, or Toronto to Duluth, across the challenging waters of the vast inland seas.

The original *Madeline* was built during the winter of 1844-1845 in Fairport, Ohio, undoubtedly for owners at Mackinac Island. The island remained her home port for the first 17 years of her life, where she served the commercial fishing industry carrying barreled fish to the lower lakes and returning with salt used to preserve fish. Apples, potatoes and lumber from the rich forests of northern Michigan also found passage on the *Madeline*, playing a big part in the development of the region.

In the winter of 1851 *Madeline* put her shipping duties on hold and journeyed to Traverse City, Michigan. On board were William, Michael and John Fitzgerald, William Bryce and Edward Chambers, all seeking an education. S.E. Waite was hired to instruct the young men in spelling, reading, writing, and arithmetic, receiving room and board on the *Madeline* in exchange for his services. *Madeline* became the first private non-Indian school in the region and her determined students went on the leave their mark on the area's history. All of the Fitzgeralds went on to serve many years as captains on the lakes. William and John became prominent in the maritime history of Milwaukee. John Fitzgerald was the grandfather of Edmund Fitzgerald, namesake of the ill-fated ore carrier lost on the Great lakes in 1975. Edward Chambers served many years as lightkeeper at Whitefish Point on Lake Superior.

After fulfilling her duties as a school, *Madeline* was returned to shipping duties on the Great Lakes and continued her service for several more years, the last few in the Milwaukee area. The life expectancy for wooden ships of her era was ten years; *Madeline* proudly served Great Lakes merchants for 20 years. She was finally abandoned to settle quietly in the mud of one of the Milwaukee rivers, taking with her a legacy of ingenuity, perseverance and the spirit of northwest Michigan pioneers.

The *Schooner Madeline's* historical importance came to the attention of the Maritime Heritage Alliance in Traverse City, an organization founded in 1982 by a group of historic wooden boat buffs with a strong determination to preserve and share the maritime history of the region. In 1985 the MHA began construction on a replica of the *Madeline*, using many of the same tools and techniques that created her namesake over a century earlier. During the five years of her construction *Madeline's* volunteer builders learned and practiced traditional boat building skills while thousands of visitors eagerly followed their progress.

The newly constructed *Schooner Madeline* was launched in 1990. Since then she has sailed over 10,000 miles to various ports on the Great Lakes as Official Goodwill Ambassador of Traverse City and the Great Lakes Region. She has also been proclaimed Official Envoy representing the area and a Michigan Historic Vessel. *Madeline* is open for tours when at her home port of Clinch Park Marina in Traverse City where she serves as a dockside interpretive center. The schooner also welcomes visitors aboard at every port she visits.

Dedicated Maritime Heritage Alliance members serve as crew, tour guides, maintenance workers and tender caregivers aboard *Madeline*. Their quest to spread Great Lakes history throughout the region is a year-round effort, requiring thousands of volunteer hours. "All these coastal communities, from Chicago to the Mackinac Straits, were settled by water first. We can't lose that significant maritime history," stresses Captain Bruce Lehmann, who has sailed the ship since it was launched.

While sailing the lakes *Madeline's* crew works side-by-side, each with their own job, efficiently guiding her from port to port. One crewmember bravely takes on galley duty for each voyage, and quite a duty it is. This person becomes the cook for the trip and their responsibilities begin long before *Madeline* sets sail. The cook plans all menus, purchases food and even prepares a few of the meals on land to be frozen and used later on board.

Bev Denyas has been a MHA volunteer for several years. She quickly became a favorite cook of her fellow members, who eagerly sign on when she is scheduled to cook. The quality and creativity of the food Bev prepares is not limited by the required use of one propane burner instead of a stove, a compact galley and limited space available for cold food storage.

Recipes for the delicious homemade food served aboard have proven themselves worthy of satisfying even the heartiest of appetites. And after a day out in the fresh air of the Great Lakes, it's hard to find a crewmember without a hearty appetite!

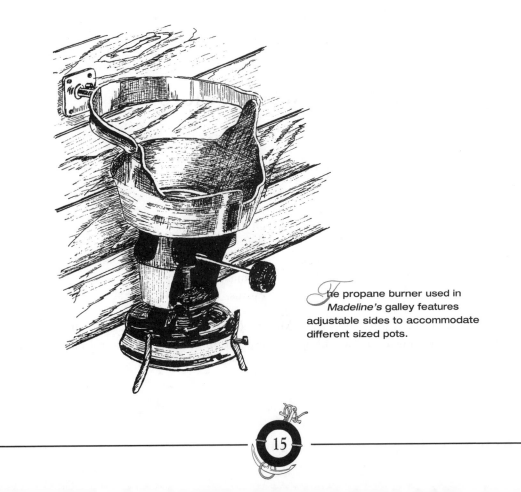

The propane burner used in *Madeline's* galley features adjustable sides to accommodate different sized pots.

Menu Favorites

Melons

Cukes

Romaine

Carrots in the Bag

Three Bean Salad

Hard Boiled Eggs –
for Breakfast and Lunch

Summer Sausage

Brownies

Tortilla Chips and Salsa

Fresh coffee and a variety of the menu favorites listed above are always handy to keep the crew happy between meals.

"Sue's Oatmeal Cookies," a recipe Bev received from the wife of Captain Jones, are a favorite snack on the *Madeline*. Fresh muffins are available for breakfast the first few days out and sandwiches accompany a cup of soup at an average noon meal. Evening meals are hot and hearty, often eaten on deck where the crew finds more room to relax

SUE'S OATMEAL COOKIES

2-1/2 sticks	margarine
1/2 c.	sugar
3/4 c.	brown sugar
1	egg
1 tsp.	vanilla
1 tsp.	cinnamon
1-1/2 c.	flour
1 tsp.	baking soda
3 c.	oatmeal
1 c.	raisins, (optional)

Cream together margarine and sugars. Mix in egg and vanilla. Combine dry ingredients and add to creamed mixture. Drop by teaspoon onto cookie sheet and bake at 350 degrees 9 minutes.

MADELINE CHILI

This is an easy recipe that takes limited time to cook on the propane burner aboard the Schooner Madeline. It may be made without the turkey for a good vegetarian meal. Served with corn bread it makes a complete protein meal. It can also be made ahead and frozen. (Bev prefers to make it ahead and always makes it vegetarian.) Cooking the spices is the difference with this recipe...it really gives it punch! Also, have fun by using different kinds of beans; it makes it a feast for the eyes as well as the appetite.

1 Tbsp.	vegetable oil
1 lg.	onion, chopped
2	garlic cloves, minced
1	red pepper, chopped
1	green pepper, chopped
1-1/2 lbs.	ground turkey or beef, (optional)
2 Tbsp.	flour
3 Tbsp.	chili powder
2 Tbsp.	ground cumin
2 tsp.	cocoa powder
1 tsp.	cayenne pepper
1/4 c.	vinegar
2 Tbsp.	strong brewed coffee
1/4 tsp.	salt
4 cans	beans, (black, kidney, pinto, etc.)

Heat vegetable oil. Add onion, garlic and peppers; sauté 5 minutes, stirring frequently. Add meat and sauté an additional 5 minutes, stirring constantly and breaking up any lumps with spoon. Stir in flour, chili powder, cumin, cocoa and cayenne pepper. Cook over low heat 3 minutes, stirring frequently, to cook spices. Add remaining ingredients, except beans, and bring to boil over medium heat. Add beans and simmer until thick.

Yield: 8 to 10 Servings

POTATO SOUP

This is an easy soup with only 4 ingredients, all of which you would have on board.

1 lg.	onion, chopped
4	potatoes, peeled, sliced
1 qt.	milk
1 Tbsp.	butter
	Salt and pepper, to taste

Place potatoes and onion in pot. Add enough water to just cover and bring to boil. Boil until tender enough to mash into a thick slurry. Add milk and butter. Season with salt and pepper to taste. Heat over medium heat. Do not let soup boil.

POTATO CHEESE SOUP

1 lb.	white potatoes, cubed
1 c.	celery, diced
1 c.	onion, diced
1	carrot, diced
1 lg. can	chicken broth
2 cans	evaporated milk
8 oz.	Velveeta cheese spread
4 Tbsp.	flour
1-1/2 c.	sour cream
	Salt and pepper, to taste

Cook potatoes, carrots, onion and celery in chicken broth until done; remove from heat. Add flour and evaporated milk; heat. Stir in cheese. Add sour cream just before serving, stirring to mix.

CARROT AND SWEET POTATO SOUP

2 Tbsp.	butter
3/4 c.	onion, chopped
1 tsp.	curry powder
2 lg.	carrots, peeled, sliced
2 c.	chicken broth, divided
1 lg.	sweet potato, peeled, sliced
	Salt and pepper, to taste
	Bacon bits

Melt butter in pan. Add onion and sauté over medium heat 5 minutes. Add curry powder, carrots, sweet potato and 1 cup chicken broth; bring to boil. Reduce heat and cook covered over medium heat until carrots are tender, approximately 15 minutes. Add remaining chicken broth. Season with salt and pepper. Mash carrots and sweet potato to desired consistency. Return to heat and bring to simmer. When ready to serve place in bowls and sprinkle bacon bits over top.

QUICK BEAN SOUP

1 lg. jar	Northern beans
1 to 2	carrots, diced
1 lg.	potato, diced
1 lg.	onion, diced
2 c.	water
	Bacon bits
	Salt and pepper, to taste

Place carrots, onion and potato in water. Bring to boil and cook until vegetables are soft. Add beans and heat thoroughly. Add bacon bits. Season with salt and pepper, to taste.

TACO SALAD IN TORTILLA SHELLS

2 tsp.	vegetable oil
1-1/2 c.	onions, chopped
1-1/2 c.	red peppers, chopped
1-1/2 c.	green peppers, chopped
1 lb.	lean ground beef
1 c.	mild salsa
1 Tbsp.	jalapeno pepper, minced
2 to 4 tsp.	chili powder
8	tortilla shells, prepared

Optional Garnishes

Lettuce, shredded
Tomatoes, diced
Black olives, sliced
Cheddar cheese, shredded
Mild salsa
Sour cream

Combine all ingredients, except tortilla shells, in pot and cook until beef is done. Place beef and vegetable mixture in prepared tortilla shells. Serve with shredded lettuce, diced tomatoes, sliced black olives, shredded Cheddar cheese, mild salsa and sour cream on the side. Crewmembers can add these toppings to taste.

MEAL IN A BAG SALAD NICOISE

This meal requires no cooking, only opening cans. It is a good hearty meal for a hot day.

1 can	tuna, in water, drained
1 can	cooked potatoes, (or boil 3 to 4 potatoes)
1 can	green beans, drained
1 can	sliced black olives
1/2 bottle	Balsamic vinegar dressing
1 tsp.	dry basil

Slice potatoes. Mix remaining ingredients with potatoes, being careful not to over mix so you have mush. Serve on lettuce leaves.

Note: Adding a sliced hard-boiled egg for garnish is nice.

Yield: 4 Servings

MEAL IN A BAG CHICKEN DINNER

This is a take aboard meal that requires no refrigeration. Like all meals on the Madeline, *it can be cooked in one pot.*

2 lg. cans	chicken or turkey, drained
2 lg. cans	mushroom soup, undiluted
3 c.	mixed wild/long grain rice
2 lg. cans	mushrooms, drained

Prepare rice according to package directions. Add remaining ingredients and heat together until hot.

Yield: 10 to 12 Servings

PAY DAY BARS

6 c.	Rice Chex
2 c.	dry roasted peanuts
1 c.	light corn syrup
1 c.	sugar
1-1/2 c.	creamy peanut butter
1 tsp.	vanilla

Place Rice Chex and peanuts in large bowl; toss together and set aside. In saucepan bring sugar and corn syrup to boil, stirring frequently. Remove from heat. Stir in peanut butter and vanilla. Pour over cereal mixture and toss to coat evenly. Spread into greased 9x13-inch baking pan. Cut into bars.

When at her home port of Clinch Park in Traverse City, Michigan, the *Schooner Madeline* welcomes visitors aboard for tours and serves as a dockside interpretive center. The schooner also welcomes visitors aboard at every port she visits.

Schooner Madeline
Maritime Heritage Alliance of Traverse City
232 E. Front Street, Traverse City, Michigan 49684
(231) 946-2647   Fax: (231) 946-6750

Sloop Welcome

The Maritime Heritage Alliance is also busy at work repairing and preserving a replica of the *Sloop Welcome*. The *Welcome* was originally constructed in 1775, at Michilimackinac by John Askin, as a private trading vessel. A few years later the sloop was purchased by the British military for use in supplying Fort Michilimackinac. Late in 1781, the *Welcome* was lost in a storm. Its final resting place still remains a mystery.

In the early 1970s a replica of the 55-foot *Welcome* was built by the Mackinac Island State Park Commission at Fort Michilimackinac for the 200th anniversary of Independence Day. It served as a window to the past for many years, offering visitors a chance to see a facet of American history often forgotten. In 1990 the sloop was found to be unseaworthy and dry-docked. Two years later the MHA became custodian of the Welcome.

Today, volunteers of the Maritime Heritage Alliance continue to reconstruct *Welcome* on the pier of the Great Lakes Maritime Academy in Traverse City. Visitors can watch the vessel take shape as traditional boat building skills are used to return the sloop to its original condition. When completed, the *Welcome* will again serve as a living museum of Michigan's maritime past from the era of the American Revolution.

Tall Ship Malabar

Traverse Tall Ship Company

Built:	1975 Bath, Maine
Former Name:	*Rachel and Ebeneezer*
Overall Length:	105'
Length on Deck:	65'
Beam:	22'
Draft:	8' 5"
Rig:	Traditional Two-Masted, Gaff Rigged, Top Sail Schooner
Mast Height:	80'
Passengers:	46 Daily Sail, 21 Overnight
Crew:	6
Retired:	Year 2000, replaced with *Tall Ship Westwind*

Captain Jim Schneider prepares to raise the flag aboard the *Malabar*.

*S*tanding on deck of the *Tall Ship Malabar*, replica of freight hauling windjammers used in the 1800s, it was easy to imagine what life on the sea may have been like. The *Malabar*, meaning "Protector Of The Sea" from ancient mythology, was brought to northern Michigan in 1987 by the Traverse Tall Ship Company. From her home port in Traverse City she sailed the beautiful water of West Grand Traverse Bay three times a day (noon, mid afternoon, and sunset), allowing passengers to step back in time in true "salty" fashion. Each two-hour trip was different, with mother nature dictating the course. Some nights local sea chanty musicians share ballads and stories, bringing to life a voyage from over 100 years ago. Other trips found passengers on deck with fresh air, a starry night and the relaxing motion of the ship as their companion. Energetic guests could pitch in and help raise the sails or take a turn at the wheel under the guidance of an experienced captain and crew.

The *Malabar* offered an adventurous overnight stay on board after the Sunset Sail for those who enjoyed something new (and old) in the way of truly unique lodging aboard a floating bed and breakfast. There were accommodations for 21 guests in 8 private staterooms which were rustic and fitting of a mid-1800s style windjammer. The rooms were bright and comfortable, with plenty of room for being lulled to sleep by the lapping waves.

Early risers were well rewarded by the day's serene sunrise over Old Mission Peninsula. Hot coffee and fresh baked goods could be found on deck while preparations for a hot breakfast were completed in the galley. Hot entrées, specialty sausages, homemade granola, fresh fruit, yogurt, juice and coffee were prepared from delicious recipes created by chefs on the *Tall Ship Malabar*. Breakfast was as memorable as the Sunset Sail the night before.

During the spring of 2000, *Tall Ship Malabar* left Grand Traverse Bay for the last time, bound for the east coast of the United States where she started her career over a quarter century ago. Traverse Tall Ship Company soon welcomed the *Tall Ship Westwind* to their docks, beginning a new era of daily sailings on Grand Traverse Bay. Guests find a new appreciation for Grand Traverse Bay after an exciting two-hour cruise aboard *Westwind*. The 66-foot long, two-masted topsail schooner *Westwind* carries 1,500 square feet of sail, weighs 38 tons, has a 14-foot beam, a mast height of 60-foot and a day sail capacity of 29 passengers. She meets or exceeds all U.S. Coast Guard regulations and is operated by our U.S. Coast Guard-licensed captain and experienced crew.

Captain Jim Schneider with Cook, Ginger Arlt.

"Beach Bards" aboard the *Tall Ship Malabar*

APRICOT PECAN SCONES

1-3/4 c.	all-purpose flour
2-1/4 tsp.	baking powder
2 Tbsp.	sugar
1/2 tsp.	salt
2	eggs, beaten
1/4 c.	cold butter
1/3 c. + 2 Tbsp.	heavy cream
1/2 c.	dried apricots, diced
1/2 c.	pecan pieces, toasted

Preheat oven to 450 degrees. Sift dry ingredients into medium mixing bowl. Cut butter into small cubes and, using a pastry cutter, cut into dry ingredients until mixture resembles coarse corn meal. Make a well in center of this mixture; pour in 1/3 cup cream, beaten eggs, apricots and toasted pecans. Combine with just a few swift strokes, working dough as little as possible. Place dough on lightly floured surface and pat into circular shape approximately 1-inch thick. Cut dough into 12 wedges, similar to cutting a pie. Place wedges on ungreased cookie sheet and brush with remaining 2 tablespoons heavy cream; sprinkle with sugar. Bake in preheated oven approximately 12 to 15 minutes. Serve warm with unsalted sweet butter and preserves.

Yield: 12 Scones
(Stacie Kohler)

MOLLY'S GRANOLA

10 c.	old-fashioned oats
1/2 lb.	coconut
2 c.	walnut pieces
1 c.	wheat germ
2 c.	sliced almonds
2 c.	pecan halves
1-1/2 c.	brown sugar
3/4 c.	canola oil
1/2 c.	molasses
2 Tbsp.	cinnamon
1-1/2 c.	water
1/2 c.	honey
1 tsp.	salt
3 tsp.	vanilla

Mix together oats, coconut, walnuts, wheat germ, almonds and pecans in large bowl. Mix remaining ingredients together in saucepan over medium heat until sugar dissolves. Pour sugar mixture over dry ingredients and mix thoroughly. Spread mixture into 2 sprayed large baking pans. Bake at 350 degrees approximately 45 minutes, stirring every 15 minutes. Granola should be slightly moist when done; it crisps as it cools down.

(Molly Carver)

CHERRY CRUMB MUFFINS

4 c.	all-purpose flour
2 tsp.	salt
1/2 c.	sugar
1/2 tsp.	cinnamon
1/4 tsp.	nutmeg
2	eggs
1/2 c.	margarine, melted
2 c.	buttermilk
1-1/3 c.	fresh cherries, pitted

Crumb Topping

1/4 c.	brown sugar
1/8 c.	flour
1/8 c.	regular oats
1-1/2 Tbsp.	margarine
1-1/2 Tbsp.	nuts, chopped

Orange Honey Butter

1/2 lb.	soft butter
1/2 c.	Orange Blossom Clover Honey
	Zest from 3 oranges

Preheat oven to 400 degrees. To prepare muffins sift all dry ingredients together in large mixing bowl. Add liquids to dry ingredients and mix with approximately 5 to 6 strokes using a wooden spoon. Chop pitted cherries and add to batter, mixing only until combined. Do not over mix or the muffins will be tough. Pour batter into lined muffin tins, filling 2/3 full. To prepare crumb topping combine all ingredients until crumbly; sprinkle over muffins. Bake 20 to 25 minutes. Let muffins cool slightly and turn out onto cooling rack. Let cool completely. Serve with Orange Honey Butter.

To prepare Orange Honey Butter simply combine butter and honey with wooden spoon until well blended and very soft. Add zest of oranges and stir until combined. Serve with Cherry Crumb Muffins or your favorite pancakes.

Yield: 24 (3 oz.) Muffins
(Stacie Kohler)

PUMPKIN PECAN BREAD

1/3 c.	shortening
1/2 tsp.	vanilla
1 c.	pumpkin
1 c.	pecan halves
1-1/3 c.	sugar
2	eggs
1/3 c.	water
1-2/3 c.	flour
1 tsp.	baking soda
1/4 tsp.	nutmeg
1/4 tsp.	baking powder
1/2 tsp.	cinnamon
1/2 tsp.	cloves

Cream together shortening, vanilla, pumpkin, pecan halves, sugar, eggs and water. In separate bowl sift together remaining ingredients. Mix dry ingredients into creamed mixture. Divide batter into 2 greased baking pans. Bake at 350 degrees 45 to 60 minutes, until knife comes out clean. Remove from pans immediately and cool on wire rack.

Yield: 2 Loaves
(Ginger Lee Arlt)

GRANDMA'S ZUCCHINI BREAD

3	eggs
2-1/2 c.	sugar
1 c.	oil
2 c.	raw zucchini, grated
3 c.	flour
1 tsp.	salt
1 tsp.	baking soda
3 tsp.	cinnamon
1 tsp.	baking powder
3 tsp.	vanilla

Combine eggs, sugar, oil and grated zucchini; mix together well. Sift together remaining ingredients, add to zucchini mixture and mix well. Pour batter into 2 or 3 sprayed bread pans. Bake at 350 degrees 55 to 65 minutes. Remove from pans immediately and cool on wire rack.

Yield: 2 to 3 Loaves
(Miranda Lee Arlt)

LEMON POUND CAKE WITH BLUEBERRY GLAZE

Pound Cake

2-3/4 c.	sugar
1-1/4 c.	butter, softened
5 lg.	eggs
3 Tbsp.	lemon zest
1 Tbsp.	lemon extract
3 c.	all-purpose flour
1 tsp.	baking powder
1/4 tsp.	salt
1 c.	evaporated milk

Blueberry Glaze

1 pt.	fresh blueberries
1 Tbsp.	water
1/2 Tbsp.	unflavored gelatin
1 c.	sugar
1 Tbsp.	lemon juice

To prepare pound cake preheat oven to 350 degrees. Grease and flour 12-cup bundt pan. Combine sugar, butter, eggs, lemon extract and lemon zest; beat with hand mixer (low speed) or wooden spoon, scraping bowl down constantly. Beat harder, or on high speed with hand mixer, approximately 5 minutes. Slowly (low speed for hand mixer) beat in dry ingredients alternately with evaporated milk. Pour batter into prepared pan and bake until wooden toothpick comes out clean, approximately 70 to 80 minutes. Cool 20 minutes and remove from pan onto cooling rack. Cool completely, and then glaze with Blueberry Glaze. Slice and serve.

To prepare Blueberry Glaze combine all ingredients, except gelatin, in small heavy saucepan. Cook over medium-high heat until all blueberries are completely cooked. Mash with small potato masher in saucepan and continue to cook until slightly thickened. Strain blueberries through a fine sieve. Soften gelatin with a teaspoon of cold water and stir into blueberry mixture. Using a pastry brush, brush glaze on cooled pound cake.

Yield: 12 Large or 22 Small Slices
(Stacie Kohler)

TROPICAL PINEAPPLE BANANA SALAD

1 lg.	fresh pineapple
4	ripe (not brown at all) bananas
1/4 c.	honey
1/2 c.	coconut, toasted
1/2 c.	sliced almonds, toasted
1 tsp.	nutmeg

Cut top and bottom off pineapple. At approximately a 30-degree angle to the pineapple, remove all outer skin. Cut out any "eyes" you missed. Eyes are the round pieces of skin that are hard to cut off. It's easy to take a paring knife and cut in a circle around them, popping them out. Cut pineapple in 4 pieces from top to bottom. Now you will have 4 wedges of pineapple. You can now cut out the core easier. Lay wedge of pineapple on flat side, with core away from you. Cut down to the fruit, removing all of core. Repeat with remaining pineapple wedges. Cut all 4 cored wedges into bite-sized pieces and put fruit and juice into medium serving bowl. Peel and cut bananas into 1/4-inch circles; add to pineapple. Stir in honey and nutmeg until all fruit is coated. Sprinkle toasted coconut and almonds over fruit. Toss lightly and serve immediately.

Yield: 6 Large Servings
(Stacie Kohler)

GRANDMA'S CRUNCHY JUMBLE COOKIES

1-1/4 c.	flour
1/4 tsp.	salt
1 c.	sugar
1 tsp.	vanilla
2 c.	butterscotch chips
1/2 tsp.	baking soda
1/2 c.	butter *or* margarine
1	egg
2 c.	rice krispies

Sift together flour, baking soda and salt; set aside. In separate bowl cream together margarine, sugar, vanilla and egg. Mix rice krispies into creamed mixture, then add dry ingredients. Dough will be very stiff. Spoon onto greased baking sheets and bake at 350 degrees 10 to 12 minutes.

(Ginger Lee Arlt)

TALL SHIP MALABAR MOCHA SWIRL

1 lb.	butter, softened
6	eggs
2 tsp.	rum *or* vodka, *or* almond flavoring
1 c.	semi-sweet chocolate, melted
3 c.	sugar
1 c.	cold coffee
4 c.	flour
1 tsp.	baking powder

Preheat oven to 350 degrees; grease and flour 2 bundt pans. Ceam together butter and sugar. Add eggs 1 at a time. Add cold coffee and rum or vodka (or almond flavoring.) Add flour and baking powder. Blend chocolate with 1/3 of mixture. Divide remaining original mixture into prepared bundt pans. Swirl chocolate batter into batter in pans. Bake at 350 degrees 30 to 45 minutes, checking with toothpick. Glaze or sprinkle with powdered sugar while warm.

(Jim Dandy)

Information on daily sailings on board the *Tall Ship Westwind* is available at Traverse Tall Ship Company at Dockside Plaza in Traverse City, Michigan. Those who cannot seem to get enough sails, wind, water, or great food should take a few days from their busy schedule to relax aboard the *Manitou*, a 114-foot, traditional two-masted, gaff rigged, topsail schooner. A replica of a nineteenth century schooner, *Manitou* sets sail from Northport, Michigan combining the romantic rusticness of old time with modern radar and equipment for an unforgettable experience.

TALL SHIP WESTWIND (TALL SHIP MALABAR-RETIRED)

Traverse Tall Ship Company
13390 S.W. Bay Shore Drive
Traverse City, Michigan 49684
(231) 941-2000
Toll-Free: (800) 678-0383
Website: www.traverse.com/tallship

Schooner Manitou
Traverse Tall Ship Company

Built:	1983 Portsmouth, New Hampshire
Former Name:	*Homer W. Dixon*
Overall Length:	114'
Length on Deck:	77'
Beam:	23'
Draft:	Board up 7', Board down 11'
Rig:	Traditional Two-Masted, Gaff Rigged, Top Sail Schooner
Mast Height:	72'
Passengers:	24 Overnight
Crew:	6
Home Port:	Northport, Michigan

Captain Dave McGinnis at the helm, sets course for Lake Michigan.

When you board the majestic *Schooner Manitou* at her home port in Northport, Michigan, you're in for three to six days of memorable sailing into the unspoiled regions of northern Michigan and beyond. *Manitou* is one of the largest sailing ships on the Great Lakes, similar in design to a nineteenth century schooner. Her romantic rusticness of yesterday combines with modern radar and equipment to provide a carefree, comfortable voyage. Possible destinations include the Manitou Islands, Cathead Bay, Power Island, Mackinac Island and Beaver Island. But, in the true style of a traditional windjammer, each day's sail course and destination are determined by the wind and weather conditions.

The *Manitou* sets sail under the watchful eye of Captain David McGinnes, one of the original captains who sailed the vessel in 1991 for Traverse Tall Ship Company to her current home port from Lake Champlain. Captain Dave studies the day's weather forecast, predicts wind speed and sets course for Lake Michigan. Life aboard ship is casual and very relaxing with very little contact from the outside world. The TV and stereo were left on shore, traded for the sights and sounds of nature. Guests are busy sharing stories, reading, playing games, taking in the sun on deck, or even pitching in raising the sails…some even take the helm under Captain Dave's guidance (passenger help is not required). The crew is always happy to teach about the ship, knot tying and other "tricks of the sailor's trade" to those interested. When the *Manitou* reaches her destination for the day, guests may spend time ashore exploring coastal villages and light houses, beach combing, hiking, swimming, or using the ship's kayaks or rowing dingy.

Back on board, Chef Stacie Kohler and her assistant are busy most of the day preparing food that delights even the most finicky. She prepares all food served on board from scratch, using the best local ingredients, on a wood burning stove. Each day begins with freshly baked muffins or pastries and steaming Leelanau Coffee Roasters coffee, followed by a full breakfast. Served under way, lunches consist of hearty soups or casseroles, freshly baked breads and salads. In the early evening appetizers are followed by amazing dinners and freshly baked desserts or homemade hand-cranked ice cream.

Guests are delighted and amazed at the quality of fare served, especially after they learn there are no electrical appliances in the galley. Meals are served family style in the cozy main saloon or up on deck. After dinner, some guests have been known to help out with dishes, mainly in an attempt to finagle Stacie's secrets and a recipe or two. Others will take advantage of the long summer days and spend more time on shore, trying to walk off those irresistible desserts. After a beautiful sunset, the main salon becomes a popular gathering spot for card games or conversation. Others will retire to their cabins early for a little reading. Most will sleep early after a full day outdoors. No one wants to be the last to rise when they know that Stacie's goodies will be warm and waiting at 7:00 a.m. Each day brings new adventure.

The ship is quiet on the last morning of the voyage. Only a few short hours away from the end of the trip, each guests spends some time reflecting upon the last few days. Some are gathering addresses. Some are trying to capture the feel of the morning sun, the breeze, the motion of the waves, and to etch the scenery into their memory so that they can take this feeling with them. All are amazed at the total relaxation and peacefulness that they feel.

Schooner Manitou Sailing Day Menu

Before Breakfast Pastry	Cinnamon Rolls
Breakfast	Blueberry Buttermilk Pancakes with Pleva Cherry Pecan Sausages Fresh Cantaloupe
Lunch	Black Bean Chili served with Cheddar Cheese in Sourdough Bread Bowl Rice Salad with a Lime Vinaigrette Marinated Tomato Salad with Fresh Mozzarella and Basil Chocolate Peanut Butter Brownies
Mid-afternoon	Fruit Bowl
Hors d'oeuvres	Sesame Chicken Skewers
Dinner	Poached Salmon with Dill Garlic Butter Oven-Roasted Baby Red Bliss Potatoes Steamed Broccoli with Olive Oil and Lemon
Dessert	Apple Crisp with Caramel Sauce and Fresh Whipped Cream Coffee or Tea

Chef Stacie Kohler prepares Tea Time in *Manitou's* main cabin (left).

Former Chef Kathleen Brennan, busy in the schooner's galley (below).

Captain Dave lends a hand at the barbeque (below, center).

Manitou guests line up for a lunchtime Barbeque Buffet (far left).

CINNAMON ROLLS

1 c.	water
2 Tbsp.	butter *or* margarine
1	egg, beaten
1 pkg. (2-1/4 tsp.)	dry yeast
1/4 lb.	butter *or* margarine, melted
3 to 3-1/2 c.	all-purpose flour
1/4 c.	sugar
1 tsp.	salt

Filling

3/4 c.	sugar
1/4 c.	cinnamon

Icing

2 c.	powdered sugar
1/4 c.	milk or water

Combine water and 2 tablespoons butter in saucepan; heat just until melted. Meanwhile combine all dry ingredients, including yeast. Make well in center of dry ingredients; pour in warm water mixture and egg. Mix with wooden spoon until dough comes together into a shaggy mass. Turn dough out onto lightly floured surface. Knead until dough comes together and is smooth; dough will be soft. With a rolling pin, roll out dough into rectangle approximately 24-inches in width and 12-inches in length. Brush melted butter or margarine on dough with pastry brush, leaving 1-inch margin on bottom of dough (edge closest to you.) Mix together filling ingredients and sprinkle over buttered dough. Start rolling dough from top to bottom (towards you), similar to rolling up a piece of paper. You want the dough to be rolled tightly or it won't make a tight cinnamon roll. When you get to the bottom of the dough (the portion not buttered), butter now and seal dough. Using a serrated knife cut roll into 12 equal parts. Place cinnamon rolls in buttered rectangular baking pan. Bake in preheated 350 degree oven approximately 20 to 30 minutes or until golden brown.

Combine icing ingredients with wire whisk until smooth. Icing should ribbon off whisk, if it doesn't, adjust with additional liquid or sugar. Cool cinnamon rolls slightly and drizzle icing over top, to taste. Serve immediately.

Yield: 12 Cinnamon Rolls

BLACK BEAN CHILI

2 c.	dried black beans
6 c.	cold water
1 lg.	onion, diced
3	garlic cloves, minced
1 Tbsp.	oregano leaves
2 Tbsp.	ground cumin
2 to 3 Tbsp.	hot chili powder
1	green pepper, diced
1 (4 oz.) can	green chilies
1 (16 oz.) can	diced tomatoes
1 (8 oz.) can	sweet corn
2 Tbsp.	stone ground mustard
1/2 Tbsp.	crushed red pepper, (optional)
	Salt and pepper, to taste

Clean beans thoroughly. In large heavy soup pot bring beans and enough cold water to cover the beans to rapid boil. Boil 2 minutes at hard boil. Remove from heat and cover; let stand 1 hour. Drain beans and rinse. Cook beans with 6 cups water listed in ingredients above. Add onion, garlic, green pepper and spices to beans. Boil on medium-high heat until beans are tender, approximately 1-1/2 to 2 hours. Add tomatoes, green chilies, corn, mustard and crushed red pepper, if desired. Season to taste with salt and pepper. Lower heat to medium and continue to cook until chili is piping hot. Serve in Sour Dough Bread Bowls.

Yield: 12 Servings

SOUR DOUGH BREAD STARTER
(*Prepare Two Days in Advance*)

2 c.	water
1-1/2 c.	all-purpose flour
1/2 c.	whole wheat flour

Combine ingredients in 4-quart plastic container with tight fitting lid. It is imperative that you follow the following instructions to the detail. After all ingredients are completely combined, cover with lid and let set at room temperature 12 hours. At this point (after 12 hours) you should see some small bubbles starting to form. It is crucial that you keep up on the "feedings" now. Every six hours you must add 1-cup room temperature water, 3/4 cup all-purpose flour and 1/4 cup whole wheat flour. Continue to feed you starter a total of six times. You can either skip your feeding overnight, or if you're a real go getter, you can set an alarm. If you decide to skip the feeding, you should put the starter in the refrigerator. If your home is above 78 degrees you will need to put your starter in the refrigerator after the first 24 hours. At any time, if your starter begins to overflow from the container, you should transfer it to a larger container. Keep in mind that the longer you allow the starter to ferment, the more character your starter will have (meaning the more "sour" it will taste.) Thirty-six hours after your original starting time your starter should be ready to be used. It will be mild so don't be disappointed on the first go. After using your starter for the first time, you should keep it refrigerated.

Continue to feed your starter once every 3 days when you are not using it. When you want to use your starter again, remove from refrigerator and do an additional feeding. Then let starter sit at room temperature two hours prior to using it in the following recipe for Sour Dough Bread. Be patient, sour dough is an art. Experiment! Just always remember to feed, feed, feed. Your starter is like a baby, it needs food to survive.

SOUR DOUGH BREAD

3 c.	sour dough starter (see above)
3 c.	warm water
1-1/2 Tbsp.	dry active yeast
8 c.	all-purpose flour
4 c.	whole wheat flour
1-1/2 Tbsp.	salt

Preheat oven to 450 degrees. Combine starter, water and yeast in large mixing bowl. Incorporate salt and flours with wooden spoon until dough resembles a shaggy mass. Turn dough out onto lightly floured surface and knead until smooth and elastic. You may need to add additional flour. Place dough into lightly oiled bowl and let rise until doubled in size, approximately 2 hours. Cut dough into 12 equal portions. Round dough portions into balls. Place rolls on corn meal dusted cookie sheet, or if you have a pizza stone sprinkle it with corn meal. Let rolls rise approximately 1 hour. Bake at 450 degrees 20 minutes. A good test is to tap the bottom of the roll; if it sounds hollow it is done throughout. Let cool completely and then cut tops off with knife and hollow out center. These are served with my Black Bean Chili.

RICE SALAD WITH LIME AND CILANTRO VINAIGRETTE

4 c.	pre-cooked rice
1 c.	extra virgin olive oil
1/2 c.	lime juice, freshly squeezed
1 Tbsp.	red wine vinegar
2	garlic cloves, minced
1 Tbsp.	ground cumin
1 Tbsp.	oregano leaves
1	green pepper, diced small
1	red pepper, diced small
1	red onion, diced small
2 Tbsp.	fresh cilantro, chopped
	Salt and pepper, to taste

This is a great recipe for using leftover rice. Even rice pilaf, or mixture of white and wild rice works great, just make sure it is cold. To prepare salad combine rice, peppers and onion. Toss rice mixture with a little extra olive oil.

To prepare vinaigrette whisk together olive oil, lime juice, red wine vinegar, garlic, cumin, oregano and cilantro. Let vinaigrette sit approximately 30 minutes; taste and adjust seasonings. Add salt and pepper to your taste. Pour vinaigrette over rice mixture. Garnish with fresh cilantro leaves and lime slices.

Yield: 12 Servings

MARINATED TOMATO SALAD
WITH FRESH MOZZARELLA AND BASIL

5 to 6 lg.	ripe organic tomatoes
1 lb.	fresh buffalo Mozzarella, cubed
10	fresh basil leaves, finely chopped
2 c.	virgin olive oil
1 c.	aged balsamic vinegar
2	garlic cloves, minced
1 Tbsp.	oregano leaves
	Salt and pepper, to taste

Wash, core and cut each tomato into 6 to 8 wedges. Combine tomatoes, Mozzarella and basil. To prepare vinaigrette, whisk together oil, vinegar, garlic and oregano. Pour vinaigrette over tomato mixture; season with salt and pepper to taste. Let tomato salad marinate at least 1 hour before serving. Taste after 1 hour and adjust seasonings. Drain tomato salad, reserving liquid. Serve tomato salad over organic baby greens. Pour some of the vinaigrette over salad before serving. Serve remaining vinaigrette on the side.

Yield: 12 Servings

CHOCOLATE PEANUT BUTTER BROWNIES

2-1/2 oz. (2-1/2 sqs.)	unsweetened chocolate
1-1/2 sticks	margarine
3	eggs
1-1/2 c.	sugar
3/4 c.	all-purpose flour
1/2 tsp.	salt
1 tsp.	vanilla
1/2 c.	peanut butter

Preheat oven to 375 degrees. Melt margarine in small saucepan. While margarine is melting, cut chocolate into very small pieces. Stir chocolate into melted margarine and continue to melt over medium to low heat until chocolate is completely smooth. Scrape chocolate mixture into medium mixing bowl. Wish a whisk, combine eggs and sugar until smooth. Add egg mixture to chocolate and stir with wooden spoon until completely combined. Stir in flour, salt and vanilla. Pour half of brownie mixture into 9x12-inch pan sprayed with non-stick coating. Dot brownie mixture with peanut butter. Pour remaining half of brownie mixture over top. Bake approximately 20 to 25 minutes or until set to the touch. Let cool completely before cutting.

Yield: 12 Brownies

SESAME CHICKEN SKEWERS

2 to 3 lbs.	chicken breasts, cut into strips
1 c.	sesame oil
1/2 c.	soy sauce
1 tsp.	fresh ginger, chopped
1 Tbsp.	garlic, chopped
1 tsp.	black pepper
1 bunch	scallions, sliced
2 Tbsp.	hot chili oil
2 tsp.	crushed red pepper
24	sm. bamboo skewers
	Sesame seeds, for rolling
	Extra soy sauce, for dipping

Marinate chicken strips in sesame oil, soy sauce, ginger, garlic, pepper and 1 teaspoon crushed red pepper. Toss around and let marinate a couple hours. After marinating, weave chicken on skewers and roll in sesame seeds. Place skewered meat on cookie sheet with proper fitting meat rack on it. Arrange skewers so they do not touch. Bake at 450 degrees approximately 10 minutes.

To prepare dipping sauce combine extra soy sauce, hot chili oil and remaining crushed red pepper. Put dipping sauce in decorative serving bowl and arrange cooked skewers around it. Sprinkle serving platter with sliced scallions. Serve immediately.

Yield: 24 Skewers

POACHED SALMON WITH DILL BUTTER

6 lbs.	fresh farm raised salmon
3 c.	white wine
2	lemons, cut in wedges
1 c.	water
4 Tbsp.	capers
1 lb.	unsalted butter
4 Tbsp.	fresh dill, chopped
	Salt and pepper, to taste

Cut salmon into 12 (8-ounce) portions. Place salmon, skin side down, in deep rectangular baking dish. Cover salmon with white wine, juice of 1 lemon, water, capers and 2 tablespoons fresh chopped dill. Cover baking dish with foil and bake at 375 degrees approximately 20 minutes or firm to the touch. While salmon is baking melt butter over low heat. When fully melted remove frothy foam that has accumulated on top. To do this, skim over the top with ladle and discard down sink. Pour the golden butter into sauceboat, being cautious to only pour in the golden butter, leaving the watery weigh at the bottom. Juice the wedges of lemons into the butter; season with salt, pepper and remaining 2 tablespoons chopped dill. Serve salmon over organic baby greens. Ladle 1-ounce dill butter over salmon. Serve with Roasted Baby Red Bliss Potatoes and Steamed Broccoli with Olive Oil and Lemon.

Yield: 12 Servings

OVEN-ROASTED BABY RED BLISS POTATOES

24 to 30	baby red bliss potatoes, cut in half
1/2 c.	olive oil
2 Tbsp.	fresh rosemary
3	garlic cloves, sliced
	Salt and pepper, to taste

Preheat oven to 450 degrees. Wash potatoes thoroughly and cut in half; pat dry with clean towel. Place potatoes in large bowl. Pour olive oil over potatoes and sprinkle with rosemary, garlic, salt and pepper. Toss potatoes to mix and lay out seasoned potatoes on flat sheet pan. Bake approximately 30 to 45 minutes or until golden brown. Halfway through baking, flip potatoes over with metal spatula so they get brown on all sides.

Yield: 12 Servings

STEAMED BROCCOLI WITH OLIVE OIL AND LEMON

2 lg. heads	broccoli
1 c.	water
1/2 c.	extra virgin olive oil
1	lemon, cut into 12 wedges

This is the most simple recipe you'll ever make. Simply cut the flowerets off the stalk and steam in 1 cup water. Steam 10 to 15 minutes or until vibrantly green and al dente; drain off water. Drizzle olive oil over broccoli. Serve each portion with a lemon wedge. Serve with Poached Salmon and Oven Roasted Red Bliss Potatoes.

Yield: 12 Servings

APPLE CRISP WITH CARAMEL SAUCE

Filling
8	apples, peeled, cored, sliced
1/2 c.	Michigan apple cider
1 Tbsp.	ground cinnamon
1/2 c.	sugar
1 tsp.	nutmeg
1/4 c.	flour

Crumb Topping
1-1/2 c.	all-purpose flour
1-1/2 c.	old-fashioned oats
3/4 c.	sugar
3/4 c.	brown sugar
1 tsp.	cinnamon
2 sticks	unsalted butter, cubed

Caramel Sauce
1-1/2 c.	sugar
2 to 3 c.	heavy cream
1 stick	unsalted butter, cut into small cubes
1 tsp.	vanilla

To prepare filling combine sliced apples, sugar, cinnamon, nutmeg and flour; let stand a few minutes. This will allow some of the natural juices in the apples to come out. Butter a rectangular baking pan and put filling inside. Pour cider over apple mixture and top with crumb topping (directions follow.) Bake at 375 degrees approximately 45 to 55 minutes or until crumb topping is golden brown and filling is bubbling around edges. Serve warm with warm Caramel Sauce (recipe follows) and fresh whipped cream, if desired.

To prepare topping combine flour, oats, sugars and cinnamon. With pastry blender or your hands cut butter into dry ingredients. You do not want big clumps of butter, it will leave big pools of melted butter when baked. Put crumb topping on top of apple filling; do not pack it on, if you have extra save it to top muffins at a later time. If you pack the topping on it will be hard as a rock when cooked.

To prepare Caramel Sauce cook sugar over medium heat until it melts and becomes an amber color; let cook 1 minute. Reduce heat to low or remove from heat altogether. Add some cream, a couple tablespoons at a time, BE CAREFUL, this is VERY hot. Whisk in cream in small portions until all cream is used. Remove from heat completely and whisk in vanilla. Whisk in butter a couple chunks at a time. It may look thin but when it cools it will be very thick. Cool a little and serve warm.

The *Schooner Manitou* sets sail from her home port in Northport, Michigan for three to six days of memorable sailing on the Great Lakes several times each year. Information on *Manitou's* sailing schedule and annual specialty trips such as Mackinac Island, North Channel (Lake Huron watershed), Music Cruise and Story Teller Cruise is available at Traverse Tall Ship Company. Reservations are recommended, as only 24 guests can be accommodated.

SCHOONER MANITOU
Traverse Tall Ship Company
13390 S.W. Bay Shore Drive
Traverse City, Michigan 49684
(231) 941-2000
Toll-Free: (800) 678-0383
www.traverse.com/tallship

U.S. Brig Niagara

Erie Maritime Museum

Original Built:	1812-1813
Mast Heights:	113'4" Foremast
	118'4" Mainmast
Armament	
1813:	(18) 32-pounder carronades
	(2) 12-pounder carronades
1998:	(4) 32-pounder carronades
Crew, 1813:	155 Officers and Men
1998:	40 Officers and Sailors
	(16 professionals, 24 volunteers)
Current Home Port:	Lake Erie's Historic Bay Front Erie, Pennsylvania

The U.S. Brig Niagara at sail on the open waters of the Great Lakes.

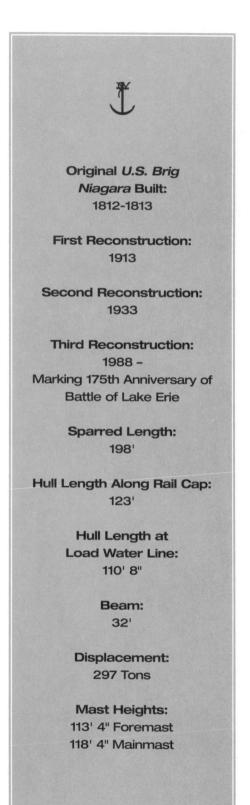

Original *U.S. Brig Niagara* Built:
1812-1813

First Reconstruction:
1913

Second Reconstruction:
1933

Third Reconstruction:
1988 –
Marking 175th Anniversary of Battle of Lake Erie

Sparred Length:
198'

Hull Length Along Rail Cap:
123'

**Hull Length at
Load Water Line:**
110' 8"

Beam:
32'

Displacement:
297 Tons

Mast Heights:
113' 4" Foremast
118' 4" Mainmast

"DON'T GIVE UP THE SHIP"

Commodore Oliver Hazard Perry – 1813

The *U.S. Brig Niagara* is a sailing reconstruction of the relief flagship used by Commodore Oliver Hazard Perry during the second and crucial Battle of Lake Erie in the War of 1812. It is a square-rigged, two-masted warship originally armed with 18 carronades and two long guns. Cramped quarters for the officers and crew, storerooms, sail bin and the galley are located on the berth deck. Magazines for the shot and gunpowder are in the hold below.

On September 10, 1813, the *Niagara* led a fleet of nine American ships in defeating a British squadron of six vessels in the Battle of Lake Erie. It was the first time in Naval history that an entire British squadron had been defeated and captured. The victory was pivotal in the War of 1812. It secured the Northwest Territory, gained control of Lake Erie and the nation's northern borders, and opened supply lines that lifted the nation's morale.

Building the American squadron in Erie during the early 1800s was a remarkable feat in itself, given Erie's mere 500 inhabitants at the time and its remote location. Experienced shipbuilders were recruited from cities such as New York and Philadelphia. Supplies were brought in from across the northeast with Pittsburgh supplying iron, rigging, and anchors and Philadelphia the canvas for sails. Cannons were brought in from Washington, D.C. As there were no sawmills, lumber was cut and squared by hand. In 1812 the U.S. Navy assigned Daniel Dobbins, a Great Lakes shipmaster living in Erie, to direct preliminary construction of the Erie fleet. In February 1813, Commodore Isaac Chauncery, Commander of U.S. Naval Forces on the Great Lakes hired Nash Brown, a New York shipbuilder, to complete the six vessels including two brigs, *Lawrence* and *Niagara*.

In March 1813, Commodore Oliver Hazard Perry took command and the vessels were completed by late July. Perry raised volunteers to augment his sailors and spent the next month training his crew at Put-in-Bay on western Lake Erie.

On September 10, 1813, six British vessels under Britain's Commodore Robert Barclay fought Perry's squadron near Put-in-Bay, Ohio. In the early stages of battle Perry's flagship *Lawrence* and her crew took most of the British fire and suffered great damage. The *Lawrence* was completely disabled and more than 80% of her crew were killed or wounded. In a final attempt at victory, Perry transferred by boat to the *Niagara* with his battle flag entitled, "Don't Give Up The Ship." Perry sailed the *Niagara* into close action, broke through the British battle line and forced Barclay to surrender his entire squadron. At the end of the battle Commodore Perry sent Major General William Henry Harrison his famous message of victory: "We have met the enemy and they are ours."

In 1813 the *Niagara* had a crew of 155 men and boys who manned her sails, 18 carronades and two long guns. In battle, men manned the guns and carronades while boys carried the black powder charges to the guns. Marines and soldiers were assigned to the fighting tops on the masts where they could fire their muskets at sailors on the enemy ships. Officers directed the setting of sails, firing of cannon and maneuvering of the brig in response to orders from the captain.

Living conditions for the crew were very poor leading to the rapid spread of sickness and disease. An iron galley stove was used to bake bread and prepare local fresh meats and vegetables to supplement normal Navy food. Fresh water for cooking, drinking and bathing was obtained by buckets directly from Lake Erie, which was and is fresh water. After disease broke out in the fleet in 1813, Commodore Perry ordered all lake water to be boiled before use.

Following the War of 1812, *Niagara* was used as a station ship in Erie serving as headquarters with officers, supplies and a sick bay. In 1820 she was deliberately sunk in Misery Bay to be preserved for future use. Erie citizens raised and restored *Niagara* on the battle's centennial in 1913 for a grand tour of the Great Lakes. The original keel and several original timbers were used in the restoration. The vessel was reconstructed again in 1933 by the State of Pennsylvania. But by the early 1980s the *Niagara* again required reconstruction to halt severe decay. In 1988, using historically accurate plans and again, several timbers from the original ship of 1812 (in non-structural areas), a third reconstruction was started. It was completed and launched September 10, 1988, marking the 175th anniversary of the Battle of Lake Erie.

Since her commissioning as the "Flagship of Pennsylvania" in 1990, the *U.S. Brig Niagara* has made summer voyages on the Great Lakes and eastern seaboard of the United States and Canada as a Goodwill Ambassador to promote the heritage of Pennsylvania. When not voyaging, *Niagara* is open to the public at the Erie Maritime Museum.

Today, the *U.S. Brig Niagara* carries a crew of 40. Although the quality and safeness of the food have improved, the cook still deals with a lack of refrigeration and one wood stove for all cooking. Not to mention cramped quarters in the galley. The meals aboard are simple but always follow the general rule of "hot, a lot and on time!" These days, actual menus and taste vary depending on each cook's ability. Recent crewmembers have experienced one cook who served nothing but canned beef stew and chili and another who prepared fresh bread every day and served rice so imaginatively that it tasted different every time. Desserts are rare, but a crewmember's birthday or other special occasion finds something special cooking below deck or smuggled on board!

The *U.S. Brig Niagara*, dockside, welcomes visitors aboard at the Tall Ship's Rendezvous in South Haven, Michigan, 1998.

STANDARD FARE ABOARD THE *U.S. BRIG NIAGARA*

Breakfast

Hot Cereal
and/or
Pancakes and Eggs

Lunch

Soup or Casserole
made with leftover
meat from the
Day before

Dinner

Roast Meat
Potatoes or Rice
Vegetable or Salad

Dessert

Desserts are infrequent unless it is a crewmember's birthday.
Otherwise, meals are capped off with cookies and fruit.

RESAPEE FOR BREAD (NAVY STYLE)

The following recipe is a result of many years of trial and error and is an exact copy of a famous bread recipe by a Navy cook:

Furst you take 5 handfulls of sugar. Enuff lard to make hevy paist when you mix it with sugar and 4 or 5 pinches of salt. If you use seawater fergit the salt. Five helmits of flour. Handfull of spud yeast (which you gotta make yerself.) Sometimes this is to much and then again it ain't. If its raining you gotta use more. One helmit of water, size 7-1/4. If usin swamp water boil furst.

Directions fer putting all this together; it don't make much difference how you mix this but do it fer quite a while. It will git reel thick. When it gits to where you can't hardly gitcha hands out, then it's done. The mixin, that is.

Now it will start puffin up. (If it don't that won't hurt non.) Us bakers calls this fermentin, there's a mess of little bugs inside makin alcahol. I think...inyway, from this point on you gotta start bein more carefull cause this doe is reel delicut. After it puffs up reel big, nock it down. Sumtimes it will fall all by itself and save you the trouble. Cut if off in chunks with yer bayonet and wad it up in balls about the size of yer hed. You shood git about 3 balls. It shood rize agin, then its reddy to eat after you bake it sum.

If you can't find iny bred pans you can wash up sum tin cans and use them. You'll find that the bottoms will burn furst so about 1/2 way thru you gotta turn them over. The furst time you make this bred it mite not be so hot but its easy after awhile.

This is enuff stuff fer about 30 min but if the furst few min in chow line duz a lot of bitchin you'll have enuff fer the hole iland.

Oh yes, if yer bakin this fer the C.O. its gotta be nicer and richer so thro in an extra handful of sugar.

Midshipmen Mess
U.S. Naval Academy

U.S. BRIG NIAGARA LUNCH CASSEROLE

25 c.	cooked rice
2 c.	margarine
2 c.	flour
2 qts.	chicken bouillon
2 qts.	milk
1/4 c.	hot sauce
12 c.	chicken, cooked, diced
1 qt.	canned mushrooms with liquid, chopped
16 oz.	pimiento, chopped
1 c.	parsley, chopped
2 lg.	onions, chopped
3 c.	stale bread cubes, buttered
	Seasoned salt
	Pepper

Melt margarine and blend in flour. Stir in liquids and cook, stirring, until thickened. Add hot sauce, seasoned salt and pepper, to taste. Mix with rice and all remaining ingredients except bread cubes. Pour into baking pan and top with bread cubes. Bake in hot oven 10 minutes or until piping hot.

Yield: 50 Servings

U.S. BRIG NIAGARA BIRTHDAY BROWNIES

4 oz.	unsweetened baking chocolate
1 c.	butter
4 lg.	eggs
1 c.	all-purpose flour
2 c.	sugar
2 tsp.	vanilla
3/4 c.	walnuts, chopped

Fudge Frosting

4 oz.	unsweetened baking chocolate
2 c.	sugar
2 lg.	eggs, well beaten
1/4 c.	lite cream or half & half
1/4 c.	butter
2 tsp.	vanilla

Preheat oven to 350 degrees; grease 9x13-inch baking pan. To prepare brownies melt chocolate and butter together over low heat; set aside to cool slightly. Beat eggs and sugar together until frothy. Add vanilla to beaten eggs and then slowly add chocolate mixture, blending well. Add flour and beat until smooth. Fold in walnuts. Spread batter in prepared pan and bake at 350 degrees 25 to 30 minutes. Cool completely on wire rack.

To prepare frosting melt chocolate over low heat in saucepan. Stir in sugar, eggs, cream, butter and vanilla; blend well. Increase heat and bring to boil, stirring constantly. Remove from heat and cool slightly. Spread frosting over completely cooled brownies. Allow frosting to set before cutting into squares.

Since her reconstruction in 1988, the *U.S. Brig Niagara* sails actively on the Great Lakes and eastern seaboard of the United States and Canada, welcoming visitors aboard at every stop. When in her home port at the Erie Maritime Museum, *Niagara* is open to the public. Live re-enactments, original artifacts, photographs, and videos bring to life the vessel's pivotal role in the war of 1812.

Visitors are welcomed aboard the **U.S. Brig Niagara** in her home port at the
Erie Maritime Museum
On Lake Erie's Historic Bay Front
150 East Front Street, Erie, Pennsylvania 16507
(814) 452-2744
Website: www.brigniagara.org

Monday – Saturday 9:00 am to 5:00 pm
Sunday Noon to 5:00 p.m.
Please call ahead for the Niagara's sailing schedule.

Also on Exhibit at the Erie Maritime Museum…

The prow of the *U.S.S. Wolverine*, originally the *U.S.S. Michigan*, has also been restored and preserved by the Erie Maritime Museum and is a permanent exhibit at the museum.

Commissioned in 1844, the *U.S.S. Michigan* was the first iron-hulled warship in the U.S. Navy and the first of her kind on the Great Lakes. Built in Pittsburgh and re-assembled in Erie, she was 167 feet long, displaced 450 tons and was powered by side-paddlers and sails. *Michigan* provided a formidable and grand Naval presence on the Great Lakes. After the War of 1812, many Americans continued to distrust British intentions in Canada and argued for continued military protection of the U.S. northern border. With the British sympathetic towards the confederacy during the U.S. Civil War, those fears worsened. During the Civil War, *U.S.S. Michigan* guarded a prison camp for Confederate soldiers on Johnson's Island, near Sandusky, Ohio. At one point, the Confederacy planned to capture *Michigan* and launch an attack on the Union from the north. The captain and crew of *Michigan* discovered and foiled the plan.

In 1905 she was renamed *U.S.S. Wolverine* when a new battleship was commissioned as *U.S.S. Michigan*. During the 1913 Centenary Commemoration of the Battle of Lake Erie, the *Wolverine* had the honor of towing the reconstructed *Niagara* around the Great lakes in a grand patriotic celebration.

Despite the personal pleas of President and former Navy man Franklin Delano Roosevelt, the *U.S.S. Wolverine* was scrapped in 1949 when local efforts to save her finally exhausted. Her prow, displayed but exposed to the weather on State Street in Erie, was saved from the scrap man's torch.

On February 26, 1998, the prow was moved to its new home on the First Mezzanine Level of the Erie Maritime Museum. The prow underwent extensive restoration that included welding, scraping, painting and refitting of her scrollwork. The *Wolverine* exhibit is popular with Naval enthusiasts, historians and local residents.

S.T.V. Pathfinder and T.S. Playfair

Tall Ship Adventures

STV Pathfinder (above)

Year Built:	1963, Kingston Shipyards
Designer:	Francis A. MacLachlin
Length Overall:	72'
Beam:	15'
Main Mast:	54'
Power:	Volvo TAMD41-H
Crew:	29 (1 Captain, 1 Exec. Officer, 3 Watch Officers, 1 Bosun, 1 Cook, 1 Chief Petty Officer, 3 Petty Officers, 18 Trainees)
Home Port:	Toronto, Ontario

TS Playfair (above, right)

Year Built:	1973, Canada Dredge and Dock Co.
Designer:	Francis A. MacLachlin
Length Overall:	72'
Beam:	15'
Main Mast:	54'
Power:	Detroit Diesel 3-71
Home Port:	Toronto, Ontario

The *TS Playfair* anchored along a scenic coastline of the Great Lakes.

*S*ister ships *S.T.V. Pathfinder* and *T.S. Playfair* are brigantine training vessels, taking their design from tall ships of the past. As part of Tall Ship Adventures, these two ships proudly embark every summer with crews including young people (aged 14 to 18), for one and two week voyages that build sailing knowledge and character. This is not a sailing school, but a non-profit organization dedicated to the development of youth. Fun, challenge and the experience of a lifetime are found as part of the crew of a tall ship.

Leaving Toronto behind, the sails are unfurled and a course set for the open waters of Lake Ontario and beyond. Living and working aboard a traditionally square rigged tall ship with other teenagers is a unique learning environment for the development of self-reliance, self-esteem, teamwork, responsibility and leadership in young people.

Both the *Pathfinder* and *Playfair* carry crews of 29, including an adult captain, an experienced youth officer staff of 10, and 18 trainees (teenagers.) Life aboard makes special demands and provides special rewards for teenage trainees from the moment they begin their hands-on adventure. Each trainee becomes a full working member of the crew, on and off watch, 24 hours a day.

As a safety precaution for the young crew, *S.T.V. Pathfinder's* galley features a propane monitor that "sniffs" for leaks and shuts off the system automatically.

The ships sail all day and all night, requiring a traditional three watch rotation. Trainees are assigned to one of the watches with duties including taking the helm, assisting with ship maneuvers (tacking, gybing, anchoring, etc.), performing ship's maintenance and assisting with food preparation and clean-up.

And…there is plenty of time for fun too, both on board and off. *S.T.V. Pathfinder* and *T.S. Playfair* usually moor or visit a port every two to three days. Shore leave allows time to take in different ports and enjoy some leisure time ashore.

Teenage crewmembers quickly master the art of cooking on board.

It is the experience of a lifetime for the young crewmembers. "When you are aboard a tall ship, all of your senses are alive." Says Maurice Smith, original captain of the *Pathfinder*. "You can smell, and almost taste, the water in the air; you can hear the crash of waves and slice of the boat, feel the wind on your face and the strong sense of motion. All of your senses are being affected by the vessel in motion that you are controlling. It is thrilling!"

Food preparation on a brigantine tall ship is not easy. The cook is a youth officer; the fresh food storage space limited and unpredictable weather conditions can make cooking (and eating!) a challenge. Nevertheless, crews eat pretty well…though admittedly not gourmet. Recipes used include helpful hints to the cook, for both preparation and creative use of leftovers. All crewmembers take a turn helping with food preparation and clean-up.

Crewmembers gather on deck for a souvenir photo to take home (above). A hungry sailor enjoys a bowl of hot pasta after an adventurous day on the open water (below). *T.S. Playfair* sails gracefully across Lake Ontario (right).

BREAKFASTS

Instructions and hints for the cook:

· Breakfasts are to include choice of cold or hot cereal, milk, apple juice and canned fruit.

· Apple juice is for the seamen and PO's

· Orange juice is for the Wardroom

· Each breakfast has one added item; this can be omitted if weather is brutal.

· People may have their one piece of fresh fruit a day at breakfast if they prefer.

· Put juice and milk in the refrigerator in the evening so it will be cold in the AM.

· As all meals, you are preparing for four sets of eaters!! Three watches and the Wardroom…keep this in mind as you heat and serve. You want stuff left for the last watch and wardroom.

MUFFINS

To be prepared according to directions on package. May be served with butter and jam.

Note: You may add things like chocolate chips, apples or cinnamon sugar but oranges will not react so well with the leavening agents in the mix.

PANCAKES

Prepare mix according to package directions.

Variation: APPLE CINNAMON PANCAKES

4 c.	apples, peeled, diced
1/2 c.	flour
2 Tbsp.	sugar
1 to 2 Tbsp.	cinnamon

Toss diced apples with flour, sugar and cinnamon. Add to prepared batter. Heat griddle to medium high (3 to 4.) Warm oven to 250 degrees to keep pancakes warm after cooking; grease pan or griddle. Using a small scoop or ladle, place 1/3 to 1/4 cup batter per pancake in pan or griddle. When rim forms and bubbles begin to break on the surface, flip cake over to brown. Spread on warming pan; if you stack them they'll get soggier. Place in oven to keep warm. Serve with syrup.

BAGELS AND CREAM CHEESE

Cut bagel in half and toast. Serve with peanut butter, jam, cream cheese and honey.

ENGLISH MUFFINS WITH HARD BOILED EGGS

Cut and toast English muffins. Serve with peanut butter, jam and honey. To boil eggs, put eggs in large pasta strainer. Put strainer in pot of cold water, enough to cover eggs; bring to boil. Turn off and leave for 30 minutes. Remove and peel.

FRENCH TOAST WITH SYRUP

30	eggs, beaten
3 to 4 c.	milk
1 Tbsp.	salt
1/4 c.	sugar
1 to 2 Tbsp.	cinnamon
60 slices	bread

Break eggs and beat with milk, salt, sugar and cinnamon. Heat large frying pan or griddle to medium. Warm oven to 250 degrees to keep toast warm after cooking; grease pan or griddle. Dip bread into egg mixture and gently lift onto pan. Cook until brown and puffy, then flip to brown other side. Keep warm in oven. Serve with syrup.

LUNCH

Note: When soup is for lunch, ask how many people want soup so you have an idea how many cans to open.
Figure 1 cup per person.

HOT DOGS AND SOUP

60	hot dogs
60	buns
	Ketchup, mustard and relish

*P*ut hot dogs in pot and cover with water. Bring water to boil; reduce heat to simmer. Serve and enjoy! If you get energetic, you could heat the buns in 200 degree oven 15 minutes or so!

GRILLIES

Bread slices
Cheese slices
Butter

*B*utter 1 side of each slice of bread. Place 1 slice cheese between 2 slices of bread, buttered side out. Grill until brown and crunchy and cheese is melted. Serve with ketchup.

PASTA SALAD

Pasta, (Penne, Rotini, Fusilli)
Oil

Cook pasta until al dente. Drain and rinse pasta with cold water. Toss pasta in oil and cool in refrigerator, stirring occasionally.

Note: Pasta salad is much better cold. Cook the pasta the day ahead and save yourself a lot of trouble.

VARIATIONS:

#1 CREAMY HAM AND VEGETABLE PASTA

Ham, diced
Vegetables, (peppers, celery, broccoli, carrots), diced
Ranch dressing

Toss ham and vegetables with cooled pasta. Add dressing, using enough to coat. Toss and season with salt and pepper, to taste. Garnish with green onions or shredded carrot. Serve cold.

#2 CREAMY CHICKEN AND VEGETABLE PASTA

Chicken, cut into bite-sized pieces
Vegetables, (peppers, celery, apples, cucumber), diced
Dressing: combine mayonnaise, Worcestershire sauce, tabasco
     sauce, salt and pepper. *Or,* use creamy Caesar salad dressing
     or creamy cucumber salad dressing.

Cook chicken in wok until no longer pink. Add vegetables, chicken and dressing to cooled pasta. Garnish with chopped green onions or cucumber bits.

#3 TOMATO BASIL PASTA SALAD

Tomatoes, diced
Green onions, diced
Peppers, diced
Parmesan cheese

Vinaigrette: combine olive oil, red wine vinegar, basil, garlic, salt and pepper. Or, use Golden Caesar salad dressing or Golden Italian salad dressing.

Add vegetables, Parmesan cheese and dressing to cooled pasta; toss to mix. Garnish with green onions or tomato bits.

#4 TOMATO, SPINACH AND CHICKPEA PASTA

Tomatoes, diced
Peppers, diced
Spinach, diced
Chickpeas, drained
Ricotta cheese, crumbled
Golden Italian salad dressing

Add vegetables, chickpeas, crumbled Ricotta cheese and dressing to cooled pasta; toss to mix. Garnish with chopped green onions or Ricotta cheese.

#5 CREAMY EGGS, CHEDDAR AND BROCCOLI PASTA

Eggs, hard boiled, chopped into bite-sized pieces
Broccoli, chopped into bite-sized pieces
Cheddar cheese, diced
Mayonnaise
Tabasco sauce
Worcestershire sauce
Salt and pepper, to taste

Combine eggs, broccoli, cheese, mayonnaise, tabasco sauce and Worcestershire sauce with cooled pasta. Season to taste with salt and pepper. Garnish with cheese bits, broccoli florets or sliced eggs.

HAM AND CHEESE PITAS OR HAMBURGER BUNS

Pitas or buns
Processed cheese slices
Ham slices
Lettuce
Mustard, mayonnaise, peanut butter and jam

Cut pitas or buns in half. Put out cheese slices. Open ham and divide between watches. Wash and break lettuce into pieces. Serve with mustard, mayonnaise, peanut butter and jam. Let people make their own great sandwiches.

TUNA MELT

Tuna
Mayonnaise
Celery, chopped
Cheese, grated
Flat bread

Mix tuna with mayonnaise and celery; spread on flat bread. Sprinkle with grated cheese. Heat at 350 degrees 15 minutes or until cheese melts.

BAKED BEANS AND FLATBREAD

Flatbread
Olive oil
Beans
Tomato paste

Brush bread with olive oil and heat in oven. Heat beans over medium heat, stirring from bottom up, until heated through. Add tomato paste. Cut bread into wedges. Serve.

Variation: For Mexican style baked beans add a jar of salsa.

DINNERS

SOUP

START EARLY…
Follow directions on can. Use medium heat and stir often from bottom.
This helps to evenly cook and heat soup.

CHILI CON CARNE

10 lbs.	ground beef
8 oz.	onions, chopped
1	garlic clove, minced
2-1/2 qts.	tomatoes, diced
2 qts.	tomato puree
1 qt.	water
3 oz.	chili powder
1-1/2 Tbsp.	cumin
1-1/2 Tbsp.	salt
1 tsp.	black pepper
2 oz.	sugar
9 lbs. + 8 oz.	Kidney beans

Cook ground beef with onion and garlic until beef loses pink color. Add tomatoes and seasonings; cook until blended. Add beans, cover and simmer 1 hour. Add water if chili becomes too thick.

GARDEN CHILI (VEGETARIAN)

3/4 c.	vegetable oil
3 lbs. + 12 oz.	onions, chopped
1-1/2 Tbsp.	garlic, minced
2 lbs. + 4 oz.	celery, chopped
1 lb.	carrots, finely chopped
2 tsp.	dried oregano
2 Tbsp.	cumin
2 Tbsp.	chili powder
2 Tbsp.	salt
1 Tbsp.	pepper
1 lb.	green peppers, chopped
2 lbs.	zucchini, chopped
1 lb. + 8 oz.	canned mushrooms
5 lbs. + 6 oz.	tomatoes, diced
1 qt.	water
5 lbs. + 6 oz.	red beans
1/3 c.	lemon juice

Heat oil. Add onions and garlic; sauté until transparent. Add celery, carrots and seasonings to onions. Cook until tender crisp. Add remaining ingredients and heat thoroughly.

HAM AND VEGETABLE FRIED RICE

4 c.	water
2 c.	rice
1/4 c.	vegetable oil
4 med.	onions, chopped
4	celery stalks, chopped
4 med.	carrots, diced
8	garlic cloves, chopped *or* 1 to 2 tsp. garlic powder
4 Tbsp.	ginger root, grated *or* 1 tsp. ground ginger
4 Tbsp.	soy sauce
4 tsp.	curry powder
4 tsp.	cumin
1 tsp.	hot pepper sauce
4	sweet green peppers, diced
4 c.	cabbage, shredded
2 c.	peas or corn kernels
8 c.	ham, cook, diced
	Salt, to taste

Boil water in saucepan; add rice. Reduce heat, cover and simmer 20 minutes or until rice is tender. DO NOT OVERCOOK. Rinse rice with cold water and drain. In large heavy saucepan heat oil over medium-high heat; cook onion until softened, stirring constantly. Add celery, carrots, garlic, ginger, soy sauce, curry powder, cumin and hot pepper sauce; cook 2 minutes, stirring constantly. Add green pepper, cabbage and peas; cook an additional 2 minutes. Add ham and rice. Cook, stirring constantly, until heated through and rice is light brown. Add salt to taste. Serve hot.

Note: Don't worry if you have to cook this in batches and keep it in the oven.

CHICKEN STIR FRY WITH VEGETABLES

6 lbs. + 4 oz.	chicken breasts, cubed
3 lbs. + 8 oz.	broccoli
3 lbs.	carrots, sliced
1 lb. + 4 oz.	mushrooms, sliced
12 oz.	green onions, sliced
3 lbs.	water chestnuts, sliced
	PC *or* VH stir fry sauce

Cook chicken in wok over medium-high heat until no longer pink. In separate saucepan stir fry vegetables until tender crisp. Add salt and pepper to taste. Add sauce to meat. Serve hot.

SWEET AND SOUR CHICKEN
Use pre-made Sweet and Sour Sauce or use recipe below.
Prepare same as for Chicken Stir Fry

Sweet and Sour Sauce

1-1/4 c.	sugar
1/4 c.	corn starch
1 c.	cider vinegar
2-1/2 c.	water
1/4 c.	soy sauce
3/5 c.	ketchup

Combine sugar and corn starch. Add vinegar, water and soy sauce; stir until smooth. Add ketchup and cook in saucepan until translucent, stirring constantly, approximately 5 to 10 minutes.

PASTA WITH TOMATO SAUCE
Use prepared pasta sauce and add available additions (onions, peppers, etc.)
OR, prepare following sauce:

5 (28 oz.) cans	diced tomatoes *or* spaghetti sauce
3 to 5	green peppers, diced
3 to 5	onions, diced
4 to 8	garlic cloves, minced *or* 1 to 2 tsp. garlic powder
1 to 2 cans	mushrooms
5 Tbsp	basil
2-1/2 Tbsp.	oregano
1 to 2 Tbsp.	sugar, depending on acidity of tomatoes
1 Tbsp.	salt
3 tsp.	pepper
5 (28 oz.) cans	crushed tomatoes
1 to 2 Tbsp.	vegetable oil

Heat oil in saucepan; add onions and cook until translucent. Add green peppers and mushrooms. Add garlic, basil and oregano. Add diced tomatoes and cook over medium heat 5 minutes. Add crushed tomatoes. Add sugar and flavorings. Add salt and pepper, to taste. Serve hot over pasta. Chunky pastas work best with this sauce.

SHEPHERD'S PIE

4 to 5 lbs.	lean ground beef
4	onions, chopped
4 (500ml) cans	vegetables
	Mashed potatoes
	Cheese, grated, (optional)

Preheat oven to 350 to 400 degrees. Brown ground beef with onion. Prepare mashed potatoes (peel, quarter and boil potatoes 20 to 30 minutes and mash) or use Idahoan instant potatoes for 30 and prepare according to package directions. Divide meat into 4 pans. Place thin layer of vegetables over meat in each pan. Top with thick layer of mashed potatoes. Sprinkle grated cheese over top, if desired. Heat in oven until very hot, approximately 30 minutes.

LAST NIGHT SOUP

This soup is a hearty soup that uses up any leftover vegetables and meat from the course. Some other things that you might want to add to the soup are pasta or rice, or if there is any leftover meat such as ham you can throw it in as well. Make sure the meat is still good! And, if you do add meat, make sure it is cooked before you add it.

15 c.	water + bouillon cubes (according to ratio on package)
10 c.	vegetables, diced (potatoes, onions, carrots, celery, corn kernels, green beans, peas, lentils, kidney beans, etc.)
	Salt and pepper, to taste

Heat water; add bouillon cubes or powder envelopes to make stock. Dice vegetables and add to water. Bring soup to boil. Reduce heat and simmer until potatoes are tender. Remember, the smaller you cut things, the faster they cook. Season and serve with warm flatbread.

FARMER'S SAUSAGE

Sausages

Boil sausages 10 minutes, then fry to brown. Serve hot.

MEXICAN CASSEROLE

1/4 c.	vegetable oil
2-1/2 c.	water
4 to 5	onions, chopped
8 to 10	garlic cloves, minced *or* 2 to 3 tsp. garlic powder
3 cans	mushrooms, sliced
4 to 6	green peppers, chopped
5 c.	rice
5 cans	kidney beans, rinsed, drained
5 cans	tomatoes
5 Tbsp.	chili powder
2 Tbsp.	cumin
1 tsp.	cayenne pepper
5 c.	Mozzarella cheese, grated

Heat oil and water over medium heat. Add onion, garlic, mushrooms and green peppers. Simmer, stirring often, until onion is tender; approximately 10 minutes. Add rice, beans, tomatoes, chili powder, cumin and cayenne pepper. Cover and simmer 40 minutes or until rice is tender and most of liquid is absorbed. Transfer to lasagna pans, sprinkle with cheese and bake until cheese is melted.

LASAGNA CASSEROLE

5 lbs.	ground beef
12 oz.	onions, minced
2	garlic cloves, minced
3 qts.	tomato sauce
1 qt.	tomato paste
1 tsp.	pepper
1 tsp.	basil
1 Tbsp.	oregano
2 lbs. + 8 oz.	noodles
2 gal.	boiling water
2 lbs. + 8 oz.	Mozzarella cheese, grated
6 oz.	Parmesan cheese
2 lbs. + 8 oz.	Ricotta cheese or cottage cheese

Cook ground beef with onion and garlic until meat has lost pink color; drain off fat. Add tomato sauce, tomato paste and seasonings to meat. Continue cooking approximately 30 minutes, stirring occasionally. Cook noodles until al dente; store in cold water and drain when ready to use. Combine cheeses. In lasagna pans arrange layers of sauce, noodles and cheese. Sprinkle tops with cheese. Bake at 350 degrees 35 to 40 minutes.

LAST NIGHT CASSEROLE

This is the same idea as the Last Night Soup. Use the Tuna Casserole as your base recipe and add leftover vegetables or meats. If you have leftover meat you want to use, make sure it is enough to substitute entirely for the tuna.

TUNA CASSEROLE

(As Last Night Casserole) or Other Available Meat

3 kgs.	canned tuna
2 to 3 med.	onions, chopped
2 liters *or* 2 (46 oz.) cans	cream of chicken soup, condensed
1-1/2 liters	milk
1/2 kg.	Cheddar cheese, grated
2.5 kgs.	egg noodles

Put water on to boil; preheat oven to 350 to 400 degrees. Mix together soup, milk and 1/2 cheese in saucepan; heat to melt cheese. Add tuna and onions to sauce. Cook noodles 5 to 7 minutes in boiling water; drain and add to casserole. Divide mixture into 4 lasagna pans. Sprinkle remaining 1/2 cheese over top. Heat in oven until heated through, approximately 20minutes.

BEEF STROGANOFF

2.5 kgs.	round steak
6 med.	onions, sliced
3 to 6	celery stalks, diced
48 to 60 oz.	condensed mushroom soup
3 to 4 c.	milk or water
2 to 3 cans	mushrooms, drained
1 to 2 c.	mayonnaise
	Egg noodles

Cut round steak into thin strips. Fry meat with onions and celery in oil over medium heat until cooked (you should do this in 4 to 6 batches.) Mix mushroom soup with milk or water and heat; blend in mayonnaise. Add mushrooms. Mix together meat and sauce; heat but do not boil. Cook egg noodles; they require less time than regular spaghetti.

CUCUMBER SALAD

8	cucumbers, thinly sliced
1/4 c.	sugar
2 c.	rice wine vinegar

*C*ombine all ingredients. Chill and serve.

LETTUCE SALAD

3 to 4	heads lettuce, washed, broken into small pieces
	Carrots, chopped
	Celery, chopped
	Peppers, chopped
	Tomatoes, chopped
	Salad dressing

*C*ombine lettuce with chopped vegetables. Serve with salad dressing.

RICE

Rice
Water

*P*ut rice and water in pot; bring to boil and simmer. Check with fork, stirring makes rice mushy and gross.

SNACKS

Follow package directions for cakes, brownies, etc.

RICE KRISPIE SQUARES

6 c.	rice krispies
40	marshmallows
1/2 tsp.	vanilla
1/4 c.	butter *or* margarine

Melt butter or margarine with marshmallows over low heat, stirring frequently. Remove from heat when melted and stir in vanilla. Add cereal, stirring until coated. Transfer mixture to greased pan and press down. Cool and cut into squares. Serve and enjoy!

RICE PUDDING

1 kg.	rice
3 liters	milk
300 g.	sugar
1 to 2 Tbsp.	vanilla
2	orange peels
3 tsp.	ground ginger
2 Tbsp.	fresh ginger

Combine rice with sugar and 2 liters of milk in pot; bring to boil. Reduce heat to simmer. Add orange peel and ginger. Add remaining 1 liter milk, if necessary, to make a smooth and creamy pudding. Add vanilla to taste. Serve hot, but remember to remove orange peel and chunks of ginger.

Life aboard the *S.T.V. Pathfinder* or *T.S. Playfair* makes special demands and provides special rewards for teenage trainees from the moment they begin their hands-on adventure. Contact Tall Ship Adventures to sign on for the experience of a lifetime.

TALL SHIP ADVENTURES
Operated by Toronto Brigantine, Inc.
283 Queen's Quay West
Toronto, Ontario M5V 1A2
Telephone: (416) 203-9949   Fax: (416) 203-0725
Email: torbrig@the-wire.com
Website: www.the-wire.com/torbrig

Tall Ship Windy

"Chicago's Tall Ship"

Year Built:	1995, Detyens Shipyard, Charleston, SC, for Robert Marthai
Maiden Voyage:	June 1996
Sparred Length:	148'
Length on Hull:	109'
Sails:	11
Sail Area:	4839 sq. ft.
Beam:	25'
Draft:	8.5'
Rig:	Four-Masted Gaff Topsail Schooner, (Class "B" Tall Ship)
Mast Height:	84'
Power:	Cummins 6C TA 300 hp
Crew:	Up to 17
Passengers:	150
Current Home Port:	Navy Pier, Chicago, Illinois

Windy's great room and galley in the aft cabin, a favorite gathering spot for hungry sailors.

From the 1800s through the 1920s more than 3,000 schooners sailed the Great Lakes, many docking in the Chicago River to unload goods and bring immigrants to the end of their journey. As a true sailing ship, *Windy of Chicago*, as she was christened, has all the character and charm of the great romantic days of sail. Like the old trading schooners and sail training ships, she is silently pushed by the winds once her sails are set and engines turned off. This four-masted schooner has been a dream of her designer and owner, Robert Marthai, for several years. "Captain Bob," as he is affectionately known, brought *Windy* to her home at Navy Pier in Chicago in 1996, bringing with her memories of what commercial sailing on the Great Lakes used to be like.

Robert Marthai—Captain, owner, designer and builder of *Windy*.

Bob's love of sailing and fascination with the history of tall ships and the Great Lakes is evident in the design of *Windy*. His schooner combines sailing tradition with his concern for safety, including being built of modern materials under close U.S. Coast Guard inspection and testing. *Windy* is the only certified four-masted sailing vessel in the United States. The Marthai family shares Bob's love of sailing. His wife, Janine, is the ship's Purser and 18-year-old daughter Sonya (who has been sailing for 17 years) serves as perhaps the youngest, but most experienced crewmember.

As an authentic sailing ship, the *Windy* sails with the winds so every cruise is unique. Passengers find the experience exciting, yet relaxing. Daily cruises allow plenty of time and space on deck to take in the view and trade winds. Guests may help by raising and trimming the sails, or even taking a trick at the wheel. Below deck the aft cabin, with its large galley and mess room, is a favorite gathering spot for hungry sailors or those looking to escape the weather.

During the winter months *Windy* embarks on week long Caribbean cruises complete with daily island hopping and evening sunsets from the deck. The sights and sounds of active ports are balanced with the serenity of unspoiled nature and wildlife while under way. Unlike typical passenger vessels, all of *Windy's* passengers are invited to serve as quasi-crew, learning the ropes and procedures of tall ship sailing. There are watches to serve, sails to trim and stars to steer by. Everyone takes part to the degree of their ability and interest.

Captain Bob with his crew aboard the *Windy* in 1998. Left to right: Captain Bob, Nikki, Aubry, Kelly, Libby, Sonya, Peter and Janine.

Windy's fulltime cook stays busy in the galley from sun-up to sundown, whipping up a delicious variety of hot and hearty crew favorites. "Captain Bob," a sailor since 1960, looks forward to the cook's Chicken Divan. Sonya prefers the Pineapple Casserole, but the cook is quick to claim Pumpkin Pie Squares as the best food on board.

Tall Ship Windy at sail on the open waters of the Great Lakes.

'CREW FOOD'
Nibbling Crackers

1 (11 oz.) box	oyster crackers
3/4 c.	oil
1 pkg.	Hidden Valley Ranch original dressing mix
1 tsp.	lemon pepper
1 tsp.	dill weed

*W*arm oil; stir in seasonings. Add crackers and mix to coat. Drain on paper towels. Store in airtight container.

SUFFERN INN SALAD
A Great Alternative to Tossed Salad

	juice of 1 lemon
6 Tbsp.	mayonnaise
1 sm.	onion, finely minced
2 c.	frozen peas
1 c.	Swiss *or* Cheddar cheese, shredded
2 c.	lettuce, torn in bite-sized pieces
8	bacon slices, crisply fried, crumbled *or* 1 jar Hormel real bacon pieces (saves time)
	Salt and pepper, to taste

*C*ombine lemon juice, mayonnaise, onion, peas, cheese, salt and pepper; cover and refrigerate overnight. Add bacon and lettuce just before serving.

Yield: 6 Servings

APPLE SALAD

4 to 6	tart apples, peeled, chopped
1 sm. can	pineapple chunks, drained
1/2 c.	golden raisins

Dressing

	juice of 1 lemon
2 to 3 Tbsp.	mayonnaise
	whipped topping, to coat

Mix together salad ingredients. Combine dressing ingredients and stir into salad. Refrigerate several hours before serving.

ZUCCHINI PINEAPPLE BREAD

3	eggs
2 c.	sugar
1 tsp.	vanilla
1 c.	oil
2 c.	zucchini, peeled, seeded, grated or finely chopped, drained
1/2 c.	raisins
3 c.	flour
1 tsp.	baking powder
1 tsp.	salt
1 tsp.	baking soda
1 c.	crushed pineapple, drained
1 c.	nuts, chopped

Mix together eggs, sugar and vanilla. Add oil and beat well. Add zucchini, flour, baking powder, salt and baking soda. Stir in pineapple, raisins and nuts. Pour batter into 1 large or 2 small greased loaf pans. Bake at 325 degrees 1 hour in 2 small pans; 1-1/2 hours for 1 large pan.

90-MINUTE BUTTERCRUST BREAD

Start-to-finish in approximately 90 minutes. A traditional, basic white bread made easy by a streamlined method. And, made extra-special with butter in the dough, plus melted butter over the top of each loaf.

4-1/2 to 5 c.	all-purpose flour
2 pkgs.	rapid rise yeast
2 Tbsp.	sugar
2 tsp.	salt
1 c.	milk
3/4 c.	water
2 Tbsp.	butter *or* margarine
1 Tbsp.	butter *or* margarine, melted

Preheat oven to 400 degrees. In large mixer bowl combine 2 cups flour, yeast, sugar and salt; mix well. In saucepan heat milk, water and 2 tablespoons butter until warm (120 to 130 degrees); butter does not need to melt. Add warm milk mixture to flour mixture. Beat at low speed until moistened; beat 3 minutes at medium speed. By hand, gradually stir in enough remaining flour to make firm dough. Knead on well floured surface until smooth and elastic, approximately 5 to 10 minutes. Place in greased bowl, turning to grease top. Cover; let rise in warm oven (turn oven to lowest setting for 1 minute, turn off) for 20 minutes. Punch down dough; divide into 2 parts. On lightly floured surface, roll or pat each half into 7x14-inch rectangle. Starting with shorter side, roll up lightly, pressing dough into roll with each turn. Pinch edges and ends to seal. Place in 2 greased 4x8-inch or 5x9-inch loaf pans. Cover; let rise in warm oven until light and doubled, approximately 30 minutes. With very sharp knife, make slash across top of each loaf; pour melted butter into each slash. Bake at 400 degrees 20 to 30 minutes until golden brown. Remove from pans; cool.

Yield: 2 Loaves

CHICKEN DIVAN
The Captain's Favorite – a Sailor Since 1960

2 (10 oz.) pkgs.	frozen broccoli, cooked, drained
2 c.	cooked chicken, diced
1 can	cream of mushroom soup
1 can	cream of chicken soup
1 c.	mayonnaise
1 tsp.	lemon juice
1/2 tsp.	curry powder
1 c.	sharp cheese, shredded
	Bread crumbs
	Butter

Arrange broccoli in 9x13-inch pan; cover with chicken. Combine soups, mayonnaise, lemon juice and curry powder. Spread soup mixture over chicken. Sprinkle cheese over top. Sprinkle bread crumbs over cheese. Dot with butter. Bake, uncovered, at 350 degrees 25 to 35 minutes.

Note: We always double the recipe, or more. Some to eat and some to freeze, with the preparation and clean up only once!

Yield: 6 Servings

PINEAPPLE CASSEROLE

The Senior Deckhand's Favorite – She's 17 and Has Been Sailing for the Last 16 Years!

1 (20 oz.) can	pineapple chunks
3 Tbsp.	flour
1/2 c.	sugar
1 c.	Cheddar cheese, shredded
1/4 c.	butter, melted
1/2 c.	cracker crumbs

Drain pineapple, reserving 3 tablespoons of juice. Combine flour and sugar; stir in juice. Add cheese and pineapple. Transfer to greased 1-quart casserole. Combine melted butter with cracker crumbs and sprinkle over top. Bake at 350 degrees 20 to 30 minutes or until lightly browned.

Note: This is good hot or cold. We always double or triple this recipe!

Yield: 4 to 6 Servings

CHINESE RICE

Fast and Easy!

1 stick	margarine, melted
1 c.	rice, uncooked
1 sm. can	sliced mushrooms
1 can	water chestnuts, with liquid
1 can	onion soup *or* beef consommé
1 soup can	water

Combine all ingredients in 2-quart casserole. Bake at 350 degrees 1 hour.

PUMPKIN PIE SQUARES
The Cook's Favorite – Feeds More Than a Pumpkin Pie Does!

Crust

1 c.	flour
1/2 c.	quick cooking oatmeal
1/2 c.	brown sugar, packed
1/2 c.	margarine

Filling

2 c.	pumpkin *or* 1 (1 lb.) can
1 (12 oz.) can	evaporated milk
2	eggs
3/4 c.	sugar
1/2 tsp.	salt
2 tsp.	cinnamon
1/2 tsp.	ginger
1/4 tsp.	cloves

Topping

1/2 c.	walnuts *or* pecans
1/2 c.	brown sugar
2 Tbsp.	margarine

Combine crust ingredients and mix until crumbly; press into ungreased 9x13-inch pan. Bake at 350 degrees 15 minutes. Combine filling ingredients and beat well. Pour filling onto baked crust. Bake at 350 degrees an additional 20 minutes. Combine topping ingredients and sprinkle over baked filling. Return to oven and bake an additional 15 to 20 minutes, until filling is set. Cool in pan on rack. Cut into squares.

Yield: 18 Servings

NO BAKE CHOCOLATE ECLAIR CAKE

1 box	graham crackers
8 to 9 oz.	Cool Whip
2 pkgs.	instant vanilla pudding
2-1/2 to 3 c.	milk
1 container	milk chocolate frosting

Mix pudding with milk; beat together well. Fold in Cool Whip. Line 9x13-inch pan with graham crackers. Pour 1/2 pudding onto crackers. Add layer of crackers over top. Pour remaining pudding over crackers and cover with another layer of crackers. Frosting can be softened in microwave 20 to 30 seconds before spreading over top. Refrigerate several hours.

PLUM CAKE

2 c.   sugar
1 c.   oil
3   eggs
2 c.   self-rising flour
1 tsp.   nutmeg
2 tsp.   cinnamon
2 sm. jars   baby food plums
        Nuts *or* raisins

Combine sugar, oil and eggs. Add flour a little at a time. Add spices, plums and nuts or raisins. Transfer batter to greased and floured tube pan. Bake at 350 degrees 1 hour. Frost with Cool Whip, if desired.

WINDY'S EASY AS PIE

The Cook's Favorite Pie

1 can   sweetened condensed milk
1 (6 oz.) can   frozen limeade *or* lemonade concentrate
8 oz.   Cool Whip
1   graham cracker pie crust

Mix together condensed milk, lemonade and Cool Whip. Pour into crust, freeze and serve.

Tall Ship Windy sails several times daily with up to 150 guests on board from Navy Pier — at the east end of Grand Avenue — in Chicago . Each cruise offers plently of time and space on deck to take in the view and trade winds of Lake Michigan. During the winter months *Windy* embarks on week-long Caribbean cruises. Cruise times vary daily. Fares are paid at the ticket booth and reservations are not accepted. Frequent sailors earn discounts, as do large groups. Navy Pier is a delightful family fun spot with many wonderful shops, classic park rides, crystal tropical garden and much more nearby.

Windy of Chicago, Ltd.
Navy Pier
600 E. Grand Avenue · Chicago, Illinois 60611
(312) 595-3555 or (312) 595-5474
Website: Search for "Tall Ship Windy"

Freighters
of the
Great
Lakes

Freight Hauling Ships of the Great Lakes

Shipping on the Great Lakes has provided an enormous service to American growth and its economy for centuries. As the size of ships and their cargos has steadily increased, so has the importance of shipping in the region. Today's freight hauling vessels carry millions of tons of local resources and products across the fresh waters of the Great Lakes and beyond every year.

Lakers, freighters, ships, vessels, boats…by whatever name they're called, they inspire awe and we never tire of watching their passage. In fact, we rush to shorelines for a fleeing glimpse and thrill to the sound of their whistles. We gather at docks to wish them bon voyage and pray for their safe return. These vessels not only capture our interest, they own a piece of our hearts.

Each Great Lakes freighter is masterfully built with cold hard steel, powered by massive engines and carries tons of cargo, but the similarities end there. The differences begin with each ship's crew, the 20 to 30 men and women who serve on board and become a family for most of the year. Crew's that become the heart and soul of each ship, proud of the work they do together and the ship they call home.

Nowhere on board is this pride more evident than in the galley. And no place else on board will you find crewmembers more willing to go the extra mile to please their shipmates. Stewards, chief cooks, 2nd cooks and porters devote their days to satisfying the hearty appetites of their crewmates. A freighter's galley is organized, shiny, filled with the aroma of fresh baked goods and a favorite gathering spot on the ship. Homemade food, all prepared freshly on board from scratch, is common fare on a daily basis. Menus full of variety, grand holiday buffets and 14-hour days in the galley are also considered standard.

Each galley takes its personality from the steward and the talent he or she brings to the ship. Some come naturally from long lines of seafaring forefathers, some from distinguished careers in the culinary field, and some gathered their cooking talents along the way as they aimed for a life on the Great Lakes. Their menus and recipes reflect their differences, each unique and each deliciously satisfying. But regardless of their differences many things remain constant; they're great cooks, crewmates, and friends and they're devoted to the happiness and well being of their fellow shipmates. All agree that their favorite reward of the job is not a paycheck; it's a smile on a crewmember's face after a good meal!

How Do You Feed a Crew of 20 to 30?..

You restock the pantry and commercial-sized refrigerators every three to seven days, and hope it lasts until you reach port. The stewards and chief cooks featured in this section helped put it in perspective by sharing their average "grocery lists"…

45 doz. eggs	50 lbs. ground beef
2 cases oranges	100 lbs. roasting chickens
2 cases apples	20 lbs. chicken breasts
2 cases bananas	20 lbs. lamb
100 lbs. flour	50 lbs. turkey
1 case tomatoes	50 lbs. smoked ham
100 lbs. steak	50 loaves bread
20 lbs. pork chops	

Welcome aboard a Great Lakes freighter! The awe inspired in a vessel's passage is at least equaled with a glance at their dinner menus and grand holiday buffets. Their recipes are sure to become favorites and the story behind each steward is sure to add a "favorite ship" to each of our lists.

M.V. Algosoo
Algoma Central Marine

Year Built:	1974 Collingwood Shipyards Ltd. Collingwood, Ontario
Length:	730'
Beam:	75'
Draft:	44'6"
Cargo:	Bulk Ore, Stone, Coal
Cargo Capacity:	31,300 Tons
Crew:	29
Chief Cook:	Lois Sutch

*L*ois Sutch combined her love of sailing with her culinary talents and came up with the perfect profession…cooking on the Great Lakes. Her love of sailing was inherited from her father who started as a deck hand in 1935. Five years later, in 1941, he joined the Navy. After returning home he settled down to a shore job, but sailing remained his first love, and he passed it on to Lois. Up until his death in 1993, her father knew the name of every ship on the seaway, what company owned it, what cargo was carried and what ports it stopped at. His vast library on ships and the seaway, along with his love of the open waters, now belong to Lois.

Lois has been chief cook aboard the M.V. *Algosoo* for over a decade, signing on in 1988 after only two months as 2nd cook on the *Algorail*. Crewmembers on the *Algosoo* may face unpredictable weather conditions on the Great Lakes, but the food they look forward to three times a day is as predictable as the morning sunrise. Menus are full of variety, with everything from the soups and entrees to the breads and desserts prepared freshly on board. Lois is quick to share the praise received for the wonderful meals and gives special thanks to the galley staff on the *Algosoo*. She relies on their efficiency and willingness to work with her, not against her, and credits all of them with making daily life on board enjoyable. Cleanliness, preparation, common sense and cooperation keep the *Algosoo* galley running smoothly. Tracey, who has worked with Lois for over ten years, is especially helpful in the smooth operation of feeding this hungry crew of 29 three times a day.

Menus are prepared a day ahead of time and handwritten on a chalkboard. Even bad weather does not change the full menus offered, except for the rare occasion when high seas warrant not using the deep fryer. There are three dining areas on board the *Algosoo;* a crew mess room, an officer's mess room and the captain and chief's mess room. Lois serves the crewmembers cafeteria style. She prefers to serve them by herself because she has come to know what they're going to order before they do, and knows the portions they prefer. The 2nd cook serves the captain and chief individually in their own dining room. Guests of the captain dine with him and receive the same individual service.

Every day starts early in the galley to have a fresh hot breakfast ready and waiting by 7:30 am. While the 2nd cook prepares breakfast, Lois starts preparing lunch and supper. They both bake in the morning too! They both end up eating lunch on the run, as they follow their busy routine to make sure lunch is ready by 11:30 am. After a three-hour break, it's back to the galley to start the potatoes and vegetables. By 4:30 pm they are busy grilling steaks, pork chops, crab cakes, fish, or the special of the day, for supper. Even after all of that, Lois is always sure to have cookies, cakes, pies, bananas, apples, oranges, a meat tray, cheese, tomatoes, yogurt, tuna, salmon and ice cream handy for the hungry crewmember that occasionally wanders in for a snack.

After a busy day, the galley is cleaned and readied for the next morning meal before Lois retires to her room. A nice long bath is first on her list, followed by a little TV or reading until 9:00 or 10:00 pm. Morning always comes too soon, but once started, it's another full day of preparing and serving food and mingling with the close crew. Lois enjoys being her own boss…her brain is always active with purchasing and menu planning. She enjoys making the choices and having the freedom to do it! Having a good captain or chief makes doing a good job very enjoyable for Lois. *Algosoo* crewmembers work three months on and then one month off. Lois truthfully admits she's exhausted after three months without a day off and usually spends her first week at home quietly relaxing.

Many of Lois' recipes have become crew favorites, including her Crab Cakes, Pierogies, Yellow Split Pea Soup, Chocolate Brownies, Butterscotch Fudge, Apple Streusel Coffee Cake and Mexican Tacos. But regardless of what appears on the daily menu, the crew knows it will be fresh, homemade and good…and there will be plenty to choose from!

ᴍENUS

Breakfast

Bran Muffins
Oatmeal Cereal
Grapefruit
Bacon
Ham
Bologna
Eggs, any style
Cheddar Cheese Omelette
Fried Potatoes

Lunch

Beef Barley Soup
Roasted Leg O' Lamb with
Rosemary Sauce
Hamburgers or Cheeseburgers
with Tomato, Lettuce and Onion
Salmon Salad Sandwich
Boiled Potatoes
French Fries with Gravy
Peas
Bread Pudding
Cream
Reese's Bars

Special Holiday Menu

Shrimp Cocktail
Cheese Platter
Waldorf Salad
Fruit Salad
Pickle Tray
Fresh Homemade Rolls
Roast Prime Rib and Gravy
Baked Virginia Ham with
Pineapple Glaze
Roast Duck a la Orange
Cornish Hens with Wild Rice
Whipped Potatoes
Baked Yams and Apples
Peas and Corn
Black Fruit Cake
Christmas Pudding
Assorted Cookies and fudge
Assorted Squares
Strawberry Cheese Cake
Homemade Chocolates

Dinner

V8 Juice
Beef Barley Soup
Homemade Bread
Tossed Salad
Roast Chicken, Cranberries and Gravy
Italian Spaghetti with Meat Sauce
Mashed Potatoes
Broccoli with Cheese Sauce
Vegetable Fried Rice
Lemon Meringue Pie
Chocolate Brownies
Carrot Loaf

YELLOW SPLIT PEA SOUP

1 lg.	ham bone
8 c.	water
3 c.	yellow split peas
1 Tbsp.	chicken base
1 lg.	onion, chopped
3	celery stalks, chopped
2	potatoes
2	carrots
	Salt and pepper, to taste

Place ham bone in large soup pot. Add peas, chicken base, onion and celery. Bring to boil; reduce heat and simmer, covered, 2 to 3 hours. Remove ham bone and take off any remaining meat. Return meat to soup pot. Mixture should be a rich yellow color and slightly thick. Grate potatoes and carrots into soup pot; stir. Add pepper to taste. I do not recommend adding any salt. Cook until vegetables are done. Serve.

MARINADE FOR PORK ROAST

1/2 c.	soy sauce
2	garlic cloves, crushed
1 Tbsp.	dry mustard
1 tsp.	ginger
1 tsp.	thyme
2 c.	apple juice

Mix all ingredients together and pour over roast (pork leg or loin.) Bake at 450 degrees 40 minutes. Reduce temperature to 300 degrees and roast slowly, covered, 30 minutes per pound. This makes a delicious gravy!

CAJUN RED BEANS AND RICE

1 can	crushed tomatoes
2 cans	kidney beans
3 Tbsp.	tomato paste
3	celery stalks, sliced into 1/4-inch chunks
1 lg.	green pepper, cubed
1	zucchini, sliced in half circles
1 lg.	onion, chopped
2 Tbsp.	Matouk *or* hot pepper sauce
	Salt and pepper, to taste

Mix all ingredients together in large pot; bring to boil. Reduce heat and simmer 1 hour. Serve over hot rice.

PASTA PRIMAVERA

1 pkg.	fettuccini, boiled, drained
3 c.	broccoli florets
2 c.	snow peas
1 c.	frozen peas
2 c.	zucchini, sliced
6 Tbsp.	olive oil
3 tsp.	garlic, chopped
2 c.	mushrooms, fresh *or* canned
2/3 c.	butter, melted
3 Tbsp.	basil
3	tomatoes, diced
1 c.	Parmesan cheese
2 c.	light cream
	Salt and pepper, to taste

Sauté tomatoes and mushrooms in olive oil. Toss with broccoli, snow peas, frozen peas, zucchini, garlic, butter and basil. Season with salt and pepper. Toss all ingredients with Parmesan cheese and light cream. Heat and serve.

MEXICAN TACOS

5 lbs.	ground beef
1 lg.	onion, chopped
2	garlic cloves, minced
3 c.	salsa sauce
4 Tbsp.	taco spice
1	green pepper, chopped
	Tortilla shells
	Cheddar cheese, shredded
	Tomatoes, cubed
	Onion, diced
	Lettuce, shredded
	Sour cream, (optional)

Brown ground beef with onion and garlic; put in strainer and remove all fat. Add salsa, taco spice and green pepper. (When I make Chili Con Carne, I freeze any leftovers in 1-pound margarine containers. When preparing tacos, I defrost one container of chili, put it through blender or processor and add it to my beef mixture. It adds much flavor!) Lay out tortilla shells and place approximately 4 tablespoons beef mixture in middle of each. Sprinkle with cheese, tomatoes, onion and lettuce. Roll up tortillas and heat in microwave 1 to 2 minutes. Add a dollop of sour cream, if desired.

CRAB CAKES

2 lbs.	imitation *or* real crab meat, finely chopped in food processor
1 c.	bread crumbs
1 Tbsp.	lemon juice
2	eggs
2 c.	mashed potatoes
2	green onions, chopped
1 Tbsp.	Matouk's hot chili peppers
4 Tbsp.	fresh parsley, chopped
1/4 c.	corn meal
1/4 c.	flour

Combine all ingredients except corn meal and flour; mix together on slow speed. Shape mixture into patties; cover with or roll in corn meal and flour. Fry patties in butter or margarine over medium heat until golden brown. Serve with tartar sauce, salsa sauce or lemon.

LIGHT FISH BATTER

3-1/2 c.	flour
5 tsp.	baking powder
1 tsp.	baking soda
2-1/2 tsp.	salt
2-1/2 c.	milk
2-1/2 c.	water

Mix together flour, baking powder, baking soda and salt. Add milk and water; mix well with whisk. Coat fish filets with batter and drop into deep fryer at 350 degrees. Fry until golden; turn over and fry other side.

ORANGE BRAN MUFFINS

1/4 c.	oil
5	eggs
2 tsp.	vanilla
1/2 c.	molasses
1-3/4 c.	sugar
4 c.	flour
4 c.	bran flakes
2 c.	natural bran
2 tsp.	baking powder
2 tsp.	baking soda
1 tsp.	salt
2 c.	orange juice
2 c.	milk

Mix together oil, eggs, vanilla, molasses and sugar until creamy; set aside. In separate bowl combine flour, bran flakes, natural bran, baking powder, baking soda and salt. Add dry ingredients to creamy mixture alternately with orange juice and milk. Let mixture set overnight. Fill muffin cups 3/4 full. Bake at 400 degrees 20 minutes.

APPLE CINNAMON TOAST

5 Tbsp.	butter
3	apples, sliced
1 c.	brown sugar
2 Tbsp.	corn syrup
1 tsp.	cinnamon
8	thick slices French bread
3	eggs
1 c.	milk
1 tsp.	vanilla

Cook apple slices with butter, brown sugar, corn syrup and cinnamon; pour into 9x13-inch pan. Arrange bread slices over apples. Beat together eggs, milk and vanilla; pour over bread. Sprinkle top with cinnamon and sugar. Refrigerate overnight. Bake at 350 degrees 45 minutes.

APPLE STREUSEL COFFEE CAKE

Streusel

1-1/4 c.	brown sugar
3/4 c.	flour
1/2 c.	cold butter
2 tsp.	cinnamon
1 c.	walnuts, chopped

Cake

3-1/4 c.	flour
1-1/2 tsp.	baking powder
3/4 tsp.	baking soda
3/4 c.	butter
1-1/4 c.	sugar
3	eggs
2 tsp.	vanilla
16 oz.	plain yogurt
2	Granny Smith apples, sliced

Mix together Streusel ingredients and set aside. To prepare cake batter, mix together flour, baking powder and baking soda; set aside. At medium speed whip butter, sugar, eggs and vanilla. Add yogurt. Add flour mixture, beating between additions. Pour half cake batter into large bundt cake pan. Lay apple slices over batter. Sprinkle 3/4 Streusel mixture over apples. Repeat layers and add remaining Streusel over top of cake. Bake at 350 degrees 1 hour or until done. If cake gets too brown before thoroughly done, cover lightly with foil.

MARMALADE LOAF

2	eggs
3/4 c.	sugar
1/4 c.	butter
3/4 c.	milk
1/2 c.	marmalade
2 Tbsp.	vinegar
2-1/2 c.	flour
1 tsp.	baking soda
1 tsp.	baking powder
1 tsp.	salt
	Rind of 1 lemon *or* orange, grated
2 Tbsp.	sugar, for top

Mix together eggs, sugar and butter until creamy. Add milk, marmalade and vinegar. In separate bowl sift together flour, baking soda, baking powder and salt; add to marmalade mixture. Add grated rind and mix well. Pour batter into loaf pan and sprinkle sugar over top. Bake at 350 degrees 1 hour.

KENTUCKY GINGERBREAD

5	eggs
1 c.	sugar
1 c.	molasses
1 c.	oil
1 tsp.	cloves
1 tsp.	ginger
1 tsp.	cinnamon
2 tsp.	baking soda dissolved in 2 Tbsp. hot water
2 c.	flour
1 c.	hot water

Combine eggs, sugar, molasses, oil, cloves, ginger and cinnamon; beat well. Add baking soda mixture. Beat in flour. Add hot water. Pour batter into greased 9x12-inch pan. Bake at 350 degrees 1 hour.

OATMEAL COCONUT COOKIES

1 c.	shortening
1 c.	sugar
1 c.	brown sugar
2	eggs
1/2 tsp.	baking powder
1 tsp.	baking soda
1/2 tsp.	salt
1 tsp.	vanilla
1 c.	coconut
2 c.	oatmeal
2 c.	flour

Cream together shortening, sugars and eggs. Add baking powder, baking soda, salt and vanilla, mixing well. Mix in coconut, oatmeal and flour. Shape dough into small balls and place on baking sheet. Flatten balls and bake at 350 degrees 10 to 12 minutes.

CHOCOLATE SOUR CREAM CAKE

1-3/4 c.	flour
1-3/4 c.	sugar
3/4 c.	cocoa
1-1/2 tsp.	baking soda
1 tsp.	salt
2/3 c.	butter
1-1/2 c.	sour cream
2	eggs
1 tsp.	vanilla

Mix together butter, sour cream, eggs and vanilla until creamy. In separate bowl combine dry ingredients. Mix dry ingredients with creamy mixture at medium speed. Pour batter into 2 greased round pans. Bake at 350 degrees 30 to 40 minutes.

SUNSHINE SNACK CAKE

2	eggs
1/4 c.	oil
1/2 c.	sugar
2-1/2 c.	flour
1/2 tsp.	baking soda
1/2 tsp.	salt
1-1/2 c.	orange juice
1 c.	raisins

Mix together eggs, oil and sugar until creamy; set aside. In separate bowl combine flour, baking soda and salt. Add orange juice alternately with flour mixture to creamy mixture. Add raisins and mix well. Pour batter into 9x13-inch pan. Bake at 350 degrees 1 hour.

COCONUT POUND CAKE

1 c.	butter
3 c.	sugar
6	eggs
3 c.	flour
1/4 tsp.	baking soda
1/4 tsp.	salt
8 oz.	sour cream
1 c.	coconut
1 tsp.	vanilla
1 tsp.	coconut extract

Mix together butter, sugar and eggs until creamy. In separate bowl combine flour, baking soda and salt; add to creamy mixture. Add remaining ingredients and mix well. Pour batter into large bundt pan. Bake at 350 degrees 1 hour.

CHERRY POUND CAKE

1 c.	butter
1 (8 oz.) pkg.	cream cheese, softened
1-1/2 c.	sugar
1-1/2 tsp.	vanilla
4	eggs
2 c.	flour
3 tsp.	baking powder
1/4 c.	nuts, chopped
1/4 c.	flour
1 c.	cherries

Mix together butter, cream cheese, sugar, vanilla and eggs until creamy. Combine 2 cups flour with baking powder and add to creamy mixture. Stir in nuts. Toss cherries in 1/4-cup flour to coat; stir into batter. Pour into large bundt pan. Bake at 350 degrees 1 hour.

M.T. Anglian Lady
Purvis Marine LTD.

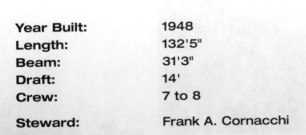

The M.T. Anglian Lady "dressed to the nines" for her spot in the Annual Tug Boat Parade.

Year Built:	1948
Length:	132'5"
Beam:	31'3"
Draft:	14'
Crew:	7 to 8
Steward:	Frank A. Cornacchi

Barge PML #2501

Year Built:	1997
Length:	295'
Breadth:	52'
Draft:	17'
Cargo Capacity:	4800 Tons

*L*ittle ships that can…the sturdy, small when compared to freighters, hardworking tugs that haul cargo loaded barges from port to port on the Great Lakes. Often less than one-tenth the size of a modern freighter, these workhorses of the Great Lakes have a heart and crew that stand up to any of their giant steel counterparts and a history of dependability to match. With their ability to visit many ports too small or too shallow to accommodate a freighter, tugs are depended upon to keep commerce in the bustling region going.

The 132-foot *M.T. Anglian Lady*, previously an anchor-handling vessel in Scotland, is among the hardworking tugs in the Purvis Marine LTD fleet. With a cargo of petroleum products on the tow aboard Barge PML #2501, *Anglian Lady* is a common sight in the ports of Detroit, Marathon, Hamilton, Chicago, Sarnia, Toronto and Windsor. As with her "sister-tugs," she is beloved by her crew and her faithful following of land-based ship watchers. Crewmembers themselves marvel at Captain Jeff Stewart's ability to turn the tug "on a dime" and maneuver in and out of ports. "He handles her like a Volkswagen." Due to potential hazards posed to the Great Lakes by the petroleum products she hauls, a Coast Guard escort accompanies *Anglian Lady* through the Soo to DeTour passage during the spring and fall when ice is present in the area. The cost of this mandatory precaution is $6,000 per one-way trip, and only one of many shipping regulations in place to protect the integrity of the lakes.

Above, crewmembers aboard *Anglian Lady* lower the Zodiak in preparation to get *Barge PML #2501* ready for notch.

View from the stern (right) as *Anglian Lady* backs up to *Barge PML #2501*.

Jack Purvis, a retired schoolteacher, started Purvis Marine LTD with the 73-foot tug *The Rocket*. He soon became known in the region as a fair man and hard worker, and quickly saw his fleet grow to over a dozen tugs and 20 barges. Described by his employees as "among the best to work for in the shipping industry," Jack's crewmembers share an atmosphere of "family" both on and off the tugs. His son, Scott, receives equally high praise for his hard work, fairness and ability since the age of 12 to operate any piece of equipment on board. In 1995, when *Anglian Lady* secured her place in Great Lakes' history by participating in the dive down to the final resting place of the Edmund Fitzgerald in Lake Superior, Scott was on board. He was also inside the Atmospheric Dive System used to view the Fitzgerald and retrieve her ship's bell. The bell was carefully hoisted from the site to the deck of *Anglian Lady*, and the tug proudly carried it safely to its new home at the Great Lakes Shipwreck Museum. (See page 427.)

"Daily life aboard a tug is so much different than life aboard a freighter," explains Frank Cornacchi, steward on the *Anglian Lady*. After enjoying years on the Great Lakes in the large galleys of freighters (see page 226), he joined Purvis Marine and the much smaller galleys and crews of tugs. "With only 7 to 8 shipmates on board, compared with 25 to 30 on a freighter, quantities of food prepared are smaller but variety is greater. We do all of our own shopping, at stores of our choice, so I am able to offer many new tastes to my shipmates." Frank works from 5:30 am to approximately 6:30 pm, with as many breaks as he wants, but finds cooking for his appreciative crewmates so enjoyable he seldom notices time. "The crew is so much like family, you want them to enjoy their meals. The rewards are great because they're always telling me how great the meals are, and they are so willing to lend a helping hand if asked!"

Planning ahead on a tug is a must, especially in the galley. Rough weather on the Great Lakes will cause the smaller vessel to roll much more and much longer than a large freighter, sometimes slowing forward progress to less than one-mile an hour. A short trip on the lakes can turn into a two-day voyage. Meals must be plentiful, at the same time cooking on board is all but impossible. Frank's shipmates never go hungry though, in fact they dine quite well on meals he prepared ahead of the storm. And they always marvel at the fresh hot meal he sets before them less than 45 minutes after the lakes have calmed. A galley full of happy, well fed friends is Frank's favorite perk aboard *Anglian Lady*.

After a long hard day and a good hot meal, Frank's thoughts turn to tomorrow's meals. Special requests are always prepared and shipmate's favorites become regular menu items. Because the *Anglian Lady* sits closer to the water line than a freighter, fishing is a pastime enjoyed on board. At a crewmate's request, the fresh catch of the day is often enjoyed that evening, using one of Frank's many recipes for preparing the region's tasty natural resource.

SALMON WITH LEMON AND GARLIC

2	salmon fillets
3 Tbsp.	butter
2	garlic cloves, minced
1 tsp.	lemon pepper
1	lemon

Season salmon with lemon pepper. Melt butter over high heat; stir in garlic. Add salmon to pan and cook 5 minutes. Turn salmon over and cook an additional 5 minutes or until fish flakes. Sprinkle with lemon juice before serving.

SALMON BAKED IN FOIL

3 to 4 lbs.	salmon
2 Tbsp.	butter, softened
1	lemon, sliced
	Salt and pepper, to taste
	Aluminum foil

Grease aluminum foil with butter. Place 3 lemon slices on foil. Lay salmon over lemon and season to taste with salt and pepper. Place 3 lemon slices on top of salmon. Wrap foil loosely but securely around salmon. Place on baking tray and bake at 350 degrees 30 to 40 minutes. Remove from oven and let stand 10 to 15 minutes.

BAKED SALMON FILLETS

4 Tbsp.	vegetable oil
1-1/2 to 2 lbs.	salmon fillets, boneless, skinless
1 Tbsp.	lemon juice
1/2 tsp.	salt
1/2 tsp.	pepper
4	green onions, finely chopped
4	carrots, shredded
3/4 c.	chicken stock

Grease baking dish with small amount of vegetable oil. Cut salmon fillets into 6 pieces and place in baking dish, in 1 layer. Brush remaining vegetable oil over salmon. Season salmon with salt, pepper and lemon juice. Sprinkle vegetables over top. Pour chicken stock over all. Bake at 350 degrees 10 to 15 minutes.

MARINATED GRILLED SALMON

1 lb.	salmon fillets, cut into 4 pieces
1/3 c.	peanut oil
3 Tbsp.	soy sauce
2 Tbsp.	vinegar
2 tsp.	brown sugar
1	green onion, finely chopped
1	garlic clove, minced
1/2 tsp.	ginger
1/2 tsp.	sesame oil
	Salt and pepper, to taste

Combine all ingredients, except salmon, and whisk together until well mixed. Place salmon in glass dish and pour marinade over top. Cover and refrigerate 5 to 6 hours. Remove salmon from marinade and grill 5 minutes per inch of thickness on each side. Fish is done when it flakes with a fork.

M.T. Atlantic Hickory

Atlantic Towing LTD

*J*eff Wilcox takes a break on the Bridge Wing across the river from Detroit.

Year Built:	1973
Length:	153'
Beam:	38'10"
Draft:	22'
Cargo:	Grain, Iron Ore
Cargo Capacity:	886 Tons
Crew:	17 during summer, 9 to 11 during winter on North Atlantic
Chief Cook:	Jeff Wilcox

Atlantic Hickory's crew gathers together after off loading grain at Ogilvee Flour Mill in Midland, Ontario. Left to right: J. Wilcox, Cook; D. Parmeter, Chief Engineer; C. Kilfoy, 2nd Mate; D. Thompson, 1st Mate; R. Morairty, 2nd Engineer; S. Dorey, Oiler; K. Nicholson, Seaman; G. Llewellyn, Master.

Unique food prepared from original recipes is standard fare aboard the *M.T. Atlantic Hickory*, thanks to Jeff Wilcox who has served as chief cook on the ship for over two years. He brought 17 years of experience with him, including a wealth of recipes and culinary secrets. Jeff began his cooking career in New Brunswick hotels and went on to train under Heinz Bauer, Cordon Bleu Chef from Germany, currently on River Casinos in the southern United States.

Jeff enjoys his life on the Great Lakes and the wonderful people that go along with it. Captain Glenn Llewellyn, Captain Robert Grahmm, and the crews of both the *Atlantic Hickory* and the *Sarah Spencer* have all made Jeff feel right at home. He returns the favor by preparing their favorite foods and having their favorite snacks freshly baked and waiting. Jeff particularly enjoys the opportunity to travel as well as the great joy of meeting different people and seeing different ways of life. He considers the Great Lakes a wonderful addition to any travel log, and he should know. His maritime career has taken him to the Islands in the Caribbean, the West Indies, Spain, Portugal and England.

Life aboard the *Atlantic Hickory* is hectic, especially is the galley. Jeff rises each day at 5:00 am to have breakfast ready between 7:30 and 8:30 am After breakfast has been cleared away the baking begins, and continues while lunch is prepared. Lunch is followed by a much needed, and appreciated break, and then it's back to work preparing dinner. If all goes well, clean up is finished by 8:00 pm and Jeff's day in the galley is done. That is, of course, if he found time during his busy day to prepare menus and order supplies. To insure freshness and variety, groceries are restocked every 10 to 12 days. His orders always include plenty of fresh fruits and produce.

Daily menus aboard the *Atlantic Hickory* are displayed on a chalkboard and always offer plenty of variety. When a crewmember's birthday comes around, Jeff has their favorite meal ready…complete with a birthday cake! Tables are set and waiting at all meals for both the officers and crew, in the same mess, where they are all served individually. Cooking on a small tugboat is definitely affected by the weather, but Jeff considers it just another challenge of life on the Great Lakes. High winds and rough seas may cause changes to a planned menu, but the variety and quality of food he serves never suffer.

Guest Menu

Broiled or Poached Haddock
Hollandaise Sauce
Oven Browned Potatoes
Fresh Garden Beans
Broccoli Spears
Apple Crisp and Lemon Meringue Pie

Menus

Special Holiday Menu

Glazed Ham
Scalloped Potatoes
Garden Mixed Vegetables
Baked Potatoes and Sour Cream
Apple Strudel
Ice Cream or Whipped Cream

Breakfast

Cereal
Fresh Fruit
Ham, Bacon and Sausage
Fresh Bologna
Omelets and Eggs
Pancakes
Toasted Sandwiches

Lunch

Homemade Soup
Freshly Baked Rolls and Bread
Assorted Sandwiches
Main Course – Meat and Potatoes
Pies and Cakes

Dinner

Roast Turkey Dinner
Mashed Potatoes
Fresh Carrots and Peas
Stuffing
Black Forest Cake

Just in case anyone on board gets the urge to snack between meals, Jeff always has freshly baked sweets, cookies, doughnuts and fresh fruit ready and waiting. Following are a few of Jeff's recipes that have become *Atlantic Hickory* favorites:

OLD-FASHIONED SPOON BREAD WITH MAPLE BUTTER

Spoon Bread

2 Tbsp.	butter *or* margarine, softened
2 c.	milk
1 c.	yellow corn meal
1 tsp.	baking powder
1/2 tsp.	salt
1 c.	milk
3	eggs, separated

Maple Butter

1/2 c.	butter, softened
2 Tbsp.	maple syrup
1/8 tsp.	cinnamon

To prepare Spoon Bread preheat oven to 350 degrees. In 2-quart saucepan combine 2-cups milk and corn meal. Cook over medium heat, stirring constantly, until all milk is absorbed and mixture is of cooked cereal consistency, approximately 8 to 11 minutes. Remove from heat; add butter, baking powder and salt. Stir until well mixed and butter is melted. Beat in remaining 1-cup milk and egg yolks with wire whisk until smooth. Transfer mixture to large bowl and set aside. In small mixer bowl beat egg whites at high speed until peaks form, scraping bowl often, approximately 1 to 2 minutes. Fold egg whites into corn meal mixture until uniform and no lumps are visible. Carefully pour into greased casserole dish. Bake 40 to 50 minutes, until golden brown and top springs back when lightly touched.

To prepare Maple Butter combine all ingredients in small bowl and stir to mix. Serve with warm Spoon Bread.

CHOCOLATE CHIP BISCUITS WITH STRAWBERRIES AND BANANAS

2 c.	all-purpose flour
1/2 c.	sugar
1 Tbsp.	baking powder
1/2 tsp.	salt
1/2 c.	butter *or* margarine
1/4 c.	shortening
2/3 c.	whipping cream
1/2 c.	semi-sweet chocolate chips

Toppings

Whipped cream
Bananas, sliced
Sweetened strawberries

Preheat oven to 400 degrees. Combine flour, sugar, baking powder and salt. Cut in butter and shortening until crumbly. Stir in whipping cream with fork until moistened. Stir in chocolate chips. Turn dough onto lightly floured board and knead until smooth, approximately 1 minute. Roll out dough to 3/4-inch thickness and cut with floured cutter. Place 1-inch apart on floured cookie sheet and bake 10 to 15 minutes, until golden brown.

To serve, cut biscuits in half. Spoon whipped cream on bottom half. Place sliced bananas over whipped cream and cover with other half of biscuit. Spoon sweetened strawberries over top.

Yield: 8 to 10 Biscuits

BRAISED PORK CHOPS AND CABBAGE

This crew favorite comes from Jeff's training under Chef Heinz Bauer.

2 Tbsp.	vegetable oil
4 (1-inch thick)	pork chops
1 med.	onion, sliced
1 med. head	cabbage, cut into 1/2-inch slices
1 c.	tomato juice
2 tsp.	beef bouillon granules
1/2 tsp.	caraway seed
1/4 tsp.	pepper
2 Tbsp.	all-purpose flour
3 Tbsp.	water

Heat oil in 10-inch skillet. Add pork chops and cook over medium heat, turning once, until brown; approximately 3 to 4 minutes on each side. Top with onion and cabbage. In small bowl stir together tomato juice, bouillon, caraway seed and pepper; pour over pork chops. Cover and reduce heat to low. Continue cooking until pork chops and cabbage are tender, 30 to 35 minutes. Set pork chops, cabbage and onions on serving platter; keep warm. Leave juice in pan.

In small bowl whisk together flour and water until smooth; stir into pan juices. Cook over medium heat until mixture comes to full boil, approximately 2 to 3 minutes. Boil 1 minute. Serve over pork chops and vegetables.

M.V. Canadian Enterprise

Upper Lakes Group

Year Built:	1979, Port Weller Dry Docks St. Catharines, Ontario
Length:	730'
Beam:	75'8"
Draft:	46'6"
Cargo:	Coal
Cargo Capacity:	35,100 Tons
Crew:	27 to 30
Steward:	Nikki Caldwell

*N*ikki Caldwell brought 24 years of experience with her to the galley of the *M.V. Canadian Enterprise,* where she finds the entire crew fabulous! She especially appreciates their willingness to try different recipes and a diverse menu. Other than the traditional "Saturday Steak Night," Nikki's fellow crewmembers are treated to menu surprises on a daily basis.

The busy Galley Staff usually find themselves eating on the run as they go from breakfast preparations to baking fresh breads, rolls and desserts all before noon. Nikki starts lunch and supper preparations at 7:00 a.m. every morning, allowing time for the homemade soups and entrees to be ready when needed. Tomorrow's menu and restocking with groceries are always on her mind, as is remembering special requests from crewmembers for a favorite meal. To keep up with demand on board, Nikki restocks with groceries every 8 to 10 days. She is always sure to get plenty of chips, popcorn, tortilla chips and other favorite snacks for her crewmates.

Nikki displays her daily menus on a chalkboard and cafeteria-style meals are enjoyed in the crew or officer's dining areas. Rough weather causes menu changes only "once in a blue moon." Otherwise it's three freshly prepared meals a day, with plenty of variety, seven days a week.

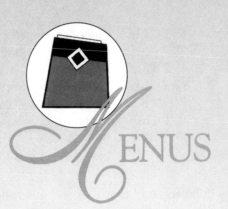

MENUS

Breakfast
Fruit Juice
Bacon and Eggs
Hot Cereal
Fruit Muffins
Pancakes
Sausages

Lunch
Homemade Soup
Hot Entrée of the Day
Sandwiches
Potatoes
Vegetable
Salad
Dessert

Dinner
Homemade Soup
Roast Beef, Gravy and Yorkshire Pudding
Cold Cuts
Mashed *or* Roasted Potatoes
Mashed Carrots and Turnips
Salad
Dessert

Special Holiday Menu

Shrimp Cocktail

Roast Beef or Ham and Turkey

Potatoes

Two Types of Vegetables

Homemade Rolls

Salads

Desserts

Assorted Candies and Specialties

Cheese, Crackers, Pickles

CAPTAIN PERCY GARRICK'S FAVORITE TOMATO SOUP

2 lg.	onions, chopped
2	celery stalks, chopped
2 Tbsp.	butter
2 (28 oz.) cans	chopped tomatoes
8 c.	water
1/2 Tbsp.	baking soda
4 c.	milk
	Salt and pepper, to taste

Sauté onions and celery in butter. Add tomatoes and water; boil 10 to 15 minutes. Add baking soda and then add milk. Do not boil after adding milk, just heat through. Season with salt and pepper, to taste.

M.V. Canadian Miner

Upper Lakes Group

Year Built:	1966
	Canadian Vickers Shipyards
	Montreal, Quebec
Length:	730'
Beam:	75'
Draft:	39'1"
Cargo:	Grain, Iron Ore
Cargo Capacity:	28,050 Tons
Crew:	23
Chief Cook:	Bernice Piercey

Bernice Piercey joins Wheelman Austin Fleet in the Crew's Mess when she worked aboard the *Canadian Prospector*.

*B*ernice joined the *M.V. Canadian Miner* early in 1998 as chief cook after working herself up through the ranks preparing food on Great Lakes vessels since 1994. In addition, she is busy working on her Chef Papers, which will require another year or two of schooling. When not on board the *Canadian Miner*, Bernice leads an equally busy, if not busier, life. Her children, Jodyann 25 and Janine 23, plus her three grandchildren Samantha 7,

Joann 20 months and Gordon 3, are a constant source of joy and activity. Bernice collects postcards for them from every port she visits and admits being away from home is the hardest part of her job. Her days off are filled with family and friends, including Kevin Ossinger, chief cook aboard the *S.S. Montrealais*. She is thrilled with her busy life on the Great Lakes, enjoying the guidance, help and friendship of Captain Gerald M. Greig, Chief Mate William R. Sullivan, 2nd cook Lorraine Shaw, Porter Robin Dewling and Shore Steward in Charge of Galley Staff, George Fenner.

The *Canadian Miner* passes gracefully through Lock One at St. Catharine, Ontario.

Seeing that her shipmates aboard the *Canadian Miner* are eating well and not complaining about the food pleases Bernice. She knows that if the food were not good, she would be the first to know. The new "Heart Smart" menus put in place by U.L.S. Group are great and ensure Bernice her fellow crewmembers are getting hearty and healthy meals.

Bernice makes sure fresh fruit, cheese, yogurt, ice cream, cookies, chips and popcorn are always on hand for the crewmate who wanders in between meals!

Guests aboard the *Canadian Miner* are welcomed with fresh flowers and fruit baskets in their rooms. They dine in the Officer's Mess Room with the captain. The crew dines cafeteria style in their own mess room where the variety and quantity of fresh hot food satisfies even the "pickiest" sailor!

Bernice and her co-workers go all out for holidays, special days and ordinary days they decide to make special. Grand buffets, decorations and sometimes even costumes fill the mess rooms and galley! The entire galley staff is up and working by 6:30 am. Immediately after breakfast is completed, the baking is started.

Chief Cook Kevin Ossinger and then 2nd Cook Bernice Piercey take part in Halloween festivites aboard the *S.S. Montrealais* in 1996. The buffet table was also decorated for the occasion.

Chief Cook Kevin Ossinger adds finishing touches to a buffet aboard the *S.S. Montrealais* (below).

Officers and crew dine together at Christmas Dinner aboard the *S.S. Montrealais* in 1997.

Canadian Miner Porter, Robin Dewling (left), always has a smile on his face!

Easter Dinner includes all the favorites from home, including trays of freshly prepared deviled eggs and rolls.

The *J.W. Westcott* mail boat, always a welcome sight to sailors, pulls up alongside the *Canadian Miner* in July, 1998.

By 8:30 am the galley is ready for Bernice to starting preparing meals for the rest of the day. Being organized is half the battle; it also allows time for a break when needed. On days when everything goes according to schedule, the galley staff takes a well-deserved break from 12:30 to 3:30 pm. Supper is then prepared and served, the galley is cleaned and the long day is done.

As with most Great Lakes freighters, the daily menu is handwritten on a chalkboard. The new Heart Smart menu Bernice follows offers 21 days of variety and so far…no complaints!

Breakfast

Apple Juice and Orange Juice
Assorted Cold Cereals
Stewed Prunes
Cream of Wheat
Eggs, any style
Grilled Bacon and Bologna
Baked Beans
Wheat Germ Biscuits and Toast

Lunch

Cream of Celery Soup
Veggie Platter
Poached Salmon Steaks with
Lemon Wedges & Tartar Sauce
Eggs, any style
O'Brien Potatoes
Baby Carrots and Peas

Dinner

Navy Bean Soup
Tossed Salad
Roast Leg of Lamb with Mint Sauce
Pizza, "All Dressed" and Veggies
Assorted Cold Meat Sandwiches
Boiled Potatoes
Yellow Beans
Homemade Apple Cake
Caramel Pudding

Special Holiday Menu

Assorted Appetizers
Tomato Juice
Roast Turkey with Cranberry Jelly
Walnut Dressing and Giblet Gravy
or Picnic Ham with Raisin Sauce
Potatoes: Oven Browned, Creamed
Buttered Kernel Corn, Brussel Sprouts
Relish Tray
Hot Rolls
Pumpkin or Hot Mincemeat Pie
Ice Cream
Cheese and Crackers
Nuts, Chocolates and Candies
Coffee, Tea and Soft Drinks

Homemade Bread, Jigg's Dinner and Figgy Duff have become favorites on the *Canadian Miner*. They are included here, along with some other favorites from their "Heart Smart" file:

PEACH CRUMB COFFEE CAKE

6 c.	Kellogg's Bran Flakes cereal
1 c.	brown sugar, packed
1/2 c.	margarine, melted
6 c.	all-purpose flour
1/4 c	baking powder
1-1/2 tsp.	salt
1 Tbsp.	ground cinnamon
1-1/2 tsp.	ground nutmeg
8 c.	Kellogg's Bran Flakes cereal
3 c.	milk
1-1/2 c.	margarine, softened
3 c.	sugar
6	eggs
2 Tbsp.	vanilla extract
7 c.	canned peaches, sliced, well drained, cut into bite-sized pieces
8 c.	low-fat plain yogurt, (optional)

Combine 6 cups cereal with brown sugar and melted margarine. Mix on low speed with wire whip attachment; set aside for topping. Combine flour, baking powder, salt, cinnamon and nutmeg; set aside. Lightly crush remaining 8 cups cereal and combine with milk. Let stand until cereal softens; set aside. Cream margarine and sugar until light. Beat in eggs and vanilla. Add flour mixture alternately with cereal mixture, mixing well after each addition. Spread into greased 18x26x1-inch baking pan. Distribute peaches evenly over surface and press down lightly. Sprinkle with topping. Bake at 350 degrees 40 to 45 minutes or until cake tests done. Serve warm or cold, cut into rectangles. Top with 2 tablespoons plain yogurt, if desired. Refrigerate unused portions.

Yield: 60 Servings

HOMEMADE BREAD

2 (8 g.) pkgs.	yeast
8 to 10 c.	warm water
4 tsp.	sugar
7 lbs.	flour
1 c.	molasses
1 c.	brown sugar
2 tsp.	cloves
3 tsp.	nutmeg
4 tsp.	Cinnamon
8 tsp.	Salt
1 lb.	raisins
1 lb.	currants
2 c.	powdered milk
2	eggs, beaten
1 c.	butter, melted, cooled

Put 2 cups warm water in pan. Add yeast and sugar; let stand 5 to 10 minutes. Add remaining warm water, brown sugar, salt, milk and spices; blend well. Add 1/2 flour and mix. Add butter and mix. Add molasses, raisins, currants and beaten eggs. Add remaining flour gradually and knead. Let dough rest 10 minutes. Put in warm place and let rise until double in bulk, 1 to 1-1/2 hours. Punch down and shape into loaves. Let rise an additional 1 to 1-1/2 hours. Bake at 350 degrees 45 to 50 minutes.

Yield: 4 to 6 Loaves

FIGGY DUFF

1/4 c.	butter
1 c.	sugar
1	egg
2 c.	flour
4 tsp.	baking powder
1/3 tsp.	salt
1 c.	milk
1/4 tsp.	Vanilla
1 c.	raisins

Cream together butter, sugar and egg. Add flour, baking powder and salt. Stir in milk, vanilla and raisins. Boil in pudding bag or mold 2 hours. Water should cover pudding half-way in large 1-quart saucepan. A saucer may be placed under pudding to keep it from resting on bottom of pot.

TURKEY NOODLE SOUP

3 c.	onions, diced
2 oz.	butter *or* oil
2 c.	celery, diced
2 c.	carrots, diced
1 c.	green pepper, diced
1-1/4 gal.	chicken stock
1/2 lb.	noodles
2-1/2 c.	cooked turkey meat, diced
1 tsp.	salt
1/2 tsp.	pepper

*S*auté onions in butter or oil until soft but not brown. Add celery, carrots, green peppers and stock; bring to boil. Reduce heat and simmer until vegetables are almost tender. Add noodles and simmer 10 minutes. Add diced turkey meat and heat through. Season with salt and pepper.

Yield: 25 Servings

Note: 1 cup packed chicken soup base = 1-1/4 gallons chicken stock.

Modifications: Use margarine instead of butter or oil.

SAUSAGE AND RICE CASSEROLE

2 c.	onions, finely chopped
2 c.	celery, finely chopped
2 c.	green pepper, finely chopped
2 (28 oz.) cans	tomatoes, chopped
6 c.	cooked rice
4 lbs.	sausages, cooked, cut in 3 pieces
1 tsp.	salt
1/2 tsp.	pepper
1/4 tsp.	thyme

*S*auté onions, celery and green pepper in small amount of butter until soft but not brown. Combine tomatoes, rice and sausage. Mix in cooked vegetables. Add seasonings and heat in moderate oven 15 to 20 minutes.

Yield: 25 Servings

BEEF CURRY

8 lbs.	stewing beef, cubed
4 oz.	fat
4 c.	onions, diced
2	garlic cloves, minced
2-1/2 to 3 Tbsp.	curry powder
1 c.	all-purpose flour
1 gal.	water *or* beef stock
1 c.	green pepper, chopped
1 c.	tomatoes, chopped
1 c.	red pimientos, chopped
2 tsp.	salt
1/4 tsp.	cayenne pepper
	Bouquet Garni: 2 bay leaves, 3 cloves, 1/2 tsp. thyme and 5 parsley sprigs tied in cheesecloth

Brown meat lightly in hot fat. Add onions and minced garlic; cook until soft and lightly browned. Stir in curry powder and flour. Cook over low heat 10 minutes. Add water or beef stock, stirring continuously until sauce is smooth. Add bouquet garni and simmer 1-1/2 to 2 hours or until meat is tender. Remove bouquet garni and add remaining vegetables; cook 15 minutes. Add salt and cayenne pepper. Serve with plain boiled rice.

Yield: 25 Servings

Modifications: Trim all visible fat. Use cooking oil in place of fat to cover cooking surface only.

TOURTIERE

5 lbs.	ground pork
4 sm.	onions, finely chopped
4	garlic cloves, minced
1 tsp.	salt
1 tsp.	celery salt
1 tsp.	ground cloves
2 c.	water
1 to 2 c.	bread crumbs
4 (9-inch)	double crust pie shells, unbaked

Place all ingredients except bread crumbs in pot. Bring to boil and cook 20 minutes. Remove from heat and add 1 cup bread crumbs; let stand 10 minutes. If all fat is absorbed, do not add remaining bread crumbs. If not absorbed, add bread crumbs until all fat is absorbed. Cool mixture and then spoon evenly into 4 pie shells. Cover with top crusts and bake at 400 degrees until golden brown.

Yield: 4 (9-Inch) Pies

Modifications: Skim off excess fat after cooking. Remove any fat remaining after adding bread crumbs.

SWEET AND SOUR SPARE RIBS

20 lbs.	spare ribs
1 c.	onions, finely chopped
1/2 c.	green pepper, finely chopped
1/2 c.	celery, finely chopped
2 oz.	butter
6 c.	pineapple juice
3/4 c.	tomato ketchup
3 c.	brown sugar
3 c.	vinegar
2 Tbsp.	soy sauce
1/2 c.	corn starch

Cut spare ribs into serving-sized pieces and place in baking pan. Brown lightly at 375 degrees 30 minutes; pour off fat. Sauté onions, green pepper and celery until soft. Add 5 cups pineapple juice, ketchup, brown sugar, vinegar and soy sauce; bring to boil. Dissolve corn starch in remaining 1 cup of pineapple juice and stir into sauce. Cook until thick and clear. Pour sauce over spare ribs, cover pan and bake at 325 degrees 1-1/2 hours.

Yield: 25 Servings

Modifications: Trim all visible fat. Use margarine instead of butter and reduce amount.

TANDOORI CHICKEN

18 lbs.	chicken pieces
7-1/2 c.	Caribbean Jerk Sauce
7-1/2 c.	plain yogurt
1/4 oz.	ground cumin
1/4 oz.	ground ginger
1/2 oz.	ground turmeric

Combine Jerk Sauce, yogurt, cumin, ginger and turmeric. Divide chicken pieces evenly into 5 non-aluminum 12x20x2-inch full counter or baking pans. Pour marinade over chicken. Marinate covered in refrigerator 2 to 24 hours. Bake chicken, uncovered, at 375 degrees 1 hour and 15 minutes, or in convection oven at 325 degrees 60 minutes. Cover during last 15 minutes if getting too brown.

Yield: 25 Servings

Note: Tandoori ovens are made from brick and clay producing a very high heat. In this adaptation the hot oven or grill produces a similar effect. Instead of grilling, bake the chicken at 375 degrees 45 to 60 minutes or until cooked.

BARBEQUED CHICKEN

18 lbs.	chicken pieces, raw
1 c.	flour
2 Tbsp.	salt
1-1/2 tsp.	white pepper
1 tsp.	paprika
4 oz.	oil
2 qts.	barbeque sauce

Mix together flour, salt, white pepper and paprika. Dredge chicken is seasoned flour; shake off excess. Sauté coated chicken pieces in oil until golden brown. Transfer to baking pan. Add barbeque sauce, cover and bake at 325 degrees approximately 1 hour or until tender.

Yield: 25 Servings

CHICKEN CACCIATORE

2 c.	onions, chopped
2 c.	green pepper, chopped
2	garlic cloves, minced
4 oz.	butter *or* margarine
2 (48 oz.) cans	tomatoes
1 qt.	water
2-1/2 Tbsp.	salt
1/2 Tbsp.	chili powder
1 tsp.	thyme
1	bay leaf
18 lbs.	chicken pieces, raw
2 c.	all-purpose flour
2 tsp.	salt
1/2 tsp.	pepper

Sauté onions, pepper and garlic in butter until soft but not brown. Add tomatoes, water, 2-1/2 tablespoons salt, chili powder, thyme and bay leaf; simmer 1 hour. Combine flour with 2 teaspoons salt and 1/2 teaspoon pepper. Dredge chicken in seasoned flour; brown and remove to roasting pan. Cover chicken with sauce. Cover and bake at 325 degrees 1 hour or until chicken is tender. Serve over spaghetti.

Yield: 25 Servings

Note: Seven 2-1/2 pound chickens, cut into 8 pieces each will allow 2 chicken pieces per serving.

Modifications: Use margarine instead of butter and reduce amount. Remove skin from chicken.

ROTINI WITH FRESH TOMATOES, BASIL AND PARMESAN

3 lbs.	Rotini, (corkscrew pasta), *or* any tubular pasta
3/4 c.	vegetable oil *or* margarine
24	green onions, chopped
24	tomatoes, coarsely chopped
12	garlic cloves, minced
6 c.	cooked ham, turkey, *or* chicken; strips *or* cubes, (optional)
1 qt.	fresh parsley, coarsely chopped
1-1/2 c.	fresh basil, coarsely chopped *or* 6 tsp. dried basil
3 c.	Parmesan cheese, grated
	Salt and pepper, to taste

In large pot of boiling water, cook pasta until al dente (tender but firm); drain. If sauce isn't ready when pasta is done, rinse pasta under warm water a few seconds to prevent it from sticking together.

Meanwhile, in large heavy saucepan or Dutch oven, heat oil over high heat. Add onions, tomatoes and garlic. Cook, stirring, 2 to 3 minutes or until tomatoes are just heated through but still hold their shape. Stir in Rotini, ham (if using), parsley, basil and Parmesan cheese. Reduce heat to medium. Cook, stirring gently, approximately 2 minutes or until heated through. Season with salt and pepper to taste.

Yield: 24 Servings

MARINATED VEGETABLES WITH PASTA

1 lb.	cauliflower flowerets
1 lb.	broccoli flowerets
1/2 lb.	green beans, cut
1/2 lb.	carrots, peeled, sliced
1/2 lb.	fresh button mushrooms
1/4 lb.	red peppers, cut in strips
1/2 lb.	small white pickling onions
1 lb.	Rotini pasta, cooked, chilled

Marinade

16 oz.	red wine vinegar
2 tsp.	dried oregano
2 tsp.	dried tarragon
1/2 tsp.	pepper, freshly ground
4 oz.	olive oil

Garnish

Cherry tomatoes
Fresh parsley, chopped

Blanch prepared flowerets, beans and carrots. Plunge immediately into cold water; drain. In bowl combine cauliflower, broccoli, mushrooms, red peppers, green beans, onions and carrots. Gently fold in cooked, chilled pasta. To prepare marinade heat vinegar and seasonings in saucepan. Add oil, whisking briskly to blend. Cool slightly and pour over vegetables and pasta. Cover and refrigerate 24 hours before serving. Drain marinade. Serve on salad bar in bowl lined with lettuce or as a small side salad served in a see-through container.

Yield: 25 Servings

PASTA PRIMAVERA

10 lbs.	asparagus spears, cut into 1-inch pieces
1 lb.	margarine
8	red bell peppers, seeded, cut in strips
8	carrots, cut in thin strips
8	leeks, cut in thin strips
6	garlic cloves, minced
2 c.	chicken stock
1 c.	white wine *or* lemon juice
2 tsp.	salt
2 tsp.	pepper
8 c.	frozen green peas
5 lbs.	Primo linguine, fine
2 c.	Parmesan cheese, grated
1 c.	fresh Italian parsley, chopped

*I*n large pot of boiling, salted water cook asparagus 2 to 3 minutes or until tender-crisp. Remove with slotted spoon, refresh under cold water, drain and set aside. Melt butter in skillet over medium heat. Stir in red bell peppers, carrots, leeks and garlic. Cook 5 minutes or until vegetables begin to soften, stirring occasionally. Pour in stock, wine, salt and pepper. Simmer 5 to 7 minutes or until vegetables are tender-crisp. Stir in peas and cooked asparagus. Meanwhile, in same pot of boiling, salted water, cook pasta 7 to 9 minutes or until tender but firm. Drain pasta and toss with hot sauce. Sprinkle with Parmesan cheese and parsley; toss until well coated. Serve immediately.

Yield: 25 Servings

Note: Any combination of vegetables works. Sweet onions works as well as leeks.

CARIBBEAN JERK STEAK

24 (8 oz.) steaks	3/4-inch thick (eye of the round, rib *or* sirloin)
4 c.	Caribbean Jerk Sauce
9 oz.	soy sauce

*P*lace steaks in non-aluminum pan. Mix Caribbean Jerk sauce and soy sauce together; pour over steaks and marinate covered in refrigerator 3 to 24 hours. Grill 5 minutes on each side for medium-rare. Brush with marinade as desired.

Yield: 25 Servings

Note: Jerk cooking has become very popular today, but relates to several hundred years ago when Jamaican slaves who were constantly on the move developed a technique of cooking meat with a mixture of spices that helped preserve it. Today similar spices and peppers are blended to flavor meats and are often grilled or can be smoked in a pit.

Variation: Substitute 48 pounds of shrimp or halibut for the steak and marinate 30minutes. Grill 8 to 10 minutes, depending on the size of shrimp and thickness of halibut.

PORK SCALOPPINI

8 lbs.	pork cutlets
1-1/2 c.	all-purpose flour
3/4 tsp.	salt
1-1/2 tsp.	black pepper
1 tsp.	Italian seasoning
1 tsp.	basil
1 tsp.	rosemary
3	eggs
1 pt.	milk
1 qt.	bread crumbs

Mix salt and pepper together; sprinkle on cutlets. Pound cutlets paper-thin between waxed paper. Mix flour and herbs together. Coat cutlets with flour mixture. Combine eggs and milk to make egg wash; beat well. Dip floured cutlets in egg wash. Coat cutlets with bread crumbs; shake off excess. Sauté in very shallow oil until golden brown and slightly crisp. Serve with tomato sauce over noodles.

Yield: 25 Servings

Note: Recipe can be modified (less herbs and tomato sauce) and served as Weiner Schnitzel with suitable accompaniments such as fried egg and noodles.

CREW'S FAVORITE "JIGG'S DINNER"

1 (7 lb.) pail	salt beef navels
1 head	cabbage
2 lbs.	carrots
3 med.	turnips
7 lbs.	potatoes

You will need a very large pot, one that will hold enough water to cover salt beef. Soak salt beef in large pot of water overnight, changing water 2 times. Cover salt beef and bring to boil; reduce heat and simmer 1-1/2 hours. Clean, peel and prepare vegetables as follows: cut cabbage and turnips in quarters, cut carrots and potatoes in half. After beef has been cooking 1 hour check broth for salt. If necessary, change water. Add vegetables according to required cooking times.

M.V. Canadian Progress
Upper Lakes Group

Year Built:	1968, Port Weller Dry Docks St. Catharines, Ontario
Length:	730'
Beam:	75'
Draft:	46'6"
Cargo:	Coal, Iron Ore, Salt, etc.
Cargo Capacity:	32,700 Tons
Crew:	28
Steward:	Tony Carter

Growing up on the Atlantic Canadian Coast and coming from a long line of seafaring forefathers, Tony's love of the Great Lakes comes naturally. He is known as a "son of a son of a sailor!" Back in the 1940s and 1950s his father was a 1st mate and captain on oil tankers. Tony himself has already enjoyed 20 years in the sailing profession, working on Great Lakes freighters, oilrigs and supply boats in the Canadian Artic. He remembers the "colorful characters" from his early days on the lakes and, of course, the colorful stories that went along with them. Tony has gone through the many changes that have taken place in the Great Lakes shipping industry over the years, enjoying the new challenges and benefits that have been put in place along the way. Traveling from port to port and meeting the locals hasn't changed, nor has his enjoyment of it.

When Tony joined the crew of the *M.V. Canadian Progress*, he quickly settled into the busy life of preparing fresh hot food for it's crew of 28. His favorite part of the job…receiving a compliment from a crewmate on a meal they enjoyed! In March 2000 Tony transferred to the *M.V. Canadian Olympic*, an updated ship with a more modern galley. He enjoys working with his new crewmates, but admits he still misses the crew on board the *Canadian Progress*.

The *Canadian Progress* has a Crew's Mess Room and Officer's Dining Room. Breakfast is usually eaten communally in the Crew's Mess. Days in the galley start early, at 6:30 am, to serve breakfast by 7:30 am. Lunch preparations start at 7:30 am and dinner is started at 2:30pm. Baking and salad preparations are an ongoing job handled by the 2nd cook, who also prepares breakfast. If all goes well, the galley crew takes a two-hour break in the afternoon.

Rough weather or food shortages caused by waiting at anchor longer than expected have been know to change the menus, but it doesn't happy often. Tony always keeps the galley well stocked with cookies, ice cream, yogurt, individual cheese packs and crackers…the favorite snacks of his crewmates.

Daily menus aboard the *Canadian Progress* are displayed on a chalkboard, but Tony's crew knows what to expect on certain days without even looking. They count on their favorite fish on Friday, steak on Saturday, chicken, turkey or ham on Sunday and a delicious roast beef once a week. He follows a 21-day menu cycle, but you wouldn't know it to see the variety offered.

Buffalo Style Chicken Wings are very popular aboard the *Canadian Progress*, using Tony's special recipe!

Menus

Breakfast
Fresh Juices and Grapefruit
Hot and Cold Cereals
Waffles and Pancakes
Egg "McMuffins"
Eggs, Any Style
Sausage and Bacon
Toast and Muffins

Lunch
Soup of the Day
Salads
Beef Stroganoff with Noodles
Smoked Meat on Rye Sandwiches
Fries or Mashed Potatoes
Vegetables

Dinner
Barbequed Spare Ribs with Rice
Chili con Carne with Rice or Toast
Baby Carrots with Mint
Dutch Fries
Salads
Desserts

Special Holiday Menu

Shrimp Cocktail

Hors d'oeuvres

Soup

Baked Ham with
Pineapple Sauce

Roast Turkey with Gravy

Dressing and Cranberry Sauce

Scalloped Potatoes or
Baked Sweet Potatoes

Freshly Baked Dinner Rolls

Chocolates and Candies

TONY'S BUFFALO STYLE CHICKEN WINGS

30 lbs	chicken wings, cut, separated at joints, tips discarded, (*or* save tips to make soup stock)
2 lg. bottles	Kraft Catalina salad dressing
1 lg. bottle	Kraft Russian dressing
1 bottle	Heinz 57 Sauce, (optional)
1/4 c.	white vinegar
2 Tbsp.	granulated garlic
	Frank's Red Hot Louisiana Sauce, (*or* similar sauce), to taste

Combine dressings with Heinz 57 sauce, vinegar and garlic in top of double boiler; stir and heat through. Add hot sauce last, to taste. Deep fry chicken wings in batches approximately 5 minutes at 375 degrees, until they float and are golden and done; be careful not to overcrowd fry baskets. Drain well. Place ladleful of prepared sauce into small pot with lid. Add a serving portion of chicken wings to pot (approximately 10) and cover with lid. Hold and shake to coat wings with sauce. Repeat with remaining sauce and wings. Serve with French fries or a Rice Pilaf.

Yield: Serves Crew of 28

Note: When frying wings, break up carefully with long handled tongs to prevent them from sticking together.

HUNGARIAN BEEF GOULASH

5 to 6 lbs.	stewing beef
4 c.	onions, roughly chopped
2 tsp.	garlic, minced
6 to 8 c.	beef stock, hot
4	green peppers, thin julienne cut
	Flour, as needed

Sauce

10 oz.	tomato sauce
2 Tbsp.	cider vinegar
1/3 c.	brown sugar
1	bay leaf
1-1/2 tsp.	caraway seeds, crushed
4 to 5 Tbsp.	Hungarian paprika
3/4 c.	Worcestershire sauce
1-1/2 tsp.	dry mustard
1/2 tsp.	ground black pepper
1	pinch cayenne pepper

Trim stewing beef, if necessary, of excess fat and gristle. Cut beef into 1-inch cubes; place in roasting pan and brown well in hot 450 degree oven. Stir in onions and minced garlic. Reduce oven temperature to 400 degrees and brown an additional 10 to 20 minutes, stirring occasionally. Transfer roasting pan to stovetop. Over medium-low heat, stir in enough flour to absorb fat and drippings. Cook and stir over low heat 5 minutes. Combine sauce ingredients; add to beef with hot beef stock. Stir to combine and cover pan with lid or foil. Reduce oven temperature to 300 or 325 degrees. Place covered roaster back in oven and stew 2-1/2 hours, until beef is tender. Stir in julienned green peppers during the last 1/2 hour and recover pan. Taste and adjust seasonings. If necessary, thicken juices with a corn starch and cold water slurry on stovetop until desired consistency. Serve on broad egg noodles cooked al dente and tossed with garlic powder and butter.

Yield: 24 Servings

Note: Hungarian type paprika is essential for the right flavor. DO NOT substitute Spanish paprika.

TOURTIÉRE (Tor-tee-air)

French Canadian (Quebec) Meat Pie

5 lbs.	ground pork
3 med.	onions, finely diced
4	garlic cloves, minced
3 tsp.	salt
1 tsp.	ground cloves
1 tsp.	dried thyme
1-1/2 tsp.	dried sage or dried savory
1 tsp.	ground black pepper
2 c.	water
1-1/2 to 2 c.	fine dry bread crumbs

Pie Dough
(Enough for 4 Double Crust Pies)

4 c.	flour
1 lb.	shortening
3/4 to 1 c.	ice water
1 tsp.	salt

To prepare pie dough cut shortening into flour. Mix salt with cold water. Add water mixture to flour mixture, stirring in just enough to moisten. Roll out dough and place bottom shells in 4 (9-inch) pie plates. Roll out top crusts and set aside.

Place all filling ingredients, except bread crumbs, into stock pot; bring to low boil. Stir and cook 20 minutes, breaking up the meat until "pink" disappears. Remove from heat and stir in 1 cup bread crumbs. Let stand and cool 20 minutes. If all fat and liquid is not absorbed stir in remaining 1/2 cup bread crumbs. Cool mixture well and spoon into pie shells; level out well. Mixture should not be too moist or too dry. Cover filled pies with pastry, egg washing rims first. Seal and flute edges. Bake at 400 degrees 35 minutes.

Yield: 4 (9-Inch) Pies

Variations: Beef stock can be used in place of water. Finely diced or grated boiled and cooled potatoes can be substituted for part of the bread crumbs. Seasonings can be increased or decreased, to taste.

Note: These meat pies freeze well. Thaw and then reheat.

S.S. Courtney Burton

Oglebay Norton Company

The S.S. Courtney Burton upbound on the St. Clair River.

Year Built:	1953, American Shipbuilding Company Lorain, Ohio
Previous Name:	*Ernest T. Weir* (Renamed *S.S. Courtney Burton* in 1978) Converted from bulk carrier to self-unloader in 1981
Length:	690'
Beam:	70'
Draft:	37'
Cargo:	Stone, Iron Ore, Coal
Cargo Capacity:	22,300 tons
Crew:	27
Steward:	Todd Stewart

*T*odd Stewart has served as permanent steward aboard the *S.S. Courtney Burton*, Flagship of the Oglebay Norton Fleet, since 1995. He knows his crewmate's appetites almost as well as they do. With over 11 years experience in the profession, Todd's presence on board accounts for the great food his shipmates rave about. Todd, in turn, enjoys the great crew and raves about the atmosphere they have created by working well together. Retired Captain Bobby B. Tilley, current Captain Gary Mielke and 2nd Cook Audrey Hannafius, in addition to the entire crew, have all left their mark on the *Courtney Burton* and each other. It's a pleasure to go to work and they all enjoy their jobs. Todd's time off is spent at home with his wife Diana and their daughter Sydney Marie, where his cooking skills also receive rave reviews!

Todd's days aboard the *Courtney Burton* start early and end late. Breakfast preparations begin at 6:00 a.m. and dinner preparations are not completed until 6:00 p.m. Todd is in the galley the entire twelve hours, except for the standard two-hour break from 12:30 pm to 2:30 pm. From 6:00 p.m. until midnight Todd can be found doing paperwork, planning menus, watching TV or walking the deck. By midnight he is sleeping, getting ready for another busy day in the galley. It's probably safe to assume he dreams of menus and pantry orders more than a few times a week!

Todd's menus are full of variety and surprises. The only thing his shipmates know for sure is the food will be fresh and hot, prepared from scratch and delicious! Other than the crew's favorite steak every Saturday night, every day is different. Daily menus are written on a chalkboard every morning and the galley takes its direction from there. Homemade breads, rolls and soups are started early, leaving time in the afternoon for preparing fresh pies and cakes. Crewmembers, officers and guests each have their own dining rooms, but all groups are served from the same menu. Todd is always happy to prepare a special request, fitting it in as soon as he can.

Keeping just the right amount of fresh fruits, vegetables and meat on board, in addition to keeping the pantry stocked with the basics, comes with experience. Todd orders supplies every 7 to 10 days, making sure to include the crew's favorite snack foods such as fruit, popcorn, smoked fish and ice cream novelties.

Menus from the *S.S. Courtney Burton* give us all a glimpse into an average meal on board and Todd's recipes bring us a step closer to tasting the homemade goodness his shipmates enjoy everyday. The Southern Pecan Pie and B-B-Q Beef Sauce are among his personal favorites.

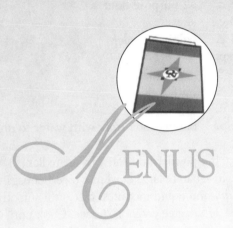

MENUS

Breakfast

Hot Cereal

Eggs and Omelets

Hot Cakes and French Toast

Fruit Crepes

Hash Browns

Bacon and Sausage

Melons and Grapefruit

Special Holiday Menu

Shrimp Cocktail

Lobster Tail

Fillet Mignon

Salads

Vegetables

Fresh Breads and Rolls

Desserts

Lunch

Homemade Soup

Sandwiches with Chips

Meat Entrée

Low-Fat Entrée

Vegetables

Fruits

Dinner

2 Meat Entrées

Potatoes or Rice

Salad

Desserts

S.S. COURTNEY BURTON BUTTERMILK HOT CAKES

5 c.	all-purpose flour
1/3 c.	sugar
1/4 c.	baking powder
1-1/4 tsp.	salt
5	eggs, beaten
5 c.	buttermilk
1/2 c.	vegetable oil
2-1/2 tsp.	baking soda (mix with water to prevent lumping)

In large bowl combine flour, sugar, baking powder and salt (dry ingredients.) Mix baking soda with small amount of water to prevent lumping. In separate large bowl mix together eggs, buttermilk, vegetable oil and baking soda mixture. Slowly combine both dry and liquid mixtures; mix until smooth. Let set at least 10 minutes before cooking. Drop batter onto lightly oiled 375 degree cooking surface. Cook until edges start to dry and surface is bubbly. Flip and cook other side.

Yield: Approximately 20 Regular-Sized Hot Cakes

CRÊPE BATTER

10 oz.	flour
8	eggs, beaten
1 qt.	whole milk
1/2 tsp.	salt
3 oz.	margarine, melted
	Fruit pie filling of choice
	Whipped cream
	Fresh fruit

Mix eggs and milk together by hand. In separate bowl sift dry ingredients together. Add dry ingredients to wet batter and mix until smooth; strain if necessary. Cook crêpes in egg skillet as you would an omelet, browning both sides. Fill with desired fruit pie filling. Garnish with whipped cream and fresh fruit.

LONE STAR DRY RUB

This is a favorite recipe of Todd's, taken from Texas Home Cooking Cookbook. It is used to prepare his favorite "Mop Sauces" (see following recipes.)

3/4 c.	paprika
1/4 c.	black pepper
1/4 c.	chili powder
1/4 c.	salt
1/4 c.	sugar
2 Tbsp.	garlic powder
2 Tbsp.	onion powder
1 Tbsp.	cayenne

Combine all ingredients and mix together well.

BEER MOP SAUCES

Beer Mop Sauce for Meat and Beer Mop Sauce for Fish are both favorites of Todd's that he uses quite often. Both were taken from Texas Home Cooking cookbook.

BEER MOP SAUCE FOR MEAT

12 oz.	beer
1/2 c.	cider vinegar
1/4 c.	corn oil
1/2 med.	onion, chopped
2	garlic cloves, minced
2 Tbsp.	Lone Star Dry Rub (recipe above)
1 Tbsp.	Worcestershire Sauce

BEER MOP SAUCE FOR FISH

12 oz.	beer
1/2 c.	lemon juice
1/2 c.	corn oil
1/2 med.	onion, chopped
2	garlic cloves, minced
2 Tbsp.	Lone Star Dry Rub (recipe above)
1 Tbsp.	white wine Worcestershire sauce

CREOLE SAUCE

4 oz.	olive oil
12 oz.	onions, chopped
8 oz.	celery, julienne
1	garlic clove, minced
36 oz.	whole tomatoes, sliced
2 c.	chicken stock *or* broth
1/2 Tbsp.	season salt
	Green pepper, chopped, to taste
1 oz.	corn starch
2 oz.	white wine
	Hot sauce, to taste

Heat olive oil in large braiser. Stir in onions, celery and garlic; simmer 15 minutes. Add sliced tomatoes, chicken stock, season salt and green peppers. Simmer 30 minutes, stirring occasionally. Dissolve corn starch in wine and stir into mixture. Add hot sauce to taste.

TODD STEWART'S FAVORITE BBQ BEEF SAUCE

2 med.	onions, chopped
1/4 c.	water
1/4 c.	vinegar
1/4 c.	sugar
1 c.	ketchup
1/2 c.	barbeque sauce
1-1/2 tsp.	salt
2 Tbsp.	margarine
1-1/2 tsp.	mustard
2 Tbsp.	Worcestershire sauce
1 tsp.	chili powder

Combine all ingredients and mix together well.

Yield: Enough Sauce for 2-1/2 Pounds of Beef

CORN BREAD DRESSING WITH OYSTERS

8 to 10 c.	corn bread, coarsely crumbled
2 slices	white bread, toasted, torn into small pieces
2	eggs, hard boiled, chopped
2 c.	celery, chopped
1 c.	onion, chopped
1 pt.	shucked oysters, drained, chopped *or*
	2 (8 oz.) cans whole oysters, drained, chopped
2	eggs, beaten
1 tsp.	poultry seasoning
5 to 6 c.	turkey *or* chicken broth

In large bowl combine all ingredients except broth. Stir in enough broth until mixture is very wet. Pour into greased baking dish and bake at 350 degrees approximately 30 minutes.

BAKED BEANS

For every 2 cans of baked beans, add:

1/2 c.	molasses
1/2 c.	brown sugar
1 c.	ketchup
2	slices bacon
1 Tbsp.	mustard
	Onion, chopped, to taste
	Salt and pepper, to taste

Combine all ingredients and mix together well. Place mixture in baking pan. Bake, uncovered, at 350 degrees 1 hour.

PUMPKIN BARS

1 c.	flour
1 tsp.	baking powder
1/4 tsp.	salt
1 tsp.	cinnamon
1 tsp.	baking soda
1 c.	sugar
2	eggs
1/2 c.	oil
1 c.	pumpkin

Frosting

1 stick	margarine
1 tsp.	milk
1 tsp.	vanilla
1-3/4 c.	powdered sugar

To prepare bars mix together flour, baking powder, salt, cinnamon and baking soda; set aside. In separate bowl mix together sugar, eggs and oil. Stir pumpkin into sugar mixture. Add dry ingredients and mix well. Spread batter in 9x13-inch pan. Bake at 350 degrees 20 to 25 minutes.

To prepare frosting combine all ingredients and mix until smooth. Spread frosting over cooled Pumpkin Bars.

PUFF PASTRY

4 c.	flour
2 c.	butter
1/4 c.	water

Combine butter with 2 cups flour. Mix together thoroughly, until very well blended. Mix in water. Work in remaining flour on table; roll out. Bake at 425 degrees 15 to 20 minutes. Fill cooled pastry with Cocoa Cream Filling or Whipped Cream Filling.

Cocoa Cream Filling for Puff Pastry

1-1/2 c.	cold heavy cream
6 Tbsp.	cocoa (sometimes 4 to 5 Tbsp. is better)
1 c.	powdered sugar

Combine all ingredients and beat until stiff.

Whipped Cream Filling for Puff Pastry

1/2 tsp.	gelatin
1 Tbsp.	cream *or* milk
1 c.	cold whipping cream
1/4 c.	powdered sugar
1 tsp.	desired flavoring

Soften gelatin in cream or milk; dissolve over hot water and set aside. Whip cold whipping cream until stiff. Beat in powdered sugar, cooled gelatin and desired flavoring.

SWEET ROLLS WITH CARAMEL NUT TOPPING

These rolls can be baked in one 10x16-inch pan or two 9-inch round cake pans.
See instructions for different pan sizes.

Sweet Roll Dough

1 pkg.	reg. *or* quick-acting active dry yeast
1/2 c.	warm water (105 to 110 degrees)
1/2 c.	lukewarm milk (scalded, then cooled)
1/2 c.	warm water
1/3 c.	sugar
1/3 c.	shortening, butter *or* margarine
1 tsp.	salt
1	egg
3-1/2 to 4 c.	flour

Caramel Nut Topping

3/4 c.	brown sugar, firmly packed
3/4 c.	butter or margarine, softened
3 Tbsp.	light corn syrup
3/8 c. (6 Tbsp.)	nuts, chopped

Filling

2 Tbsp.	butter *or* margarine, softened
1/4 c.	sugar
2 tsp.	cinnamon

Glaze

1 c.	powdered sugar
1 Tbsp.	milk
1/2 tsp.	vanilla

To prepare dough dissolve yeast in 1/2-cup warm water (105 to 110 degrees.) Combine 2 cups flour with all ingredients and beat until smooth. Stir in enough remaining flour to make dough easy to handle. Knead dough until smooth and elastic, approximately 5 minutes. Place dough in greased bowl and rotate, leaving greased side up. Cover and let rise until doubled in size, approximately 1-1/2 hours.

If preparing in (2) 9x9-inch pans, roll out dough into (2) 9x15-inch rectangles; roll out into (2) 8x15-inch rectangles if using 10x16-inch pan. Combine filling ingredients, spread over rectangles of dough and roll up. Cut 9x15-inch pieces into 9 rolls each; cut 8x15-inch pieces into 8 rolls each. Place rolls in greased pans (sometimes I don't grease.) Combine ingredients for Caramel Nut Topping and sprinkle over rolls. Let rise until double in size, approximately 40 minutes. Bake at 375 degrees 25 to 30 minutes or until golden brown. Mix glaze ingredients together until smooth and drizzle over top of rolls.

Yield: 16 to 18 Rolls

SOUTHERN PECAN PIE

Todd's favorite pecan pie!

1 c.	sugar
4 Tbsp.	butter *or* margarine, melted
4	eggs
1/2 tsp.	salt
2 tsp.	vanilla
2 c.	Karo syrup
3 c.	pecans
2 Tbsp.	flour
2 (9-inch)	pie shells, unbaked

Mix together all ingredients. Gently pour mixture into two pie shells. Bake at 375 degrees 10 minutes. Reduce oven temperature to 325 degrees and bake an additional 40 to 45 minutes.

Yield: 2 (9-Inch) Pies

ABIGAIL VAN BUREN'S PECAN PIE

1 c.	white corn syrup
1 c.	dark brown sugar
1/3 tsp.	salt
1/3 c.	butter, melted
3 lg.	eggs, slightly beaten
1 tsp.	vanilla
1 c. lg.	whole pecans
1 (9-inch)	pie shell, unbaked

Mix together white corn syrup, dark brown sugar, salt and butter. Add slightly beaten eggs and vanilla. Spread whole pecans in pie shell. Pour syrup mixture over pecans. Bake at 350 degrees approximately 45 minutes.

Yield: 1 (9-Inch) Pie

GRAMS CAKE

1 (20 oz.) can	crushed pineapple, undrained
1 can	cherry pie filling
1 pkg.	yellow cake mix
1 c.	walnuts, chopped
1 c.	butter, melted
	Coconut

Grease 9x13-inch pan. Spread crushed pineapple evenly in pan. Cover pineapple with cherry pie filling. Sprinkle dry cake mix over pie filling. DO NOT STIR. Sprinkle chopped walnuts and coconut over top. Drizzle with butter and bake at 350 degrees 1 hour.

DUMP CAKE

1 can	cherry pie filling
1 (15 oz.) can	crushed pineapple, undrained
1 box	white or yellow cake mix
1 stick + 2 Tbsp.	margarine
1/2 stick (4 Tbsp.)	butter
	Cool Whip

Dump pie filling and pineapple into 9x13-inch pan; mix together. Sprinkle dry cake mix over top. Cube margarine and butter; place over cake mix. Bake at 350 to 375 degrees 1 hour. Top cooled cake with Cool Whip.

CHERRY SOUR CREAM CAKE

3/4 c.	butter
1-1/2 c.	sugar
3	eggs
1/2 tsp.	almond extract
1-1/2 tsp.	baking soda
3 c.	flour
1 (8 oz.) container	sour cream (1 c.)
1 can	cherry pie filling

Streusel Topping

1/2 c.	flour
1/4 c.	sugar
1/2 tsp.	cinnamon
1/4 c.	butter

Spray 9x13-inch baking pan with Pam. Cream butter and sugar. Beat eggs until light and fluffy; add to creamed mixture. Mix in almond extract. In separate bowl combine baking soda and flour. Add flour mixture alternately with sour cream to creamed mixture. In food processor, process cherry pie filling until smooth. (Do not use entire can of pie filling, it will be too much.) Spread half of cake batter in prepared pan. Spread cherry pie filling over batter and top with remaining batter. In bowl, cut in ingredients for Streusel Topping and sprinkle over top of batter. Bake at 375 degrees 30 minutes. Check for doneness.

TOMATO CAKE

1/2 c.	Crisco
1 c.	sugar
10 oz.	tomato soup
2 c.	flour
1 tsp.	baking soda
1 tsp.	baking powder
1 tsp.	cinnamon
1 c.	raisins, chopped if desired
1 tsp.	nutmeg
1/2 tsp.	cloves
	Nuts, chopped
	Raisins, cut up, (optional)

Cream together Crisco and sugar. Mix in tomato soup until well blended. Combine dry ingredients in separate bowl. Stir dry ingredients into creamed mixture. Spoon batter into tube pan. Bake at 350 degrees; check at 40 minutes.

BANANA BREAD

2 to 3	bananas
1/2 c.	shortening
1 c.	sugar
3	egg yolks
1 tsp.	baking soda
2 Tbsp.	hot water
1 tsp.	vanilla
1/4 c.	nuts, chopped, (optional)
1-3/4 c.	flour
1/4 tsp.	salt

Mash bananas in bowl. In separate bowl cream together shortening, sugar and egg yolks; add to bananas. Dissolve baking soda in hot water and add to banana mixture. Add nuts and vanilla. Sift flour and salt together; add to banana mixture. Bake at 325 degrees 1 hour and 15 minutes in greased 5x9x3-inch pan or 45 to 55 minutes in two greased 5x8x3-inch pans.

Yield: 1 (9-Inch) Loaf or 2 (8-Inch) Loaves

GRAHAM CRACKER CRUST

1 lb.	graham cracker crumbs
8 oz.	sugar
1 Tbsp.	cinnamon
1 Tbsp.	nutmeg
8 oz.	margarine, melted

Mix together graham cracker crumbs, sugar, cinnamon and nutmeg by hand. Add melted margarine and mix together very well. Mixture should be moist enough to hold together when clutched in your hand. Press mixture into 4 pie pans. Bake at 350 degrees 5 minutes.

Yield: 4 Pie Crusts

MAKE YOUR OWN SWEETENED CONDENSED MILK

1 c. + 2 tsp.	powdered milk
1/2 c.	lukewarm water
3-1/2 Tbsp.	butter, melted
3/4 c.	sugar

Combine all ingredients in blender or food processor; blend until smooth. Store in refrigerator. Keeps well for 2 to 3 weeks.

Yield: Equivalent of 1 Can of Sweetened Condensed Milk

BEST FRUIT CAKE EVER!

Although not a member of the galley staff on the S.S. Courtney Burton, Joe "The Boat" Mokry, Wheelsman aboard ship, has a few hidden culinary talents and graciously shared one of his favorite recipes!

1 c.	butter
1 c.	sugar
4 lg.	eggs
1 c.	dried fruit
1 tsp.	baking powder
1 tsp.	salt
1 c.	brown sugar
1 to 2 qts.	Whiskey
	Lemon juice

Before you start, sample the whiskey to check for quality. Good, isn't it? Now go ahead.

Select a large mixing bowl, measuring cup, etc. Check the whiskey again, as it must be just right. To be sure the whiskey is of the highest quality, pour 1 level cup into a glass and drink it as fast as you can. Repeat. With an electrix miser, beat up 1 cup of better in a large fluffy bowl. Add 1 teaspoon of thugar and beet again. Meanwhile, make sure that the whiskey is of the finest quality! Add 2 arge leggs, 2 cups fried druit and beat till high. If druit gets stuck beaters, just pry loose with drewscriver. Sample the whiskey again, checking for tonscisity. Next, sift 3 cups of salt or anything, it really doesn't matter. Sample the whiskey, cheking fer quality. Sift 1/2-pint lemon juice. Fold in chopped butter and strained nuts. Add 1 babble spoon of brown huger or whatever colors you can find, and wix mel. Grease oven and turn cake pain to 350 grades. Now pour the whole mess into oven and ake. Check the whiskey again and bo to ged!

M.V. English River
Canada Steamship Lines

Year Built:	1962
	Collingwood Shipyards
	Collingwood, Ontario
Length:	405'
Beam:	60'
Draft:	36'6"
Cargo:	Cement
Cargo Capacity:	7,450 Tons
Crew:	19
Steward:	Roderick Sandiford Sr.

Roderick Sandiford stands at ease after preparing Roast Turkey, Pineapple Glazed Ham, Rock Cornish Hens and Standing Rib Roast for a holiday buffet on board the *M.V. English River.*

As longtime steward aboard the *M.V. English River*, Roderick Sandiford knows what this crew of 19 likes to eat... he has been working with them for over a decade! He has spent more than 20 years in this profession, preparing hot and hearty meals three times a day, so he has quite a collection of recipes. His favorite reward of the job has always been a smile on the faces of fellow crewmembers after a good meal. Judging by his menus and recipes, he must receive his reward quite often! Roderick enjoys this crew he has come to know so well, as he enjoys his daily life on board with Captain R. Richard, 2nd Mate Gordon Connelly, A.R. Joe Tannis, Chief Engineer K. Renault and his own staff Paul Penny and Ivan Hulan.

Throughout his many years on the lakes, the rough weather and the long days, when courage was required from everyone on board, Roderick has always held his wife Ingrid as his hero. He marvels at her ability to balance her own demanding career as a Bank Manager with being a great mother to their three active children Jackie, Roderick Jr. and Matthew without complaining. His time at home makes all his work worthwhile and he thanks Ingrid.

Roderick's busy days aboard the *English River* are spent creating menus, making sure the galley is well stocked and preparing three hot meals a day (with the dependable help of Paul and Ivan, he is quick to add.) In addition to the full menus offered, this crew likes to snack. Plenty of cold cuts, fresh fruits, canned fish, yogurt, and carrot and celery sticks are always on hand.

Daily menus are displayed on menu pads and a chalkboard. Saturday is always "Steak Night" and it wouldn't be Sunday on the *English River* without Roderick's full Turkey Dinner. Baking starts first thing in the morning, with breads, rolls, muffins and desserts made fresh every day. Roderick's Fruit Salad Cake has become a favorite dessert on board. Both the crew and officer's mess rooms stand ever ready to serve a hungry mate.

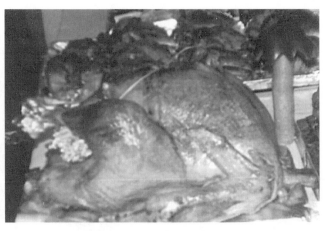

Not a detail is overlooked when presenting a holiday buffet. Table accents, cleverly carved from fresh vegetables, add a finishing touch to the spread.

MENUS

Special Holiday Menu

Chef's Salad

Shrimp Cocktail

Seafood Chowder and French Onion Soup

Elegant Duckling a la Orange

Rock Cornish Hens with Red Raisin Sauce

Pineapple Glazed Baked Ham

Poached Salmon with Aspic

Standing Rib Roast with Yorkshire Pudding

Potatoes Au Gratin

Mashed Potatoes

Candied Sweet Potatoes

Rice Pilaf

Glazed Carrots, Peas Amandine

Black Forest Cake, Pumpkin Pie

Fruit Cream Tarts, Plum Pudding

Fresh Fruit, Ice Cream

Breakfast

Assorted Juices

Grapefruit

Rolled Oats

Eggs, any style

Bacon and Sausages

Home Fries

French Toast

Tomato Sandwiches

Bran Muffins

Coffee and Tea

Lunch

Beef Barley Soup

Tossed Salad

Spaghetti with Meat Sauce

Garlic Bread

Braised Veal Chops with Gravy

Boiled Potatoes, Steamed Rice, Corn

Chocolate Cake

Fruit Salad

Ice Cream

Dinner

Navy Bean Soup

Caesar Salad

Prim Rib with Gravy and Yorkshire Pudding

Pork Fricassee

Sausage Rolls with Gravy

Mashed or Stuffed Potatoes

Steamed Rice

Broccoli with Cheese Sauce

Lemon Squares, Cinnamon Rolls

Cherry Turnovers, Ice Cream

BEEF PAPRIKA

6-1/2 lbs.	roast beef, cooked, cubed *or* cut in strips
3	med. onions, chopped
1/4 c.	butter
4 c.	heavy cream
4 c.	medium white sauce
1/3 c.	paprika
2 tsp.	parsley, finely chopped
	Pepper, to taste

Sauté onions in butter until tender; drain off excess fat. Add cream and simmer 5 minutes. Blend in white sauce, beef, paprika and parsley; heat thoroughly. Serve over noodles.

Yield: 20 Servings

MATAMBRE

2-1/4 lbs.	flank steaks
1 c.	wine vinegar
1/2 c.	oil
1	garlic clove, minced
12 oz.	fresh spinach
4	carrots, blanched, cut in half
4	eggs, hard cooked, quartered
2	sweet red peppers, sliced
1 lg.	onion, sliced
1/4 c.	parsley, chopped
2 tsp.	salt
1/4 tsp.	pepper
15 c.	beef stock

Split each steak in half lengthwise to within 1/2-inch to form 1 layer of steak (do not slice apart completely.) Place open steaks on cutting board; pound meat to 1/4-inch thickness. Mix together vinegar, oil and garlic. Marinate steaks in vinegar mixture 6 hours in refrigerator. Place opened steaks end-to-end, overlapping approximately 2-inches, to form one long piece. Pound overlapping edges to seal. Layer spinach, carrots, eggs, peppers, onion, parsley and seasonings evenly across meat. Carefully roll meat jelly roll fashion; tie securely at 1-inch intervals, crosswise and once lengthwise. Place meat roll in roasting pan. Add beef stock to cover 2/3 of roll. Add more stock or water if necessary. Cover tightly and bake at 375 degrees 2 hours or until meat is tender. Let stand 10 minutes before untying strings and slicing. Thicken sauce, if desired.

Yield: 10 Servings

MEAT-ZA-PIE

4.4 lbs.	ground beef
2 c.	milk
1-1/2 tsp.	garlic salt
1-1/2 c.	dry bread crumbs *or* cracker crumbs
2 c.	tomato sauce *or* ketchup
2 tsp.	oregano
1 c.	green peppers, chopped
1-1/2 c.	canned mushroom pieces, drained
3 c.	Cheddar cheese, grated
	Parmesan cheese, grated, to taste

Mix together ground beef, milk, garlic salt and crumbs. Divide beef mixture evenly into 4 (9-inch) pie plates; press on bottom and sides of pan to form shells. In center of each shell, layer ingredients in following order: Ketchup or tomato sauce sprinkled with oregano, green peppers, mushroom pieces and Cheddar cheese. Top with grated Parmesan cheese. Bake at 375 degrees approximately 35 minutes.

Yield: 4 Pies

Note: Recipe may also be prepared in large 12x20-inch pan; bake 45 to 55 minutes.

EASY BEEF WELLINGTON

6.6 lbs.	rib-eye beef
1/2 c.	butter
4 c.	fresh mushrooms, sliced
1/2 c.	onion, chopped
1/4 c.	sherry
1/2 c.	parsley
1/2 lb.	liver sausage *or* paté
1	egg, beaten
	Flaky pastry, enough for 4 double crust pies

Preheat oven to 425 degrees. Place beef on rack in open roasting pan and cook 50 minutes or until thermometer registers 120 degrees. Remove from oven and let stand 30 minutes. Melt butter in frying pan; sauté mushrooms and onion until tender. Add sherry and parsley. Cook until all liquid evaporates; cool. Roll pastry in rectangle large enough to wrap meat completely. Spread liver sausage or pate over surface leaving a 2-inch margin around edges. Spoon mushroom mixture down center of pastry. Place roast, top side down, in middle of the pastry. Wrap meat completely with pastry, sealing edges with beaten egg. Decorate with extra pieces of pastry. Place roast, seam side down, on baking sheet. Brush top and sides with egg. Bake at 425 degrees 30 minutes. Let cool 10 minutes before serving.

Yield: 12 Servings

Note: This recipe may be completely prepared ahead of time and reheated at 300 degrees 1/2 to 1 hour.

APRICOT BEEF BRISKET

1 (4.4 lb.)	beef brisket
1 c.	water
1 c.	beer
2 c.	canned apricot halves, drained, finely chopped
1 Tbsp.	sugar
1/2 tsp.	salt
1 dash	ground cloves

Place brisket in roasting pan. Add water and beer, adding more if necessary to cover bottom of pan. Sear uncovered at 425 degrees 30 minutes. Cook tightly covered at 350 degrees 2-1/2 to 3 hours or until meat is tender; drain liquid. Combine apricots, sugar, cloves and salt. Spread sauce over meat. Broil 10 minutes, basting frequently.

Yield: 12 Servings

MEAT BALL HOAGIES

Seasoned meat balls, cooked
Individual crusty *or* submarine loaves, split, toasted
Spaghetti sauce
Green pepper, chopped
Lettuce, shredded
Cheddar *or* Mozzarella cheese, shredded
Parmesan cheese

For each serving spread a crusty loaf with spaghetti sauce. Top with meat balls and then another layer of sauce. Cover with green pepper and lettuce. Sprinkle with cheese. Broil until cheese melts.

ROAST BEEF HOAGIES

Roast beef, rare, thinly sliced
Individual crusty *or* submarine loaves, split, toasted
Tomato sauce
Tomatoes, sliced
Green pepper rings
Green onions, sliced
Mozzarella cheese, sliced *or* shredded

For each serving spread a crusty loaf with tomato sauce. Layer roast beef slices, tomato and green pepper over roast beef. Sprinkle with green onion and top with cheese. Broil until cheese melts.

STIR FRY BEEF ORIENTAL

5-1/2 lbs.	lean chuck *or* round beef, boneless, cut into strips
1-1/2 c.	soy sauce
1-1/2 c.	cider vinegar
1 c.	brown sugar
3/4 c.	oil
10	carrots, thinly sliced *or* shredded
5	green peppers, sliced
8	onions, sliced
8 c.	mushrooms, sliced
5 to 6 Tbsp.	corn starch
1 lb.	bean sprouts
1-1/4 c.	water chestnuts, (optional)
	Salt and pepper, to taste

Combine soy sauce, vinegar and brown sugar. Pour marinade over beef strips; marinade must cover beef. Marinate in refrigerator at least 12 hours. Drain meat, reserving marinade. Heat 1/2 of oil in frying pan or wok. Stir-fry meat in hot oil 2 to 3 minutes or until brown. Season with salt and pepper to taste. Remove meat from pan. Add remaining oil to pan. Stir fry carrots, green peppers, onions and mushrooms in hot oil 2 to 3 minutes or until tender-crisp. Return meat to pan. Dissolve corn starch in marinade; stir into beef mixture. Add bean sprouts and water chestnuts. Continue cooking until sauce thickens.

Yield: 20 Servings

BEEF CRÊPES WITH CURRIED APRICOT BEEF FILLING

4.4 lbs.	beef, cooked, cut into strips
1 c.	green onions, sliced
3 c.	apricot nectar, canned, *or* juice from apricots with food coloring
1/4 c.	curry powder
2 tsp.	salt
1 tsp.	garlic powder
1 tsp.	ginger
1/4 c.	corn starch
1/4 c.	lemon juice
4 c.	canned apricots, sliced
18	med. crepes
	Oil

Sauté green onions in oil. Add apricot nectar, curry, salt, garlic and ginger. Dissolve corn starch in lemon juice; add to apricot mixture. Cook over low heat, stirring constantly, until slightly thickened. Add beef and apricots; heat thoroughly. Fill each crêpe with beef filling. Fold crêpes and serve topped with additional sauce, if desired.

Yield: 18 Crêpes

BRAISED BEEF A LA MODE

1 (10 lb.)	beef shoulder clod *or* chuck roll
1-1/2 Tbsp.	salt
2 tsp.	pepper, coarsely ground
1 tsp.	garlic, finely chopped
3/4 tsp.	thyme
3/4 tsp.	marjoram
1/2 tsp.	tarragon
1-1/2	celery stalks, coarsely sliced
3 med.	carrots, coarsely sliced
2 med.	onions, sliced
1/2 c.	tomato paste
2 c.	red wine
4 c.	beef stock

Rub salt and other seasonings into surface of beef. Brown beef in hot fat until richly colored on all sides. Remove meat to roasting pan. Brown sliced vegetables in same fat. Stir in tomato paste and wine. Heat slowly as sauce thickens. Add beef stock and bring to boil; pour over meat. Cover and cook slowly at 300 degrees 4-1/2 hours or until desired doneness. Turn meat periodically while cooking. Remove cooked beef; strain sauce and skim off excess fat. Reduce sauce to half its volume. Season if desired and thicken if necessary.

A la Bourgoise: After browning the roast, brown 12 carrots cut in strips and 30 to 40 peeled pearl onions. Brown as evenly as possible, and then transfer vegetables to a baking dish. While roast is cooking, bake carrots and onions uncovered 30 to 40 minutes or until barely tender. After meat is cooked and sauce strained and reduced, add vegetables to sauce and heat thoroughly. Thicken sauce, if necessary, and serve sauce and vegetables with the roast.

A la Mode: Prepare as for Bourgoise. To get a rich glossy sauce, cook 3 calf's feet alongside roast.

Yield: 20 Servings

BROCCOLI CREAM QUICHE

2 bunches	Ontario broccoli
12 oz.	lite cottage cheese
16 oz.	cream cheese
6	eggs
1/3 c.	35% cream
1-1/2 c.	Mozzarella cheese, grated
3 Tbsp.	Parmesan cheese, grated
	Salt and pepper, to taste

Short Crust

1-1/2 c.	flour
6 Tbsp.	butter
1	egg
1/4 tsp.	Salt

To prepare short crust mix together flour, butter and salt. Slightly beat egg; add to flour mixture. Let stand 30 minutes. Line bottom and sides of buttered 10-inch springform pan with pastry.

Cuts stems off broccoli and break into individual flowerets. Steam until halfway cooked and cool in cold water. Beat together cottage cheese, cream cheese, eggs, cream, salt and pepper. Pour 1/2 cottage cheese liquid mixture onto pastry and sprinkle evenly with 1/2 of the cheeses. Spread broccoli evenly over mixture. Add remaining cottage cheese liquid and top with remaining cheese. Bake at 350 degrees 50 to 60 minutes. Let rest 5 minutes. Unmold, cut and serve.

Yield: 12 Servings

Tips: Soft cream cheese is mush easier to work with. This can also be served cold as an appetizer.

VEGETABLE FETTUCINI WITH DILL SAUCE AND CURRIED COTTAGE CHEESE

2 lbs.	Ontario carrots
1 lb.	leeks
1-1/2 lbs.	Ontario zucchini
1/2 bunch	fresh dill
1 bunch	shallots
5 c.	35% cream
24 oz.	cottage cheese
2 tsp.	curry
1-1/2 c.	lite sour cream
	Salt and pepper, to taste

Wash and peel carrots; trim ends. Cut dark green from tops of leeks. Trim zucchini ends. Slice all vegetables into long flat ribbons (fettuccini shaped.) Steam all vegetables separately until al dente and cool immediately. Pat vegetables dry on paper towels. Pick 12 large sprigs from dill bunch and reserve for garnish. Chop shallots and remaining dill finely. Sauté shallots in non-stick frying pan. Add cream and reduce to half. Add chopped dill; continue reducing to one-third. Cool slightly. Mix cottage cheese with 1 teaspoon curry. Add sour cream to sauce and bring to slow boil. Add vegetables. Place vegetables on dinner plate and garnish with cottage cheese mixture. Sprinkle with curry and a sprig of dill. Serve immediately.

Yield: 12 Servings

SHAKE YOUR OWN CAESAR SALAD

5 oz.	Ontario Romaine lettuce
1 oz.	Parmesan cheese, freshly grated
1-1/2 oz.	fresh bacon bits
1/2 oz.	croutons
1-1/2 oz.	Caesar dressing, *or* to taste

Also required

1 (6x2x9-inch)	poly bag *or* large sandwich bag
4 (2 oz.)	plastic portion cups with lids
1	paper towel
1	napkin
1	plastic fork
1 lg.	hinged dome container

Wash and break Romaine into bite-sized pieces; dry in paper towel. Place bacon bits, croutons, Parmesan cheese and dressing in individual portion cups; cover with lids. Place paper towel and Romaine in poly bag, folding so Romaine is showing. Place all ingredients (including fork rolled in napkin) into hinged container. When ready to prepare individual serving, simply toss everything in plastic bag, shake and enjoy!

Yield: 1 Serving

CREW'S FAVORITE FRUIT SALAD CAKE

2 c.	all-purpose flour
1-1/2 c.	sugar
1/2 tsp.	salt
1	egg
1 (19 oz.) can	fruit salad
1 tsp.	vanilla extract
2 tsp.	baking soda
1 Tbsp.	all spice
1/2 c.	brown sugar

Sauce

1 can	Carnation milk
3/4c.	sugar
1/2 c.	butter
	Favorite extract, to taste
	Corn starch

Grease and flour a funnel cake pan. Mix together flour, baking soda, sugar, all spice and salt; set aside. In separate bowl beat egg with fork; add vanilla and fruit salad. Add fruit mixture to dry ingredients, mixing together well with wooden spoon. Pour batter into prepared pan. Sprinkle brown sugar over top. Bake at 350 degrees approximately 1 hour or until done.

To prepare sauce mix together milk, sugar and butter in saucepan; heat until melted. Thicken with corn starch and add your favorite extract. Serve sauce over cake.

M.V. George A. Stinson

American Steamship Company

Year Built:	1978
	American Shipbuilding Co.
	Lorain, Ohio
Length:	1004'
Beam:	105'
Draft:	50'
Cargo:	Taconite (Iron Ore Pellets)
Cargo Capacity:	59,700 Ton
Crew:	28
Steward:	Cornelius J. Gleason

*C*ornelius J. Gleason, steward aboard the *M.V. George A. Stinson*, and 2nd cook Mary Babino take a well deserved break in the ship's organized galley.

After serving 20 years in the U.S. Air Force, Cornelius Gleason joined the American Steamship Company where he has enjoyed every aspect of life on the Great Lakes for over two decades. The last few years have found him as steward aboard the *M.V. George A. Stinson*, creating menus and meals that both surprise and delight his fellow crewmates. Cornelius has four children, (Cornelius P., Cathern, Debbra and Dagni) who are also delighted with his culinary talents and help assure his time off ship is at least as busy as his time aboard.

With the dependable help of 2nd cook Mary Babino and porter Dennis Carrile the galley on board the *George A. Stinson* runs like clockwork. They are in the galley seven days a week, at least eight hours a day spread out over a 12-hour period, going about business as usual. Business as usual includes preparing and individually serving crewmates three fresh hot meals a day. It also includes baking fresh breads, pastries and desserts every day, which keeps the 2nd cook hopping. In addition, Cornelius keeps the ship stocked with plenty of popcorn, chips, assorted ice cream bars and fresh fruit to hold his hungry crewmates over between meals. The pantry is restocked once a week.

Packers Thanksgiving
November 26, 1998

Appetizers
Simmered Mountain Oysters
Poke Salad
Sardines (Canned)

Soup
Cheese Soup

Entrées
Boiled Crabs Als Itch with
Drawn Oleo
Fried Big Bologna
Grilled Road Kill with Fresh Fungus
Tail Gate Brats

Vegetables
Sautéed Road Apples
Boiled Field Corn
Potatoes a la Raw

Desserts
Fresh Crab Apple Pie
Choke Cherry Cake
Assorted Ice Cream with
Tomato Sauce

Holiday Favors
Pigs Eye or Blatz Beer
All You Can Chug
Rot Gut Whiskey
Cheese Soda

GOD SAVE THE FAVRE!

Cornelius displays his daily menu on a chalkboard and it always includes something different for the crew to try. His sense of humor shines through quite often, as it did when he prepared a special "Packer's Thanksgiving Dinner Menu" for the Green Bay football fans aboard. This special menu featured Packer favorites such as Grilled Road Kill, Cheese Soup and Tail Gate Brats!

Captain
Robert J. Gallagher

Chief Engineer
Thomas Sufak

Steward
Cornelius J. Gleason

Mate
Daniel Bensoni

Mate
Kevin R. Johnson

Mate
James M. Luke

Engineer
Martin M. Kowalski

Engineer
Ralph Biggs

Engineer
Richard Evertt

The Crew
Thomas P. Hainley
Michael E. Hill
Kenneth D. Goetz
Ken Grothe
Leonard W. Lackey
Robert Benson
David S. Grieg
Jason J. Sharpe
Michael A. Sitter
Toribio O. Lopez
Richard A. Tanner
Robert J. Jamison
Joseph J. Pajtash
Anthony J. Delphia
Mary E. Babino
Kristin Haack
Kenneth E. Young

*M*any of Cornelius' recipes have become favorites aboard the *George A. Stinson*. Below is an average day's menu and following are three recipes that always receive rave reviews!

Breakfast
Assorted Dry Cereal
Oatmeal
Melon, Prunes and Grapefruit Sections
Sausage and Corned Beef Hash
Hot Cakes and French Toast
Assorted Juices
Milk, Coffee and Tea

Lunch
Homemade Soup of the Day
Salad Bar
Omelets – Eggs to Order
Rubin Sandwiches and
Sloppy Joes
Roast Pork Loin
Mashed Potatoes with Pork Gravy
Apple Pie and Ice Cream

Dinner
Homemade Soup of the Day
Salad Bar
Roast Prim Rib Au Jus
Grill Ground Round
Broiled Half Chicken with
Cranberry Sauce
Baked Potatoes and Sour Cream
Steamed Broccoli
Lemon Butter Sauce
Carrot Cake
Ice Cream

CRANBERRY BREAD

12 c.	flour
6 c.	sugar
6 Tbsp.	baking powder
6 tsp.	salt
3 Tbsp.	baking soda
4-1/2 c.	orange juice
6 Tbsp.	orange peel, grated
12 Tbsp.	shortening
6	eggs
6 c.	cranberries, halved
6 c.	nuts, chopped

Grease bottoms only of 6 loaf pans; set aside. Combine flour, sugar, baking powder, salt and baking soda; stir to mix well. Add orange juice, orange peel, shortening and eggs; mix until well blended. Stir in cranberries and nuts. Turn into prepared loaf pans. Bake at 350 degrees 55 to 65 minutes, until toothpick inserted in center comes out clean. Cool thoroughly before slicing.

Yield: 6 Loaves

CAPTAIN BOB GALLAGHER'S
RENOWNED CHARBROILED PORK LOIN

1 (8 lb.)	pork loin, boneless
	Vidalia onion vinaigrette
	Lemon pepper
	Garlic

Combine vinaigrette with lemon pepper and garlic; marinate pork loin overnight. Broil over charcoal 45 minutes, turning meat approximately every 5 minutes.

MEXICAN LIME TORTILLA SOUP
With Diced Chicken

2 Tbsp.	vegetable oil
2 med.	onions, chopped
1 med.	tomato, chopped
1/2 lg.	green pepper, chopped
1	jalapeno, diced
3	limes, (1 thinly sliced for garnish)
8 c.	chicken stock
2 c.	cooked chicken, chopped
1 lg.	Ripe avocado, peeled, chopped

Heat oil in large soup pot; add onions and saute 3 to 4 minutes, until soft. Add tomato and green pepper; saute an additional 2 minutes. Add jalapeno, juice of 2 limes, shell of 1 lime and chicken stock. Simmer 2 minutes and then remove lime shell. Taste soup; add juice of another lime if needed. Add cooked chicken and simmer until all is heated through. Season to taste with salt, garlic, salsa, pepper, etc.

When serving place 2 tablespoons avocado in bowl with a small handful of tortilla chips. Ladle hot soup into bowl. Garnish with thin lime slice.

Note: To make this soup quick, delete onions, tomato, green pepper and jalapeno; substitute with salsa.

M.V. Indiana Harbor

American Steamship Company

Year Built:	1979, Bay Shipbuilding Corp. Sturgeon Bay, Wisconsin
Length:	1000'
Beam:	105'
Draft:	56'
Cargo:	Coal, Iron Ore
Cargo Capacity:	78,850 Tons
Crew:	30, Plus 4 passengers during summer months
Steward:	Dawn M. Weymouth

Dawn Weymouth, steward aboard the M.V. Indiana Harbor, thoroughly enjoys daily life in her shiny galley and on the Great Lakes.

*D*awn Weymouth started sailing on Great Lakes freighters in 1990 with only one goal in mind…to become a steward on board one of the magnificent ships. She achieved her goal four short years later and has been dishing out fresh and delicious meals to her crewmates aboard the *M.V. Indiana Harbor* ever since. Cooking for a crew of 30 makes for very busy days and Dawn enjoys every minute of it. She also enjoys visiting different ports, taking in the beautiful scenery of the region and catching up with fellow crewmates over a cup of fresh coffee. Life on the Great Lakes is everything Dawn dreamed it would be. She is pleased that more and more women are entering the merchant marine life in every department; deck, engine and galley.

Dawn credits Captain James Van Dongen and Chief Engineer William Rudder for the smooth operation of the *Indiana Harbor*. Their great supervision not only keeps the ship running, but also is directly responsible for the great attitude of this crew. When not on board, Dawn is kept busy with her four children and three grandchildren, all residents of Florida.

Meals aboard the *Indiana Harbor* are full of homemade soups, salads, entrées and desserts, and they're all prepared fresh daily. Dawn's day starts at 6:00 am, and if all goes well, ends at 6:00 pm She has lunch and dinner preparations well underway while breakfast is being served. The 2nd cook on board prepares fresh salads and baked goods throughout the day, keeping up with the appetites of this hungry crew. To keep up with the supplies necessary, Dawn restocks with groceries every seven to ten days. In addition, a variety of cold cuts, cheese, ice cream, popcorn, juices, cookies and fresh fruit are always plentiful for the snackers aboard.

Daily menus aboard the *Indiana Harbor* are displayed on a marker board, and they are always full of surprises. Dawn's crewmates usually don't know what she has up her sleeve until they see it posted. Shrimp Butter, Corn Chowder, and Beef and Green Bean Casserole are a few of this crew's favorites. The Walnut Bars and Oh Henry Bars don't last long on board either!

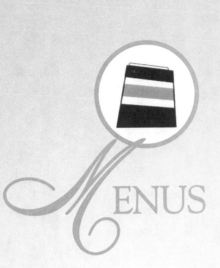

Menus

Captain
James N. Van Dongen
Chief Engineer
William B. Rudder
Steward
Dawn M. Weymouth

First Mate
David Griggs
First Asst.
Paul Newhouse
2nd Mate
William Boyd
2nd Asst.
Gerald Anderson
3rd Mate
James F. Bremer
3rd Asst.
Ralph Biggs III
3rd. Asst.
Jim A. Arlt

Boatswain
David Barber
Wheelsman
Charles Schoop
David Sungling
Robert Hidien
Watchman
Robert Derke
Evin Early
Russ Luther
Deckhand
Larry Kauti
Leonard Kauti
Allen Johnson
Qmed
Steve Furst
Todd Buckingham
John P. Schafer
Conveyorman
Daryl Overby
Gateman
Jeff Johnson
Wiper
Jack Povaser
2nd Cook
Maryann Gleason
Porter
Jim Martinesu

Thanksgiving 1999

Appetizers

Stuffed Mushroom Caps
Shrimp Cocktail
Shrimp Butter with Crackers
Deviled Eggs
Veggie & Relish Tray
Assorted Fruit Bowl

Soups

Oyster Stew
Homemade Turkey Nugget

Salads

Garden Fresh Salad
Waldorf Salad
Cole Slaw

Entrées

Roast Turkey with Sage Stuffing
and Cranberry Mold
Broiled Beef Tenderloin with
Sautéed Mushrooms
Broiled Lobster Tail with Drawn Butter
Buttered Acorn Squash
Asparagus Spears with
Hollandaise Sauce
Whipped Potatoes with Gravy
Candied Yams
Twice Baked Potatoes

Desserts

Apple Pie a la Mode
Mincemeat Pie
Pumpkin Pie with
Whipped Cream Topping
Pecan Pie
Assorted Ice Cream

Holiday Favors

Soda Pop, Apple Cider and Egg Nog
Fruit Cake
Gum, Assorted Chocolates
and Hard Candy
Mints and Nuts

THAT'S ALL FOLKS!

Chicago vs.
Detroit
12:40

Miami vs.
Dallas
16:15

Breakfast

Fresh Fruit
Hot Cereal
Eggs Made to Order
Assorted omelets
Hot Cakes and French Toast
Fried Potatoes
Bacon, Sausage, Spam-Ham

Lunch

Soup
Salad Bar
Sandwiches
Hot Entrées
Potatoes
Vegetables
Desserts

Dinner

Soup
Salad Bar
Prime Rib Au Jus
Cajun chicken
Assorted Casseroles
Bake Potatoes with Sour Cream
Broccoli with cheese Sauce
Desserts
Ice Cream

*H*oliday menus go beyond the variety already offered on a daily basis, rivaling any grand event planned on land. Dawn plans a day full of activity and FOOD for her *Indiana Harbor* crewmates!

WALNUT BARS

Crust

1 c.	flour
1/2 c.	butter
2 Tbsp.	powdered sugar

Filling

2	eggs, beaten
1-1/2 c.	brown sugar
2 Tbsp.	flour
1/4 tsp.	baking powder
1/2 tsp.	salt
1 tsp.	vanilla
1 c.	walnuts, chopped
1/2 c.	coconut

Frosting

1/2 c.	powdered sugar
2 Tbsp.	butter
2 Tbsp.	orange juice
1 tsp.	lemon juice

To prepare crust combine all ingredients and press onto bottom of 9x13-inch pan. Bake at 350 degrees 12 to 15 minutes or until slightly golden. Combine filling ingredients and mix together well. Spread filling over crust. Return to oven and bake an additional 25 minutes; check after 18 minutes, it may be ready. Combine frosting ingredients and mix until smooth. Spread frosting over cooled filling.

OH HENRY BARS

1 c.	sugar
1 c.	white syrup
1-1/2 c.	creamy peanut butter
6 c.	corn flakes
1/2 c.	chocolate chips
1/2 c.	butterscotch chips

In saucepan combine sugar and syrup; bring to rolling boil and remove from heat. Add peanut butter and corn flakes; mix together thoroughly until coated. Spread mixture into 9x13-inch pan. Melt chocolate chips and butterscotch chips together. Spread chocolate mixture over base while still warm. This is very easy!

SHRIMP BUTTER

1 can	shrimp salad
1/4 lb.	butter
1 (8 oz.) pkg.	cream cheese
	Horseradish, to taste

Combine all ingredients and mix together well; refrigerate. Use as dip or spread on crackers, croissants or grilled Italian bread slices.

CORN CHOWDER

1	Polish sausage, sliced
1 can	creamed corn
1 can *or* pkg.	frozen whole kernel corn
2	potatoes, cubed
1	onion, diced
1 can	chicken broth
1/4 c.	milk
1/4 c.	butter
	Salt and pepper, to taste

Combine all ingredients in crock pot. Cook on low 3 to 7 hours.

Yield: 2 Servings

BEEF AND GREEN BEAN CASSEROLE

1 lb.	ground beef, cooked
1 can	cream of celery soup
1/2 c.	sour cream
1 pkg.	frozen green beans
1 can	mushrooms
1/2 tsp.	thyme
1 dash	pepper

Topping

2 tsp.	margarine
	Bread crumbs *or* potato chips

Mix all casserole ingredients together and place in baking dish. Combine topping ingredients and sprinkle over top. Bake at 350 degrees until heated through.

M.V. Oglebay Norton

Oglebay Norton Company

Year Built:	1978, Bay Shipbuilding Corp. Sturgeon Bay, Wisonsin
Length:	1000'
Beam:	105'
Draft:	56'
Cargo:	Coal, Iron Ore
Cargo Capacity:	78,850 Tons
Crew:	28
Steward:	Calvin Statham, Sr.

Calvin Statham, Sr., steward aboard the *M.V. Oglebay Norton* always has a fresh supply of homemade cookies and snacks ready for his crewmates.

Calvin Statham has been sailing the Great Lakes with Oglebay Norton Company for over 25 years, enjoying every minute of it. "Everybody has been great! I have never been treated as well, or been as highly respected, as I am here. The money and benefits are good too, but it's the daily life I enjoy. I've met some great people and made some good friends." In 1999, after receiving a beautiful clock from Oglebay Norton Company in recognition of his 25 years of service, Calvin's first thought was, "I can't believe it's been that long!"

Growing up in Georgia, Calvin acquired the philosophy "if you're good to it, it will be good to you." This hardworking attitude remains the foundation of his life and it shows in the enthusiasm he brings to the galley of the *M.V. Oglebay Norton* everyday. He is proud of the fact that he got where he is today the good old-fashion way...hard work! "When I look in the mirror every morning I like what I see, knowing I haven't hurt anyone along the way. I feel lucky for being able to spend my days doing what I enjoy."

ONCO
Breakfast Menu

Hot Cereal * Eggs to Order
Bacon * Sausage * Ham
Spam * Fried Bologna
Pancakes Plain or
Blueberry * Bagels
French Toast * Waffles
Omlets * B.L.T. * Hash
Grilled Cheese * Toast
Fried Potatoes * Melon
Grapefruit
Juice

Calvin enjoys surprising his crewmates with new menus, and being rewarded with their compliments makes all his hard work worthwhile. After returning from 30 days off — the standard "family leave" granted to all Oglebay Norton Company crewmembers after 60 days on ship — he loves to hear that the crew has been asking, "when will Calvin be back?" And no wonder they anxiously await his return, every meal is a bounty of homemade variety. Calvin displays his daily menu on a chalkboard and the crew never knows what to expect until they see it posted. Calvin says sometimes he doesn't even know, he just keeps the surprises coming! It's no surprise, however, that *Oglebay Norton's* crew looks forward to every meal Calvin prepares. "Menus change, but nothing changes when it comes to the cook. There are no excuses for the crew not eating well," is Calvin's rule in the galley.

Days start early aboard the *Oglebay Norton*. Every morning Chief Robert Calder and Chief Donald Beaudour bring Calvin fresh coffee made from their "special blend" because they know he will make them their favorite breakfast...Eggs Benedict. "We've got to take care of Cal because, boy, we love those Eggs Benedict," is their explanation. It's hard to tell what Calvin enjoys most, the coffee or seeing their faces light up when he serves them their special breakfast.

Calvin gets right into preparing lunch and dinner as soon as breakfast is cleared away. The 2nd cook starts the daily baking while the porter is busy making beds for officers and distributing linen to the crew. They are all in the galley at least 8 hours a day, spread out over 12 to 14 hours. When he's finally done in the galley, Calvin prepares menus and gets his order for fresh supplies ready.

"A lot of the work is done on your own time, just to keep up," explains Calvin, "but you can always find time to enjoy the good company on board. And there is plenty of good company to be found on the *Oglebay Norton*. In addition to his morning "coffee group" Calvin credits Captain Constantine Mark, 1st Mate Leonardo DiCeffeli, Bosun Charles Lindberg III and Watchman David Cook with creating the great atmosphere on board. Another shipmate that always brings a smile to Calvin's face is Bill Sunderlin. Calvin has known Bill for over 20 years and cannot recall a day he wasn't wearing his cowboy boots (custom made in Texas, of course.) Bill's fashion statement dates way back to when Roy Rogers first became his hero and he used to travel all the way to California to have lunch with him. To this day, amidst all the wonderful food available to Bill, his favorite foods remain grilled cheese sandwiches, hot dogs and hamburgers. So, in true *Oglebay Norton* style, Calvin always has a hot dog or hamburger handy. Each crewmember is different, but as a group they form a perfect crew.

Nothing makes Calvin happier than a smile on a fellow crewmember's face after a good meal!

Calvin's menus and recipes, ever changing and always full of surprises, delight *Oglebay Norton*'s crew and nothing could make Calvin happier. His spaghetti, stir-fry, stuffed peppers and prime rib have become crew favorites. Calvin and the entire galley staff go all out to make holidays on board special, with menus and all the trimmings that rival any dinner their crewmates are missing at home.

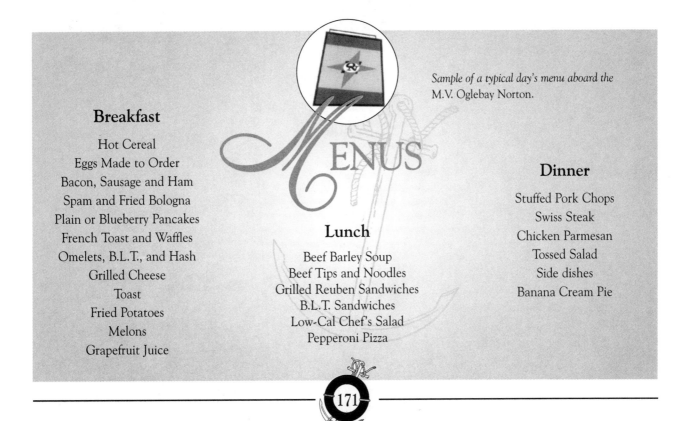

Sample of a typical day's menu aboard the M.V. Oglebay Norton.

Breakfast

Hot Cereal
Eggs Made to Order
Bacon, Sausage and Ham
Spam and Fried Bologna
Plain or Blueberry Pancakes
French Toast and Waffles
Omelets, B.L.T., and Hash
Grilled Cheese
Toast
Fried Potatoes
Melons
Grapefruit Juice

Lunch

Beef Barley Soup
Beef Tips and Noodles
Grilled Reuben Sandwiches
B.L.T. Sandwiches
Low-Cal Chef's Salad
Pepperoni Pizza

Dinner

Stuffed Pork Chops
Swiss Steak
Chicken Parmesan
Tossed Salad
Side dishes
Banana Cream Pie

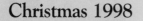

Christmas 1998

Soup
Chicken Noodle Soup

Appetizer
Shrimp Cocktail

Salads
Chef's Salad · Waldorf Salad

Vegetables
Mashed Potatoes with Gravy
Sweet Potatoes · Acorn Squash
Asparagus · Cauliflower and Cheese Sauce

Entrées
Lobster Tail and Drawn Butter
Filet Mignon
Country Baked Ham with Raisin Sauce
Stuffed Cornish Hens with Wild Rice Dressing

Desserts
Pumpkin Pie · Mincemeat Pie
Apple Pie · Cherry Pie
Fruit Cake · Ice Cream

Beverages
Egg Nog, Milk
Kool-Aid and Pop

CHRISTMAS
MENU
1998

MOTOR VESSEL
OGLEBAY NORTON

DINNER WILL BE
SERVED FROM
1400 TO 1600.
CHRISTMAS DAY

APPETIZERS
Chicken Noodle Soup
Shrimp Cocktail
Chef Salad
Waldrof Salad

VEGETABLES
Mashed Potatoes W/ Gravy
Sweet Potatoes
Acorn Squash
Asparagus
Cauliflower & Cheese Sause

BEVERAGES
Egg Nog
Milk
Koolaid
Pop

ENTREES
Lobster Tail And Drawn Butter
Fillet Mignon
Country Baked Ham W/ Raisin Sause
Stuffed Cornish Hen W/Wild Rice
Dressing

DESSERT
Pumpkin Pie-Mincemeat Pie
Fruit cake-Apple pie
Cherry Pie-Ice Cream

Christmas Continues on
Saturday the 26th with the entree
of Steak.
Sunday the 27th with the entree
of Turkey

CHEESY CHICKEN QUESADILLAS

6	chicken tenderloins, boneless, skinless
1-3/4 c.	water
1 box	Uncle Ben's Spanish rice
6	(8-inch) flour tortillas
1/4 c.	ripe olives, sliced
1-1/4 c.	Mexican-style cheese, shredded
3/4 c.	salsa
1/3 c.	sour cream

Preheat oven to 450 degrees. Cut chicken tenderloins into 1-inch pieces. In large skillet combine water, rice and contents of seasoning packet from rice; add chicken. Bring to boil. Cover, reduce heat and simmer 10 minutes. Spray both sides of tortillas with non-stick cooking spray. Place 3 tortillas on large baking sheet. Top each tortilla with 1/3 cup cooked rice mixture, 1/3 of olives and 1/3-cup cheese. Top with remaining tortillas and sprinkle with remaining 1/4 cup cheese. Bake 5 to 7 minutes or until light brown. Cut into wedges to serve. Top with salsa and sour cream.

Yield: 2 to 3 Servings

CHEESE BALL

A Favorite from Kathy Davis

16 oz.	cream cheese, softened
1 pkg.	corned beef
1/4 tsp.	garlic (may substitute onions or onion powder)

Stir all ingredients together until well mixed. Shape mixture into ball and refrigerate overnight. Serve with crackers.

GREAT LAKES CHICKEN KABOBS

2	chicken breasts boneless, skinless
1 sm.	orange cut into wedges
1/4 c.	pineapple chunks
1/2	red bell pepper cut into 1-inch pieces
1/2	green bell pepper cut into 1-inch pieces
1/3 c.	teriyaki sauce

Cut chicken into 1-inch pieces. Thread chicken, orange, pineapple, red bell pepper and green bell pepper alternately onto 4 (10-inch) skewers. Brush teriyaki sauce over kabobs. Grill or broil kabobs 10 to 15 minutes, brushing occasionally with teriyaki sauce, until chicken is done; turn once. Serve kabobs over rice.

Yield: 2 Servings

CRANBERRY-GLAZED CORNISH HENS WITH WILD RICE

1 box	Uncle Ben's long grain and wild rice, fast cooking recipe
1/2 c.	celery, sliced
1/3 c.	slivered almonds, (optional)
1 (8 oz.) can	jellied cranberry sauce, divided
4	Cornish game hens
2 Tbsp.	olive oil

Preheat oven to 425 degrees. Prepare rice according to package directions. Stir in celery, almonds and 1/2 cranberry sauce; cool. Spoon approximately 3/4 cup rice mixture into cavity of each hen. Tie drumsticks together with string and place on rack in roasting pan. Brush each hen with oil. Roast 35 to 45 minutes or until juices run clear, basting with oil occasionally.

Meanwhile, heat remaining cranberry sauce in small saucepan until melted. Remove hens from oven; remove and discard string. Spoon warm cranberry sauce over hens.

Yield: 4 Servings

PARMESAN CHICKEN AND RICE

1 Tbsp.	oil
4	chicken breasts, boneless, skinless
3	garlic cloves, minced
1-1/2 c.	rice, uncooked
2 (14-1/2 oz.) cans	chicken broth
1 c.	Parmesan cheese, shredded
1 c.	frozen peas, thawed

Heat oil in medium skillet. Add chicken and cook over medium-high heat 5 to 7 minutes or until light brown. Season with salt and pepper, if desired. Add garlic and cook briefly. Stir in rice and chicken broth; bring to boil. Cover, reduce heat and simmer 20 minutes or until chicken juices run clear. Remove from heat; stir in Parmesan cheese and peas. Cover and let stand 5 minutes.

Yield: 4 Servings

BEEF STROGANOFF

1 lb.	round steak, cut in cubes
	Onions, chopped, to taste
1	garlic clove, minced
1 c.	mushrooms, sliced
1 c.	sour cream
2 cans	tomato sauce
1 can	mushroom soup
1 Tbsp.	Worcestershire sauce
1 tsp.	oregano
	Salt and pepper, to taste

Brown round steak in skillet. Add remaining ingredients and simmer together until steak is cooked. Serve over egg noodles.

SWEET POTATO PUFF
A Favorite from Kathy Davis

3 c.	sweet potatoes, mashed
1/2 c.	sugar
1/2 c.	butter
2	eggs
1/3 c.	milk
1 tsp.	vanilla
1/2 c.	coconut

Topping

1/2 c.	brown sugar
1/4 c.	flour
2 Tbsp.	butter
	Nuts, chopped

Combine mashed sweet potatoes with sugar, butter, eggs, milk, vanilla and coconut. Transfer mixture to casserole. Combine topping ingredients and sprinkle over top. Bake at 350 degrees 35 to 40 minutes.

Yield: 8 Servings

WHITE BREAD

2	qts. warm water, (105 to 110 degrees)
1/3 c.	(or 6 pkgs.) dry yeast *or* 1/4 lb. cake yeast
1 c.	oil *or* shortening, melted
1 c.	sugar
2	Tbsp. salt
1 c.	powdered milk
6 qts.	flour, as needed

Mix together warm water, yeast, oil, sugar and salt until yeast is dissolved. Add powdered milk and flour. Mix 5 minutes, or longer, until dough leaves sides of bowl. Let rise until double in size. Knock dough down and let rest 5 minutes. Cut dough into loaf-size pieces and let rest an additional 5 minutes. Shape dough into loaves and place in greased pans. Let rise in warm place until double in size. Bake at 400 degrees 10 minutes. Reduce temperature to 350 degrees and bake 30 minutes, until bread sounds hollow when tapped with fingers.

Yield: 8 (1-1/2 Pound) Loaves

RYE BREAD

2 qts.	warm water, (110 degrees)
1/2 c.	yeast
1 c.	brown sugar
1 c.	oil *or* shortening, melted
2 Tbsp.	salt
1/2 c.	molasses
1-1/2 qt.	rye flour
3-1/2 to 4 qts	reg. flour, as needed
1/3 c.	caraway seed

Prepare Rye Bread using same method as for White Bread. May be baked as a round loaf or regular long loaves.

ZUCCHINI BREAD

5 c.	salad oil
3-3/4 lbs.	sugar
5 Tbsp.	salt
3 c.	eggs
10 c.	zucchini, shredded
48 oz.	bread flour
2 Tbsp.	cinnamon
2 Tbsp.	nutmeg
5 Tbsp.	baking powder
4 Tbsp.	baking soda
5 c.	walnuts, chopped

Combine salad oil, sugar and salt; mix together on low speed 2 to 3 minutes. Add eggs and mix 2 to 3 minutes. Add shredded zucchini and mix 2 to 3 minutes. Sift together flour, cinnamon, nutmeg, baking powder and baking soda. Add dry ingredients to zucchini mixture; mix 2 minutes, scraping bowl. Add walnuts last, stirring to mix. Pour into greased and floured loaf pans. Bake at 375 degrees until bread tests done.

AMERICAN APPLE BREAD

2 lbs., 12 oz.	sugar
2 lbs.	oil
14 oz.	eggs
3 lbs., 12 oz.	bread flour
4 tsp.	baking soda
4 tsp.	salt
4 tsp.	cinnamon
4 tsp.	vanilla
8 lbs.	apples, diced
18 oz.	walnuts, chopped

Mix sugar together with oil 3 to 5 minutes; scrape bowl. Mix in eggs, a few at a time, mixing well after each addition; scrape bowl. Sift together flour, baking soda, salt and cinnamon; add to sugar mixture. Stir in vanilla. Fold in apples and nuts. Bake in greased loaf pans at 375 degrees until bread tests done.

OATMEAL BREAD

17 oz.	hot water
8-1/2 oz.	oatmeal
11-1/2 oz.	brown sugar
1 oz.	salt
5 oz.	margarine
23 oz.	water, room temp.
2 oz.	yeast
4 lbs., 5 oz.	bread flour

Blend together hot water, oatmeal, brown sugar, salt and margarine with mixer 5 minutes. Dissolve yeast in room temperature water and add to oatmeal mixture. Add flour and mix 10 minutes on second speed. Bake in greased loaf pans at 350 degrees 30 to 40 minutes.

BANANA NUT BREAD

2-1/4 c.	butter *or* margarine
4-1/2 c.	sugar
12	eggs
12	bananas, mashed
9 c.	flour
5 tsp.	baking soda
4-1/2 tsp.	salt
2 c.	nuts, chopped
3 Tbsp.	vanilla

Combine butter, sugar, eggs and bananas; mix 2 minutes. Sift flour with baking soda and salt. Add dry ingredients to butter mixture. Stir in vanilla. Fold in nuts. Bake in greased loaf pans at 375 degrees until bread tests done.

BLUEBERRY MUFFINS

1 lb.	butter
1 lb., 4 oz.	sugar
3 oz.	dry milk
1/2 oz.	salt
12 oz.	eggs
1 lb., 14 oz.	water
2 lbs., 8 oz.	cake flour
2 oz.	baking powder
1 lb., 4 oz.	blueberries

Cream butter, sugar and salt. Add eggs and mix until blended. Mix in dry milk, cake flour, baking powder and water. Fold in blueberries. Transfer to muffin tins. Bake at 400 degrees until muffins test done.

BRAN MUFFINS

1 lb.	sugar
8 oz.	shortening
1/2 oz.	salt
1 lb.	eggs
1 lb., 8 oz.	milk
8 oz.	bran
1 lb., 8 oz.	bread flour
1-1/2 oz.	baking powder
4 oz.	honey
4 oz.	molasses
1 lb.	raisins

Cream sugar, shortening and salt. Add eggs and milk. Add bran. Add bread flour and baking powder, then add honey and molasses. Stir in raisins. Bake in muffin tins at 425 degrees until muffins test done.

CORN MUFFINS

1 lb., 4 oz.	pastry flour
1 lb., 4 oz.	corn meal
6 oz.	sugar
2-1/2 oz.	baking powder
3/4 oz.	salt
8 oz.	eggs, beaten
2 lbs., 2 oz.	milk
12 oz.	butter, melted

Combine flour, corn meal, sugar, baking powder and salt. Mix in eggs, milk and melted butter. Bake in muffin tins at 400 degrees until muffins test done.

BASIC MUFFINS

1-1/2 lbs.	sugar
1/2 oz.	salt
1 lb.	shortening
2 c.	whole eggs
2-1/2 lbs.	pastry flour
1-1/4 oz.	baking powder
2 c.	milk

Cream together sugar, salt and shortening with electric mixer on second speed 3 to 5 minutes; scrape bowl. Add eggs a few at a time; scrape bowl again. Sift together flour and baking powder; add alternately with milk to creamed mixture. Bake in muffin tins at 400 degrees until muffins test done.

Yield: 6 Dozen

PIZZA DOUGH

8 c.	warm water
4 Tbsp.	dry yeast
1/3 c.	salad oil
3/4 oz.	salt
1 oz.	sugar
7 lbs.	bread flour

Dissolve yeast in warm water. Add remaining ingredients to yeast mixture; let rise. Shape onto pizza pans and cover with toppings of choice.

SOFT ROLL DOUGH

1 c.	warm water
2 oz.	yeast
6 oz.	sugar
6 oz.	shortening
1 oz.	salt
3 c.	warm milk
3 lbs.	bread flour

Dissolve yeast in 1-cup warm water. In separate bowl combine sugar, shortening and salt; mix on low speed 3 to 5 minutes. Add dissolved yeast to sugar mixture along with milk; mix together, scraping bowl. Add flour and mix 3 to 5 minutes on low speed.

CROISSANT DOUGH

2 qts.	warm milk
8 oz.	yeast
6 oz.	sugar
1-1/2 oz.	salt
1 lb.	butter
6 lbs.	bread flour
4 lbs.	butter

Dissolve yeast in warm milk. Combine sugar, salt and butter; mix on low speed 3 minutes. Add yeast mixture. Add bread flour and mix 2 to 3 minutes; rest dough. Roll dough with butter.

SWEET DOUGH

2 qts.	warm milk, (105 to 110 degrees)
1/3 c.	dry yeast
2 c.	oil *or* margarine, melted
2 c.	sugar
8 Tbsp.	salt
8	eggs
1/2 tsp.	yellow food coloring
3 tsp.	vanilla
6 to 7 qts.	flour, as needed

Dissolve yeast in milk. Add remaining ingredients and mix until smooth; dough will be soft and sticky. Let dough rise in warm place until double in size. Roll out on floured surface for sweet rolls or raised donuts. Raised donuts should be rolled to approximately 3/4-inch thick; sweet rolls less than 1/4-inch thick. Use large donut cutter for donuts. Let donuts rise until double in size before frying at 360 degrees. Spread sweet roll dough with melted butter and sprinkle with filling of choice; roll jellyroll style and cut. Sweet rolls also have to rise to double in size before baking at 375 degrees. To frost donuts prepare a glaze combining powdered sugar, milk and vanilla. Glaze donuts and sprinkle with coconut or topping of choice.

ZUCCHINI OR CARROT BREAD

2 lbs.	whole eggs
4 lbs.	sugar
3 lbs.	salad oil
2 lbs., 8 oz.	bread flour
1 lb., 8 oz.	cake flour
1-1/2 oz.	baking soda
1-1/2 oz.	baking powder
1-1/2 oz.	salt
1-1/2 oz.	cinnamon
3 lbs., 6 oz.	zucchini *or* carrots, finely chopped
1 lb., 3 oz.	walnuts, finely chopped

Whip eggs, oil and sugar together until smooth. Sift dry ingredients together and fold into egg mixture. Blend in zucchini or carrots and walnuts; do not over mix. Grease and flour loaf pans and fill half full. Bake at 375 degrees until bread tests done.

BANANA ORANGE BREAD

3 lbs.	pastry flour
1 lb., 4 oz.	sugar
2-1/2 oz.	baking powder
2 tsp.	baking soda
4 tsp.	salt
12 oz.	walnuts, finely chopped
1 lb., 4 oz.	eggs
3 lbs.	ripe bananas, mashed
1 lb.	oil
1-1/2 oz.	orange rind, grated

Combine flour, sugar, baking powder, baking soda and salt. In separate bowl mix together eggs and oil. Combine egg mixture with dry ingredients. Stir in bananas, orange rind and walnuts, mixing just until all dry ingredients are moistened. Bake in greased and floured loaf pans at 375 degrees until bread tests done.

ORANGE NUT BREAD

1 lb., 8 oz.	sugar
2 oz.	orange rind, grated
3 lbs.	pastry flour
4 oz.	dry milk
2 oz.	baking powder
4 tsp.	baking soda
4 tsp.	salt
1 lb., 8 oz.	walnuts, chopped
10 oz.	eggs
12 oz.	orange juice
2 lbs.	water
6 oz.	oil

Combine sugar, orange rind, pastry flour, dry milk, baking powder, baking soda and salt. In separate bowl mix together eggs, orange juice, water and oil. Combine egg mixture with dry ingredients and walnuts, mixing until blended. Baked in greased and floured loaf pans at 375 degrees until bread tests done.

BANANA CHEESE CAKE

Crust

1 lb.	quick cooking oatmeal
7 oz.	pecans, finely chopped
12 oz.	brown sugar
1/2 c.	margarine, melted

Filling

3 lbs.	cream cheese
18 oz.	sugar
1	lemon rind, grated
1/4 tsp.	salt
2-1/2 c.	eggs
2-1/4 c.	ripe bananas, mashed
2 c.	whipping cream
	Juice from 1 lemon

To prepare crust mix together oatmeal, pecans and brown sugar. Add melted butter to oatmeal mixture and rub together. Divide crust mixture evenly into 4 (9-inch) springform pans; gently press onto bottom.

To prepare filling cream together cream cheese, sugar, lemon rind and salt on second speed of mixer 5 minutes. Scrape bowl a few times during creaming. Add eggs a few at a time; scrape bowl several times. Add mashed bananas and mix a few minutes. Add whipping cream and mix a few more minutes. Mix in lemon juice by hand. Pour filling over 4 prepared crusts. Bake at 350 degrees 35 minutes.

Yield: 4 (9-Inch) Cheese Cakes

CHEESE CAKE

3 lbs	cream cheese
12 oz.	sugar
1/2 tsp.	salt
1/2 tsp.	lemon rind, grated
2 c.	whole eggs
1 Tbsp.	vanilla extract
2 c.	whipping cream
	Juice from 1/2 lemon

Cream together cream cheese, sugar, salt and lemon rind on second speed of mixer using paddle for 5 minutes. Scrape bowl and paddle at least 2 times during creaming. Gradually add eggs and vanilla to creamed mixture, scraping bowl. Add whipping cream and cream 2 minutes. Mix in lemon juice by hand. Pour over prepared crusts in springform pans. Bake at 350 degrees 30 to 35 minutes.

CHEESE CAKE

5 lbs.	cream cheese
20 oz.	sugar
1 oz.	salt
2 oz.	corn starch
8 oz.	cake flour
4 oz.	butter, melted
4 c.	whole eggs
1 c.	hot water
4 c.	egg whites
26 oz.	sugar
1 Tbsp.	cream of tartar

Mix together cream cheese, 20-ounces sugar, salt, corn starch and cake flour with wire whisk. Gradually add melted butter and eggs, mixing together well. Add hot water and mix well. In separate bowl combine egg whites with 26-ounces sugar and cream of tartar; whip on high speed until stiff but not dry. Fold egg white mixture into cream cheese mixture. Line baking sheet with short dough and bake lightly, approximately 10 minutes. When cooked, spread dough evenly and then add filling. Sprinkle crumbs over top. Bake at 350 degrees 45 to 60 minutes.

MARBLE CHEESE CAKE

3 lbs.	cream cheese
12 oz.	sugar
6	eggs
1 lb.	semi-sweet chocolate, melted
1 c.	strong black coffee
1 c.	sour cream
2 Tbsp.	vanilla extract
2 Tbsp.	salt

Beat together cream cheese and sugar; add eggs and mix well. Add sour cream, vanilla extract and salt. Place crumbs in bottom of pan. Spread filling evenly over crumbs. Mix melted chocolate with coffee. Pour chocolate mixture on top of filling and marbleize. Bake at 350 degrees 35 to 45 minutes, until done.

CHOCOLATE CHEESE CAKE

3 lbs.	cream cheese
20 oz.	sugar
1/2 Tbsp.	salt
2 oz.	cocoa
2-1/2 c.	whole eggs
1 Tbsp.	vanilla
2 c.	whipping cream

Cream together cream cheese, sugar, salt and cocoa on second speed of mixer using paddle approximately 5 minutes. Scrape bowl and paddle at least 2 times while creaming. Gradually add eggs and vanilla to mixture, scraping bowl and paddle a few more times. Add whipping cream and cream on second speed approximately 2 minutes. Pour over prepared crust and bake at 350 degrees 35 to 45 minutes, until set in center.

JELLY ROLL

3 c.	eggs
3-1/2 c.	sugar
2 tsp.	salt
1/2 c.	powdered milk
4 c.	flour
4 tsp.	baking powder
1 c.	hot water
2 tsp.	vanilla
	Jelly

Beat eggs on high speed until light in color. In separate bowl combine sugar with salt and powdered milk; add to eggs and beat until fluffy. Sift flour with baking powder and fold into egg mixture. Add hot water and vanilla quickly; mix. Slowly pour batter into sheet pan that has been lined with waxed paper or foil. Bake at 350 degrees approximately 15 minutes; check for doneness by inserting toothpick in center. Turn jellyroll cake upside down onto towel that has been sprinkled with powdered sugar. Roll up with towel and let cool. Unroll, spread with jelly and roll up again. Slice when ready to serve.

GERMAN CHOCOLATE CAKE

8 oz.	hot water
8 oz.	sweet chocolate, melted
24 oz.	sugar
8 oz.	butter
8 oz.	Sweetex
1/2 oz.	salt
8 oz.	egg yolks
1 Tbsp.	vanilla
19 oz.	cake flour
1/2 oz.	baking soda
17 oz.	buttermilk
8 oz.	egg whites
4 oz.	sugar
	Coconut Frosting

Dissolve melted chocolate in hot water; let cool. Cream together 24-ounces sugar, butter, Sweetex and salt on second speed of mixer for 5 minutes. Gradually add egg yolks and vanilla; mix 5 minutes. Sift flour and baking soda together; add alternately to creamed mixture with chocolate mixture and buttermilk on first speed of mixer. Whip egg whites with 4-ounces sugar until stiff but not dry; fold into first mixture. Grease, paper and flour cake pans. Pour batter into prepared pans and bake at 350 degrees 25 to 30 minutes. Cool and frost with Coconut Frosting.

⚓

COCONUT FROSTING
(for German Chocolate cake)

2 lbs.	evaporated milk
28 oz.	brown sugar
8 oz.	egg yolks
2 lbs.	margarine, melted
1 lb.	pecans, chopped
1 lb.	coconut, chopped *or* shredded

Combine evaporated milk, brown sugar and egg yolks with melted margarine in large saucepan; cook slowly, stirring constantly until mixture coats spoon (approximately 15 minutes). Add pecans and coconut; mix thoroughly. Refrigerate overnight. Next day, beat on medium speed with paddle.

SPONGE CAKE

3 c.	whole eggs
1 c.	egg yolks
24 oz.	sugar
1/4 oz.	salt
1 Tbsp.	vanilla
3/4 c.	milk
8 oz.	butter
24 oz.	cake flour
1/2 oz.	baking powder

In saucepan combine whole eggs, egg yolks, sugar, salt and vanilla. Heat only until warm and then whip on low speed 5 minutes. Turn to second speed and beat an additional 10 minutes. In separate saucepan melt butter with milk. Sift flour with baking powder and fold into egg mixture by hand. After all flour is mixed in, fold in milk and butter mixture. Grease and flour 6 (9-inch) baking pans. Pour batter into prepared pans and bake at 350 degrees 30 to 40 minutes, until done.

ANGEL FOOD CAKE

4-1/2 c.	egg whites
4-1/2 tsp.	cream of tartar
1 tsp.	salt
4-1/2 tsp.	vanilla extract
2 tsp.	almond extract
1-1/2 lbs.	sugar
15 oz.	cake flour
22 oz.	powdered sugar

Combine egg whites, cream of tartar, salt and extracts in mixing bowl. Whip with wire whip on third speed until stiff but not dry. Add sugar slowly and whip until whites hold a stiff peak. Sift flour and powdered sugar; fold into egg white mixture. Pour into 3 (9-inch) greased tube pans and bake at 350 degrees 35 to 40 minutes. Be sure to double pans.

BANANA CARROT CAKE

1-1/2 c.	salad oil
1 lb.	sugar
1/2 tsp.	salt
3	eggs
2 tsp.	vanilla extract
15 oz.	cake flour
1 tsp.	baking powder
1 tsp.	baking soda
1/2 tsp.	cinnamon
2 c.	bananas, pureed
2-1/4 c.	carrots, grated

Mix together oil, sugar, salt, eggs and extract. Add dry ingredients, mixing well. Fold in bananas and carrots. Bake in greased cake pans at 350 degrees 35 to 45 minutes.

CARROT CAKE

2 lbs.	sugar
3 c.	salad oil
2 c.	eggs
20 oz.	bread flour
4 Tbsp.	baking powder
4 Tbsp.	baking soda
4 Tbsp.	cinnamon
6 c.	carrots, grated

Icing

16 oz.	cream cheese
12 oz.	margarine
2 lbs.	powdered sugar
4 Tbsp.	vanilla

To prepare cake, mix sugar and oil together on low speed 3 minutes. Add eggs 1 at a time, mixing approximately 3 minutes after each addition. Sift dry ingredients and add to sugar mixture. Add grated carrots and mix 1 minute. Spread batter evenly into greased and floured pans. Bake at 350 degrees 40 to 45 minutes.

To prepare icing, cream together margarine and cream cheese 5 minutes. Add powdered sugar and vanilla, mixing well. Frost cooled cakes.

APPLE CARROT RAISIN CAKE

8 oz.	margarine
2 lbs.	sugar
4 Tbsp.	cinnamon
1 Tbsp.	nutmeg
4	apples, grated
8	carrots, grated
2 c.	raisins, soaked
4 Tbsp.	vanilla
20 oz.	bread flour

Glaze

10 oz.	powdered sugar
8 Tbsp.	fresh lemon juice

To prepare cake, cream together margarine, sugar, cinnamon and nutmeg on second speed 3 to 5 minutes. Add apples, carrots, raisins and vanilla; mix 1 to 2 minutes on low speed. Sift bread flour and add to batter, mixing 1 to 2 minutes. Bake at 350 degrees 40 to 45 minutes.

Combine glaze ingredients and spread on top of warm cake.

PUMPKIN CAKE

3/4 c.	margarine
2 c.	sugar
3	eggs
1 c.	milk
1-1/2 c.	canned pumpkin
1/4 c.	unsulfured molasses
3/4 tsp.	baking soda
3 c.	cake flour
4-1/2 tsp.	baking powder
1/4 to 1/2 tsp.	salt
3/4 tsp.	cinnamon
3/4 tsp.	ginger
3/4 tsp.	nutmeg

Blend margarine with sugar until creamy. Add eggs 1 at a time, beating well after each addition. In separate bowl mix together milk, pumpkin, molasses and baking soda; set aside. In another bowl mix together flour, baking powder, salt, cinnamon, ginger and nutmeg. Add wet and dry mixtures alternately to butter mixture until all ingredients are combined. Bake at 350 degrees 25 to 30 minutes.

FRUIT CAKE

10 lbs.	mixed glazed fruits, (preferably cherries and pineapple)
5 lbs.	white raisins
1 (No. 5) can	pineapple juice
6 Tbsp.	vanilla
3 Tbsp.	almond extract
2 c.	brandy
3 lbs.	sugar
3 lbs.	butter
3 lbs.	eggs
3-3/4 lbs	bread flour
1-1/2 c.	milk
3 lbs.	walnuts

Glaze

2 lbs.	Karo syrup
1 lb.	water

Combine pineapple juice, vanilla, almond extract and brandy. Marinate mixed glazed fruits and raisins in pineapple juice mixture 3 days. Cream sugar with butter 5 minutes. Slowly add eggs and cream an additional 5 minutes. Add flour and milk alternately to creamed mixture, 1/3 at a time; start with dry and end with liquid. Add walnuts to fruit mixture. Mix batter and fruit mixture together by hand. Using 16-ounces of batter per cake, pour into greased baking pans. Bake at 350 degrees 1-1/2 hours. Check by color and toothpick. Brush with brandy after baking.

To prepare glaze, boil syrup and water together. Glaze cakes while glaze is hot.

FRUIT CAKE

20 lbs.	glazed fruit
10 lbs.	raisins
9 c.	pineapple juice
3 c.	wine *or* brandy
32 oz.	bread flour
4 lbs.	sugar
2 oz.	salt
4 lbs.	butter
4 lbs.	eggs
1/2 c.	vanilla
3 lbs.	bread flour
4 lbs.	walnuts

Combine pineapple juice with wine or brandy. Soak glazed fruit and raisins in pineapple juice mixture at least 3 days; stir twice a day. Combine 32-ounces bread flour with sugar, salt and butter; mix on low speed 5 minutes. Gradually add eggs and vanilla; mix 5 minutes. Add remaining 3 pounds of bread flour and mix 2 minutes. Mix fruit mixture and walnuts into batter by hand. Divide batter evenly into greased baking pans. Bake at 350 degrees 1-1/2 hours. Check by color and toothpick.

CHOCOLATE CUP CAKES

2 c.	cocoa
4 c.	hot water
7 c.	all-purpose flour
6 c.	sugar
2 tsp.	baking powder
4 tsp.	baking soda
2 tsp.	salt
2 c.	margarine, softened
8	eggs

Mix cocoa with hot water until smooth; set aside. Beat sugar with margarine until creamy; beat in eggs and set aside. In large bowl mix together flour, baking powder, salt and baking soda. Combine all ingredients and mix 2 minutes. Bake in muffin tins at 375 degrees until done.

CHOCOLATE BROWNIES

4 c.	whole eggs
4 lbs.	sugar
1 Tbsp.	salt
2 Tbsp.	vanilla
1 lb.	margarine, melted
1 lb.	bitter chocolate, melted
12 oz.	bread flour
1 lb.	walnuts, chopped

Combine eggs, sugar, salt and vanilla; mix on second speed of mixer 10 minutes. Combine melted margarine and melted chocolate. Add chocolate mixture to egg mixture and mix 1 to 2 minutes. Mix bread flour with walnuts; add to batter and mix on low speed 3 minutes using wire whip. Heavily grease baking sheet. Place silicone paper over greased sheet. Spread batter evenly over silicone paper. Bake at 350 degrees 35 to 40 minutes.

Yield: 1 Baker Sheet

CHOCOLATE BROWNIES

2 lbs., 4 oz.	cake crumbs
1 lb., 6 oz.	sugar
1 lb.	corn syrup
1 lb.	high-ratio shortening
1 lb.	bitter chocolate, melted
1 lb., 6 oz.	whole eggs
13 oz.	cake flour
1 Tbsp.	salt
1 lb.	walnuts, chopped

Mix cake crumbs only long enough to break up. Add sugar and corn syrup to crumbs; mix thoroughly. Add shortening and chocolate; mix until uniform. Add eggs and mix 2 to 3 minutes, scraping bowl. Sift flour and salt; mix into batter only long enough to blend. Add walnuts and mix 1 to 2 minutes. Bake at 350 degrees 35 to 40 minutes.

CREAM CHEESE BROWNIES

3-1/2 c.	eggs
3 lbs., 6 oz.	sugar
2 Tbsp.	vanilla
1 lb.	margarine
1 lb.	butter
20 oz.	flour
8 oz.	cocoa
8 oz.	walnuts, chopped

Cream Cheese Filling

2 lbs.	cream cheese
8 oz.	sugar
1 Tbsp.	vanilla
2	eggs

To prepare chocolate batter combine eggs with sugar and vanilla; mix on second speed of mixer 15 minutes. Melt margarine and butter; add to egg mixture on low speed 2 minutes. Sift flour and cocoa; add to batter with walnuts.

To prepare filling, mix cream cheese with sugar until smooth. Add eggs and vanilla to cream cheese mixture slowly, scraping bowl often. Grease full baker sheet and cover with silicone paper. Spread half chocolate brownie batter into pan. Spread cream cheese filling over top. Cover with remaining chocolate brownie batter. Bake at 350 degrees 45 to 60 minutes (closer to 60 minutes.)

COCONUT SQUARES

24 oz.	bread flour
24 oz.	shortening
4 oz.	brown sugar
4 lbs.	brown sugar
2 lbs.	macaroon coconut
1-1/2 lbs.	walnuts, ground
1-1/2 Tbsp.	baking powder
4-1/2 c.	eggs
3 Tbsp.	vanilla

To prepare crust rub together bread flour, shortening and 4-ounces brown sugar by hand to form a paste. Spread paste onto greased baker sheet. Bake at 350 degrees approximately 10 minutes, until light brown. Cool.

Mix 4-pounds brown sugar with coconut, walnuts and baking powder on low speed using paddle until no longer lumpy. Add eggs and vanilla to coconut mixture. Mix on low speed 1 minute. Spread coconut mixture over cooled crust and spread evenly. Bake at 350 degrees until golden brown and firm in center.

Yield: 1 Baker Sheet

BUTTERSCOTCH NUT SQUARES

3/4 lb.	butter
1 lb.	brown sugar
1 c.	eggs
2 Tbsp.	vanilla
14 oz.	bread flour
5/8 oz	baking powder
2 Tbsp.	salt
5 oz.	walnuts, chopped

Cream butter on low speed 5 minutes. Gradually add brown sugar and mix on low speed an additional 5 minutes. Gradually add eggs and beat 3 minutes on second speed. Add vanilla. In separate bowl sift dry ingredients together. Add walnuts to dry ingredients. Add dry ingredients to creamed mixture and spread 1/2-inch thick on greased 14x20-inch pan. Bake at 325 degrees 35 minutes. Cut into squares to serve.

DATE SQUARES

2 lbs.	dates
10 oz.	brown sugar
1 qt.	water
1-1/2 oz.	corn starch
1-3/4 lbs.	brown sugar
1-3/4 lbs.	shortening
2-1/2 lbs.	quick cooking oatmeal
1-1/2 lbs.	bread flour
3/4 oz.	salt

In saucepan combine dates, 10-ounces brown sugar, water and corn starch; cook and cool. Rub together 1-3/4 pounds brown sugar with shortening, oatmeal, flour and salt. Pack oatmeal mixture on bottom of baker's sheet, reserving some crumbs for top. Spread cooled date mixture over oatmeal mixture layer. Cover with reserved crumbs. Bake at 350 degrees 45 to 50 minutes.

ALMOND BARS

3 lbs.	sugar
3 lbs.	sliced almonds
2 Tbsp.	salt
2 Tbsp.	cinnamon
2 Tbsp.	vanilla
2 c.	egg whites
1 c.	Karo syrup
	Jelly

Combine all ingredients, except jelly, in steam kettle and heat until warm. Spread thin layer of jelly on baking sheet. Spread batter over jelly. Bake at 350 degrees until golden brown.

ALMOND SLICES

1-1/2 lbs.	sugar
1-1/2 lbs.	almond paste
6 oz.	bread flour
4 c.	whole eggs
1-1/2 lbs.	butter
3	lemon rinds, grated
3 Tbsp.	vanilla
	Jelly

Cream sugar with almond paste, bread flour and a few eggs (not entire volume of eggs) on second speed until fluffy; approximately 5 minutes. Add butter with lemon rind and cream together 5 minutes. Add remaining eggs and vanilla slowly; cream an additional 5 minutes. Spread thin layer of jelly on cookie sheet. Spread filling evenly over jelly. Bake at 350 degrees until golden brown. After cool, spread thin layer of jelly and Fondant Icing over top.

ICE BOX COOKIE DOUGH

2 lbs.	brown sugar
2 lbs.	margarine
1 c.	whole eggs
1 Tbsp.	vanilla
3 lbs.	bread flour
1 oz.	baking soda
8 oz.	chocolate chips
8 oz.	butterscotch chips

Mix brown sugar and margarine together on low speed using paddle 3 minutes. Add eggs and vanilla; mix 2 to 3 minutes. Sift bread flour and baking soda; add to brown sugar mixture, mixing only long enough to blend. Divide dough in half. Add chocolate chips to half of dough. Add butterscotch chips to remaining half of dough. Shape rectangle of chocolate chip dough into pan. Shape rectangle of butterscotch chip dough and press over first layer. Remove from pan and wrap in plastic wrap or foil; refrigerate or freeze. When ready to bake, slice dough and place on cookie sheet. Bake at 350 degrees 10 to 12 minutes, or until done.

OATMEAL COOKIES

1 lb.	brown sugar
1 lb.	margarine
1/2 c.	whole eggs
1 Tbsp.	vanilla
8 oz.	raisins, soaked
10 oz.	bread flour
1/2 oz.	baking soda
1 lb.	oatmeal

Mix brown sugar and margarine together on low speed using paddle 3 minutes. Add eggs and vanilla; mix 2 to 3 minutes. Add raisins and mix 1 minute. Sift flour and baking soda; combine with oatmeal. Add oatmeal mixture to margarine mixture, mixing only long enough to blend dry ingredients. Bake at 350 degrees 10 to 12 minutes, or until done.

PEANUT BUTTER COOKIES

13 oz.	sugar
13 oz.	brown sugar
22 oz.	peanut butter
1 lb.	margarine
1 c.	whole eggs
20 oz.	bread flour
1 Tbsp.	baking soda
1 Tbsp.	baking powder

Combine sugars, peanut butter and margarine; mix on low speed 3 minutes using paddle. Add eggs and mix 2 to 3 minutes. Sift dry ingredients. Add dry ingredients to sugar mixture, mixing only long enough to blend dry ingredients. Roll dough into balls and dip in sugar. Place balls on baking sheet and flatten crisscross with fork. Bake at 350 degrees 10 to 12 minutes, or until done.

MOLASSES COOKIES

28 oz.	sugar
12 oz.	margarine
4	eggs (1 c.)
1 c.	honey
1 c.	molasses
1 c.	milk
3-1/4 lbs.	pastry flour
1-1/2 oz.	baking soda
2 Tbsp.	cinnamon
1 Tbsp.	ginger
24 oz.	cake crumbs

Mix sugar with margarine on low speed using paddle 3 minutes. Add eggs and mix 2 minutes. Add honey, molasses and milk; mix 1 minute. Sift flour, baking soda, cinnamon and ginger together. Add dry ingredients with cake crumbs to sugar mixture, mixing only long enough to blend. Bake at 350 degrees 10 to 12 minutes, or until done.

THUMBPRINT COOKIES

16 oz.	brown sugar
2 lbs.	margarine
3/4 c.	egg yolks
1 Tbsp.	vanilla
32 oz.	bread flour
	Jelly

Cream brown sugar and margarine on low speed using paddle 3 minutes. Add eggs and vanilla; mix 2 minutes. Add bread flour, mixing only long enough to blend. Refrigerate before using. Roll chilled dough into balls and place on baking sheet. Flatten balls with thumb to leave indent. Bake at 350 degrees 10 to 12 minutes. Fill indents with jelly.

SUGAR COOKIES

1 lb.	sugar
12 oz.	margarine
1	egg
1/2 c.	sour cream
1 Tbsp.	baking soda
20 oz.	bread flour
1/2 Tbsp.	nutmeg

Mix sugar with margarine on low speed 3 minutes. Add egg and mix 3 minutes. In separate bowl combine sour cream and baking soda; let stand 5 minutes. Add sour cream mixture to sugar mixture; mix 3 minutes. Sift bread flour and nutmeg together. Add flour mixture to sugar mixture, mixing only long enough to blend. Roll out dough and cut into desired shapes. Bake at 350 degrees 10 to 12 minutes, or until done.

SUGAR COOKIES

32 oz.	sugar
1 lb.	margarine
1	lemon rind, grated
1 c.	eggs
1 c.	milk
3 lbs.	pastry flour
1 oz.	baking powder

Mix sugar with margarine and lemon rind on low speed using paddle 3 minutes. Add eggs and mix 2 minutes. Add milk and mix 1 minute. Sift flour and baking powder; add to sugar mixture, mixing only long enough to blend. Roll out dough and cut into desired shapes. Bake at 350 degrees 10 to 12 minutes, or until done.

CHOCOLATE FUDGE BROWNIE COOKIES

2 lbs.	powdered sugar
8 oz.	butter
10 oz.	margarine
6 oz.	cocoa
1-1/2 c.	eggs
1 Tbsp.	vanilla
10 oz.	cake flour
	Walnuts, chopped

Combine powdered sugar with butter, margarine and cocoa; cream on second speed 5 minutes. Gradually add eggs and vanilla; mix 3 minutes, scraping bowl. Sift cake flour and add to dough by hand. Grease baking sheet with butter. Place sheet of buttered silicone paper on top of buttered sheet. Spread batter evenly on pan. Sprinkle walnuts over top. Bake at 350 degrees 15 to 20 minutes.

CHOCOLATE CHIP OR BUTTERSCOTCH CHIP COOKIES

12 oz.	sugar
12 oz.	brown sugar
1 lb.	butter
1 c.	eggs
1 Tbsp.	vanilla
1 Tbsp.	water
20 oz.	bread flour
4 c.	chocolate chips *or* butterscotch chips

Mix sugars with butter on low speed 5 minutes. Gradually add eggs, vanilla and water; mix 3 minutes. Sift flour and add along with chocolate or butterscotch chips to sugar mixture. Mix on low speed 1 minute. Bake at 350 degrees 10 to 12 minutes, or until done.

TOLL HOUSE COOKIES

12 oz.	sugar
12 oz.	brown sugar
8 oz.	margarine
1 c.	eggs
1 Tbsp.	vanilla
22 oz.	bread flour
2 Tbsp.	baking soda
12 oz.	chocolate chips
1 c. (4 oz.)	walnuts, chopped

Combine sugars with margarine and mix on low speed 5 minutes. Add eggs and vanilla; mix 3 minutes. Sift flour and baking soda together. Add flour mixture with nuts and chocolate chips to sugar mixture; mix 1 minute. Bake at 350 degrees 10 to 12 minutes.

APRICOT NUT COOKIES

4 lbs.	pastry flour
2-1/4 lbs.	butter
1 c.	egg yolks
1 oz.	dry yeast
1 c.	warm water
1 c.	milk
8 c.	walnuts, ground
2 Tbsp.	cinnamon
20 oz.	sugar
	Apricot preserves
1-1/2 c.	egg whites
12 oz.	sugar

Rub pastry flour and butter together; set aside. Beat eggs slightly; set aside. Dissolve yeast in water; set aside. Mix milk with eggs and yeast mixture. Add to flour mixture and make as pie dough; chill. To prepare nut filling mix together ground walnuts, cinnamon and 20-ounces sugar. Divide dough into 3 pieces. Roll first piece 17x25-inches and place on greased baker sheet. Evenly spread 1/2 nut filling over top; reserve remaining nut filling. Roll out second piece of dough the same size and place over nut filling. Spread apricot preserves over second piece of dough. Roll out third piece of dough and cover apricot layer. Cut holes in top of dough and bake at 350 degrees 45 minutes. Whip egg whites with 12-ounces sugar; spread over top of baked cookies. Cover with reserved nut filling and bake an additional 10 minutes.

BUTTERSTAR COOKIES

4 lbs.	powdered sugar
5 lbs., 10 oz	margarine
2-1/4 c.	egg whites
3 Tbsp.	vanilla
1-1/2 Tbsp.	lemon extract
6 lbs.	bread flour

Cream sugar and margarine together on medium speed approximately 10 minutes. Slowly add egg whites with vanilla and lemon extract; cream an additional 10 minutes. Sift flour and add to creamed mixture. Mix 1 minute at low speed. Drop cookies onto baking sheet with pastry bag. Bake at 350 degrees until golden brown.

COCONUT MACAROONS

2-1/2 lbs.	sugar
3 lbs.	macaroon coconut
1 Tbsp.	salt
2 c.	egg whites
2 Tbsp.	vanilla
4 oz.	bread flour

Heat all ingredients together in steam kettle until warm to the touch. Drop onto baking pans covered with silicone paper and bake until golden brown.

Variation: For Chocolate Coconut Macaroons, add melted bitter chocolate.

RICH NUT COFFEE CAKE

6	eggs, beaten
2-1/2 c.	sugar
3/4 c.	oil
1 Tbsp.	vanilla
4-1/2 c.	flour
1-1/2 tsp.	salt
6 tsp.	baking powder
1-1/2 c.	milk

Topping

6 Tbsp.	margarine, melted
1-1/2 c.	brown sugar
3 tsp.	cinnamon
1 c.	nuts, chopped

To prepare batter add sugar, oil and vanilla to beaten eggs; beat until smooth. Sift together flour, salt and baking powder. Add dry ingredients alternately with milk to sugar mixture. To prepare topping combine melted margarine with brown sugar and cinnamon. Stir nuts in by hand. Grease and flour 12x15-inch cake pan. Place 1/2 batter in prepared pan; sprinkle 1/2 topping mixture over batter. Pour remaining batter over top. Sprinkle remaining topping mixture over batter. Bake at 350 degrees 40 to 50 minutes, until center springs back when touched.

CREAM PUFF SHELLS

1 qt.	water
2 c.	margarine
1 qt.	flour
16	eggs

*B*ring water and margarine to rolling boil. Stir flour in vigorously; if boiling too hard remove from heat. Continue stirring in flour until mixture leaves sides of pan. Transfer mixture to mixing bowl. Using mixing paddle mix in eggs 1 at a time, mixing thoroughly after each addition (have eggs ready in quart container before hand.) Continue to beat until smooth. Drop by spoon or ice cream scoop onto ungreased baking sheet. Bake at 400 degrees 50 minutes; cool. Fill with whipped cream, or chocolate or vanilla pudding. Dust with powdered sugar.

Yield: 38 to 40 Puffs

PUFF PASTRY FOR TURNOVERS

4-1/2 qts.	flour
2 Tbsp.	salt
1-1/2 qts.	cold water
2 c. (1 lb.)	puff paste
4 lbs.	puff paste

*M*ix flour, salt, 2-cups puff paste and cold water together with mixer. Transfer dough to floured surface and roll out into rectangle 1/4-inch thick. Cover 2/3 of dough with remaining 4 pounds of puff paste. Fold dough 3 times; roll out again. Fold dough 3 times again. Store in refrigerator until ready to use; will keep several days if covered. When ready to use, cut into triangles and bake at 375 degrees 30 minutes. Use for turnovers or Napoleons, or use a whipped cream filling.

DANISH PASTRY

12 oz.	sugar
8 oz.	shortening
1 lb.	flour
1 oz.	salt
8 oz.	compressed yeast
1/2 oz.	mace
5 oz.	powdered milk
10 oz.	eggs
2 lbs.	cold water
3 lbs.	flour
1-1/2 lbs.	margarine

Cream together sugar and shortening. Blend in 1-pound flour, salt, yeast, mace and powdered milk. Mix in eggs a few at a time, beating well after each addition. Add water and mix well. Add remaining 3-pounds flour, mixing until blended. Roll dough out into rectangle on floured surface. Spread margarine over 2/3 of dough; let rest. Fold dough into thirds and let rest again. Roll out again into rectangle. Dough is now ready for use as desired.

OATMEAL CRUST
Great for Leftover Fruit

1-1/2 c.	margarine, softened
2 c.	brown sugar
3-1/2 c.	flour, sifted with 1 tsp. baking soda
2 tsp.	salt
3 c.	rolled oats

Mix all ingredients together until well blended. Put 1/2 mixture in bottom of 12x20 inch pan; pack onto bottom and up sides slightly. Combine fruit, such as pie filling, with sugar, cinnamon and a little nutmeg to taste. Use approximately 2 (No. 2-1/2) cans of fruit with juice. Thicken with tapioca or corn starch. Place fruit mixture over crust. Sprinkle remaining crust mixture over top. Bake at 350 degrees until slightly browned, approximately 20 minutes. This crust may also be used for making Date Bars.

PUMPKIN PIE

12	eggs, beaten until smooth
2 (No. 2-1/2) cans	pumpkin
3 c.	sugar
2 tsp.	salt
2 tsp.	cinnamon
1 tsp.	ginger
1/2 tsp.	cloves
3/4 tsp.	nutmeg
5-1/2 c.	milk
4	pie shells, unbaked

Combine all ingredients and mix together 1 minute. Divide pumpkin mixture into 4 unbaked pie shells. Bake at 350 degrees 1 hour, or until filling puffs up. Pie is done when knife inserted near center comes out clean.

Yield: 4 Pies

PIE CRUST

3-1/2 qts.	flour
1-1/2 qts.	shortening, (lard preferred)
4 Tbsp.	salt
4 Tbsp.	sugar
4	eggs
2 c.	water

Combine flour with shortening, salt and sugar. Mix together just long enough to resemble meal. Mix eggs with water; add to flour mixture. Mix just until all ingredients are worked together. Over mixing will cause tough crust. Roll out for pie crusts.

FRENCH TOPPING FOR OPEN FACE APPLE PIE

4 c.	flour
1 tsp.	salt
2 c.	brown sugar, *or* use 1 c. brown sugar and 1 c. white sugar
2 c.	margarine, softened

Blend all ingredients together until mixture resembles meal. Sprinkle over open face apple pie and bake.

Yield: Topping for 4 Pies

FUDGE SAUCE

1 gal.	Milk
8 oz.	bitter chocolate, melted
4 lbs.	sugar
1 lb.	honey
1 tsp.	salt
8 oz.	butter
6 oz.	corn starch

*M*ix all ingredients together very well.

FRUIT SAUCE

2 c.	fruit, prepared for pie filling
4 c.	water
1 lb.	sugar
1/4 tsp.	salt
1	lemon, juice and rind, grated
2 oz.	clear gel
1 c.	water

*P*ut fruit in steam kettle with 4 cups water, sugar, salt and lemon; bring to boil and let simmer approximately 2 minutes. Dissolve gel in 1-cup water and strain. Add gel mixture to fruit mixture while stirring. Let simmer approximately 2 minutes. Add food coloring, if needed.

POPPY SEED FILLING

1 lb.	poppy seed, ground
12 oz.	sugar
1/2	lemon rind, grated
	Seedless raisins, (optional)

*C*ombine all ingredients and mix together very well.

ALMOND FILLING

2 lbs.	sugar
1 lb.	almond paste
1 lb.	margarine
1-1/2 c.	whole eggs
1 Tbsp.	vanilla
1 lb.	bread flour

Cream together sugar, almond paste and 1 or 2 eggs on medium speed until mixture in smooth; scrape bowl. Add margarine and cream on second speed 2 to 3 minutes, scraping bowl. Add remaining eggs, a few at a time, mixing at second speed. Mix in vanilla. Add flour on low speed and mix 2 minutes.

PECAN FILLING

2 lbs.	brown sugar
1-1/2 lbs.	pecans, chopped
8 oz.	margarine
8 oz.	pastry flour

Mix all ingredients together with paddle on low speed until mixture starts to get crumbly.

BUTTER CREAM FILLING FOR DANISH

2 lbs.	powdered sugar
12 oz.	margarine
1 c.	whole eggs
2 Tbsp.	vanilla

Cream powdered sugar and margarine together 3 minutes. Add eggs and vanilla to creamed mixture slowly; mix approximately 2 minutes on medium speed.

FONDANT ICING

6 to 8 c.	hot water
1 Tbsp.	vanilla
1 Tbsp.	almond extract
1 Tbsp.	salt
10 lbs.	dry fondant
10 lbs.	powdered sugar

Place hot water, vanilla, almond extract and salt in large bowl. Add dry fondant and mix with paddle. Add powdered sugar and mix with paddle. After blending, mix on low speed approximately 10 minutes or until smooth.

STREUSEL CRUMB TOPPING

20 oz.	sugar
24 oz.	margarine
20 oz.	cake flour
20 oz.	bread flour
1 Tbsp.	vanilla

Rub all ingredients together by hand or use paddle with mixer on first speed. Be careful not to over mix, it will easily become a paste.

OATMEAL CRUMB TOPPING

1 lb.	brown sugar
1 lb.	oatmeal
8 oz.	bread flour
8 oz.	pastry flour
1 lb.	margarine

Rub all ingredients together by hand or use paddle with mixer on first speed. Mix only long enough to form crumb mixture. Do not over mix or it will turn to paste.

M.V. Paul R. Tregurtha

Interlake Steamship Company

Year Built:	1981, American Shipbuilding Company, Lorain, Ohio
Length:	1014'
Beam:	105'
Draft:	56'
Cargo:	Coal
Cargo Capacity:	68,000 Tons
Crew:	26 + 2 Cadets
Passengers:	Average of 6 The *Paul R. Tregurtha* carries passengers from May through October
Chief Cook:	John R. Duning

Chief Cook John Duning with 2nd Cook Sandy VanTassel and Porter Yvette Gordon in the *M.V. Tregurtha's* shiny galley.

The M.V. *Paul R. Tregurtha's* friendly Chief Cook John Duning is organized, busy and focused while keeping his kitchen and dining areas loaded with eating opportunities. The happy culinary zone is well stocked at all times with handsome salad bar, jammed cookie jars, refrigerated snack center and bulging ice cream freezer.

"To give a meal that's well accepted by 30 crew members, and maybe six to eight guests, is a challenge I enjoy," claims John, who is well experienced as a former resort owner in menu planning, purchasing, budgeting and supervision for 200 to 300 guests on a weekend.

John adds finishing touches to the evening's offerings.

In concern for the health of personnel, Interlake Steamship Company expects John to offer low-cal, low-fat food; no salt or whole milk is used in cooking. A salad bar is always available as an alternative and lean meats, with plenty of chicken and fish, are used. "The heavy meals of the past are gone. As a regular menu breakfast and lunch include seventeen different offerings, many of them cooked to order."

"A complication in meal preparation on a boat is that 50% of the crew, at any given time, are in bed. Some are just going to work while others are coming back. I don't believe in wasting food in our world today, and I won't use steam tables, which overcook food and drain away its nutrients. So individualized plates of food are at the ready, covered with Saran Wrap and labeled with a name tag, ready to be micro-waved," explains John. Second Cook Sandy VanTasssel and Porter Yvette Gordon are ever present and essential in the smooth operation of *Tregurtha's* Steward's Department.

As with other crewmembers, John has had multi-careers, not only running a resort lodge in Rogers City, but as a social worker in the Detroit area for 15 years. He also served in Vietnam. John thoroughly enjoys his work on the *Tregurtha* and the independence that comes with it. His leisure time activities include cruising in the Georgian Bay area in his cabin cruiser and winter skiing in Michigan and Utah.

Menus on the *Tregurtha* are printed and sent to crew and passengers. Everyone on board is served individually in the crew's, officer's or passenger's dining areas. The galley comes to life at 0530 and remains a hub of activity preparing crew and passenger meals until 1330. After a short break it's back to work serving the evening meal in six settings, starting with an array of fresh hors d'oeuvres served to passengers at 1600. John's menus and recipes are as memorable as the M.V. *Paul R. Tregurtha* itself.

M/V PAUL R. TREGURTHA

MEMORIAL DAY PICNIC

24 May 1989 1130

Minnesota Onion Soup

Barbecue Pork Ribs
Or
Barbecue Chicken Breast

Featuring Maple Syrup Barbecue Sauce

Coney Island Hot Dogs or Coney Island Cajun Dogs

Arizona Baked Beans
Wisconsin Potato Salad
Michigan Green Beans

HORS D'OEUVRES BUFFET

Complete With Apple, Rhubarb or Pumpkin Pies
Ean Rolls and Beverages

Not gold, but only man can make
A people great and strong;
Men who for truth and honor's sake,
Stand fast and suffer long.

Brave men who work while others sleep,
Who dare while others fly-
They build a nation's pillars deep
And lift them to the sky.
-- Ralph Waldo Emerson, A Nation's Strength

MENUS

M\V Paul R. Tregurtha

THANKSGIVING DAY BUFFET

28 NOVEMBER 1996 1130

Oyster Stew

Caesar Salad
Cranberry Apple Conserve

Herb-Roasted Turkey
Snap and Pull Crap Legs with Drawn Butter
Baked Virginia Ham
Mashed Potatoes and Giblet Gravy
Sweet Potatoes With Apples
Oyster Dressing
New England Bread Stuffing
Scalloped Corn

Complete With Pumpkin Pie, Apple Pie, Mincemeat Pie
and Creme Brulee'

HORS D'OEUVRES BUFFET

Rolls - Breads and Beverages

Happy Thanksgiving

Never eat more than you can lift.
-- Miss Piggy

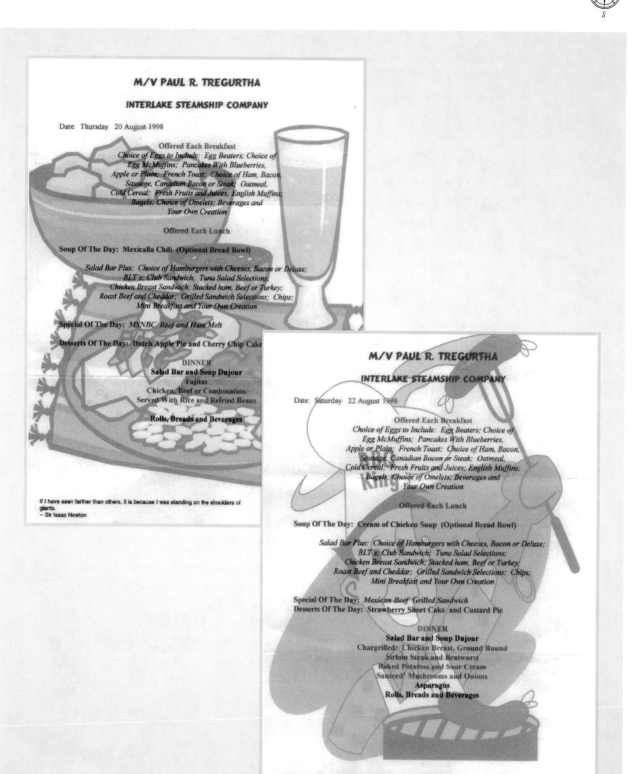

M/V PAUL R. TREGURTHA

INTERLAKE STEAMSHIP COMPANY

Date: Thursday 20 August 1998

Offered Each Breakfast
Choice of Eggs to Include: Egg Beaters; Choice of
Egg McMuffins; Pancakes With Blueberries,
Apple or Plain; French Toast; Choice of Ham, Bacon,
Sausage, Canadian Bacon or Steak; Oatmeal,
Cold Cereal; Fresh Fruits and Juices; English Muffins;
Bagels; Choice of Omelets; Beverages and
Your Own Creation

Offered Each Lunch

Soup Of The Day: Mexicalla Chili (Optional Bread Bowl)

Salad Bar Plus: Choice of Hamburgers with Cheeses, Bacon or Deluxe;
BLT's; Club Sandwich; Tuna Salad Selections;
Chicken Breast Sandwich; Stacked ham, Beef or Turkey;
Roast Beef and Cheddar; Grilled Sandwich Selections; Chips;
Mini Breakfast and Your Own Creation

Special Of The Day: MSNBC Beef and Ham Melt

Desserts Of The Day: Dutch Apple Pie and Cherry Chip Cake

DINNER
Salad Bar and Soup Dujour
Fajitas
Chicken, Beef or Combination
Served With Rice and Refried Beans

Rolls, Breads and Beverages

If I have seen farther than others, it is because I was standing on the shoulders of giants.
-- Sir Isaac Newton

M/V PAUL R. TREGURTHA

INTERLAKE STEAMSHIP COMPANY

Date: Saturday 22 August 1998

Offered Each Breakfast
Choice of Eggs to Include: Egg Beaters; Choice of
Egg McMuffins; Pancakes With Blueberries,
Apple or Plain; French Toast; Choice of Ham, Bacon,
Sausage, Canadian Bacon or Steak; Oatmeal,
Cold Cereal; Fresh Fruits and Juices; English Muffins;
Bagels; Choice of Omelets; Beverages and
Your Own Creation

Offered Each Lunch

Soup Of The Day: Cream of Chicken Soup (Optional Bread Bowl)

Salad Bar Plus: Choice of Hamburgers with Cheeses, Bacon or Deluxe;
BLT's; Club Sandwich; Tuna Salad Selections;
Chicken Breast Sandwich; Stacked ham, Beef or Turkey;
Roast Beef and Cheddar; Grilled Sandwich Selections; Chips;
Mini Breakfast and Your Own Creation

Special Of The Day: Mexican Beef Grilled Sandwich
Desserts Of The Day: Strawberry Short Cake and Custard Pie

DINNER
Salad Bar and Soup Dujour
Chargrilled: Chicken Breast, Ground Round
Sirloin Steak and Bratwurst
Baked Potatoes and Sour Cream
Sauteed' Mushrooms and Onions
Asparagus
Rolls, Breads and Beverages

Only in America.....do we buy hot dogs in packages of ten and buns in packages of eitht.

NEW ENGLAND SEAFOOD CHOWDER

I don't know of a recipe that better represents our area than chowder. I adapted this from my mom's clam chowder recipe and guests often request it.

1 lb.	whitefish
1 c.	celery, diced
1 lg.	onion, diced
5	med. potatoes, peeled, diced
3 Tbsp.	all-purpose flour
1/3 c.	cold water
2 (6-1/2 oz.) cans	minced clams with liquid
1 (4 oz.) can	tiny shrimp
1 can	crab meat
2 tsp.	salt
1/2 tsp.	pepper
2 Tbsp.	butter *or* margarine
1 (12 oz.) can	evaporated milk
1/2 (1 oz.) jar	pimiento, drained
	Fresh parsley, chopped

Place fish in large Dutch oven with enough water to cover. Cook over medium heat until fish flakes with fork, approximately 10 minutes. With slotted spoon remove fish and break into bite-sized pieces; set aside. Measure cooking liquid and add enough additional water to equal 4 cups. Cook celery, onions and potatoes in the liquid until tender. Combine flour and water to make a paste; stir into chowder. Cook and stir until mixture boils. Add reserved fish, clams with liquid, shrimp, crab meat, salt, pepper, butter, milk and pimiento. Heat through, stirring occasionally. Garnish with parsley.

Yield: 3-1/2 Quarts

HONEY-MUSTARD GLAZED MEAT BALLS

1/4 c.	honey
1/2 tsp.	lemon rind, grated
2 Tbsp.	low-sodium soy sauce
1 Tbsp.	Dijon mustard
1 Tbsp.	fresh lemon juice
2 tsp.	vegetable oil
1 c.	onion, finely chopped
1 c.	green bell pepper, finely chopped
2	garlic cloves, minced
1-1/2 lbs.	raw chicken thighs, freshly ground
1/2 c.	fine dry bread crumbs
1/2 c.	zucchini, coarsely shredded
1/2 tsp.	salt
1/2 tsp.	lemon rind, grated
1/4 tsp.	pepper
2 tsp.	Dijon mustard
2 tsp.	fresh lemon juice
1 tsp.	low-sodium soy sauce
	Vegetable cooking spray

Combine honey, 1/2 teaspoon lemon rind, 2 tablespoons soy sauce, 1 tablespoon mustard and 1 tablespoon lemon juice; stir well with wire whisk and set aside. Coat large non-stick skillet with cooking spray; add oil and place over medium heat until hot. Add onion, bell pepper and garlic; sauté 5 minutes or until tender. Let onion mixture cool. Combine onion mixture with ground chicken and remaining ingredients (except honey mixture); stir well. Shape mixture into 48 (1-1/4-inch) balls. Recoat skillet with cooking spray and place over medium heat until hot. Add half of meat balls to skillet and cook 15 minutes or until browned, turning frequently. Remove from skillet and keep warm. Repeat with remaining meat balls. Return cooked meat balls to skillet. Pour honey mixture over meat balls; cook 3 minutes or until thickened, stirring constantly.

Yield: 4 Dozen

GARLIC-ROSEMARY ROASTED CHICKEN

1 (5 to 6 lb.)	roasting chicken
1 Tbsp.	rosemary, chopped
8	garlic cloves, crushed
8 med.	red onions
2 whole	garlic heads
2 tsp.	olive oil
	Fresh rosemary, (optional)

The beauty of roasted chicken is its versatility.
Try rubbing it with paprika and add some fresh tomatoes 20 minutes before chicken is done.

To prepare Garlic-Rosemary Roasted Chicken preheat oven to 450 degrees. Remove giblets and neck from chicken; discard. Rinse chicken under cold water and pat dry; trim excess fat. Starting at neck cavity, loosen skin from breast and drumsticks by inserting fingers and gently pushing between the skin and meat. Place chopped rosemary and crushed garlic cloves beneath skin on breasts and drumsticks. Lift the wing tips up and over back; tuck under chicken. Place chicken, breast side up, on broiler pan. Cut thin slice from end of each onion. Remove white papery skins from garlic; do not peel or separate cloves. Cut tops off garlic, leaving root end intact. Brush onions and garlic with olive oil. Arrange onions and garlic around chicken. Insert meat thermometer into meaty part of thigh, making sure not to touch bone. Bake at 450 degrees 30 minutes. Reduce oven temperature to 350 degrees and bake an additional 1 hour and 15 minutes or until meat thermometer registers 180 degrees. Discard skin.

Yield: 8 Servings

Note: Spread the roasted garlic on French bread, if desired.

BUFFALO-STYLE CHICKEN WINGS

2-1/2 lbs. (12 to 15)	chicken wings
1/4 c.	Durkee red hot sauce
1 stick (1/2 c.)	butter *or* margarine
	Celery sticks
	Bleu cheese dip

Split wings at joint and discard tips; arrange on rack in a roasting pan. Cover wing pieces with sauce on both sides. Bake at 425 degrees 1 hour, turning halfway through cooking time. Wings can be deep fried at 400 degrees for approximately 12 minutes and then dipped into hot sauce until completely coated. Serve with celery and Bleu cheese dip.

BEEF BURGUNDY

2-1/2 lbs.	lean round steak, boneless
4	garlic cloves, minced
2 c.	Burgundy *or* other dry red wine
1 (10-3/4 oz.) can	condensed reduced-sodium, low-fat cream of mushroom soup, undiluted
1 (10-1/2 oz.) can	beef consommé, undiluted
1 (1 oz.) env.	onion recipe soup mix
6 c.	fresh mushrooms, sliced
1 (16 oz.) pkg.	frozen pearl onions
3 Tbsp.	all-purpose flour
1/2 c.	water
2 (12 oz.) pkgs.	medium egg noodles, uncooked
1/4 c.	Parmesan cheese, grated
3/4 c.	non-fat sour cream alternative
	Vegetable cooking spray

Trim fat from steak. Cut steak into 1-inch cubes. Coat large, ovenproof Dutch oven with cooking spray; place over medium heat until hot. Add steak and cook 9 minutes, until steak loses pink color. Drain well and set aside. Wipe drippings from pan with paper towel. Recoat pan with cooking spray and place over medium heat. Add garlic and sauté 1 minute. Add wine, mushroom soup, beef consommé and onion soup mix; stir well and bring to boil. Return steak to pan; stir in mushrooms and onions. Remove from heat; set aside. Place flour in small bowl. Gradually add water, blending with wire whisk; add to steak mixture. Cover and bake at 350 degrees 1-1/2 hours.

Cook noodles according to package directions, omitting salt and fat. Drain noodles well and place in large bowl. Add cheese and sour cream; toss gently to coat. Serve steak mixture over noodles.

Yield: 12 Servings

GRILLED CHICKEN CAESAR

1 Tbsp.	chili powder
2 Tbsp.	Worcestershire sauce
1 tsp.	ground cumin
1/4 tsp.	pepper
1	garlic clove, crushed
1 lb.	chicken breasts, skinless, boneless, cut into 1-inch wide strips
3/4 c.	low-fat buttermilk
3 Tbsp.	Romano cheese, grated
1 Tbsp.	lemon juice
1 tsp.	anchovy paste
1/2 tsp.	dry mustard
1/4 tsp.	pepper
1	garlic clove, minced
1 (10 oz.) pkg.	ready-to-eat Romaine salad
2 c.	cherry tomatoes, halved
3/4 c	plain croutons
	Vegetable cooking spray

Combine chili powder, Worcestershire sauce, cumin, 1/4 teaspoon pepper, 1 crushed garlic clove and chicken strips in medium bow; stir well and set aside. Prepare grill or broiler. Place chicken strips on grill rack or broiler pan coated with cooking spray and cook 5 minutes on each side or until chicken is done. Combine buttermilk with cheese, lemon juice, anchovy paste, dry mustard, 1/4 teaspoon pepper and 1 minced garlic clove in large bowl; stir well. Add Romaine salad, tomatoes and croutons; toss gently to coat. Spoon salad mixture onto each of 4 plates. Top salad mixture with chicken strips.

Yield: 4 Servings

Note: Substitute 12 cups sliced Romaine lettuce for 1 (10-ounce) package ready-to-eat Romaine salad, if desired.

Year Built:	1970, Lithgows, Port Glasgow, Scotland
Length:	642'10"
Beam:	74'10"
Draft:	42'
Cargo:	Salt
Cargo Capacity:	23,900 Tons
Crew:	25 to 28
Steward:	Linda Orr

*L*inda Orr is in the middle of her sixth season as a steward on the Great Lakes and can't think of anything she would rather be doing. After sailing off and on for over 25 years, the lakes seem like home. And after years spent perfecting her culinary skills while cooking for large groups, the hectic galley of a Great Lakes freighter is a natural second home. Her training at truck stops, restaurants, tourist camps and with the Canadian Coast Guard is put to good use everyday aboard the *M/V Sauniere*.

After a quick 6:00 am glance at the daily menu Linda prepared earlier, *Sauniere's* galley crew is off and running. Second Cook Siobhan McDowall handles breakfast and then immediately starts filling ovens with the day's baked goods and desserts. Linda is convinced Siobhan makes the best cream puffs on the lakes! Cedric Mohammed is the porter on board and runs circles around the galley, sun-up to sundown, cleaning and serving the crew meals. Preparing lunch and dinner, creating menus, and ordering groceries to ensure the pantry is always well stocked keeps Linda busy throughout the day and beyond. She usually restocks supplies every two weeks with an average order including hundreds of pounds of potatoes, beef, and poultry.

Daily menus written on a dry-erasable board are posted in the crew's mess, where shipmates dine at long tables set with condiments and utensils. Officers aboard the *Sauniere* are presented with printed menus at smaller tables in the Officer's Dining Room. Everyone on board is served individually and no one goes away hungry. If hunger pains strike between meals this crew knows where to find their favorite Kipper snacks, fresh fruits and cheeses, lunchmeat, ready made sandwiches, bagels, cookies and ice cream!

Linda's menus are filled with homemade variety and always include an assortment of freshly baked desserts. With a little advance notice, Linda or Siobhan prepare a special cake for a shipmate's birthday or other celebration. Friday is fish day, along with other choices, Saturday is steak night and Sundays feature turkey, ham or prime rib. Always conscious of cost, Linda usually serves fresh homemade ham subs within two days of a Virginia ham dinner.

Experience has taught Linda not to use the deep fryer or attempt bread baking when the Great Lakes are churning out their notorious storms. Once, when baking bread, the ship began to roll shortly after she placed fresh dough in the oven. A few minutes later all of the loaves were stuck to the oven wall! Weather aside, nothing comes between the crew and their favorite food. The following menus and recipes are much-enjoyed on board and bring a taste of the *M.V. Sauniere* to shore.

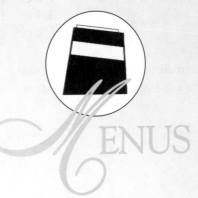

Breakfast

Oatmeal
French Toast
Bacon and Sausage
Egg McMuffins
Grape Fruit Halves
Fruit Juice
Coffee
Milk

Lunch

Homemade Soup of the Day
Chicken Pot Pie
Pepperoni and Mushroom Pizza
Tuna Salad Sandwich
French Fries
Steamed Rice
Kernel Corn
Beets
Assorted Desserts

Dinner

Homemade Soup of the Day
Seasoned Ribs with Honey Garlic Sauce
Fiesta Chicken Pie
Cold Cuts
Parsley Boiled Potatoes
Steamed Rice
Mashed Turnips
Green Beans
Assorted Desserts

Special Holiday Menu

Shrimp Cocktail
Scallops Newburg
Prime Rib of Beef Au Jus
Stuffed Cornish Hens with Gravy
Roast Duck a la Orange
Mashed Potatoes
Rice Pilaf
Candied Yams
Green Beans Almandine
Assorted Squares and Pies
Nuts, Chocolates, Candies
Relish Tray, Deviled Eggs
Soft Drinks

IMPOSSIBLE PIE (Coconut Custard)

6 c.	milk
8	eggs
1-1/2 c.	sugar
1/2 c.	butter
3/4 c.	flour
1-1/2 c.	coconut

Beat all ingredients together. Pour mixture into large greased baking pan. Bake at 350 degrees 45 minutes. This forms its own crust on the bottom.

NORWEGIAN COOKIES

1-1/3 c.	sugar
1 c. + 2 Tbsp.	butter
1 tsp.	vanilla
2	eggs
3 c.	all-purpose flour
1 tsp.	baking powder
1 pkg.	chocolate chips
4 tsp.	sugar
1 tsp.	cinnamon

Combine 1-1/3 cups sugar with butter, eggs and vanilla; beat until fluffy. In separate bowl mix together flour, baking powder and chocolate chips. Stir flour mixture into sugar mixture. Divide dough into 4 equal parts. Shape each part into a roll 14-inches long and 1-inch wide. Place each roll on ungreased cookie sheet and flatten with fork. Combine 4 teaspoons sugar with 1-teaspoon cinnamon and sprinkle over flattened rolls. Bake at 350 degrees 15 minutes. Slice diagonally while warm.

RAINBOW JELLO SQUARES

First Layer

1 lg. or 2 sm. pkgs.	lime Jello
1-1/2 c.	boiling water
1/2 tsp.	salt
1 c.	cold water
1/2 c.	Carnation milk
2 Tbsp.	vinegar

Second Layer

1 sm. pkg.	lemon Jello
1/2 c.	boiling water
1 (8 oz.) pkg.	cream cheese
1 c.	whipped cream (*or* ready whipped, not too stiff)

Third Layer

1 lg. or 2 sm. pkgs.	red Jello
1-1/2 c.	boiling water
1/2 tsp.	salt
1 can	fruit cocktail, well drained
1 c.	cold water
2 Tbsp.	vinegar

To prepare first layer dissolve Jello and salt in boiling water. Stir in cold water, Carnation milk and vinegar. Pour into 9x13-inch dish and let set. To prepare second layer dissolve Jello in boiling water; let cool. Beat cream cheese until creamy and fold into cooled Jello. Fold in whipped cream. Place over top of first layer and let set 3 hours. To prepare third layer dissolve Jello and salt in boiling water. Add well-drained fruit cocktail, cold water and vinegar. Pour mixture over top of second layer and let set until firm. Cut into squares to serve.

PUFF SHORTBREAD

Base
1 c	flour
1 Tbsp.	sugar
1/2 c.	butter
1 Tbsp.	water

Topping
1 c.	water
1 c.	flour
1 Tbsp.	sugar
1 tsp.	almond flavoring
3	eggs

Glaze
1 c.	powdered sugar
1 Tbsp.	cream
1 Tbsp.	butter
2 tsp.	almond flavoring

 To prepare base, mix together flour and sugar. Cut in butter. Add water and mix into a dough. Shape dough into a ball and divide in half. Spread each half into a rectangle on ungreased cookie sheet, forming a fairly thin layer. To prepare topping bring water to a boil. Mix flour with sugar and beat into water. Add almond flavoring. Remove from heat and beat until mixture leaves sides of pot; cool 15 minutes. Add eggs 1 at a time, beating well after each addition. Spread half of mixture over each rectangle. Bake 15 minutes in preheated 425-degree oven. Reduce temperature to 350 degrees and bake an additional 20 to 30 minutes, until browned. Puff will fall a bit after removing from oven. Combine glaze ingredients and drizzle over each puff. Cut into fingers to serve.

Yield: 16 Servings (8 Servings per Rectangle)

M.V. Steven B. Roman

Canada Steamship Lines

The Steven B. Roman's steward, Frank Cornacchi, also served as steward aboard the *M.V. Tadoussac* for over 11 years. The *Tadoussac*, built in 1969, measures 730 feet from bow to stern.

Built:	1965
Length:	488' 9"
Beam:	56'
Draft:	35' 6"
Cargo:	Cement
Cargo Capacity:	7,600 Tons
Crew:	19
Steward:	Frank A. Cornacchi

Frank Cornacchi brought a wealth of experience with him to the galley of the M.V. *Steven B. Roman*, where he proudly worked for over six years serving his crewmates the food they loved. He has worked over 53 years in the food industry, 19 of those years sailing. He also worked many years as an Executive Chef at hotels and catering services in the Toronto area. Prior to joining the *Steven B. Roman*, Frank worked 11 years aboard another ship owned by Canada Steamship Lines, the *M.V. Tadoussac*. He considers the two vessels the most important ships in his life, feeling honored to have walked their decks and a better person for having been a member of their crews.

In 1999 Frank began a new chapter in his life on the Great Lakes when he signed on with Jack Pruvis as steward aboard his fleet of tugboats. He is currently aboard the *Anglian Lady*, a tug with a crew that quickly found a place in Frank's heart and on his list of "most important ships." (See page 95.) His anchor in life remains his close-knit family. Frank and his wife, Vera, have been married for over 43 years, raising their children in the beautiful region of the northern Great Lakes.

Frank's years aboard the *Steven B. Roman* were full of busy days creating menus, preparing favorite foods and cementing lifelong friendships. Less hectic days allowed time for Frank to enjoy his favorite "unofficial duties," including filling in as mother, banker, doctor and "good listener" for a shipmate far away from home. Listening well and trying to help out with problems is part of the closeness that comes naturally to those that sail the lakes. Facing challenges together and understanding unspoken thoughts also comes naturally. One day that sticks out in Frank's mind found the crew without engines for 44 minutes during a storm on Lake Superior. The day happened to be the anniversary of the tragic loss of the *S.S. Edmund Fitzgerald*, and their ship happened to be almost directly above the spot where the *Fitzgerald* now rests, 16 miles from Whitefish Point. Frank and his *Steven B. Roman* crewmates quietly shared their unspoken thoughts.

Frank always gave 2nd cook Bev Brown a lot of credit for the smooth operation of their successful galley aboard the *Steven B. Roman*. "The finest 2nd cook I have sailed with," is the way he describes her. "We could read each other's

Delicious appetizers, salads, entrées and side dishes too numerous to name, are presented in holiday style aboard the *Steven B. Roman*.

minds when it came to what needed to be done next." They were both very proud of their menus and were the first to admit, "we could not afford to eat at home as we did on the *Steven B. Roman!*"

A daily menu was displayed on a chalkboard, but Frank is pretty sure no one ever read it. He served cafeteria style and there was always plenty of variety. He admits some days even he may not have known what was for dinner until he started the day. If a crewmember mentioned at breakfast something that sounded good for dinner, Frank would change his plans and prepare it. The only pattern really followed was "some kind of steak" every Saturday. He would change his menu when the weather got rough (definitely no deep-frying) and prepared food that could be eaten later. He knew…"The crew's appetite would eventually come back after a good roll!"

When it came to snacking, Frank and his crewmates had a household-style refrigerator in the mess stocked each day with cold cuts, cheese, salmon, tuna, yogurt and a variety of fresh fruit. This crew never went hungry! Groceries were restocked every two weeks to ensure everything needed was always on hand. Potatoes were one of the least used items in Frank's galley; he used more rice and fresh vegetables. He had it figured out that each crewmember would consume approximately two pounds of food per day including breakfast, lunch, supper and snack time.

Although Frank is no longer aboard the *Steven B. Roman*, he assures us the crew is still eating well. The menus and recipes may have changed but the homemade variety offered everyday remains the same. Frank's daily menus and Special Holiday Menu illustrate the homemade goodness his friends aboard the *Steven B. Roman* are accustomed to. His recipes allow us to bring some of that homemade goodness into our own kitchens.

An array of homemade desserts and breads — fresh from the galley — add the finishing touch to a bountiful Christmas Buffet.

Breakfast

Juice

Muffins – Made Fresh Everyday

Eggs, Any Style

Bacon and Ham

Home Fries

Pancakes

Bologna

Tomato Sandwiches

Lunch

Homemade Chicken Soup

Curried Lamb Chops and Rice

Salt Pork Riblets and Boiled Mashed Potatoes

Brussel Sprouts and Frozen Peas

Zucchini Bread

Pineapple Upside Down Cake

Pudding

Special Holiday Menu

*We usually prepare a Buffet and Serve
11:30am-1:00pm and 4:30-6:00pm*

4 Salad Choices

Baked Ham

Stuffed Atlantic Salmon

Cornish Hens

Prime Rib

Turkey

Yams, Turnips, Baked Pepper Squash

Roasted and Mashed Potatoes

Shrimp Bowl

All Fruits Available

Deviled Eggs

Nuts and Chocolates

Soda Pop

Dinner

Beef Barley Soup

Grilled N.Y. Steak w/Mushrooms

Fried Bologna

Spaghetti and Meat Sauce

Braised Veal Chops

Cold Ham

Baked Potatoes with Sour Cream

Steamed Rice

Kernel Corn

Fresh Fruit Salad

Lemon Squares

Chocolate Cake

Mint Chocolate Chip Ice Cream

FRANK'S CURRIED LAMB SHOULDER CHOPS

	Lamb shoulder chops
	Salt, to taste
	Pepper, to taste
	Garlic, to taste
1 lb.	onions, diced
8 oz.	celery, diced
12 oz.	carrots, sliced
8 oz.	turnips, julienne
1	red pepper, diced
1	green pepper, diced
3 med.	tomatoes, diced
2	zucchini, diced
2 Tbsp.	garlic powder
3 Tbsp.	ginger powder
4 oz.	curry powder
1 (4 oz.) jar	curry paste
	Water or stock

Season shoulder chops with salt, pepper and garlic; sauté and set aside. Sauté onions, celery, carrots, turnips, peppers, tomatoes and zucchini. Add garlic powder, ginger powder, curry powder, and curry paste. Season with salt and pepper, to taste. Mix well and add water or stock; cook 10 minutes. Place a layer of sauce in roasting pan; add chops and cover with remaining sauce. Cover and cook in oven 1 hour. Serve with rice. Enjoy!

Note: Try this recipe with chicken breasts instead of lamb.

PARMESAN BREADED CHICKEN BREASTS

4	chicken breasts, halved
2 c.	cracker crumbs
3/4 c.	Parmesan cheese
1/2 tsp.	salt
1/2 tsp.	pepper
2 Tbsp.	dried parsley
1	egg, beaten

Flatten chicken breasts for even cooking. To prepare breading mixture mix together cracker crumbs, Parmesan cheese, salt, pepper and parsley. Dip breasts into beaten egg and then into breading mixture. Brown in skillet using olive oil to prevent sticking; transfer to baking sheet. Bake at 350 degrees approximately 20 minutes to finish cooking. Serve with potatoes and vegetable of choice. This is also great with pasta!

Yield: 8 Servings

CHICKEN PICANTE

1/2 c.	medium-hot chunky taco sauce
1/4 c.	Dijon-style mustard
2 Tbsp.	fresh lime juice
3	whole chicken breasts, split, skinless, boneless
2 Tbsp.	butter *or* margarine
	Cilantro, chopped, for garnish
	Plain yogurt

Combine taco sauce, mustard and lime juice in large bowl. Add chicken, turning to coat. Cover; marinate in refrigerator at least 30 minutes. Melt butter in large skillet over medium heat until foamy. Remove chicken from marinade, reserving marinade. Add chicken to skillet and cook approximately 10 minutes or until brown on both sides. Add marinade; cook approximately 5 minutes or until chicken is tender and marinade glazes chicken. Remove chicken to serving platter. Boil marinade over high heat 1 minute; pour over chicken. Garnish with cilantro. Serve with yogurt.

Yield: 6 Servings

CURRIED CHICKEN

1/4 c.	all-purpose flour
1/2 tsp.	curry powder
1/2 tsp.	ground cinnamon
1/2 tsp.	ground ginger
1/4 tsp.	garlic powder
2	whole chicken breasts, split, skinless, boneless
1/4 c.	vegetable oil
1 c.	plain yogurt
2 Tbsp.	lime juice
	Peel of 1 lime, grated
	Lime slices, for garnish
	Mint sprigs, for garnish

Combine flour, curry powder, cinnamon, ginger and garlic powder in shallow dish. Add chicken, 1 piece at a time, dredging to coat. Heat oil in large skillet over medium heat. Add chicken; cook until brown on both sides. Cover and reduce heat to low. Cook 15 minutes or until chicken is tender. Combine yogurt and lime juice in small saucepan. Cook over low heat, stirring constantly, until warm. Arrange chicken on serving platter. Spoon approximately 1/2 yogurt sauce over chicken; sprinkle with grated lime peel and garnish with lime slices and mint. Pass remaining sauce.

Yield: 4 Servings

STIR-FRIED CHICKEN

2	whole chicken breasts, split, skinless, boneless
2 Tbsp.	vegetable oil
1 c.	celery, sliced diagonally
1 med.	carrot, sliced diagonally
1 med.	green bell pepper, cut into thin strips
1 c.	mushrooms, sliced
1/2 sm.	onion, thinly sliced
1 tsp.	salt
1/4 tsp.	ground ginger
1 (16 oz.) can	bean sprouts, drained
1 (5 oz.) can	water chestnuts, drained, sliced
1/4 c.	water
2 tsp.	corn starch
2 Tbsp.	soy sauce
3 c.	hot cooked rice
3/4 c.	peanuts

Slice chicken crosswise into 1/4-inch strips. Heat oil in wok or large skillet over high heat. Add celery, carrot, green pepper, mushrooms, onion, salt and ginger. Stir-fry approximately 3 minutes or until vegetables are tender-crisp; remove from wok and keep warm. Add chicken to wok; stir-fry 3 to 5 minutes or until tender. Return vegetables to wok; stir in bean sprouts, water chestnuts and water. Blend corn starch with soy sauce until smooth, then gradually stir into chicken and vegetables. Cook, stirring constantly, until thickened. Mound rice onto serving platter. Spoon chicken and vegetables over rice. Sprinkle with peanuts and serve immediately.

Yield: 6 Servings

BEV BROWN'S CHEESE CAKE

	Graham cracker crumb crust mixture
2 lbs. + 4 oz.	Cream cheese
1	lemon rind, grated
1	orange rind, grated
6	eggs
10 oz.	sugar
1 Tbsp.	vanilla
20 oz.	sour cream
2 oz.	sugar
1 tsp.	vanilla
Topping of choice:	cherry, blueberry, pineapple, etc.

*L*ine sides and bottoms of 3 (8-inch) cake tins with graham cracker crumb crust mixture. Cream grated rinds with cream cheese until smooth. Slowly add eggs to cream cheese while beating. Add 10-ounces sugar and 1 tablespoon vanilla, beating on high speed approximately 5 minutes. Pour mixture into prepared tins and bake at 350 degrees 30 to 35 minutes. Do not overbake. Mix sour cream with 2-ounces sugar and 1 teaspoon vanilla until blended. Spread over 3 cakes. Sprinkle a few graham cracker crumbs over top and bake an additional 10 minutes. When ready to serve, top with your choice of cherry, blueberry, pineapple, etc.

Note: This cake can be kept in freezer for future use.

Yield: 24 Servings

United States

Coast Guard

United States Coast Guard

"Semper Paratus" — Always Ready to Meet the Call

Since the 1790's the United States Coast Guard has been at work protecting American lives, shores and interests at home and around the world. Every day the dedicated men and women of the Coast Guard make a difference in America. In fact, at the end of an average day, they have...

- Saved 14 lives
- Conducted 180 search-and-rescue missions
- Kept $7 million worth of narcotics from hitting American streets
- Responded to 32 oil spills or hazardous chemical releases
- Stopped hundreds of illegal migrants from setting out on the ocean, and compassionately enforced American law for those who have set out

So, in a year, that's 4,380 people saved, 65,700 rescue missions, $2.6 billion worth of narcotics, 11,680 environmental clean-ups or responses to pollution, and tens of thousands of illegal migrants stopped.

NINTH COAST GUARD DISTRICT

"GUARDIANS OF THE GREAT LAKES"

The Great Lakes region is proudly served by the Ninth Coast Guard District, boundried by the shores of the states of Minnesota, Wisconsin, Michigan, Illinois, Indiana, Ohio, Pennsylvania and New York.

The Ninth District includes 92 units in all, responsible for boating safety, military readiness, search and rescue, aids to navigation, ice breaking, law enforcement, environmental protection and port security on the Great Lakes, including nearly 6,700 miles of American shoreline. There are 48 stations (with 188 small boats) dotting the shoreline, two air stations, one air facility, 10 cutters and more.

To facilitate commerce on the Great Lakes during the winter months, the Ninth District employs five 140-foot ice breaking tugs, the 290-foot ice breaker *Mackinaw*, and three 180-foot ice breaking buoy tenders, one of which is the *Bramble*. During an average winter season the cutters work closely with the Canadian Coast Guard, clearing the way for approximately $62 million worth of commercial cargo. During the winter of 1993-94, when all five Great Lakes were frozen over for the first time since the 1970s, they kept commerce flowing with an estimated cargo value of $124 million.

The district maintains more than 3,300 buoys, navigational lights and fixed aids throughout the Great Lakes. Additionally, the district has a combat-trained port-security unit which can be deployed to any location in the world. Such was the case during the Persian Gulf War and the Haitian operation "Uphold Democracy."

What keeps the men and women of the Ninth Coast Guard District going?...

Judging by the menus and recipes shared on the following pages by the *USCGC Mackinaw* and *USCGC Bramble*, our guess is the food! Their menus overflow with variety and their recipes represent the fresh hot food prepared on board every day, for crews of 50 and 70 no less! Proof that even the galleys on these beloved sturdy ships stand "Always Ready to Meet the Call!"

THE COAST GUARD FESTIVAL
Grand Haven, Michigan - "Coast Guard City U.S.A."

Last Weekend of July through First Full Weekend of August

Every year tens of thousands of visitors are welcomed to "Coast Guard City U.S.A.," home of the annual Grand Haven Coast Guard Festival. This event, which began as a community picnic in 1924, has blossomed into an annual week long festival in honor of the U.S. Coast Guard. This unique celebration commemorates the ideal all Coast Guard men and women share: saving lives at sea, in peace and in war, both here at home and around the world.

Grand Haven has celebrated its unique relationship with the Coast Guard since the early 1900s, when the U.S. Life Saving Service established a station in this Lake Michigan shoreline community. Today, Grand Haven is known as "Coast Guard City U.S.A." in recognition of her special relationship with the longest continuous seagoing service of our nation.

The first cutter home ported in Grand Haven was the *USCGC Escanaba* (WPG-77). She arrived, coated with ice, in the winter of 1932 to a warm welcome by the community and the Grand Haven High School Band. She was a "Michigan" ship from the beginning, built at Defoe Works in Bay City and commissioned soon after for the arduous duty of ice breaking on Lake Michigan. In early 1942, *Escanaba* was transferred to war duty in the North Atlantic and assigned to the "Greenland Patrol."

While carrying out escort duties for many of the Allied convoys bound for Greenland and Iceland, *Escanaba* rescued survivors of two torpedoed ships, the *U.S.S. Cherokee*, rescuing 22 men on June 15, 1942, and the *S.S. Dorchester*, rescuing 133 more on February 3, 1943. Four months later, *Escanaba* was

The original *USCGC Escanaba*, lost in 1943 during war duty in the North Atlantic, is memorialized every year at Escanaba Park in Grand Haven during the Festival.

steaming in company with the cutters *Mojave, Tampa, Storis, Algonquin* and *Raritan*, providing protection to a convoy enroute to Newfoundland. During the early morning hours of June 13, 1943, *Escanaba* was herself torpedoed and quickly sank. *Raritan* picked up the only two survivors, while 101 friends and neighbors of Grand Haven were lost forever to both the perils of war and the sea.

The anguish of this small, close-knit community over the devastating loss of *Escanaba* was channeled into raising $1 million in war bonds to purchase a replacement cutter the following year. The third, and most recent *Escanaba*, a 270-foot Famous class cutter, was commissioned during festival week in Grand Haven in 1987. The highlight of the annual Coast Guard Festival celebration is the National Memorial Service at Escanaba Park on the Grand Haven waterfront. This annual service commemorates the tragic loss of the first *Escanaba* in World War II and the sacrifice of all Coast Guard members who have died while fulfilling the Coast Guard motto "SEMPER PARATUS" – (Always Ready).

USCGC Bramble

WLB-392

Year Built:	1943 – Zenith Dredge Company Duluth, Minnesota
Type:	Class "C" Buoy Tender
Length:	180'
Beam:	37'
Draft:	13'
Displacement:	1,025 Tons
Propulsion:	Diesel Electric, Single Screw, 1,200 Shaft Hp
Max. Speed:	13 knots
Crew:	8 Officers, 42 Enlisted
Food Service Officer:	FSI Brian P. Jackman

Food Service Specialist 1st Class Brian P. Jackman in *USCGC Bramble's* galley. The shiny utensils hanging over his shoulder were used to prepare thousands of meals under his direction.

A familiar sight on the Great Lakes, and at her current home port in Port Huron, Michigan, is the *United States Coast Guard Cutter (USCGC) Bramble*. Aids to navigation is *Bramble's* primary mission; aids to navigation assist the merchant fleet and private vessels in safely navigating waterways. *Bramble's* area of responsibility covers Lake Ontario, Lake Erie and southern Lake Huron including Saginaw Bay. She is currently responsible for maintaining 220 buoys, 1 NOAA weather buoy, 6 lighthouses, 3 fog signals, 2 radio beacons and 22 shore sidelights. During winter months *Bramble's* capabilities as an icebreaker enable her to escort ships through ice, assist ships in distress and break ice for flood relief.

Bramble's Deck Force readying buoys for Haiti.

The *USCGC Bramble* primarily deploys twice a year for buoy operations. In late fall and early winter she spends 8 to 10 weeks on "buoy decommissioning" – removing buoys and installing temporary winter marks (smaller buoys not normally damaged by ice.) In early spring, as the lake ice begins to subside, *Bramble* starts the 8 to 10 week "buoy commissioning" season to replace winter marks with regular buoys. When not icebreaking, her winter months are spent undergoing maintenance and training. During the summer *Bramble* attends regularly scheduled dry-dock or dockside activities, training conferences and festival celebrations throughout the lakes. She has frequently served as Patrol Commander for the Port Huron-to-Mackinac Island sailboat race. This race originated in 1925 and is one of the largest freshwater sailboat races in the county. She also sets buoys in the Detroit River for the International Freedom Festival.

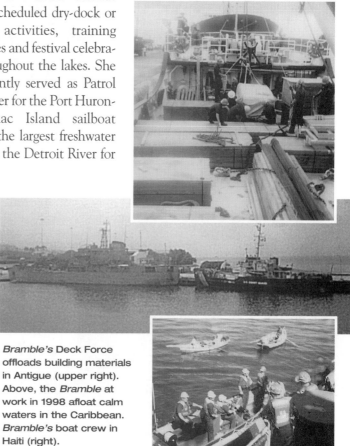

The *USCGC Bramble* began her distinguished career of service for the Coast Guard in 1945 as she departed the Great Lakes to perform navigational duties at her first home port of San Pedro, California. Later that year she was transferred to Juneau, AK for supply and aids to navigation work around the Aleutian Islands. After World War II, *Bramble's* home port changed to San Francisco. Except for a brief stay in Hawaii in 1946, she remained assigned to San Francisco until 1949. From July to October 1947 *Bramble* participated in "Operation Crossroads," the first test of an atomic bomb's effect on surface ships, at Bikini Island.

Bramble's Deck Force offloads building materials in Antique (upper right). Above, the Bramble at work in 1998 afloat calm waters in the Caribbean. Bramble's boat crew in Haiti (right).

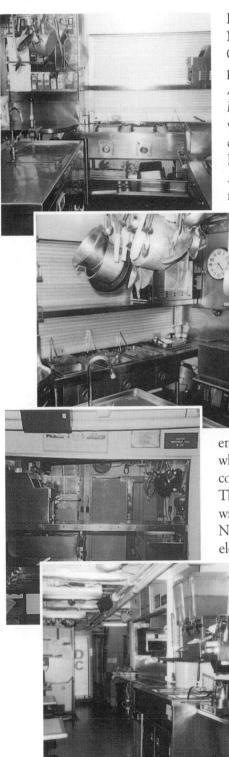

In 1953, while assigned to Miami, Florida, a renewed interest in the fabled Northwest Passage brought about another mission for *Bramble*. The *Coast Guard Cutters Bramble, Spar* and *Storis* were selected to attempt a forced passage along the northern shore of Canada from the Pacific to the Atlantic Ocean. Preparations for the difficult voyage included fitting *Bramble* with a stainless steel propeller and strengthening her bow to withstand tremendous pressures created by the Arctic ice pack. She departed Miami on May 24, 1957 en route for Seattle, Washington via the Panama Canal. On July 1, 1957 the task force departed Seattle for the Atlantic. The ships traveled through 4500 miles of semi-chartered water to recross the Arctic Circle into the Atlantic. On December 2, 1957 *Bramble* safely returned to Miami. The success of the mission distinguished the three cutters as the first surface ships to circumnavigate the North American Continent.

In 1962 *Bramble* was transferred to Detroit, Michigan to perform the missions of aids to navigation, search and rescue, and icebreaking throughout the Great Lakes. Upon completion of a major renovation in 1975 (her engines were removed and rebuilt, her berthing areas were expanded and modernized, and a new hydraulic boom was installed) *Bramble* reported to Port Huron, Michigan, her current home port.

From December 1986 to April 1987 *Bramble* performed law enforcement duties in the Caribbean. She was involved in six cases during which one vessel was seized, three persons arrested and 50 tons of marijuana confiscated. In 1989 *Bramble* again underwent major renovations in Toledo. This time her original Cooper Bessemer main diesel engines were replaced with General Motors Electromotive Division EMD-645 V-8 diesel engines. New 200 KW ship's service generators, boilers, associated plumbing and electric cable were also part of the project.

The Golden Anniversary of USCGC *Bramble's* commissioning was marked in 1994, along with her Great Lakes sister ships *Acacia*, home ported in Charlevoix, Michigan and *Sundew*, home ported in Duluth, Minnesota. Winter of 1996 found her conducting relief ferry operations for Harsen's Island. As always, *Bramble* is "Semper Paratus" – Always ready to meet the call.

FSI Brian P. Jackman was Food Service Officer aboard the *Bramble* for over three years, where he and three junior cooks took full responsibility for the planning and preparation of three hot and hearty meals a day for the crew of 50. He also stood Officer of the

Bramble's galley and mess deck stand shining and "at ease," waiting for the next meal to begin.

Day Duty, where he was the direct representative of command for the ship for 24-hour periods of time, making him responsible for the safety and care of *Bramble*. Petty Officer Jackman has been in the service for over 17 years, beginning as a cook in the U.S. Army from 1979 to 1982. He joined the Coast Guard in 1985.

An average day for a cook aboard the *Bramble* begins at 4:30 am prepar-ing breakfast, which is served at 6:00 am; the noon meal is served at 1:00 pm (1300) and the evening meat at 5:00 pm (1700.) Petty Officer Jackman planned meals using a five-week cycle menu, which accounted for the variety of food available on board. Supplies were ordered on a monthly basis, so planning ahead was necessary, but since the government works on a credit card basis he was able to go ashore to a grocery store when the galley ran short. Even with three cooks working under his direction, Petty Officer Jackman often found himself over the stove lending a hand to keep up with demand. If all went well, the hectic day ended by 6:00 pm (1800.) It's no wonder he looked forward to time off relaxing with his wife Karen, daughter Heather and son Paul. Judging by his recipes, surely they must at least try to get him to cook while he's home.

Petty Officer Jackman's menus for holidays and special occasions aboard the *Bramble*, such as the Retirement Reception Menu displayed on the next page, included a wide variety of favorites, all prepared fresh on board. The care given by the galley staff in preparing and presenting the special buffets added to the festivities.

Empty tables in the Mess Deck await the jovial crowd and noise of the next meal.

A steaming fresh lunch sits ready in *Bramble's* serving line.

Christmas Dinner 1997 aboard the *USCGC Bramble* included a festive table of appetizers.

MENUS

Retirement Reception

Sweet-n-Sour Meatballs
BBQ Beef Slices
Chicken Wings, Hot and BBQ
Pigs and Blanket
Fresh Cooked Fish
Stuffed Mushrooms
Shrimp Cocktail
Pasta Salad
Assorted Breads
Cheese and Crackers
Fresh Vegetables and Dips
Decorated Cake

Daily breakfast, lunch, and dinner menus show
how well the hard working men of the *Bramble*
eat and the variety they are offered every day.
The recipes shared by Petty Officer Jackman
became favorites and he enjoyed preparing
them for his fellow crewmembers.

Lunch

Cream of Potato Soup
Roast Pork Loin with Gravy
Baked Potato Wedges
Cauliflower with Cheese
Dinner Rolls
Bramble Salad Bar
Apple Sauce
Frosted Spice Cake
Assorted Beverages

*Other lunch favorites aboard the USCGC
Bramble are Newport Fried Chicken, Philly
Steak Subs with Sautéed Mushrooms and
Onions, Marinated Beef Tenderloin
and Ginger Pot Roast.*

Breakfast

Assorted Fruit Juices
Assorted Fresh Fruit
Assorted Dry Cereals
Eggs to Order, Omelets and Boiled
Oven Browned Bacon
Waffles and Syrup
Home Fries
Coffee, Tea and Milk

*Other regulars on the breakfast menu are
Creamed Beef and Hot Biscuits, Egg English
Muffins, Canadian Bacon, Grilled Sausage
Patties and Hash Browns.*

Dinner

Soup of the Day
Baked Classic Ham
Candied Sweet Potatoes
Black Eyed Peas
Corn Bread
Bramble Salad Bar
Pecan Pie with Whipped Topping
Assorted Beverages

*Sloppy Joes, Teriyaki Pork Ribs, Grilled Tuna
Steaks, Chicken Parmesan, Marinated Beef
Tenderloin and Meat Lovers Pizza are other
favorites the crew of Bramble look forward to
seeing on the menu.*

CREAMY BROCCOLI AND CHEESE SOUP

1-1/2 gal.	milk
1/2 gal.	water
2 Tbsp.	chicken base
2 c.	celery, minced
2 c.	onions, minced
2 bunches	fresh broccoli
2-1/2 lbs.	Cheddar cheese, shredded
	Garlic, to taste
	Salt and pepper, to taste

Peel broccoli stalks and chop finely. Saute chopped broccoli with onions and celery. Heat milk with water, Cheddar cheese and chicken base. Add broccoli mixture to milk mixture. Thicken with a roux. Season to taste with salt, pepper and garlic.

Yield: 50 Servings

LOBSTER BISQUE

5 lbs.	whole lobsters
3	whole bay leaves
1 Tbsp.	peppercorns
2 lg.	onions, cut into wedges
5	celery ribs, cut into 2-inch pieces
2 gal.	milk
4 oz.	white wine
1 Tbsp.	paprika
1/2 tsp.	ground white pepper
2 Tbsp.	fresh parsley, minced
1/2 c.	onions, chopped, sautéed, (optional)
1/2 c.	celery, chopped, sautéed, (optional)
	Clam base, to taste
	Salt and pepper, to taste

Boil whole lobsters in stockpot with bay leaves, peppercorns, onions wedges and 2-inch celery pieces. Remove lobsters from pot when cooked and strain stock; reserve stock. Allow 1 gallon stock to cool and then add milk, wine, paprika, white pepper, clam base, salt and pepper. Heat and thicken with a roux to medium thickness. Remove lobster from shell, chop and add to sauce; add fresh minced parsley. You may add sautéed onions and/or celery, if desired. Also, any other fresh seafood; precook before adding to stock.

Yield: 50 Servings

SLOPPY JOES

15 lbs.	ground beef
1/2 c.	celery, diced
1/2 c.	onions, diced
1/2 c.	green peppers, diced
1 (No. 10) can	crushed tomatoes
1/2 (No.10) can	tomato paste
1 gal.	water
1 c.	brown sugar
1/2 c.	white vinegar

Brown ground beef with celery, onions and green peppers; drain. Add remaining ingredients and heat until desired thickness. Adjust to taste. Mixture should have a hint of brown sugar and vinegar.

Yield: 50 Servings

VEAL WITH MUSHROOM SAUCE

Veal portions
Fresh tomatoes, sliced
Swiss cheese
Dill weed

MUSHROOM SAUCE

2 (No. 5) cans	cream of mushroom soup
1 (No. 5) can	milk
2 c.	fresh mushrooms, sautéed
1/2 c.	onions, minced, sautéed
1/2 c.	celery, minced, sautéed
2 oz.	white wine
	Salt and pepper, to taste

Pan or griddle fry veal portions; may be breaded or unbreaded. Place veal portions evenly on sheet pan. Place 2 slices fresh tomato on each portion, then 1 slice of Swiss cheese. Garnish with dill weed. Bake at 350 degrees 5 to 7 minutes, until cheese melts.

To prepare Mushroom Sauce mix soup with milk and heat. When heated add remaining ingredients. Serve sauce over veal or on the side.

Yield: 50 Servings

CRAB MEAT STUFFING

2-1/2 lbs.	imitation crab meat, chopped
2 qts.	seasoned bread crumbs
1 c.	onions, diced, sautéed
1 c.	celery, diced, sautéed
1/2 c.	green peppers, diced, sautéed
1/2 c.	carrots, shredded, sautéed
1/2 c.	fresh parsley, finely chopped
1-1/2 lbs.	butter *or* margarine, melted
1 c.	Parmesan cheese, grated
4	eggs, scrambled
2 oz.	white wine

Combine all ingredients and mix together well. When squeezed in hand mixture should form a firm moist ball, which does not fall apart. This stuffing is good for fish fillets or boneless chicken breasts.

PIZZA DOUGH

1 c.	yeast
1 gal. + 1/2 c.	warm water, (105-110 degrees)
1 c. + 2 Tbsp.	sugar
9 Tbsp.	salt
1 c. + 2 Tbsp.	shortening
3 gal. (13 lbs.)	all-purpose flour

Dissolve yeast in warm water in warmed bowl. Add sugar, salt, shortening and 2 cups flour. Turn mixer to speed 2 and mix 2 minutes or until well blended. Continuing on speed 2 add remaining flour, 1 cup at a time, until dough clings to hook and cleans sides of bowl. Knead on speed 2 an additional 6 to 7 minutes or until dough is smooth and elastic. Cut dough into 12 equal size pieces; knead into balls. Let rise to double in bulk. Grease sheet pans, roll dough out, place on pans and let rise. Then precook dough until lightly brown in 350 degree oven. Do not overcook. Place desired pizza items on baked crust. Return to oven and bake until done or cheese is lightly browned.

Note: Ingredients may need to be divided, depending upon the size of mixer used.

Yield: 6 Thick Sheet Pan Crusts or 12 Thin Crusts

SWEET-N-SOUR PORK OR CHICKEN

20 lbs.	pork loin or chicken breasts, boneless
1 c.	soy sauce
1 c.	white wine
1/2 c.	corn starch
1 Tbsp.	ground ginger
	Corn starch
	Pancake batter, prepared

Sweet-n-Sour Sauce

1 gal.	water
1 lb.	brown sugar
1 (No. 5) can	pineapple juice
1 (12 oz.) bottle	ketchup
1 Tbsp.	ground ginger
4 oz.	white vinegar
1/4 c.	sweet pickle relish
2 sm. cans	chopped pineapple
1 (16 oz.) jar	maraschino cherries, rinsed
	Corn starch

To prepare Sweet-n-Sour Sauce combine water, brown sugar, pineapple juice, ketchup, ground ginger, vinegar and pickle relish in saucepan; thicken with corn starch. Once thickened, add pineapple and cherries. Sauce may be adjusted to taste. Do not add cherry juice, as it will make the sauce bitter.

Trim excess fat from pork or chicken; discard. Cut meat into strips 1-1/2-inches long and 1/2-inch thick. To prepare marinade combine soy sauce, wine, 1/2 cup corn starch and ground ginger. Marinate meat pieces at least 2 hours; drain liquid. Place marinated meat pieces evenly on sheet pan. Cook at 350 degrees 10 to 15 minutes; drain again and allow to cool. Dredge pieces in corn starch and dip into prepared pancake batter. Preheat deep fryer to 350 degrees. Test a few pieces; batter should stick to pork or chicken when fried. Transfer to serving plate and cover with Sweet-n-Sour Sauce.

Yield: 50 Servings

USCGC Mackinaw
WAGB-83

Year Built:	1944 – Toleo, Ohio
Length:	290'
Beam:	74'6"
Draft:	19'6"
Displacement:	5,340 Tons
Propulsion:	Diesel Electric, 10,000 Shaft Hp
Max. Speed:	18 knots
Crew:	12 Officers, 67 Enlisted
Food Service Officer:	FSC Richard Reynolds

On deck of the *USCGC Macinaw* is FSC Richard Reynolds with the six Food Service Specialists that work by his side in the busy galley. Left to right, standing: FS2 Daryl Jochimsen, FS1 David Casteel, FS2 Shawn McMullen, FS3 Nathan Bell and FSC Richard Reynolds. Left to right, kneeling: FS3 Barry Wildman and FS3 Matthew Cave.

*B*ased in Cheboygan, Michigan since 1944, the *United States Coast Guard Cutter (USCGC) Mackinaw* is the largest Coast Guard vessel to sail the Great Lakes. *Mackinaw* was built at a cost of $10 million as part of a World War II effort to increase the tonnage of raw materials shipped, and to maintain essential commerce on the Great Lakes during the winter. When launched, *Mackinaw* was the most powerful and capable icebreaker in the world. She is still the standard by which other icebreakers are measured. With a hull thickness of 1-5/8 steel and six diesel engines that produce 2000 horsepower each, plus innovative design features, the *Mackinaw* is well equipped to perform any task assigned. *Mackinaw* has a top speed of 18 knots and a 346,910 gallon fuel capacity.

Mackinaw's many missions include icebreaking, search and rescue (SAR), aids to navigation, law enforcement and public relations. During the summer months *Mackinaw* attends festivals around the Great Lakes such as the Coast Guard Festival in Grand Haven, National Cherry Festival in Traverse City and the Chicago to Mackinaw Race as a SAR platform. Also during the summer and early fall, *Mackinaw* goes into a maintenance period in a shipyard to make any repairs needed before the icebreaking season. Depending on the severity of the weather *Mackinaw* may be underway for a few weeks to a couple of months at a time between December and May. She covers the entire Great Lakes region providing icebreaker assistance to commercial shipping and flood relief operations. A typical tour of duty on the *USCGC Mackinaw* is three years for enlisted personnel and 18 months to three years for officers.

FSC Richard Reynolds, Food Service Officer (FSO) is in charge of the busy Dining Facility aboard the *USCGC Mackinaw*. By his side are six capable Food Service Specialists (FS), each performing duties that keep the large crew of the *Mackinaw* raving about the food: (FS1 David Casteel – FS, is the Dining Facility Supervisor; FS3 Shawn McMullen – Duty FS; FS3 Daryl Jochimsen – Duty FS; FS3 Barry Wildman – Duty FS; FS3 Nathan Bell – Duty FS; SNFS Matthew Cave – Duty FS)

The demands of the upper Great Lakes permit very few "typical days" on the *Mackinaw*, but the galley crew always stands ready with delicious hot food. As FSO, Officer Reynolds' day runs from 7:00 am to 5:00 pm where you will find him in charge of the day-to-day running of the Dining Facility, preparing menus, ordering food and equipment, doing paperwork, working in the galley and training the Junior FS's. The Duty FS's are the people who do a majority of the meal preparation and baking. When in port they work on a rotational basis of two days on, two days off. Their average day begins at 5:30 am and ends at 7:00 pm. When the *Mackinaw* is underway they work 15 hours on an "on" day, but only 10 to 12 hours on an "off" day.

When in home port the *Mackinaw* normally serves 30 people for breakfast and dinner, and 70 for lunch. Underway, 50 to 70 are served at each meal and 20 to 30 at the fourth meal, which is available at 11:00 pm for the oncoming and off-going watches (and the few crewmembers who stay up late to eat again!) While underway the galley is bustling with activity 20 to 24 hours a day; after meal preparations for the day are completed a night baker starts preparing the breads, rolls and desserts for the next day.

How do you feed a crew of 70?.. Officer Reynolds runs a six-week cycle menu that he updates on a regular basis. For an added change of pace he offers a "restaurant style" menu every few weeks, allowing the crew to order what they want and have it made as they go through the serving line.

Mackinaw's galley operates on a budget of $15,000 to $20,000 a month. During extended times in port a low inventory of $10,000 in grocery items is kept on hand, but two or three resupply trips a week are necessary. During the winter, because of the possible low lead-time before getting underway and the uncertainty of how long they will be gone, an inventory of $30,000 is always on board. During an average month, *Mackinaw's* crew will consume:

200 doz. eggs
250 gal. milk
750 lbs. flour
400 chicken breasts
200 lbs. meat
500 lbs. seafood
500 lbs. poultry
100 lbs. coffee beans
$2500 worth of fresh produce

Officer Reynold's well-stocked pantry holds a $30,000 inventory during winter months, in readiness for lengthy duty on the icy Great Lakes.

Holidays, parties and ceremonies aboard the *USCGC Mackinaw* bring forth the best the galley has to offer. Nothing is overlooked and everything is memorable. The recipes and menus shared on the following pages by Officer Reynolds are among the most popular on board. All of his recipes are original and developed on the ship.

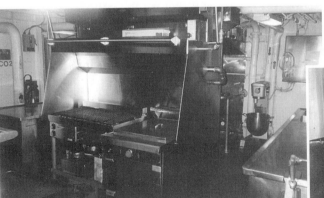

Every inch of *Mackinaw's* large galley is left clean and shiny at the end of a meal.

*M*ENUS

Portholes brighten *Mackinaw's* roomy Mess Deck.

Christmas Party

Appetizers
6:00 to 7:00 PM

Shrimp Cocktail
Crab and Swiss Baquettes
Vegetable Platter with Ranch Dip
Chickan Canapes with Sour Dough Rounds
Herbed Chicken Wings

Main Course
7:00 to 8:00 PM

Roast Prime Rib with Au Jus
Chicken Cordon Bleu with Hollandaise
Italian Red Potatoes
Wild Mushroom Risotto
Sautéed Mixed Vegetables
Hot Homemade Dinner Rolls
Caesar Salad
Seafood Pasta Salad
Horseradish Cream Sauce

Decorated Christmas Cake

Christmas Dinner

Lobster Bisque
Broiled Stuffed Mushrooms
Shrimp Cocktail
Salami and Cheese Baquettes
Fresh Fruit Platter and Relish Tray
Roast Turkey
Prime Rib with Yorkshire Pudding
Sausage and Mushroom Stuffing
Grilled Asparagus Spears
Mashed Potatoes with Giblet Gravy
Candied Sweet Potatoes
Cranberry Sauce
Caesar Salad
Homemade Dinner Rolls
Bread Pudding with Rum Sauce

Change of Command Menu

Shrimp Cocktail
Basil Chicken Canapes
BBQ Chicken Samosas
Spinach Tutiziki
Fresh Fruit Platter
Italian Sausage Pieces with Marinara Sauce
Portobello Mushroom Croustade
Vegetable Platter with Dip
Yukon Gold Potato Salad
Kalamata Olive Foccachia
Sun Dried Tomato and Herb Foccachia

Breakfast

Chilled Fruit Juice
Fresh Fruit Tray
Eggs to Order and Omelets
Sausage Links or Patties
Hash Brown
Hot Pancakes and French Toast
Butter and Syrup
Corned Beef Hash
Hard and Soft Boiled Eggs

*Other regulars on the breakfast menu are
Creamed Beef and Biscuits, Blueberry Pancakes,
Waffles, Hot Grits and Crispy Bacon*

Lunch

Cream of Broccoli Soup
Grilled Pork Loin
Roasted Baby Potatoes
Wild Mushroom Sauce
California Blend Vegetables
Dinner Rolls
Fruit Salad
Salad Bar
Potato Salad
Cucumber Onion Salad
Frosted Brownies

*A few of the other lunch favorites include
Crab Quesadillas, Chicken Florentine, Fried Perch,
Roasted Rack of Lamb, Seafood Enchiladas,
Grilled Tuna Steaks, Caribbean Chicken Wraps,
Italian Steak Wraps, Santa Fe Pork, Grilled Red
Snapper, Thai Shrimp and more!*

Dinner

Soup of the Day
BBQ'D Pork Loin Chop
Oven Browned Potatoes
Black Eyed Peas
Jalapeno Corn Bread
Garden Blend Vegetables
Salad Bar
Balsamic Salad
Pasta Salad
Fruit Salad
Chocolate Mousse

*Other dinner favorites are numerous too. They
include Chicken Lasagna, Prime Rib, Fried Halibut
Nuggets, Herb Broiled Chicken, Beef Stroganoff,
Grilled Reubens, Baked Meat Loaf, Roast Turkey
and Horseradish Crusted Salmon.*

CREAM OF MUSHROOM SOUP

1-1/4 lbs.	butter
3/4 lb.	onion, minced
3-1/3 Tbsp.	garlic, chopped
5 lbs.	fresh mushrooms, sliced
1-7/8 oz.	Morels
1-1/4 c.	hot water
2-1/2 c.	white wine
2-1/2 gal.	chicken stock
1-7/8 c.	flour
2-1/2 qts.	heavy whipping cream
2-1/2 Tbsp.	black pepper
2-1/2 tsp.	kosher salt
3-3/4 Tbsp.	chives
5/8 c.	fresh basil

Soak dry Morels in hot water 15 minutes; strain and reserve stock. Slice Morels into strips. Sauté onions, garlic and fresh mushrooms in butter until soft. Add flour to make a roux and cook 5 minutes. Add chicken stock, wine and reserved mushroom stock; cook 10 minutes. Add remaining ingredients and let cook an additional 20 minutes. Adjust seasonings to taste.

Note: This soup should be fairly thick; if not, add a little corn starch mixed with cream until desired thickness.

Yield: 75 Servings

THAI SHRIMP

3 gal.	chicken stock
1 lb.	cabbage, shredded
1 lb.	green onions, diced
3 lbs.	straw mushrooms
1/2 c.	carrots, julienne
1 Tbsp.	red pepper flakes
1 Tbsp.	ginger
1 Tbsp.	garlic, crushed
1 Tbsp.	black pepper
3 Tbsp.	soy sauce
2-1/2 lbs.	shrimp, sliced in half
1/2 c.	cilantro
1/4 c.	lime juice

Combine all ingredients except shrimp, cilantro and lime juice; simmer 30 minutes. Add remaining ingredients and cook an additional 10 minutes.

Yield: 60 Servings

VEAL WITH MUSHROOMS, CREAM AND SHERRY

12 lbs.	veal cutlets
	Seasoned flour
	Butter

Sauce

1/2 lb.	butter
1 c.	flour
2 Tbsp.	garlic
1	onion, diced
4 lbs.	mushrooms
1 oz.	Morel mushrooms
1 pt.	chicken stock
1 pt.	sherry
3 qts.	heavy whipping cream
1/4 c.	basil
	Salt and pepper, to taste

Dredge veal in flour and sauté in butter. To prepare sauce sauté mushrooms, onions and garlic in butter 10 minutes; add flour to make a roux. Add cream, wine and chicken stock; cook until thickened. Add basil and adjust seasonings.

Yield: 75 Servings

MEXICAN CLUB SANDWICH

4 lbs.	turkey roast
4 lbs.	ham slices
3 c.	Cilantro Mayonnaise
100	bacon strips
3	heads lettuce, shredded
10	tomatoes, sliced 1/8-inch thick
50	flour tortillas, cilantro and chili flavor

Cilantro Mayonnaise

1/2 gal.	mayonnaise
1 c.	cilantro
1/2 c.	green chilies
1 Tbsp.	pepper
1 Tbsp.	garlic
1 Tbsp.	chipotle peppers base

To prepare Cilantro Mayonnaise combine all ingredients; refrigerate. Spread each tortilla with 1 tablespoon Cilantro Mayonnaise. Layer on remaining ingredients. Wrap tightly and cut in half diagonally.

Yield: 75 Servings

ITALIAN STEAK WRAPS

20 lbs.	beef strip loin (R-T-C)
3 lbs.	Provolone cheese, thinly sliced
8	red peppers, roasted, peeled
8	green peppers, roasted, peeled
4	onions, roasted, sliced
3 Tbsp.	garlic, crushed
1 c.	olive oil
1 c.	balsamic vinegar
1 c.	basil
1 Tbsp.	red pepper flakes
1 Tbsp.	black pepper
3	heads lettuce, shredded
10	tomatoes, sliced 1/8-inch thick
50	flour tortillas, tomato flavor
1-1/2 c.	Basil Mayonnaise

Basil Mayonnaise

1/2 gal.	mayonnaise
1 c.	fresh basil
1 Tbsp.	pepper
2 Tbsp.	garlic

To prepare Basil Mayonnaise combine all ingredients; refrigerate. Roast whole strip loin at 325 degrees until internal temperature is 150 degrees; slice thin. Mix together peppers, onions, garlic, vinegar, oil and seasonings. Marinate meat in mixture 3 hours. To assemble, place Basil Mayonnaise on tortilla. Then add cheese, meat, tomatoes, lettuce and pepper mixture. Wrap tortilla tightly and cut in half.

Yield: 75 Servings

CHICKEN ENCHILADAS

18 lbs.	chicken breasts, skinless, boneless (R-T-C)
2 gal.	chicken broth
1 lb.	butter
3 Tbsp.	garlic, crushed
2 qts.	onions, minced
2 c.	flour
3 qts.	whipping cream
3 Tbsp.	coriander
2 Tbsp.	cumin
2 Tbsp.	chili powder
2 Tbsp.	pepper
2 lbs.	green chilies
2 c.	cilantro
1 Tbsp.	kosher salt
1 tsp.	cayenne pepper
4 lbs.	Cheddar cheese, shredded
75	tortillas

Cook chicken in stock; remove and let cool, reserving stock. Sauté onions and garlic until soft. Add seasonings, except cilantro, and cook 5 minutes. Add flour to make a roux. Add stock and cream to roux and cook 10 minutes. Add chilies and 1/2 cheese, stirring until all cheese has melted. Add cilantro and check seasoning. Slice chicken; combine with 2-quarts of sauce and mix. Coat bottom of sheet pan with sauce. Place chicken in tortilla with a little cheese and roll. Place in sheet pan; cover with sauce and extra cheese. Cook in oven 30 minutes.

Yield: 75 Servings

BUTTERNUT SQUASH

10 lbs.	butternut squash, peeled, cubed
1-1/2 lbs.	onion, chopped
1-1/2 lbs.	red bell peppers, chopped
3-1/8 Tbsp.	garlic, crushed
2-1/2 gal.	chicken stock
1/2 c.	brown sugar
1-1/3 Tbsp.	ginger, ground
1-1/3 Tbsp.	allspice
1 Tbsp.	mace
2-1/8 Tbsp.	black pepper
2-1/8 Tbsp.	kosher salt
1 Tbsp.	nutmeg
2 qts.	heavy whipping cream
1-1/2 c.	white wine
1 pt.	heavy whipping cream
8 Tbsp.	corn starch

Combine all ingredients except whipping cream, wine and corn starch in kettle. Bring to boil and simmer 1 hour or until squash is very tender. Strain squash, reserving cooking liquid. Return liquid to kettle. Puree squash and return to kettle. Add 2-quarts heavy cream and wine; bring to low boil. Mix corn starch with remaining 1 pint heavy cream; add to kettle. Cook until smooth and thick.

Yield: 60 Servings

RED SNAPPER WITH BASIL BUTTER

20 lbs.	red snapper
	Salt and pepper, to taste

Butter Mix

1 lb.	butter, softened
1 c.	basil
1 Tbsp.	garlic
4 Tbsp.	chives
1 tsp.	cayenne
4 Tbsp.	lemon juice
1 Tbsp.	oregano

Mix together all ingredients for Butter Mix; set aside. Score skin on the snapper to prevent curling; season and charbroil. When fish is done remove to an insert and top with butter mix.

Yield: 75 Servings

SANTA FE PORK

| 30 lbs. | pork top loin, boneless, cut into 2-inch cubes |

Marinade

3 qts.	red wine
3/4 c.	fresh ginger
3/8 c.	chipotle pepper
	Salt and pepper, to taste

Sauce

1-1/2 c.	olive oil
12	onions, wedged
3/8 c.	garlic, crushed
60	shallots
1-1/2 lb.	butter
12	bay leaves
1/2 c.	thyme
1-1/2 lbs.	peppers
3 qts.	chicken stock
3 Tbsp.	cumin
1-1/2 Tbsp.	coriander
3/4 c.	lime juice
2 c.	cilantro
2 qts.	tomatillos

Combine marinade ingredients; add pork and refrigerate 3 to 4 hours. Drain pork and reserve marinade. Brown pork on griddle and place in kettle along with reserved marinade. Add remaining ingredients, except cilantro, and simmer 2 to 3 hours or until pork is tender. Add cilantro and thicken with corn starch, if needed. Serve over Black Bean Cakes and top with finely diced tomatoes and sour cream.

Yield: 60 Servings

BLACK BEAN CAKES

10 lbs.	black beans, cooked
1 lb.	green onions, chopped
1 Tbsp.	garlic, crushed
3/4 c.	cilantro
1 Tbsp.	cumin
	Salt and pepper, to taste

Drain black beans and puree in batches, leaving chunks. Combine beans with remaining ingredients. With floured hands make patties approximately 3-inches wide. Dust patties with flour and place on floured sheet pans; place in freezer 1 hour. Dredge patties again in flour and sauté in butter on griddle.

Yield: 75 Servings

CHICKEN CONQUESTADOR 2

28 lbs.	chicken breasts, skinless, boneless, (R-T-C), butterflied
1 gal.	low-calorie Italian salad dressing
1 c.	cilantro
3 lbs.	Cheddar cheese, shredded
2 qts.	Black Bean Salsa, drained
	Cilantro Cream Sauce

BLACK BEAN SALSA

4 lbs.	tomatoes, diced
1 c.	canned tomatoes, crushed
2 c.	black beans, cooked
1 lb.	red onions, diced
1 lb.	red and green bell peppers, diced
1 lb.	canned chili peppers
3/4 c.	lime juice
4 Tbsp.	olive oil
1 c.	cilantro
1 Tbsp.	cumin
2 Tbsp.	chili powder
1 Tbsp.	sugar
2 Tbsp.	kosher salt
1 Tbsp.	pepper
1 Tbsp.	coriander

CILANTRO CREAM SAUCE

1 lb.	butter
2 c.	flour
1 c.	red onion, diced
3 Tbsp.	garlic, crushed
1 gal.	chicken stock
1 lb.	green chilies
3 qts.	heavy whipping cream
2 c.	cilantro
2 Tbsp.	chives
1/2 c.	parsley
1 Tbsp.	pepper
1/2 c.	lime juice

To prepare Black Bean Salsa combine all ingredients; let sit 1 hour. To prepare Cilantro Cream Sauce melt butter; add onions and garlic, sauté until soft. Mix in flour to make a roux and cook 10 minutes. Slowly add stock, stirring until smooth. Add cream and cook 10 minutes. Add seasonings and whisk until smooth. Cook 10 minutes, then add lime juice and remove from pan.

To prepare Chicken Conquestador mix dressing and cilantro together; add chicken and marinate at least 3 hours or overnight. Charbroil chicken until almost done. Pan up; spoon on Black Bean Salsa and cheese. Finish in oven until cheese has melted and beans are hot. Serve with Cilantro Cream Sauce.

Yield: 75 Servings

RISSOTO WITH WILD MUSHROOMS

6 lbs.	Arborio rice
1 gal.	chicken stock
1 qt.	white wine
1/4 c.	olive oil
1/2 lb.	butter
2 oz.	dry mushrooms, soaked, diced
2 oz.	Morels, soaked, diced
2 lbs.	mushrooms, sliced
1 lb.	Portabella mushrooms
2	red onions, diced
4 Tbsp.	garlic, crushed
2 Tbsp.	pepper
3 c.	Parmesan cheese
1 c.	basil
1 qt.	heavy whipping cream
1/2 lb.	butter

Soak dry mushrooms in 1-quart of hot stock; reserve liquid and slice mushrooms. Melt butter; add oil, onions, garlic and mushrooms. Cook 5 minutes. Add rice and cook an additional 10 minutes. Add stock, 1 cup at a time, stirring continuously. Add additional stock whenever it is absorbed. When out of stock start adding wine and reserved mushroom stock in the same manner. Rice at this moment should be almost cooked and creamy. Add whipping cream and butter; cook until rice is finished. Add additional stock, if necessary. Add cheese and serve.

Note: Rice should be very creamy when put on the line; it will thicken more as it sits.

Yield: 75 Servings

BREAD PUDDING

3 loaves	bread, torn into pieces
18 c.	brown sugar
6 c.	2% low-fat milk
12 c.	whipping cream
24	eggs
6 c.	raisins
4 Tbsp.	cinnamon
3/4 c.	butter

Preheat oven to 350 degrees. Mix all ingredients into a smooth batter. Pour into buttered full shallow pan and bake 50 minutes. Serve hot with butter sauce.

Yield: 75 Servings

PORK KALAMATA

60 lbs.	pork loin chops, (R-T-C)
1 gal.	Pork Marinade
1 lb.	Kalamata olives
1 c.	green onions, chopped
3 Tbsp.	capers
1/2 c.	olive oil
3 Tbsp.	basil
1 Tbsp.	garlic
1/2 tsp.	pepper
1/3 c.	balsamic vinegar

Pork Marinade

1/2 gal.	olive oil
2 c.	balsamic vinegar
4 Tbsp.	garlic
1/2 c.	white wine
1 c.	onions, diced
1 c.	fresh basil
2 Tbsp.	thyme
2 Tbsp.	oregano
1 Tbsp.	pepper
1 tsp.	rosemary

To prepare Pork Marinade combine all ingredients and mix well. This marinade may also be used for chicken or strip loins. Dip sliced pork loin racks into marinade; place into roasting pan and let sit overnight. Mix remaining ingredients together; let sit 3 hours. Charbroil racks and finish in 400 degree oven. Place olive mixture on top of racks and serve.

Yield: 75 Servings

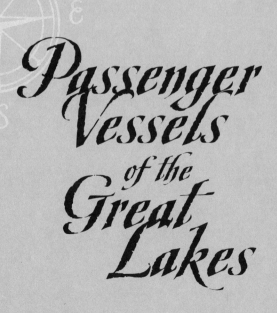

Passenger Vessels
of the
Great Lakes

Passenger Vessels of the Great Lakes

They're back…with all the elegance, luxury and legendary dining they left with years ago. The excitement of cruising the Great Lakes has returned in style, with vessels six-decks tall offering passengers comfort, entertainment and activity as they sail from port to port throughout the region.

The *S.S. Badger* was gone for only two years, returning in 1992 as a passenger and vehicle cross-lake cruise ship offering voyages reminiscent of the 1960s with today's amenities. In 1997 the German-owned *M.V. Columbus* arrived on the Great Lakes, marking the first time since World War II a foreign cruise ship had sailed through the St. Lawrence Seaway. The year 2001 marks the maiden voyage on the lakes of *MTS Arcadia*, a beautiful white cruise ship scheduled to visit 27 ports in the region several times a year.

Dining on these passenger vessels is worth the cost of the voyage itself. Bounties of homemade ship specialties, freshly created on board by talented chefs, are prepared around the clock in the galley below deck.

Welcome back to cruising the Great Lakes. Bon Voyage… Bon Appétit!

M.T.S. Arcadia

Great Lakes Cruises, Inc.

Elegantly covered tables set the stage for unique dining aboard the M.T.S. Arcadia. Service on board is very personal and attentive.

Year Built:	1969
Year Rebuilt:	1989
Length:	367'
Beam:	54'
Draft:	18'6"
Decks:	6
Crew:	115
Passengers:	224
Accommodations:	120 Cabins

*I*magine being aboard a beautiful white cruise ship, six decks tall and longer than a football field. Now imagine cruising the timeless beauty of the Great Lakes on this grand ship, stopping at bustling metropolitan ports and then heading off towards hidden islands. No, you're not thumbing through the pages of a history book, fondly recalling days gone by when passenger ships were a common sight on the lakes. The year is 2001 and the magnificent ship waiting to welcome you aboard is the *M.T.S. Arcadia.*

It has been nearly half a century since Americans and Canadians leisurely cruised their five Great Lakes aboard a luxurious passenger ship. Decades spent longing for the open fresh waters to carry them from port to port as they enjoy elegance and comfort along the way. The old world charm set to welcome passengers aboard the *M.T.S. Arcadia* for her first season on the Great Lakes will not disappoint even the best dreamers amongst us. All of the lakes will host the long awaited cruise ship at least once during her 23 scheduled voyages in 2001, and over 27 ports are anticipating her dockside arrival. Chicago, Detroit, Green Bay, Mackinac Island, Duluth, Thunder Bay, Erie and many other ports stand ready, as does the *M.T.S. Arcadia* herself, to welcome Great Lakes cruising back to the region.

Elegance and adventure await excited passengers as they embark upon a three, four or seven-night cruise aboard *Arcadia*. Guests enjoy a quiet, relaxing sail or activity filled days as they head towards scheduled shore excursions. The Library and Card Room on board provide quiet relaxation after a day of sun and fresh Great Lakes breezes on the two promenade decks and sun deck, or at the pool. A gymnasium and sauna, hairdresser, shopping, games, scheduled lectures on the region and live entertainment round out the choices of activities available. In the evening, a dance band and jazz pianist both perform, allowing guests to end their day under a shining Great Lakes moon according to how much energy they have left. The long awaited dream of cruising the Great Lakes has returned in style.

Special attention has been given to dining aboard the *M.T.S. Arcadia*. Elegantly covered tables scattered with fresh flowers and china welcome passengers into the dining room. Four meals plus afternoon tea are served daily. Each waiter is assigned only 12 guests, so service is very personal and attentive. Diners choose from menus offering everything from meticulously prepared hors d'oeuvres to delicate desserts, with an assortment of original entrées offered in between. The galley staff provides unique cuisine and the ship's crew provides entertainment for the memorable Welcome and Farwell Dinners presented at the beginning and end of each cruise. The *M.T.S. Arcadia* elevates dining standards on the Great Lakes to a new level!

The *M.T.S. Arcadia* offers a variety of areas on board for guests to gather, including the Princess Lounge, the Pool, and the Queen's Lounge.

Welcome Dinner

Hors d'oeuvres
Prosciuto with Melon
Tomatoes Farcies with Vegetables

Soups
Chicken Consomme Royal
Soup Bisque

Farinaceous
The Aroma of Genoa: Trennette with
Basil Cream or Tomato

Main Course
Fillet of Sole Almondine
Paella Valenciana
Beef Tenderloin a líAnglaise with
Mushroom Sauce
Roast Prime Rib of Kansas Beef with
Natural Juice
From Cold Buffet
Assiette Anglaise
Low Calorie Plate
Halibut Sauté
Vegetarian Plate
Fresh Vegetables Sauté Chinese Style
with Soya and Ginger

Salad Penelope
Various Dressings

Assorted Cheese Tray

Islands Floating with Strawberry Sauce
Friandiases De Dames
Coup "Romanof"
Lemon Sherbet
Black Forest Cake
Fresh Fruits in Basket

Hot Tea, Iced Tea, Coffee,
Decaffeinated, Milk, Camomille

*M*ENUS

Greek Tavern Dinner

Greek Hors d'oeuvres
Taramosalata, Tzatziki, Stuffed Grape Leaves,
Olives, Fried Kalamari, Greek Beans in
Tomato Sauce, Mini Cheese Pie, Fried Beef,
Boulette with Ouzo

Soup
Avgolemono Soup

Mousaka

Main Course
Roasted Baby Lamp Roumeli
Brochette of Beef Fillet
Shrimps Microlimano

Low Calorie Plate
Pasta al Dente with Crab Meat and
Grilled Tomatoes

Vegetarian Plate
Stuffed Tomatoes with Vegetables and
Pine Nuts

The Famous Greek Salad
(Romaine Lettuce, Kalamata Olives,
Feta Cheese, Tomatoes, Onions)

Baklava
Galaktoboureko · Kataifi Special
Ice Cream · Kaimaki
Fresh Fruits in Basket

Hot Tea, Iced Tea, Coffee, Decaffeinated,
Milk, Camomille

Dinner

Hors d'oeuvres
Antipasto
Escargots a la Bourguignone (Snails)

Soups
Browned Onion Soup with Cheese Croutons
Vegetable Consomme

Farinaceous
Fettuccini a la Putanesca
Linguini with Seafood and Cream Sauce

Main Course
Pink Trout in Sweet Savory Butter
Breaded Turkey Scallopini with Parmesan
Roast Rack of Lamb Provengale
Roast Duckling with Orange Sauce

Cold Plate
Assorted Mixed Plate

Low Calorie Plate
Poached Fillet of Trout with Lemon Sauce

Vegetarian Plate
Oriental Fried Rice with Stir Fry Vegetables

Salad Laurette

Assorted Cheese Tray

Pistachio and Strawberry Mousse Orange
Liqueur
Bavarian Apple Strudel with Vanilla Sauce
Mocca and Vanilla Ice Cream with
Chocolate Sauce
Raspberry Frozen Spumone
Variety of Little French Pastries
Hot Tea, Iced Tea, Coffee, Decaffeinated,
Milk, Camomille

Farewell Dinner

Hors d'oeuvres
Smoked Salmon with Onion Rings,
Capers, Rye Bread,
Malossol Caviar American Dressing

Soups
Consomme Ambassador
The Famous Soup Henri IV

Farinaceous
Spinach Fettucini with Primavera Sauce

Main Course
Broiled Lobster Tails with Butter
Oven Baked Halibut with Champagne Sauce
Fillet of Beef with Cream of Mushroom Sauce

Low Calorie Plate
Grilled Escalope of Turkey Breast

Vegetarian Plate
Mushroom Ragout with Pasta Tagliatelle

Caesar Salad

Baked Alaska (Flambé)
Fresh Fruits in Basket

Hot Tea, Iced Tea, Coffee,
Decaffeinated,
Milk, Camomille

AVGOLEMONO
Greek Egg and Lemon Soup

2 qts.	chicken broth
1/2 c.	raw rice
2	eggs
	Juice from 2 lemons
	Salt and white pepper, to taste

Place chicken broth in large soup kettle and bring to boil. Add rice, stirring constantly, until mixture returns to boil. Reduce heat, cover and simmer approximately 15 minutes, until rice is tender but not mushy. Remove from heat and keep warm. Beat eggs 3 minutes. Gradually add lemon juice, beating constantly. Slowly add small amount of hot rice mixture to eggs, beating. Stir egg mixture into kettle and cook over low heat until soup thickens; do not boil again. Season to taste with salt and white pepper.

Yield: 6 Servings

LINGUINE WITH SEAFOOD AND GARLIC CREAM SAUCE

1/4 c.	butter
1/2 lb.	crab meat, cut in bite-sized pieces
2	garlic cloves, minced
2	green onions, thinly sliced
1/2	tsp. pepper
1/2	tsp. rosemary
3/4 c.	whipping cream
1/2 c.	Parmesan cheese, grated
	Salt, to taste
	Fresh parsley, snipped
	Linguine

Cook linguine according to package directions; drain and set aside. Melt butter in large skillet. Add garlic, green onions, rosemary and pepper. Add cream and simmer until sauce thickens slightly. Stir in crab meat and season with salt. Add Parmesan cheese, stirring until melted. Combine crab mixture with linguine and garnish with fresh parsley.

Yield: 2 Servings

ANTIPASTO

1 lb.	cheese tortellini, fresh *or* frozen
1/4 lb.	salami, chopped
1/4 lb.	Provolone cheese, cut in strips
1 (10 oz.) pkg.	frozen spinach, thawed, drained
1 (6 oz.) jar	marinated artichoke hearts, drained, chopped
1 (6 oz.) can	sliced ripe olives, drained
1/2 c.	Parmesan cheese, grated
2 tsp.	Dijon mustard
2 c.	creamy Italian dressing

Cook tortellini according to package directions; drain. Combine tortellini, salami, Provolone cheese, spinach, artichoke hearts and olives in large bowl. In separate bowl whisk together dressing, mustard and half of Parmesan cheese. Pour dressing over tortellini mixture and toss gently. Top with remaining Parmesan cheese. Garnish with additional olives, if desired. Refrigerate at least 4 hours before serving.

STUFFED TOMATOES WITH VEGETABLES AND PINE NUTS

6	tomatoes
3 Tbsp.	olive oil
1	onion, finely diced
1 (10 oz.) pkg.	frozen spinach
1/2 lb.	Feta cheese, crumbled
1/2 c.	pine nuts
1	egg
2 tsp.	basil
	Salt and pepper, to taste

Hollow out insides of tomatoes, leaving thick wall to hold shape. Heat oil in small saucepan. Add onion to saucepan and sauté. Combine sautéed onions with spinach, Feta cheese, pine nuts, egg, basil and seasonings. Spoon filling mixture into tomatoes, pressing down lightly. Place stuffed tomatoes in baking pan and bake at 350 degrees 15 minutes.

ESCARGOTS A LA BOURGUIGNONNE
Snails

32	snails
32	snail shells
1 c.	butter, softened
1/3 c.	fresh parsley, snipped
3	green onions, finely diced
1	garlic clove, minced

Mix together butter, parsley, green onions and garlic; set aside. Place snails in shells; fill with butter mixture. Transfer to baking pan and bake at 350 degrees 15 minutes.

THE FAMOUS GREEK SALAD

Salad
Romaine lettuce leaves, torn
Spinach leaves, torn
Cherry tomatoes, halved, seeded
Black olives, halved, pitted
Feta cheese, crumbled

Dressing

2 c.	olive oil
2	garlic cloves, minced
1/2 c.	red wine vinegar
	Juice from 1 lemon
	Oregano, to taste
	Salt and pepper, to taste

Combine salad ingredients in large bowl; toss and chill. Whisk dressing ingredients together until well blended. Toss dressing with salad.

GREEK MOUSSAKA

3	eggplants, peeled, sliced 1/2-inch thick
1/2 c.	vegetable oil, divided
2	onions, diced
2 lbs.	ground beef *or* lamb
4 Tbsp.	tomato paste
1/2 c.	red wine
1/3 c.	fresh parsley, chopped
1	pinch cinnamon
1 c.	bread crumbs
1 c.	Parmesan cheese, grated
	Salt and pepper, to taste

SAUCE

1	stick butter, melted
6 Tbsp.	flour
1 qt.	milk
4	eggs, beaten
1	pinch nutmeg
2 c.	Ricotta cheese *or* cottage cheese

Heat 1/4 cup vegetable in large skillet. Add eggplant slices and brown; set aside. Heat remaining 1/4 cup oil in same skillet. Add onions and cook until tender. Add ground beef or lamb and cook through, approximately 10 minutes. Drain and set aside. In bowl combine tomato paste, wine, parsley, cinnamon, salt and pepper. Stir tomato paste mixture into meat, return to heat and simmer, stirring frequently, until all liquid has been absorbed. Remove from heat and set aside.

To prepare sauce, whisk flour into melted butter. Bring milk to boil in saucepan and gradually whisk into butter mixture until smooth. While simmering, stir in eggs, nutmeg and Ricotta or cottage cheese. Grease baking pan and sprinkle with bread crumbs. Place a layer of eggplant slices in pan; sprinkle with Parmesan cheese and bread crumbs. Layer meat sauce over top and sprinkle with Parmesan cheese and bread crumbs. Pour sauce over top and bake at 375 degrees 60 minutes or until top is golden brown. Let set 15 minutes before serving.

FRENCH BUTTER PASTRY

1	egg
3	egg yolks
1/3 c.	sugar
4 Tbsp.	butter, melted
6 Tbsp.	flour, sifted
1 tsp.	lemon rind, grated
2-1/2 Tbsp.	corn starch
1 tsp.	baking powder
1 Tbsp.	lemon juice, freshly squeezed
1/8 tsp.	salt
	Colored frostings, of choice

Combine egg, egg yolks and sugar in top of double boiler. Heat over hot water until warm (approximately 100 degrees), beating constantly. Remove from heat; beat until cool and stiff. Combine sifted flour with corn starch, salt and baking powder; sift together. Gently mix dry ingredients into cooled egg mixture. Add lemon juice and grated rind. Add melted butter slowly, stirring constantly. Pour batter into well greased baking pan. Bake at 375 degrees 20 minutes. Cut cooled pastry into shapes and frost with colored frosting.

MINIATURE NUT FILLED PASTRIES

2-1/2 c.	flour
1 c.	butter
2	egg yolks, slightly beaten
1/2 c.	sour cream

NUT FILLING

3 c.	walnuts *or* pecans, finely ground
1 c.	dark corn syrup
	Powdered sugar

Place flour in large bowl. Cut in butter with pastry blender until mixture resembles coarse crumbs. Stir in egg yolks and sour cream, mixing well. Turn dough onto floured surface and knead until smooth. Chill dough for easier handling. To prepare filling stir ground nuts together with corn syrup. Divide chilled dough in half; roll out first half to 1/8-inch thickness. Cut dough into 2-inch squares. Place 1 teaspoon nut filling diagonally across each square. Bring unfilled corners of dough together to meet in center, pinching to seal. Repeat procedure with remaining dough and nut filling. Place on greased cookie sheet and bake at 400 degrees 10 to 12 minutes, until edges are lightly browned. Let cool completely and then sprinkle with powdered sugar.

LEMON SHERBET

1 qt.   milk
1-1/2 c. sugar
1   lemon rind, grated
          Juice from 2 lemons

Stir milk and sugar together until sugar is dissolved. Freeze until mixture begins to thicken. Remove from freezer; add grated lemon rind and juice. Return to freezer until firm, stirring occasionally.

BAKLAVA

1 lb.   phyllo sheets
1 lb.   walnuts, finely chopped
1/2 c.   sugar
1 tsp.   cinnamon
1 c.   butter, unsalted, melted
1 c.   honey

Grease 9x13-inch baking pan and preheat oven to 350 degrees. Mix together walnuts, sugar and cinnamon; set aside. Place 1 sheet phyllo in prepared baking pan, draping up sides of pan; brush with melted butter. Repeat procedure to make a total of 6 layers. Sprinkle 1 cup walnut mixture over top. Cut remaining phyllo into 9x13-inch rectangles. Place 1 rectangle over filling and brush with melted butter. Repeat procedure to make at least 6 layers. Sprinkle with 1 cup of walnut mixture and cover with another 6 layers of phyllo, brushing each with melted butter. Repeat both layers 3 more times, ending with phyllo on top. Using a sharp knife, cut halfway through all layers in diamond pattern, dividing baklava into 24 sections. Bake 1-1/4 hours, until top is golden brown. Heat honey in saucepan until hot, but not boiling. Spoon hot honey over baklava after removing from oven. Cool completely in pan.

GALAKTOBOUREKO
Greek Custard Filled Pastry

1 pkg.	phyllo sheets
1 c.	butter, melted

Custard

1 qt.	milk
5	eggs
1/2 c.	farina (cereal)
1/2 c.	sugar

Syrup

1/2 c.	water
1/2 c.	honey
	Zest from 1 lemon

Butter a 9x13-inch baking pan. To prepare custard scald milk in saucepan; cool to luke warm. Add sugar and farina to milk and beat until fluffy. In separate bowl beat eggs until fluffy. Slowly beat small amount of milk mixture into eggs, then add all egg mixture into milk mixture, blending well. Cook over low heat, stirring constantly, until thick. Cool completely and chill. Brush 6 phyllo sheets with melted butter and place in prepared pan, making edges drape over sides of pan. Spread filling over phyllo sheets, then flip edges of phyllo sheets back over filling. Top with 6 more phyllo sheets overlapping, each brushed with melted butter. Using sharp knife cut halfway through layers. Bake at 350 degrees 20 to 30 minutes, until golden brown. Combine syrup ingredients in saucepan and bring to boil; boil gently 10 minutes. Pour hot syrup over cooled pastry.

FRENCH FRITTERS

4 pcs.	fruit of choice, (apples, oranges, pears, figs, etc.)
4 Tbsp.	sugar
1	lemon rind, grated
1 c.	flour, sifted
1/2 tsp.	salt
1 Tbsp.	butter, melted
2 Tbsp.	lemon juice
2	eggs, separated
2/3 c.	milk
	Powdered sugar

Slice fruit. Combine sugar with grated lemon rind, tossing to mix. Sprinkle fruit slices with sugar mixture and let stand 2 to 3 hours. To prepare batter beat egg yolks together with milk, flour, salt, butter and lemon juice. Beat egg whites until stiff and fold into batter. Dip coated fruit slices in batter and deep fry at 375 degrees; drain. Sprinkle with powdered sugar.

MINIATURE FRENCH PUFFS

1/3 c.	butter, softened
1/2 c.	sugar
1	egg
1-1/2 c.	flour, sifted
1-1/2 tsp.	baking powder
1/2 tsp.	salt
1/4 tsp.	nutmeg
1/2 c.	milk
1/2 c.	butter, melted
1 c.	sugar
2 tsp.	cinnamon

Grease 4 small muffin tins and preheat oven to 350 degrees. Combine 1 cup sugar with 2 teaspoon cinnamon; set aside. Combine 1/3 cup softened butter with 1/2 cup sugar and egg; mix thoroughly. Combine sifted flour with baking powder, salt and nutmeg; stir to mix. Add flour mixture to sugar mixture alternately with milk. Fill 48 muffin cups 2/3 full. Bake at 350 degrees 15 minutes, until golden. Dip hot puffs in melted butter and then in cinnamon and sugar mixture. Best if served warm.

⚓

The *M.T.S. Arcadia* has 23 cruises on the Great Lakes scheduled between June and October 2001, and more planned for the future. Over 27 scheduled stops are made at ports including Chicago, Detroit, Green Bay, Mackinac Island, Duluth, Thunder Bay, Erie and more. Each cruise accommodates 224 passengers with six decks of luxury, activity, entertainment and memorable dining. Information on sailing schedules and reserving passage aboard the *M.T.S. Arcadia* is available through Great Lakes Cruises, Inc.

GLCI
Great Lakes Cruises Inc.

M.T.S. ARCADIA
Great Lakes Cruises, Inc.
217 Wisconsin Ave., Waukesha, WI 53186
(877) 777-GLCI · (262) 513-1110 · Fax: (262) 513-2870
email: info@greatlakescruises.com
Website: www.greatlakescruises.com

Year Built:	1952, Christy Corporation, Sturgeon Bay, Wisconsin
Launched:	September 6, 1952
Daily Service:	March 21, 1952 thru November 1990
Resumed Cross-Lake Service:	May 18, 1992 under new ownership, Lake Michigan Carferry Service, Inc.
Length:	410'6"
Beam:	59'6"
Draft:	18'6"
Height:	7 Stories (106'9" from top of spar to bottom of keel)
Crew:	60
Passengers:	620
Automobiles:	180
Staterooms:	42 (84 Berths)

The *S.S. Spartan*, other "sister" in the "Twin Queen's of the Lake," equalled the *S.S. Badger* in length, height, and cost of $5 million to build.

*I*n May of 1992, after years of dedicated planning and millions of dollars in renovations, the *S.S. Badger* again set sail from Ludington, Michigan. Following a gala christening the carferry set out on Lake Michigan carrying hundreds of excited passengers and over a century of history on her graceful shoulders. Lazy days long gone, when Cary Grant, Jack Benny, Tyrone Power, Tammy Wynette, Agnes Moorehead, The Who and millions of other passengers spent carefree hours on the wind swept decks of the *Badger* were no longer just a memory. The Lake Michigan Carferry was back and a treasured era in the region's history was returned to the shores of Ludington.

The history of freight and passenger steamship service across Lake Michigan has been part of the region's past, and that of the country itself, since 1875, when the Flint and Pere Marquette Railway chartered the 175-foot long side-wheeler steamer *John Sherman* to shuttle grain, packaged freight and passengers between Ludington, Michigan and Sheboygan, Wisconsin. Seventeen years later, James Ashley, former governor of Montana and then president of the Ann Arbor Railroad, pushed cross-lake service into the 20th century when he ordered the 260-foot wooden hulled *Ann Arbor I* and loaded it with railroad cars. Having proven that a carferry was a viable alternative to shipping loose bulk cargo, the Lake Michigan carferry service was born.

During this period the Flint and Pere Marquette Railway went ahead with plans to develop a similar fleet of car ferries, placing an order to have the first steel hulled cross-lake car ferry designed. Launched in 1896, and ready for service by February 1897, the ship was named *Pere Marquette*, after the famed Jesuit missionary. The 350-foot long vessel was an immediate success and also proved to be a fine icebreaker. So significant was the design that it set the standard for many railroad ferries built in the 20th century on the Great Lakes and abroad.

Through the years the carferry fleet, as with its owners, expanded and retrenched as economic times demanded, but never faltered in its service to the people and businesses of the upper Great Lakes. With the outbreak of World War I cross-lake freight traffic increased substantially, as was the case with most of the nation's rail

In 1991 Charles Conrad also purchased the *S.S. City of Midland*. When launched in 1940, she was the largest carferry of her time and the first to have passenger accommodations on two decks. In 1998 the *City of Midland* was converted to a barge and renamed *PM 41*.

Excited passengers watch from deck as the *Badger* pulls into port.

***S.S. Badger's* Wheelhouse.**

systems. In the summer of 1918 the U.S. Railroad Administration created the Lake Michigan Car Ferry Association, bringing the 11 vessels of the Ann Arbor, Grand Trunk and Pere Marquette railroads under its supervision. It was anticipated that the three rival fleets could pool their ferries to provide faster and more efficient service to aid in the war effort, which proved to be true. After the war, in 1920, the carferries were returned to their respective owners.

The 1920s were a prosperous time for the United States and for the car ferries of Lake Michigan. Several new ferries were ordered by all three railroads, including two that were delivered just in time for the Great Depression. While the decrease in commerce caused by the depression forced older tonnage off the lake, not all of the events were negative. In 1931 the *City of Flint 32*, one of the ships in the Pere Marquette fleet, set a world marine record for miles traveled by traveling 101,000 miles on 1,010 crossings of Lake Michigan.

In 1951 the final additions were made to the Ludington based carferry fleet. Hailed as the "Twin Queens of the Lakes" the *S.S. Spartan* and the *S.S. Badger*, each at a cost of $5 million to build, were 410 feet in length…the largest Great Lakes carferries ever built with the most superior passenger accommodations ever witnessed. A few years later, in 1955, over 205,000 passengers and 204,460 freight cars were transported in 6,986 crossings of Lake Michigan.

***S.S. Badger's* Upper Deck Café offers buffet-style breakfast, lunch and dinner, each featuring several entrées.**

The 1960s were some of the busiest years in *S.S. Badger's* history. Excited passengers lined up daily to board and set sail on their four-hour cruise across the clear blue water of Lake Michigan. Railroad cars and guests traveled in style between Ludington and the Wisconsin ports of Manitowoc, Kewanee and Milwaukee. Time aboard was spent leisurely strolling decks, relaxing in one of the lounges or dining in one of *Badger's* two dining rooms. Sticking to railway tradition, dining aboard was an elegant event. White linen tablecloths covered tables overflowing with specialties from *Badger's* galley. All meals were freshly prepared on board using the very finest ingredients available.

Breakfast

CHOICE OF ONE
Chilled Orange or Tomato Juice
Fresh Fruit in Season   Dry or Cooked Cereal with Cream

1. GRILLED SMOKED HAM OR BACON WITH EGGS... $1.65
2. SUGAR CURED BACON, ONE EGG................. $1.30
3. TWO EGGS, FRIED, BOILED OR SCRAMBLED...... $1.30

Buttered Toast - Jelly

Coffee,   Tea, Pot   Milk   Sanka, Pot

Chilled Orange or Tomato Juice   .30   Double .50
Baked Apple with Cream   .35

Fruit in Season   .35   Dry Cereal with Cream   .45
Butter Toast - Jelly   .20   Two Eggs (Any Style) .65
French Toast or Wheat Cakes with Syrup   .60

Coffee, - Cup .15   Tea, Pot .25   Milk .20   Sanka, Pot .25

Chessie Special
LARGE GLASS ORANGE OR TOMATO JUICE...... .85
Buttered Toast - Jelly
Coffee - Tea - Milk

Chesapeake & Ohio
DINING SERVICE

During the 1950s and 60s, *Badger* guests ordered breakfast from extensive menus featuring many ship favorites.

Stewed Prunes with Cream .35

Dry or Cooked Cereal with Cream .40

Ham, Grilled or Fried .90

Bacon (4) Slices .65

Grilled Ham, Bacon or Sausage with Eggs 1.25

Eggs, Boiled, Fried or Scrambled .65

French Toast or Wheat Cakes with Syrup .50

Sweet Roll .15   Doughnuts .15

Toast, Dry or Buttered .20

Coffee, Cup .15   Tea, Pot .25   Milk .20   Sanka .25

Your comments about C & O's dining service will be welcome. Write H. T. Askew,
Passenger Traffic Manager, Chesapeake and Ohio Railway Company, Richmond, Va.

Good Morning

Number One
85c
Chilled Orange Juice
and
Dry or Cooked Cereal with Cream
Toast, Dry or Buttered   Sweet Roll
Jelly
Coffee   Tea   Milk

Number Two
$1.35
Chilled Orange Juice   Chilled Tomato Juice
or
Stewed Prunes with Cream
Bacon (3) Slices with Fried Egg
or
Chopped Ham and Scrambled Eggs
Toast, Dry or Buttered   Sweet Roll
Jelly or Marmalade
Coffee   Tea   Milk

Number Three
$1.70
Chilled Orange Juice   Stewed Prunes with Cream
or
Fresh Fruit or Melon in Season
Grilled Ham or Sausage with (2) Eggs
Toast, Dry or Buttered   Sweet Roll
Jelly or Marmalade
Coffee   Tea   Milk   Instant Sanka

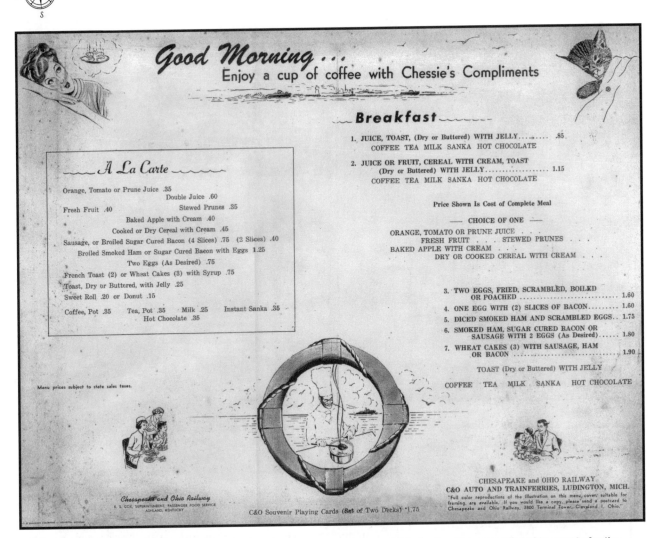

A full-color reproduction of the illustration featured on this *Badger* menu, suitable for framing, was offered to guests for the asking from Chesapeake and Ohio Railway.

Up to 60 crewmembers, most of whom lived on board for 20 days at a time between days off, shared the passenger's enthusiasm for dining on the *Badger*. Mealtime was commonly the highlight of each crewmember's day. They dined on a variety of fresh hot food including homemade breads and pastries in the crew's cheerful mess room, right off the galley. Here the crew would linger well past mealtime, sharing the day's events and their plans for the future. Card games and other pastimes often kept them in the mess room until they retired for the day.

By 1975 the Chesapeake & Ohio Railroad, which had purchased Pere Marquette Railway some years earlier, was no longer interested in operating car ferries, citing the rising costs of vessel upkeep, increasing labor and fuel costs, and advances in railroad technology. In 1983 it sold its three remaining ferries to the newly created Michigan-Wisconsin Transportation Company. The new company struggled to keep the ferries afloat, but

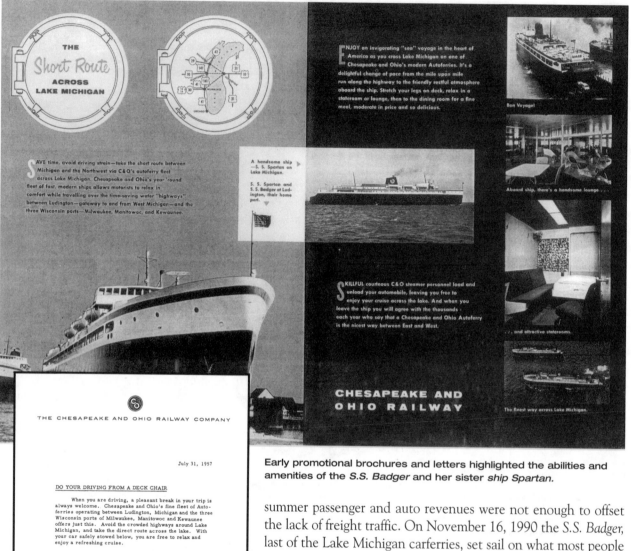

Early promotional brochures and letters highlighted the abilities and amenities of the *S.S. Badger* and her sister *ship Spartan.*

summer passenger and auto revenues were not enough to offset the lack of freight traffic. On November 16, 1990 the S.S. *Badger*, last of the Lake Michigan carferries, set sail on what most people believed would be her final trip. The local Ludington economy soon felt the absence, as did the many families who had faithfully worked on the carferries for generations.

But Lake Michigan was not to be without its ferries for long. In July of 1991 Charles Conrad, a Ludington native and retired entrepreneur, purchased the *S.S. Badger* and her sister ship the *S.S. Spartan* along with the *City of Midland*. Mr. Conrad simply refused to believe that new life could not be put back into the *Badger*. Even when the original estimate of $250,000 to renovate and update the ship jumped to several million dollars, he forged ahead with his vision. It was a fitting return to his boyhood love of the carferries. Conrad, son of a chief engineer for the former Pere Marquette Railway, had accompanied his father on many cross-lake trips as a youth and grew to love the carferries along the way.

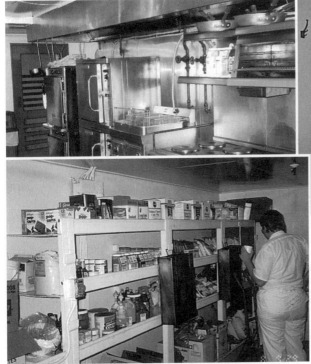

Below deck, over 1500 meals a day are prepared in the *Badger's* galley while the living room sized walk in cooler keeps the ingredients fresh. The *Badger's* crewmembers dine in their own cheerful mess room, next to the galley.

In 1992, three years before his death, Charles Conrad's dream was realized when the beautifully renovated *S.S. Badger* set sail from Ludington, Michigan to Manitowoc, Wisconsin. He always believed the ferries would forever be a part of Ludington: "They've been on the lake for the past hundred years, and I want to do whatever I can to assure they'll be running for the next hundred." His hopes for the *S.S. Badger* and the Ludington area continue to be realized, pushing the Lake Michigan Carferry Service ever closer to his goal of putting the *S.S. Spartan* into service in the near future.

Today, the *S.S. Badger* sails as a passenger and vehicle cross-lake cruise ship; rail freight is no longer ferried across the lake. Up to 620 passengers eagerly board the majestic ferry for each sailing, anticipating a voyage reminiscent of the 1960's. They are not disappointed, only pleasantly surprised to discover the many modern amenities added to the traditional comfort and service on board. In addition to strolling decks and relaxing in lounges, guests aboard the *Badger* spend their time enjoying live entertainment, a video arcade game room, Children's Story Time, the *Badger* Boutique, a maritime historical display, and even full-length feature films in the Movie Lounge. Also on board, the Badger Boatel offers passengers the convenience and adventure of spending the night in an authentic car ferry stateroom.

As always, dining aboard the *S.S. Badger* is an event. If the food on board has changed at all, it has only gotten better. Walk-in pantries and freezers (larger than an average living room) hold the fresh ingredients necessary to create a vast variety of *Badger* specialties from scratch every day. On a busy day over 1500 meals are freshly prepared for passengers in the shiny clean galley below deck. The *Badger's* Upper Deck Café offers buffet-style breakfast, lunch, and dinner, each with several entrees, side dishes, and desserts that rival any bountiful meal in the region. Plus, sandwiches, salads, snacks and beverages are available on the main deck at the *Badger* Galley. Favorite beer, wine and cocktails are served on board in the Portside Bar, Bow Bar and Upper Deck Bar. Throughout the season special Sunset Shoreline Cruises are planned on the *S.S. Badger*. These two-hour cruises along the Lake Michigan Coast bring back themes, AND FOOD, from the *Badger's* past featuring entertainment and the Badger Party Buffet.

Meals and socializing in the mess room have not lost any of their appeal to the crew either. The Lake Michigan Carferry Service operates on the philosophy that "the ship runs on the crew's stomach…" So, the *Badger* crew is fed well! A special galley staff and fulltime baker are devoted entirely to preparing favorite foods and baked goods for the *Badger's* crew of 60. Laura Fuller, 1st Cook on board during nights and weekends shares her "Herman" recipes; both are favorites of the crew. These recipes for 4 loaves of bread are usually, but not always, enough to feed this hungry crew of 60.

SOURDOUGH STARTER HOMEMADE BREAD
Chef Laura calls this "Herman"

To make your own starter:

4 c.	sugar
4 c.	flour
4 c.	water, room temperature

Mix together sugar, flour and water. Store in 1-gallon glass jar (pickle type) with a loose top; a coffee filter and rubber band works well. Leave on counter and stir daily. "Herman" takes 1 to 2 weeks to cure. "Herman" is ready when he smells like yeast or stale beer.

⚓

HOMEMADE BREAD WITH "HERMAN"

3 c.	warm water (110 degrees)
4-1/2 tsp.	yeast
1 tsp.	baking soda
2 tsp.	salt
4 Tbsp.	butter *or* margarine, (optional)
6 Tbsp.	sugar
2 c.	"Herman"
6 to 8 c.	flour

Dissolve yeast in warm water to soften. Mix in remaining ingredients in order listed. Knead 5 to 10 minutes on floured surface; knead in additional flour as needed. Let rise in buttered bowl covered with cheesecloth or a towel in a warm place with no drafts 1 hour. Punch down and let rest 10 minutes. Shape into loaves and place in buttered pans. Let rise again, as before, 1 hour. Bake at 375 degrees 30 to 35 minutes.

Yield: 4 Loaves

Variations: In place of flour you can add 1 of the following items to make unique breads (in equal measure 1 to 2 cups): oatmeal, whole wheat, wheat germ, dry minced onion (great with chili), rye flour and/or caraway seed, dried vegetable soup mix (Harvest Bread) or dry ranch seasoning.

BANANA BREAD WITH "HERMAN"

1-1/3 c.	butter
2 c.	sugar
4	eggs
4 c.	"Herman"
4 c.	bananas, mashed
8 c.	flour
1 Tbsp.	baking powder
2 tsp.	baking soda
1 tsp.	nutmeg
1 Tbsp.	salt
3 c.	walnuts, chopped

Cream butter and sugar; beat in eggs. Beat in "Herman" and bananas. Sift dry ingredients together and stir into creamed mixture. Add nuts. Pour into 4 greased loaf pans. Bake at 350 degrees 1 hour.

Yield: 4 Loaves

Living with "Herman"...

Do not use metal, except to bake with. "Herman" lives on the counter at room temperature. If he is not used regularly (weekly) he can be stored in the refrigerator, but he will need to be "fed" weekly. To feed, just stir in a tablespoon of sugar. "Herman" will also need to be "fed" after each use. For each cup of "Herman" you use mix together 1 cup each of flour, sugar and water; add to "Herman." If you plan on doing some "big baking" be sure to double feed "Herman" 3 days in advance. Once you have a healthy "Herman" you can share him with a friend, who will need to "feed" him.

Recipes reminiscent of the early S.S. *Badger* era bring back tastes from the ship's original menus.

SOUTHERN FRIED CHICKEN

1	whole fresh chicken
1-1/2 c.	all-purpose flour
1 tsp.	salt
1 tsp.	black pepper
1 tsp.	paprika
	Vegetable oil, for frying

Rinse chicken with cold water. Cut chicken into serving pieces; set aside. Combine flour, salt, black pepper and paprika in bowl or bag. Heat vegetable oil in heavy skillet. Shake chicken pieces in flour mixture, a few pieces at a time, until coated. Place chicken pieces in hot oil and fry until golden on the outside and cooked through, turning once. Drain on paper towels.

YANKEE POT ROAST

1 (3 to 4 lb.)	chuck roast
4 Tbsp.	vegetable oil
3	bay leaves
4	carrots
2	onions
4	potatoes
4	celery stalks
2 c.	water
1 c.	beef stock
	Salt and pepper, to taste

Heat vegetable oil in deep skillet. Brown chuck roast on both sides in skillet. Reduce heat; add water and bay leaves. Season with salt and pepper, to taste. Cover and simmer 3 to 4 hours, until chuck roast is tender. Cut onions, potatoes and celery into thirds. Add onions, potatoes, celery and carrots to skillet. Cover and simmer until vegetables are tender, approximately 30 minutes. Remove chuck roast to serving plate and thicken juices to make gravy.

BAKED APPLE DUMPLINGS

6	med. apples, peeled, cored
	Butter, cut into pieces
	Sugar
	Cinnamon

Dough

2 c.	flour
2 tsp.	baking powder
1 tsp.	salt
3 Tbsp.	sugar
2/3 c.	shortening
1/2 c.	milk

Sauce

1 c.	sugar, (may use 1/2 c. white sugar and 1/2 c. brown sugar)
1 c.	water
1/2 tsp.	cinnamon
1/2 tsp.	nutmeg
1/2 c.	butter

Combine sauce ingredients in pan and heat until sugar and butter are melted; set aside. To prepare dough sift dry ingredients. Cut in shortening until crumbly. Add milk and stir until just moistened. Roll dough on lightly floured surface to 1/4-inch thickness. Cut dough into 6 squares. Center 1 apple on each piece of dough. Sprinkle each apple with sugar and cinnamon, and dot with butter. Fold corners of dough over apples; moisten with water to seal. Place apples in baking pan and pour sauce over top. Bake at 350 degrees until apples are tender; approximately 45 minutes.

The *S.S. Badger* sails daily in the spring and fall, and twice a day during the summer months from Ludington, Michigan to Manitowoc, Wisconsin and back. Reservations are recommended and it is suggested you arrive 60 minutes prior to departure.

S.S. BADGER
Lake Michigan Carferry Service
701 Maritime Drive, PO Box 708, Ludington, Michigan 49431
1-800-841-4243
900 S. Lakeview Drive, Manitowoc, Wisconsin 54220
Website: www.ssbadger.com

M.V. Columbus

Hapag-Lloyd, Germany

Year Built:	1997, MTW-Shipyard, Wismar for Hapag-Lloyd, Hamburg, Germany
Country of Registry:	Bahamas
Length:	472'4" (144 MTR)
Beam:	70'6" (21.5 MTR)
Draft:	5 MTR
Decks:	6
Cabins:	205
Passengers:	423
Crew:	170
Nationality of Officers:	European/International
Board Currency:	German Marks
Board Language:	German

The M.V. Columbus sails out of port filled with excited European passengers anxious to see more of the Great Lakes.

*A*new era in Great Lakes history began on September 17, 1997 as passengers set sail from Montreal aboard the German owned cruise ship *M.V. Columbus.* It was the first time a foreign cruise ship had sailed through the St. Lawrence Seaway since World War II. Europeans are extremely interested in cruising the "inland seas" of the Great Lakes and their enthusiasm is matched by U.S. and Canadian residents who long for the days when majestic cruise ships like the *S.S. Keewatin* and *S.S. South American* were a common sight in their ports. Days before automobiles and air travel replaced leisurely cruises across the open lakes.

Hapag-Lloyd of Hamburg, Germany had long dreamed of cruising the Great Lakes, but lacked a vessel capable of the tricky maneuvering required to pass through the locks of the St. Lawrence Seaway. The need for a ship with a narrow hull, small draught and strong tenders to avoid damage as it entered and left the locks were major considerations in designing and building their ship. Their design was triumphant and the grand cruise ship *M.V. Columbus* maneuvered her first locks with flying colors, even with only a few feet to spare between the ship's sides and the walls of the locks. Another obstacle, the availability of suitable ports on the Great Lakes for a ship of this size, was solved with the help of U.S. and Canadian authorities. And lastly, to comply with restrictions placed on foreign vessels in the Great Lakes region dating back to 1886, the Passenger Services Act, the *Columbus* must continue to begin or end her cruises in alternating U.S. and Canadian ports without dropping off or adding passengers.

All obstacles solved, with passengers on both sides of the Atlantic eager to book passage on her Great Lakes cruises, the *M.V. Columbus* is becoming a familiar sight in the region. During her first two seasons, 1997 and 1998, the *Columbus* made stops at several Great Lakes ports including Duluth and Toronto. A year later, in 1999, Beaver Island, Chicago, Cleveland, Detroit, Grand Haven, Milwaukee, Thunder Bay and several other familiar ports played host to *Columbus* and her excited passengers. The reception at each port was overwhelming, complete with dockside bands, entertainment, buffets and champagne. Newspapers, radio and television followed her progress across the lakes, welcoming the return of cruise ships to the area. Passengers and crew aboard the *Columbus* were as thrilled as the thousands of visitors who turned out at ports and lined banks in anticipation of viewing the long-missed site on the waters of the Great Lakes.

One step aboard the *M.V. Columbus* assures you old world luxury has indeed returned to the Great Lakes. Several elegant restaurants, lounges, a library and a card room combine with more modern amenities such as a swimming pool and gymnasium to offer passengers everything needed for an unforgettable cruise. Elegant air-conditioned suites and cabins with private bath facilities, color television, spacious wardrobes and mini bars provide the ultimate escape after a long day of site-seeing in bustling ports.

One of the many lounges aboard the *Columbus* where passengers mingle and enjoy live entertainment.

Meals on board are all prepared from scratch by talented German chefs and their staff of many. Several restaurants with a variety of menus are popular gathering spots for passengers, which means the galley is a place of constant activity.

Early rising passengers find breakfast ready and waiting on deck, where the variety of food will satisfy any "breakfast mood" they may be in. A few hours later, a splendid lunch buffet is on deck waiting for their return. Days aboard the Columbus can be filled with pure relaxation or the bustle of enjoying the many activitied planned. An average day on board offers a hearty Bavarian drinking session with free beer at noon, then lunch, a shipboard rally, darts, tea to a musical accompaniment, bingo, a lecture, and a hobby tour. At day's end guests may be treated to one of the many "Crazy Dinners" presented on board. A favorite, "Hollywood Beauties," features stewardesses "dressed to the nines" in true Hollywood tradition, offering regional food to compliment the festive occasion. Finally, a little dancing and entertainment and even a late night snack. Whatever the meal or occasion on board, the elegance that surrounds dining is as reminiscent of past Great Lakes cruise ships as the *M.V. Columbus* herself.

Staterooms are luxurious and private, offering magnificent views of the Great Lakes.

The *Columbus* offers many forms of activity on board, including a swimming pool and exercise room.

Passengers make meal selections from a variety of festive menus on board.

DRINKS & CO

MENUS

M.V. COLUMBUS
Early Morning Favorites

Fresh From the Baker's Shop
Fruit Breads and Pastries
Croissants, Biscuits and Toast
Whole Grain Toast with Honey and Marmalade

Juice of Fresh Fruit
Orange, Grapefruit, Apple and Tomato

Fresh Fruits of the Season
Melons, Pineapple, Papaya, Mango or Grapefruit

Stewed Fruit
Plums, Prunes and Peaches

Hard Cured Fruits
Apples, Apricots, Bananas, Plums and Prunes

Cereal
Corn Flakes, Rice Krispies and Special "K"

Original Recipe Granola
With Raisins, Nuts, Honey, Apples and Yogurt

Porridge and/or Semolina Pudding

Dairy Products
Natural and/or Fruit Yogurt
Creamed Cottage Cheese
Choice of International Creams

Eggs and Omelets
Two Eggs, Prepared to Order
Served with Your Choice of Crispy Bacon,
Fried Ham and/or Sausage
Omelets
Served with Bacon, Ham, Tomatoes and
Fresh Herbs

From the Grill
Fried Bacon
Sausage
Fried Ham

Sausage and Ham Specialties
Ham, Cooked or Smoked
Salami
Liver Pasties
Cold Meats, Cooked, Smoked and/or Hard Cured

Beverages
Fresh Brewed Coffee
Fresh Brewed Decaffeinated Coffee
English Morning Tea
Orange Pekoe Tea
Geylon Tea
Choice of Herbed Teas
Hot or Cold Milk
Hot or Cold Chocolate

Recipes used to prepare dinner entrées on board the *Columbus* show the culinary talents of the ship's German chefs.

SALMON CORDON BLEU WITH EGG RICE

Courtesy of Peter Springer, Kitchen Master

4 (120 g.)	nice salmon fillets
4	slices smoked salmon
4	slices Mozzarella cheese
4	basil leaves
100 g.	bread crumbs
2	eggs
	Salt
	Pepper
	Flour
	Oil

Sauce

20 cl.	sugar water
10 cl.	tomato juice with vinegar
1 tsp.	sugar
10 cl.	pineapple juice
2 tsp.	soy sauce *or* oyster sauce
2 tsp.	sherry *or* sake
2 tsp.	potato starch *or* corn starch
50 g.	fresh pepper squares (brunoise)

Rice

160 g.	Patna rice, long grain rice or parboiled rice
50 g.	leeks, julienne
50 g.	onions, julienne
4 cl.	olive oil
2	whole eggs
	Salt and pepper, from a mill

Carefully flatten salmon fillets. Place 1 slice smoked salmon, 1 slice Mozzarella cheese and 1 basil leaf on each fillet. Spice to taste and fold up. Dip each filled fillet in egg and then in breading mixture. Cook rice in plenty of salt water until pithy (concisely done) and drain; squeeze out excess moisture.

To prepare sauce, heat sugar water in saucepan. Add remaining ingredients, except potato starch, and cook several minutes. Carefully stir in potato starch and remove from heat. Carefully bake prepared salmon until done; keep warm. Sauté vegetables for rice in oil. Over high heat add rice to vegetables. Mix eggs with whisk and add to rice mixture; toss to cook and mix. Serve salmon on rice base and top with sauce. Serve immediately.

Yield: 4 Servings

OVEN ROASTED LAMB'S BACK
WITH RATATOUILLE CREAM AND POTATO FRITTERS

1	lamb back, cleaned, bones removed
	Salt
	Rosemary
	Garlic
	Olive oil
1/4 liter	cooking juice from lamb
1/4 liter	cream
1/8 liter	sour cream
1/2	red pepper, cut in squares
1/2	yellow pepper, cut in squares
1 sm.	melanzane, cut in squares
4 c.	olive oil
1	garlic clove, minced
1 twig	thyme
1 Tbsp.	ketchup
20 cl.	liquid, as needed
	Tomatoes, cut into squares, (optional)
8 lg.	potatoes
2	eggs
	Marjoram
	Nutmeg
	Salt and pepper, to taste

Clean lamb and remove bones. Combine olive oil, garlic and rosemary. Rub garlic mixture over lamb and let marinate. Season to taste with salt and pepper. Roast in oven at 200 degrees approximately 10 minutes, to desired doneness. Let lamb cool and then carve.

Ratatouille Cream

Sauté peppers, melanzane and minced garlic in olive oil. Stir in lamb drippings, cream and sour cream; let cook and thicken. Add additional liquid if needed. Add thyme and ketchup. Add tomato squares just before serving, if desired. Spoon sauce over carved lamb.

Potato Fritters

Peel potatoes and grate small with vegetable grater. Mix potatoes with eggs. Season with salt, pepper, marjoram and nutmeg to taste. Cook on griddle until browned.

Variation: May also serve with a brown rosemary sauce and a clove of white garlic.

Yield: 8 Servings

CRÊPES WITH SPRING MORELS ON A PARSLEY-GARLIC SAUCE

Crêpe Batter

80 g.	flour, sieved
2 dl.	milk
2	eggs
2 Tbsp.	sunflower oil
1	pinch nutmeg
	Salt

Filling

500 g.	fresh morels
500 g.	white asparagus
1	shallot
	Flour, as needed, small amount
1/2 dl.	white wine
1 dl.	poultry bouillon
2 dl.	heavy cream
	Salt and pepper, to taste

Sauce

20 g.	butter
1	shallot
1-1/2	spring garlic cloves
2	bundles smooth parsley
	Few basil and tarragon leaves
2 dl.	bouillon
2 dl.	cream

To prepare crêpes blend all ingredients together; let stand 15 minutes. Stir again. Cook on both sides in coated pan. Transfer to salad plate and let cool.

To prepare filling remove stems from morels. Carefully clean morels and chop into large squares; set aside. Wash asparagus, peel and remove lower end. Cut asparagus sticks into squares and cook in salted water until soft. Cut shallot into squares and sauté in butter. Dust cleaned morels lightly with flour and stir in with shallots. Add wine and bouillon. Season with salt and pepper, cover and cook until soft; let cool. Put morel mixture through sieve and return to pan to reheat. Add heavy cream. Taste and adjust seasonings. Mix in cooked asparagus.

To prepare sauce cut shallot into squares and sauté in butter with garlic, parsley, basil and tarragon leaves. Add bouillon and cook to reduce; cool. Put mixture through sieve and return to pan to reheat. Add cream and reduce again. Mix in a slice of cold butter.

To assemble, lay crêpes out flat and spread with filling. Roll up crêpes and place in covered ovenproof dish. Place sauce over top of crêpes. Cover and bake in middle of hot oven 12 to 15 minutes. Decorate with stems and leaves. Serve.

Yield: 4 Servings

Information on the *M.V. Columbus,* including cruise dates and scheduled Ports of Call
can be obtained through:

CRUISING THE GREAT LAKES
The Mariport Group Ltd.
P.O. Box 1758
Cambridge, ON NIR 7G8
Canada
Telephone: (519) 624-5513 · Fax: (519) 624-5569
Email: info@cruisingthegreatlakes.org
Website: www.cruisingthegreatlakes

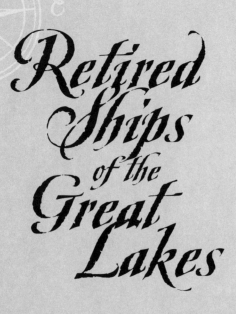

Retired
Ships
of the
Great
Lakes

Retired Ships of the Great Lakes

Sailing the Great Lakes has always been an adventure with more than its fair share of danger, purpose, luxury and heroic rescues. The size and beauty of the largest bodies of fresh water in the world are rivaled only by the shipping legends they have gathered over the centuries.

Early bulk hauling freighters amazingly carried thousands of tons of cargo in one load from port to port on the Great Lakes, aiding tremendously in the region's growth. Car ferries transported hundreds of vehicles at a time safely across waterways.

Luxurious passenger ships provided elegant week-long cruises. And Coast Guard vessels stood ready year round to weather storms, aid in navigation and break through ice, keeping vessels and their passengers safe.

Over the decades shipbuilding techniques and materials improved at a rapid pace, as did the technology available for navigation. One by one, some of the grandest vessels ever to sail the Great Lakes were retired and replaced by more cost efficient, state-of-the-art ships. Majestic cargo hauling freighters were replaced with self-unloading ships, requiring less manpower and time to transport goods. Shiny car ferries were replaced with bridges allowing thousands of cars an hour to pass over waterways at 55 miles per hour. Luxurious coal burning passenger ships became obsolete. And rugged Coast Guard vessels and lightships became outdated. Today's ships have removed many of the dangers associated with shipping on the Great Lakes, but have not replaced the historical significance and special place in our hearts reserved for the ships of yesterday.

The proud ships featured in this section were all rescued from the scrap piles and painstakingly preserved, with the exception of the Michigan State Car Ferries, which live on in the memories of those fortunate enough to have walked their decks. Many of the legends associated with these grand ships revolve around how, where and on what their crews and passengers dined. The stories of finest quality, freshly prepared homemade food in limitless quantities are true. So are the stories of less-than-modern cooking devices available and precautions necessary for cooking on high seas.

As dedicated historical groups and individuals went about the task of preserving, restoring and researching these retired ships, they did not overlook the galleys and dining areas. Original menus stand as proof that the men and women on board ate well, and quite often, with plenty of variety to satisfy their appetites. Treasured recipes, once used in the galleys, offer us all a taste of their culinary legends.

Museum Ship Alexander Henry

Canadian Coast Guard

The Alexander Henry at work off the coast of Canada shortly before her retirement in 1985.

Built:	1959, Port Arthur Shipbuilding Co., Thunder Bay, Ontario
Built For:	Canadian Coast Guard
Length:	210'
Beam:	40'
Draft:	19'
Crew:	34
Retired:	1985, Replaced with the *Samuel Risley*
Current Name:	Museum Ship *Alexander Henry*
Current Home Port:	Kingston, Ontario

*W*inters in the northern Great Lakes region are long and hard, and no one knows it better than past crews of *Canadian Coast Guard Ice Breaker Alexander Henry*. She was named in honor of the fur trader, explorer and writer, who from about 1803, led annual summer expeditions to Kaministiquia, now Thunder Bay. For 25 years this tough ship and her proud crew worked the region, getting all loaded ships out before the winter freeze-

Maintenance and care are given year round to ensure the Museum Ship *Alexander Henry* remains in authentic condition.

up and ensuring an early opening of the shipping season each spring. During the winter she assisted local tugs in moving large 730-foot lakers that needed assistance due to heavy ice conditions in the area. The ship's primary role was the full range of heavy-duty navigation aids servicing – buoy work, beacon servicing, construction support, station and site resupply, and personnel transfer. Her second role was to provide both shipping route and harbor facility icebreaking for the movement of ships. *Alexander Henry's* early career was devoted to these tasks in the Georgian Bay area, and then later in Thunder Bay. Situated at the head of the Great Lakes/St. Lawrence Seaway

System, Thunder Bay is the world's largest grain handling port.

Over the course of time, major advances in marine technology made operating the *Alexander Henry* very expensive compared to newer ships. Her specialized layout and heavy construction limited her use for other functions, forcing the Canadian Coast Guard to remove her from its fleet in 1985. Shortly after the announcement of her retirement was made, the Marine Museum of the Great Lakes at Kingston contacted the Coast Guard and their local Member of Parliament, expressing their hope that this icebreaker could be preserved as a fine example of Canadian Great Lakes shipbuilding. The museum received a phone call from the Coast

Guard a few months later, announcing the *Alexander Henry* would arrive at their dock in a few day's time.

The *Alexander Henry* arrived safely alongside the museum dock in the spring of 1985, which is where she proudly sits today. Resources are not available to take the ship on cruises, but constant work ensures she is maintained in the most authentic way possible. The Museum Ship *Alexander Henry* stands as a tribute to the sailors of the Canadian Coast Guard and is used to demonstrate life on the Great Lakes.

Daily tours allow guests to visit each area of the ship, viewing rooms, decks and equipment as they were on her

The stainless steel galley appears today just as it did when the *Alexander Henry* made her final voyage in 1985.

The baking area was constantly in use preparing the homemade breads, rolls and desserts served on board.

final voyage in May of 1985. The *Alexander Henry* was among the last of the Great Lakes ships to be finished in natural materials; quarter sawn oak, mahogany and birch. Even the well-equipped galley remains in its same shiny, organized and natural state. It is here

Each officer had a designated seat in the Officer's Mess.

that the cook, assistant cook and steward, under the supervision of a Store's Officer, prepared and served up to 150 fresh hot meals a day. The galley closed down at night but coffee, juice and sandwiches were always available in the pantry for the night watches.

In the Officer's Mess each officer had a designated seating area. A steward

Alexander Henry's crew looked forward to gathering for meals in the crew's mess.

The cook's cabin provided comfort and privacy at the end of busy day.

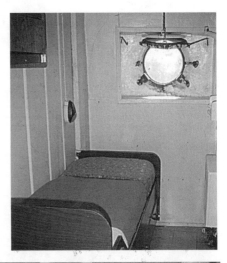

The captain's berth was furnished with a double bed surrounded by natural wood paneling.

The lounge area in the captain's quarters provided room to stretch out and catch up on paper work.

hovered nearby at mealtime, usually in the pantry, ready to take an order but seemingly oblivious to officer's conversations. As on any other Great Lakes ship, the hard working crew of the *Alexander Henry* looked forward to their freshly prepared meals and they were never disappointed. Lake Baked Fish Supreme and Great Lakes Swiss Steak quickly became crew favorites. Authentic recipes for both of these favorites are supplied here, straight from the galley aboard the Museum Ship *Alexander Henry*. Both recipes are shown in 6-serving portions and also 60-serving portions. The 60-serving recipe was used aboard ship when she sailed with a crew of 58; try it when you're expecting a full crew of hungry sailors!

The galley crew preparing one of the last meals served aboard the *Alexander Henry* while she was in service.

The engine room (above center) and captain's cabin on the final vonyage, May 1985.

LAKE BAKED FISH SUPREME

6 Servings

	Olive oil
6 lbs.	fish fillets
1	garlic clove, minced
1	onion, diced
4	carrots, diced
3	celery ribs, diced
3	potatoes, diced
2	green peppers, diced
3	med. ripe tomatoes, diced
1	lemon, thinly sliced
	Salt, pepper and oregano, to taste

Cover bottom of roaster with olive oil. Lay fish fillets side by side in bottom of roaster, skin side down. Layer spices, garlic, onion, celery, potatoes, carrots, tomatoes, peppers and lemon on top. Re-spice. Bake at 300 degrees until vegetables feel soft.

LAKE BAKED FISH SUPREME

60 Servings

	Olive oil
24 lbs.	fish fillets
8	garlic cloves, minced
5	onions, diced
40	carrots, diced
18	celery ribs, diced
15	potatoes, diced
15	green peppers, diced
35	med. ripe tomatoes, diced
6	lemons, thinly sliced
	Salt, pepper and oregano, to taste

Cover bottom of roaster with olive oil. Lay fish fillets side by side in bottom of roaster, skin side down. Layer spices, garlic, onion, celery, potatoes, carrots, tomatoes, peppers and lemon on top. Re-spice. Bake at 300 degrees until vegetables feel soft.

GREAT LAKES SWISS STEAK
6 Servings

6 lbs.	inside round steak
1/2 tsp.	paprika
1/2 c.	flour
1 c.	mushrooms, sliced
1 c.	green peppers, sliced
1/2 c.	onions, sliced
1 c.	ketchup
1 c.	water
	Salt and pepper, to taste

Paprika flour pounded steak; season with salt and pepper. Brown floured steak in pan of oil. Drain fat and transfer to casserole dish. Fry vegetables in pan; add water and ketchup. Pour vegetable mixture over steak. Bake at 350 degrees approximately 1 hour.

GREAT LAKES SWISS STEAK
60 Servings

30 lbs.	inside round steak
1 Tbsp.	paprika
1 c.	flour
10 c.	mushrooms, sliced
10 c.	green peppers, sliced
5 c.	onions, sliced
10 c.	ketchup
10 c.	water
	Salt and pepper, to taste

Paprika flour pounded steak; season with salt and pepper. Brown floured steak in pan of oil. Drain fat and transfer to casserole dish. Fry vegetables in pan; add water and ketchup. Pour vegetable mixture over steak. Bake at 350 degrees approximately 1 hour.

CCGC ALEXANDER HENRY CINNAMON ROLLS

(Bed and Breakfast guests aboard the Museum Ship Alexander Henry *wake up to fresh cinnamon rolls every morning, similar to those prepared using this recipe.)*

Dough

1 (1/4 oz.) pkg.	active dry yeast
1 c.	warm milk (105 degrees)
1/2 c.	sugar
1 tsp.	salt
2	eggs
1/3 c.	butter, melted
4 c.	all-purpose flour

Filling

1 c.	brown sugar, firmly packed
2-1/2 tsp.	cinnamon
1/3 c.	butter, softened

Frosting

8 Tbsp.	butter, softened
1-1/2 c.	powdered sugar
1/4 c.	cream cheese
1/2 tsp.	vanilla
1/8 tsp.	salt

To prepare dough dissolve yeast in warm milk. Add sugar, salt, eggs, butter and flour; mix well. Dust hands lightly with flour and knead dough into large ball. Put ball in bowl, cover and let rise in warm place approximately 1 hour, until doubled in size. Roll dough out on lightly floured surface to 1/4-inch thick 16x21-inch rectangle.

Preheat oven to 400 degrees. To prepare filling, combine brown sugar and cinnamon in bowl. Spread softened butter over surface of dough and sprinkle evenly with brown sugar mixture. Begin with a 21-inch side of dough and carefully roll to other 21-inch edge. Cut rolled dough into 1-3/4-inch strips and place at least 3-inches apart in lightly greased baking pan Bake 10 minutes or until lightly browned. Combine frosting ingredients and beat until fluffy. Coat each cinnamon roll with frosting as soon as removing from oven.

Today, the Museum Ship *Alexander Henry* is permanently located dockside at the Marine Museum of the Great Lakes at Kingston in Ontario, Canada. In addition to enjoying tours to every area of the ship, guests are also invited to stay on board overnight. The *Alexander Henry* offers a unique Bed amd Breakfast experience, with lodging in a choice of authentic cabins from the chief officer's cabin to the cook's cabin. All cabins are on the outside of the ship, offering a view. The cabins, mostly officer's, are modest but comfortable and are kept "Shipshape and Bristol Fashion." A delicious continental breakfast is served every morning to overnight guests. Other attractions in the area include Fort Henry, Agnes Etherington Art Centre, Murney Tower Museum, Hockey Hall of Fame, Kingstone Harbour, Market Square and the Farmer's Market.

THE MUSEUM SHIP *ALEXANDER HENRY*
Marine Museum of the Great Lakes at Kingston
55 Ontario Street
Kingston, Ontario, Canada K71 2Y2
Telephone: (613) 542-2261 Fax: (613) 542-0043
Email: mmuseum@stauffer.queensu.ca
Website: www.MarMus.Ca

Open to the Public Daily
Tours from the third weekend in May (Victoria Day) through the end of September

Huron Lightship

United States Coast Guard

Built:	1920 Consolidated Ship Building Co. Morris Heights, New York
Built For:	United States Lighthouse Service
Length:	96'5"
Beam:	24'
Draft:	9'6"
Crew:	11 to 12, Rotating (7 to 9 on Duty at a Time)
Retired:	1970
Current Name:	Huron Lightship Museum
Home Port:	Port Huron, Michigan

Former crewmember and Chief Cook Donald Thurow is currently an active volunteer and tour guide on the *Huron Lightship* Museum. Donald joined the U.S. Coast Guard shortly after Pearl Harbor was attacked. He spent 39 months on the Coast Guard Vessel *Roger B. Taney*, the only ship in the area still afloat after the attack on December 7, 1941. The *Roger B. Taney* was decommissioned December 7, 1986 after 50 years of distinguished service and three wars. The ship was designated a National Historic Landmark and is open to the public in Baltimore, Maryland.

*L*ightships served as floating lighthouses, anchored in areas where it was too deep, expensive or impractical to construct a lighthouse, but where navigational aid was definitely needed. For 50 years, the *Huron Lightship* faithfully performed her duties as a floating lighthouse, guiding thousands of Great Lakes sailors safely through obstacles and fog that could last for days. Originally launched in 1920 as Lightship 103 of the United States Lighthouse Service, she was later renamed U.S. Coast Guard WAL 526 in 1950, eleven years after the Coast Guard took over the Lighthouse Service in 1939, and WLV 526 in 1965.

In 1943, while serving aboard the *Taney*, Donald had a quick photograph taken to send home to his mother.

After being stationed at various shoals on Lake Michigan, the *Huron Lightship* arrived at Corsica Shoals in Port Huron in 1935. It was here, approximately six miles north of the Blue Water Bridge connecting Canada and United States, and three miles east of the Michigan shoreline, that the *Huron Lightship* and her crew of 11 to 12 spent 36 years guiding mariners into the narrow dredged channel of lower Lake Huron leading to the St. Clair River. It was here, every year at Corsica Shoals, that the lightship arrived by April 1st and stayed through December 15th. And it was here, that the main light atop her 52'6" mast dependably replaced the sun seven days a week, shining from one hour before sunset until one hour after sunrise. When visibility was less than five miles, her foghorn, powered by steam in the early days and air compressors in later years, would sound a three-second blast every 30 seconds. The foghorn would continue to sound until visibility improved, which could be days. This prompted locals to nickname her "Old B.O." because of the familiar sound her horn made.

Over the years *Huron Lightship* underwent many changes and upgrades, the most notable taking place after the 1948 shipping season. Decking was redone, the Deck House was moved to allow relocation of the radio beacon transmitting equipment, quick acting water-tight doors were installed, the steam boat hoist was replaced with an electric hoist and the huge black stack with the foghorn at top was replaced with two deck mounted foghorns and a stubby stack. Below deck a new electric anchor windlass was installed and the galley was moved and remodeled with stainless steel. Crew's quarters were also enlarged and a crew lounge area and mess deck were added. The biggest changes took place below in the engine room with the installation of new modern fuel tanks, diesel engines, air compressors, generators, a heating system and a water system. In later years the foghorns were changed to diaphones and new radar was installed.

In the late 1960s it was deemed no longer cost effective to maintain the *Huron Lightship*. In 1970 she lifted her three-ton mushroom anchor and was retired from active service, proudly taking with her the distinction of being the last lightship on the Great Lakes. A lighted horn buoy replaced the *Huron Lightship*.

The *Huron Lightship* Museum "decked out" for the holidays.

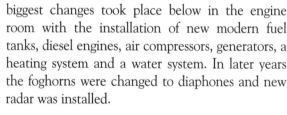

In 1972, after being acquired by the City of Port Huron by mandate of area residents, the *Huron Lightship* was enshrined at Pine Grove Park as a tribute to her vigilance and in fond memory of a bygone era. But after a few years, interest and affection for the retired ship began to fade, replaced with neglect, vandalism and thievery. This faithful lightship sat on the verge of ruin until a group from the Lake Huron Lore Marine Society came to her rescue. Restorations began in 1989 with the combined help of volunteers from the Lake Huron Lore Marine Society, Port Huron Museum of Arts and History, former U.S. Coast Guardsmen and other concerned citizens. In 1989 the *Huron Lightship* was designated a National Historic Landmark. She is the only lightship on the Great Lakes to be so honored.

In 1990, with her dignity restored, the *Huron Lightship* opened to the public once again. Today, the ship welcomes visitors aboard to see an accurate restoration complete with original furnishings, equipment, uniforms, bedding and many artifacts relating to maritime history. The *Huron Lightship* is staffed by a group of dedicated volunteers who are constantly updating displays and stand ready with in-depth explanations about daily life aboard a "floating lighthouse."

During her 50 years of service, daily life on board the *Huron Lightship* was always active for the crew. All hands stood watch in addition to their other responsibilities, as many times there were only four or five crewmembers aboard. An average number on board was seven or eight. Watches consisted of monitoring radio beacon transmitters, checking visibility, firing the boiler, tending the water in the boiler and tending the fire in the galley stove. Duty was 21 days on and 7 days off, with the crew rotating. The time off was known as compensatory leave.

Donald Thurow served as Chief Cook on the *Huron Lightship* for 22 months from 1946 to 1948. As a former crewmember, he remembers first hand the busy schedule and deep sense of comradeship shared by all on board. When not on watch, time was spent keeping things "ship shape" and listening to the radio; Arthur Godfrey or the ball game were favorites. In good weather the crew often sat on deck telling war stories or sea stories and sharing the latest scuttlebutt (gossip.) As most of the crew had considerable sea duty and war experiences, these stories could go on for hours. The skipper while Donald was on board was an old-time cutter man and often talked of rum running days from the past.

The compact galley aboard the *Huron* was kept clean, shiny and full of supplies.

The Ward Room, located at the ship's stern, was a favorite spot on board for relaxing and watching television.

311

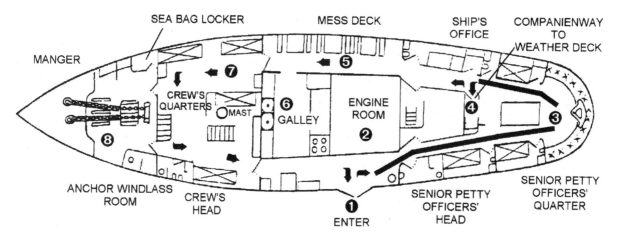

Sketch of the lightship's layout below deck, "home" to her crew.

The ship was always active, someone was always on watch. As cook, Donald's days started at 5:30 am, when the night watch woke him. By 6:30 am he had a hot breakfast ready and the crew was together at the large oak table in the Ward Room enjoying it. At 8:00 am the American Flag was raised, signaling the beginning of another day aboard. Seaman cleaned and washed the decks and general maintenance was performed while Donald cleaned the galley and started dinner (the noon meal and largest of the day.) At least three times a week, at 1:00 pm, the crew participated in mandatory drills, officially called "Quarters." Quarters included practicing procedures to be followed in the event of one of many emergencies that could arise in the course of an average day.

The galley on the *Huron Lightship* in the 1940s was clean, organized and featured a coal burning stove. Donald had quickly mastered the "5-Count" method of determining the temperature of a coal-burning oven and was notorious for turning out several homemade pies a week. How do you bake a pie at 375 degrees when you can't set an oven temperature? "Stick your hand in the oven; if you can hold it there for a count of 5, you're at the right temperature, otherwise adjust the coal!" He does admit cakes were rare; the rolling of the ship usually caused them to flop.

Good solid nourishment was the order of the day, and Donald planned meals around what the crew asked for. "Everyone likes the cook, especially when the food is good. We ate very well!" He estimates 90% of the men in the Coast Guard ate better on board the ship than they did at home. The supply boat was taken to the Coast Guard Station at Fort Gratiot Light at least once a week for fresh groceries, mail and crew needs. It was a one-hour trip from the *Huron Lightship* to the Coast Guard Station on shore. With years of practice at filling out the standard Coast Guard purchase orders, Donald was always able to squeeze out extra money to stock the ship with the favorite snacks and candy of his crewmates. Those snacks came in handy when three meals a day just weren't enough for the hungry sailors. The galley was always open, with two rules…"If you make a mess, clean it up, and…if you take the last cup of coffee, make a fresh pot!"

The *Huron Lightship* Museum sits proudly at her current home port in Port Huron, Michigan. The small boat on deck, called the Liberty Boat, transported off-duty sailors to shore.

The lightship sailors shared humble accommodations, which consisted of nine bunks and several lockers.

Donald retired from the U.S. Coast Guard after almost eight years of service, taking with him many fond memories of the unique and colorful crew from the *Huron Lightship*, and also the recipes for their favorite foods on board.

Breakfast
Bacon
Sausage
Eggs, Any Style
Hot Cakes and French Toast for the asking

Dinner
Steak, Roast Beef or Pork Chops
Homemade Soup
Salad
Vegetable
Dessert

Supper
Spaghetti, Stew or Hamburgers
Side Dishes

Special Fare...

Sunday on the *Huron Lightship* was always "Chicken Day", roasted, fried or once in a while "fancied up" with cream of mushroom soup. Saturday Night was always "Wienies & Beans" and Sunday Night it was "Every Man for Himself!" Macaroni and Cheese was common on Friday evening, along with salmon patties. Thanksgiving was celebrated in style featuring a "full Turkey Dinner with all the trimmings!"

LIGHTSHIP PANCAKES

3 to 4 c.	flour
2 tsp.	baking powder
1	egg
1	pinch salt
1/4	stick butter, melted
	Water, as needed

Combine all ingredients in large bowl. Whip the daylights out of the batter until all lumps are gone. Pour batter into hot greased griddle. When small bubbles form, flip and briefly cook other side.

Note: Use water, not milk, in the batter. Milk stops the pancakes from rising.

BEAN SOUP

4 to 5	ham or pork hocks
2 lbs.	dried beans, soaked, washed
3	onions, quartered
4 to 5	carrots, thinly sliced
2 gal.	Water
	Salt and pepper, to taste

Combine all ingredients in large soup pot. Simmer and cook 2 to 3 hours, until beans are soft; skim off fat. Remove ham hocks and cut off meat. Return meat to soup.

CHIPPED BEEF ON TOAST
Commonly Referred to as "S.O.S."

1 lb.	dried chipped beef
1 qt.	water
1 pt.	milk
1/4 lb.	butter
1 pinch	pepper
1 c.	flour
	Cold water, as needed
	Small amount pepper

Combine beef, with 1-quart water, milk, butter and pepper in pan; bring to slow boil. Mix flour with cold water and whip the daylights out of it until smooth. Slowly add to pan, stirring constantly, until thicken. Spoon over toast or potatoes.

Note: This can also be prepared with canned salmon; stir gently as salmon is delicate. Donald also used to prepare this on board with boxed salted catfish.

DONALD'S SPAGHETTI SAUCE

3 (No. 2-1/2)	cans tomatoes
	Garlic
	Onions, finely diced
	Salt, pepper and oregano, to taste

Brown onions with garlic in hot oil. Add tomatoes, salt, pepper and oregano. Simmer slowly 3 to 4 hours. If sauce is too thick add 1/2 cup ketchup.

RIB ROAST

1 (7 to 8 lb.)	roast
	Salt
	Pepper, coarsely ground
	Garlic clove
	Water

Rub roast with salt and coarsely ground black pepper. Insert 1/2 garlic clove in each end of roast. Place roast in baking pan with 1/2-inch water; do not cover. Cook in hot 400 degree oven 1 hour or until desired doneness. Roast will be medium-rare in the middle and well-done around the outer edges. Serve with freshly cooked potatoes and carrots.

Note: This is also an excellent way to cook a pork loin roast. Less cooking time is required for a pork loin roast.

CHERRY PIE

2 cans	cherries
2 c.	sugar
1/2 c.	corn starch
	Cold water
1/2 c.	milk
1	egg

Combine cherries and sugar in saucepan; bring to slow boil. Dissolve corn starch in cold water and stir until all lumps are gone. Add corn starch mixture to cherries. Pour into unbaked pie shell and cover with top crust. Sprinkle cold water around edges of top and bottom crust; crimp or seal with fork. Mix milk with egg and brush over top. Bake at 375 degrees 45 minutes.

COCONUT CREAM PIE

2 c.	milk
1/4 c.	coconut
2	eggs
1/2 c.	sugar
6	egg whites
1/4 c.	powdered sugar

Combine milk and coconut in saucepan; bring to slow boil. Slowly stir eggs and sugar into milk mixture. Partially bake a pie crust 15 to 20 minutes, until lightly browned; let cool. Pour coconut mixture in pie crust. Whip eggs whites with powdered sugar. Spread over top of pie and return to oven for a few minutes, until slightly browned.

PIE CRUST

4 c.	flour
1	pinch salt
1 c.	shortening
	Cold water

Mix together flour, salt and shortening; knead together. Add small amount of cold water, a little at a time, until dough resembles small peas. With well floured hands roll dough into ball. Roll ball out and place in pie tins.

Huron Lightship
1920-1970

Lightship Museum
Port Huron, Mich.

Today, Donald Thurow is an active volunteer aboard the *Huron Lightship* Museum. Most days you will find him busy updating displays, working on renovations and helping with the maintenance required to keep this proud vessel "ship shape." He is always happy to stop what he's doing and conduct a personal tour through the ship, proud to have a part in preserving the *Huron Lightship's* important role in Great Lakes Maritime History. He also shares a favorite poem of his by C. Tucker, bringing to life the dangers of serving on a lightship.

Perils of the Lighthouse

When a sailor gets to thinking
he is one of the best,
let him ship out on a lightship
and take the acid test.
If he still feels like bragging,
I don't think that all his tales
will be of deep sea sailing,
but of the ship that never sails.

— C. Tucker

Everyday the dedicated men and women of the United States Coast Guard put their lives at risk in service to their country. Most of us only see them in dress uniforms aboard shiny ships at festivals, safely anchored in harbors with colorful flags hanging from decks. We do not see the sea-battered ships, covered with ice, carrying exhausted sailors further out into the treacherous waters of the Great Lakes. We do not experience the danger they face or the loss they feel when a crewmate gives his life in the line of duty.

The *Huron Lightship* experienced such a loss when crewmember Robert J. Gullickson was lost at sea on May 7, 1958. He was riding in a small boat with fellow crewmember Vincent Disch, delivering mail to the *Huron* as it was stationed in Lake Huron about two miles off shore. Their boat was capsized by waves, throwing both men into the high seas. The two held hands and talked in the water before a wave separated them, taking Robert Gullickson with it He was the only crewmember lost during the 35 years the *Huron Lightship* guided freighters through the lower lake into the river.

Robert J. Gullickson, BM3, USCG, was honored in a memorial service aboard the *Huron Lightship* on July 12, 1998. A poem, "The *Huron Lightship*" was written by fellow crewmember Neil C. Hamilton and dedicated in honor of his friend, expressing the feelings of all who had proudly served aboard the *Huron Lightship*. Neil served aboard the lightship for 26 months. He retired from the military in 1981, after 30 years of service, including two tours to Vietnam.

THE *HURON LIGHTSHIP*

By
Neil C. Hamilton
Crewmember, 1957-1959

Winds a'howling, seas running high,
the *Huron Lightship* is still standing by
through gale storms and November's might,
the *Huron* survived the storm tossed night.

Nine months a year on her station she stands,
her foghorn sounding all the way to the lands.

Listen!…hear her foghorn's blast
and see her main light so bright,
always vigilant, it shines on still
through the long, dark night.

Her crew may change, the 'old man' too,
but her missions the same,
to guide the ships through.

For fifty years she's done her duty,
guiding the mariners to the lee.
Now she lies enshrined forever
here by Port Huron's sea.

A memorial now to all who served,
we commit their memory unto thee.
Please Lord, we pray, accept them
…and always keep them free.

'Semper Paratus' was their guide,
their right to liberty,
these crewmen of the *Huron*.
these brave Coast Guardsmen of the sea.

The *Huron Lightship* Museum is open for tours, allowing visitors to experience life on a floating lighthouse first-hand. A self-guided tour has guests follow a blue line through the shipside entry on the main deck, down to the engine room, Senior Petty Officers' quarters at the stern, up the companionway (stairwell) to the weather deck, and on through the mess deck, galley and crew's quarters. The lightship's unique 6,000-pound "mushroom" anchor is on display with plenty of history to go along with it.

HURON LIGHTSHIP MUSEUM
Pine Grove Park, Port Huron, Michigan 48060
(810) 982-0891

Open May, June and September: Weekends Only
July and August: Wednesday through Sunday, 1:00pm – 4:30 pm
Other Times by Appointment

S.S. Keewatin

Canadian Pacific Railway Company

The S.S. Keewatin's Flower Well Lounge is two-decks high with Italian hand-etched and painted skylights, welcoming sunlight into the potted plants.

Launched:	September 14, 1907
Length:	350'
Beam:	43'8"
Draft:	16'
Passengers:	288
Crew:	86
Retired:	November 29, 1965
Current Name:	*S.S. Keewatin* Maritime Museum
Home Port:	Douglas, Michigan

*T*he S.S. *Keewatin* was majestic, elegant, grand, and gracefully sailed the Great Lakes as recent as 36 years ago. Launched five years before the S.S. *Titanic*, the *"KEE"* (as she was affectionately called) and her sister ship, the S.S. *Assiniboia*, offered guests the romance of cruising the world's largest inland waterways in unrivaled elegance for 57 years. The trips were either short holidays in themselves, or the water route portion of a guest's Canadian

The Dining Saloon accommodated 120 passengers in Edwardian elegance surrounded by walnut paneling and polished brass.

Pacific Railway journey across Canada and northern regions of the United States. Whatever their destination, passengers enjoyed memorable cuisine, first-class service and state-of-the-art accommodations aboard the luxurious *Keewatin*. Deck sports included shuffleboard, bull board and deck quoits, with swings and slides nearby to entertain children. Morning Bouillon and Afternoon Tea were served in the Observation Lounge of the Promenade Deck Aft, and later there was dancing on the polished oak dance floor. Best of all, and also reminiscent of this bygone era, an "Inland-Sea Cruise" aboard the S.S. *Keewatin* from Port McNicoll to Fort William and back, including berth and meals, was available for only one hundred dollars!

Dining aboard the S.S. *Keewatin* was an "event." Attention to detail was evident everywhere from menu preparation to the galley crew, serving staff and setting. The meals were known for quality and quantity. A 1927 travel brochure describes, "Dinner served on the white ship is not a meal – it is an epicurean delight." The Dining Saloon seated 120 passengers in Edwardian elegance surrounded by walnut paneling and polished brass. All of the tables and chairs were bolted to the floor, but for passenger convenience and comfort, the chairs swiveled out and back. Each chair

was labeled with an ivory number plate to coincide with meal tickets issued to passengers upon boarding. Meals were served in one, two or three settings, depending on the number of passengers aboard and each setting received the same careful attention. It was the Purser's responsibility to inform guests of their dining arrangements, ensuring each meal went smoothly.

The eighteen waiters, in Canadian Pacific Railway tradition, were not allowed to write down food orders but had to memorize what each person had ordered at his tables. According to Jack Neilson, a waiter from the 1945 season: "We learned to remember the complete order

Morning Bouillon and Afternoon Tea were served in the Observation Lounge of the Promenade Deck Aft. Later in the day, the lounge was transformed into a ballroom and guests danced on the polished oak floor.

for seven people at each sitting. We learned how to use our waiter's wrist napkin to unobtrusively blot a spill and wipe away crumbs as we removed a serving dish. We learned to set the table correctly – which silverware went where and why. We also learned to vacuum our table stations after the last dinner, polish the woodwork and brass fittings, and to clean the window at our station to be as clear as crystal. As we had three sittings at each meal, we carefully laid snow white linen clothes in layers of three, for quick changes between sittings, praying all through the meal no one would spill a liquid during the first sitting that would soak through all three layers."

The Canadian Pacific Railway was renowned for the quality of their food and the strict daily routine of the galley crew never changed. Even breakfast was offered from an extensive printed

Guests in the Dining Saloon choose dinner entrées from an extensive menu as their waiter commits each selection to memory. The Canadian Pacific Railway did not allow waiters to write down food orders.

Breakfast

Blended Fruit Juice
Orange juice · Tomato Juice

Stewed Prunes · Half Grapefruit
Rolled Oats · All Bran · Bran Flakes
Shredded Wheat · Corn Flakes · Grape Nuts

Fried Lake Fish
Pork Sausage
Grilled Ham · Bacon

Griddle Cakes with Maple Syrup

Omelette · Eggs to Order
French Fried Potatoes

Corn Bread · Toast
Marmalade or Jam · Honey

Tea · Coffee · Cocoa

COFFEE WILL BE SERVED FIRST,
IF DESIRED

Lunch

Chilled Apple Juice
Green Onions · Pickled New Beats

Chicken Noodle Soup · Consomme Clear

Fried Lake Superior Trout, Maitre d'Hotel

Combination Salad
Sliced Tomatoes · Sliced Cucumbers
Mayonnaise or French Dressing

Fricassee of Veal with Green Peas
Fried Sugar Cured Ham, Apple Jelly
Grilled Loin Steak, Mushroom Sauce

Assorted Cold Cuts
Potato Salad

Boiled or French Fried Potatoes

Strawberry Sponge Pudding, Fruit Sauce
Cream Coconut Pie · Ice Cream
Sliced Pineapple · Scotch Shortbread
Stilton Cheese, Wine Cured · Imperial Cream Cheese

Tea · Coffee · Milk

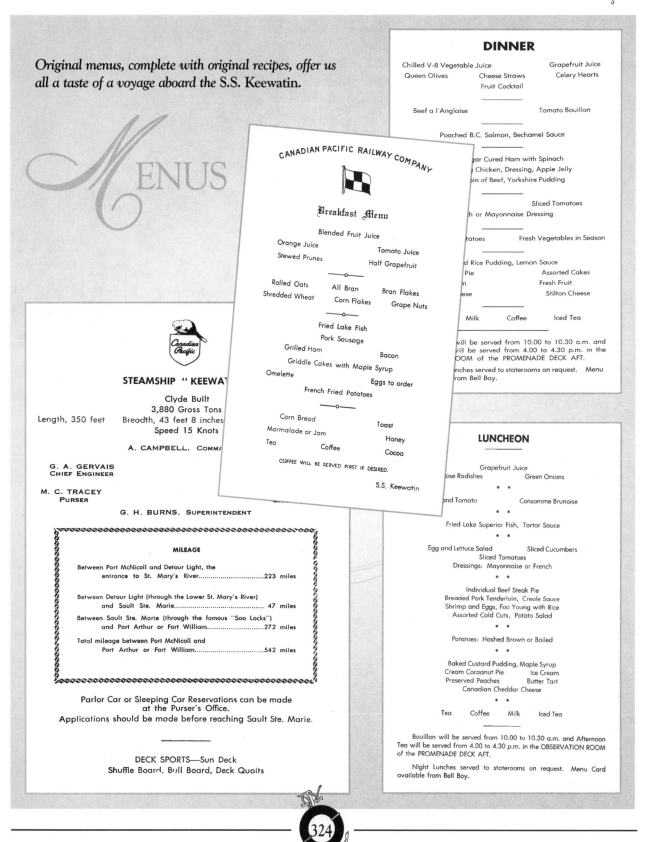

Original menus, complete with original recipes, offer us all a taste of a voyage aboard the S.S. Keewatin.

MENUS

DINNER

Chilled V-8 Vegetable Juice	Grapefruit Juice
Queen Olives Cheese Straws	Celery Hearts
Fruit Cocktail	

Beef a l'Anglaise   Tomato Bouillon

Poached B.C. Salmon, Bechamel Sauce

...gar Cured Ham with Spinach
... Chicken, Dressing, Apple Jelly
...in of Beef, Yorkshire Pudding

     Sliced Tomatoes
...h or Mayonnaise Dressing

...tatoes   Fresh Vegetables in Season

...d Rice Pudding, Lemon Sauce
... Pie   Assorted Cakes
...m   Fresh Fruit
...ese   Stilton Cheese

Milk   Coffee   Iced Tea

...will be served from 10.00 to 10.30 a.m. and
...ill be served from 4.00 to 4.30 p.m. in the
...OOM of the PROMENADE DECK AFT.

...nches served to staterooms on request. Menu
...rom Bell Boy.

CANADIAN PACIFIC RAILWAY COMPANY

𝔅reakfast 𝔐enu

Blended Fruit Juice

Orange Juice
Stewed Prunes   Tomato Juice
Half Grapefruit

Rolled Oats   All Bran
Shredded Wheat   Bran Flakes
Corn Flakes   Grape Nuts

Fried Lake Fish
Pork Sausage
Grilled Ham   Bacon
Griddle Cakes with Maple Syrup
Omelette   Eggs to order
French Fried Potatoes

Corn Bread   Toast
Marmalade or Jam
Tea   Coffee   Honey
Cocoa

COFFEE WILL BE SERVED FIRST IF DESIRED.

S.S. Keewatin

STEAMSHIP "KEEWAT...

Clyde Built
3,880 Gross Tons
Length, 350 feet   Breadth, 43 feet 8 inches
Speed 15 Knots

A. CAMPBELL, COMMA...

G. A. GERVAIS
CHIEF ENGINEER

M. C. TRACEY
PURSER

G. H. BURNS, SUPERINTENDENT

MILEAGE

Between Port McNicoll and Detour Light, the
entrance to St. Mary's River.................223 miles

Between Detour Light (through the Lower St. Mary's River)
and Sault Ste. Marie............................ 47 miles

Between Sault Ste. Marie (through the famous "Soo Locks")
and Port Arthur or Fort William.....................272 miles

Total mileage between Port McNicoll and
Port Arthur or Fort William.................542 miles

Parlor Car or Sleeping Car Reservations can be made
at the Purser's Office.
Applications should be made before reaching Sault Ste. Marie.

DECK SPORTS—Sun Deck
Shuffle Board, Bull Board, Deck Quoits

LUNCHEON

Grapefruit Juice	
...ose Radishes	Green Onions
...and Tomato	Consomme Brunoise

Fried Lake Superior Fish, Tartar Sauce

* *

Egg and Lettuce Salad   Sliced Cucumbers
Sliced Tomatoes
Dressings: Mayonnaise or French

* *

Individual Beef Steak Pie
Breaded Pork Tenderloin, Creole Sauce
Shrimp and Eggs, Foo Young with Rice
Assorted Cold Cuts, Potato Salad

* *

Potatoes: Hashed Brown or Boiled

* *

Baked Custard Pudding, Maple Syrup
Cream Cocoanut Pie   Ice Cream
Preserved Peaches   Butter Tart
Canadian Cheddar Cheese

* *

Tea   Coffee   Milk   Iced Tea

Bouillon will be served from 10.00 to 10.30 a.m. and Afternoon
Tea will be served from 4.00 to 4.30 p.m. in the OBSERVATION ROOM
of the PROMENADE DECK AFT.

Night Lunches served to staterooms on request. Menu Card
available from Bell Boy.

menu with all of the pastry and breads freshly prepared aboard ship. Luncheon, an informal gathering, always included fresh fish, delicious soups and salads. Dinner was more formal with special meat or fish entrees and beautifully prepared desserts.

Cooks on both the S.S. *Keewatin* and the S.S. *Assiniboia* were Canadian citizens but usually of Chinese ancestry. The Canadian Pacific Railway had brought in Chinese laborers to help construct the railbed and discovered the Chinese were also excellent cooks. It took special patience to prepare as many as one thousand meals a day for the passengers and crew, especially as the boats rolled and pitched. To add to the challenge, cooking was done on an 11-1/2-foot cast iron coal-burning stove, making it necessary for the cooks to run their hands about an inch over the surface to find the right cooking temperature.

Fresh flowers on the night stand and crisp white bed linens added comfortable elegance to the Deluxe Suites aboard the *S.S. Keewatin*.

Dinner

Chilled V-8 Vegetable Juice · Grapefruit Juice
Queen Olives · Cheese Straws · Celery Hearts
Fruit Cocktail

Beef a l'Anglaise · Tomato Bouillon
Poached B.C. Salmon with Bechamel Sauce
Boiled Sugar Cured Ham with Spinach
Roast Young Chicken with Dressing and Apple Jelly
Roast Sirloin of Beef with Yorkshire Pudding

Chef's Salad · Sliced Tomatoes
French or Mayonnaise Dressing

Boiled or Mashed Potatoes
Fresh Vegetables in Season

Baked Rice Pudding with Lemon Sauce
Walnut Cream Pie
Assorted Cakes
Ice Cream · Fresh Fruit
Canadian Cheese · Stilton Cheese

Tea · Milk · Coffee · Iced Tea

Night Snacks served to staterooms on request.
Menu Cards available from Bell Boy.

Canadian Pacific

NIGHT SNACK MENU

Sandwiches:

Cold Ham	- - - - - -	40c
Cold Turkey	- - - - -	40c
Cold Beef	- - - - - -	40c
Tomato	- - - - - - -	30c
Cheese	- - - - - - -	30c

Includes

Coffee, Tea or Milk

GREAT LAKES STEAMERS

The 86 crewmembers dined in the Crew's Mess, just off of the galley. They ate in shifts of eighteen and were served by their own waiter. This being a favorite gathering area of the crew, there were usually card games in the Crew's Mess each evening. Being next to the galley made late night snacking not only delicious, but also convenient.

As the decades quickly passed in carefree luxury aboard the *S.S. Keewatin*, so did the feasibility of keeping the beloved coal burning ship in operation. Her final voyage in November of 1965 brought an abrupt end to elegant passenger steamship travel in the region, and left the *"KEE"* with an uncertain future.

Rescuing the *S.S. Keewatin* from the scrap pile had an unlikely beginning in a 1966 Christmas gift from Diane Peterson to her husband, Roland. The gift was a book entitled *"Farewell To Steam,"* by David Plowden. The book featured a photo essay on the retired Canadian Pacific Railway Steamships that impressed the Petersons and sparked on ongoing effort to preserve the bygone era of elegant passenger steamships that sailed the Great Lakes. They arranged to have the *Keewatin* towed to southwestern Michigan (a feat in itself!) and immediately began their preservation, restoration and research. Today, the *S.S. Keewatin* rests gracefully in the Douglas-Saugatuck area of Southwestern Michigan. Her beauty and history have been carefully preserved with original furnishings and memories of past crewmembers, bringing to life the lazy days of sailing the inland seas.

The *S.S. Keewatin* sailed under the command of eleven different Masters during her 57 years on the Greak Lakes, each leaving his mark on the grand passenger vessel.

James Gillies	1907	Joseph Bishop	1941-1946
E.B. Anderson	1907	Reginald Walter Jarman	1947-1951
Alexander Brown	1908	Robert Mitchell	1951-1953
Malcolm McPhee	1909-1929	Ernest H. Ridd	1954-1956
Francis J. Davis	1930-1938	Alexander Campbell	1957-1965
John Parker Pearson	1939-1941		

A full Dining Saloon shows attentive waiters standing unobtrusively behind their guests, ready to accommodate requests.

The 11-1/2-foot cast iron, coal-burning stove in the galley offered plenty of space for the large kettles used on board.

The *S.S. Keewatin* at the Port McNicoll dock.

OMELETTE

4	eggs
1 Tbsp.	light cream
1 tsp.	butter
1 tsp.	vegetable oil
	Salt, to taste
	Pepper, to taste

Beat together eggs and light cream until light and fluffy. Add salt and pepper to taste; set mixture aside. Heat butter and vegetable oil together in omelet pan over HIGH heat, then remove from heat. Pour egg mixture into pan and return to heat. When eggs begin to set, lift edges with spatula so that uncooked egg will run to the bottom of the pan. Shake pan occasionally to prevent sticking. When egg mixture is completely set, roll omelette onto warm plate and serve at once.

Yield: 2 Servings

STEWED PRUNES

"Canadian Strawberries" According to the Crew

Packaged prunes do not need soaking. Follow directions on the package.

Cover bulk prunes with hot water. Use 2 cups water to 1/2 pound prunes. Let stand 2 hours and cook slowly in same water until prunes are plump and tender.

POACHED SALMON

1	whole salmon *or* 1 (4 to 6 lb.) center cut of fish
2 to 3 qts.	salted water
3 to 4	peppercorns
1	bay leaf
	Few slices of lemon
	Lemon, for garnish
	Parsley, for garnish

Wash and clean salmon or center cut of fish. Wrap fish securely in a piece of cheesecloth cut long enough to help remove it from broth when cooked. Bring salted water to boil (the amount of water you use depends on the amount of fish.) Add peppercorns, bay leaf and a few slices of lemon. Add fish to boiling water and boil approximately 15 minutes. Reduce heat and let simmer until cooked. Cook approximately 6 to 8 minutes per pound. Do not overcook. The fish should flake easily when fully cooked. When done, lift fish from broth and remove cheesecloth. Place on hot serving platter and skin very carefully. Garnish with lemon and parsley.

BÉ CHA MEL SAUCE (White Sauce)

Bé cha mel (ba´shä mel´) steward of Louis XIV, a white sauce made of cream, butter, flour, etc.

2 Tbsp.	butter
2 Tbsp.	flour
1 c.	milk
	Salt
	White pepper
	Nutmeg, (optional)

Melt butter in saucepan. Stir in flour until smooth and cook over low heat a few minutes; be sure not to brown. Stir in milk and continue cooking over low heat, stirring constantly until sauce bubbles. Cook very gently several minutes until sauce has thickened. Season with salt, pepper and a pinch of nutmeg.

Yield: 1 Cup

ROAST BEEF SIRLOIN CUT

1	Sirloin cut roast
	Salt and pepper, to taste

Place roast, fat side up, on rack in shallow baking pan. Do not cover. Preheat oven to 325 degrees and roast approximately 18 to 35 minutes per pound for medium to well done. Use a meat thermometer to register 140 degrees for rare, 160 degrees for medium and 180 degrees for well done. Make a slice in center of meat; when done the dial will register the temperature. Season with salt and pepper to taste after roasting. Remove from pan and place on warm platter; let stand 10 to 15 minutes. Carve to serve.

YORKSHIRE PUDDING

2	eggs
1/2 tsp.	salt
1 c.	all-purpose flour
1 c.	milk
2 Tbsp.	roast beef drippings

In blender combine eggs, salt, flour and milk; blend at high speed 2 to 3 seconds. Turn off blender, scrape down sides and blend again 40 seconds. Refrigerate 1 hour.

Preheat oven to 400 degrees. Heat beef drippings in 10x15x2-1/2-inch roasting pan over moderate heat until drippings splutter. Briefly beat batter again and pour into pan. Bake in middle of oven 15 minutes. Reduce temperature to 375 degrees and bake an additional 15 minutes, until pudding has risen over top of pan and is crisp and brown. Divide pudding into portions with sharp knife. Serve immediately.

SOFT AND CREAMY RICE PUDDING

4 c.	milk
2/3 c.	sugar
1/4 c.	rice, uncooked (not quick cooking)
1/2 tsp.	salt
1 tsp.	vanilla *or* 1 dash nutmeg *or* grated rind of 1/2 lemon
1/2 c.	raisins

Combine all ingredients except raisins in casserole dish. Bake uncovered at 300 degrees 3 hours. Stir 3 times with a fork during the first hour of baking to prevent rice from settling. After first hour stir in raisins.

Note: For a firmer pudding stir in 1 or 2 well-beaten eggs 30 minutes before pudding is done.

Yield: 6 Servings

LEMON SAUCE

1/2 c.	sugar
1 Tbsp.	corn starch
1 c.	boiling water
2 Tbsp.	butter
1-1/2 Tbsp.	lemon juice
1 dash	nutmeg
	Few grains of salt

Mix sugar and corn starch together in small saucepan. Add boiling water, stirring constantly. Boil 5 minutes. Remove from heat and stir in butter, lemon juice, nutmeg and salt.

Yield: Approximately 1 Cup

GINGERSNAPS

3/4 c.	shortening
1 c.	brown sugar
1/4 c.	molasses
1	egg
2-1/4 c.	all-purpose flour, sifted
2 tsp.	baking soda
1/2 tsp.	salt
1 tsp.	ground ginger
1 tsp.	ground cinnamon
1/2 tsp.	ground cloves

Preheat oven to 375 degrees. Cream together shortening, brown sugar, molasses and egg until fluffy. Sift together dry ingredients and stir into molasses mixture. Form dough into small balls. Roll balls in sugar and place 2-inches apart on greased cookie sheet. Bake at 375 degrees approximately 12 minutes.

Yield: 5 Dozen

SCOTCH SHORTBREAD

1 c.	butter
1/2 c.	sugar
2-1/2 c.	all-purpose flour, sifted

Preheat oven to 300 degrees. Cream butter and sugar together until light and fluffy. Stir flour into butter mixture. Chill several hours. Roll dough 1/4 to 1/2-inch thick on floured surface. Cut with 1-3/4-inch cookie cutter or cut into 2-1/2-inch strips. Bake on ungreased cookie sheet at 300 degrees approximately 30 minutes. Cool slightly and remove from cookie sheet.

Yield: Approximately 3 Dozen

CREAM COCONUT PIE

3/4 c.	corn starch
1 Tbsp.	flour
1/2 c.	half & half
3	eggs
3	egg yolks
3/4 c.	sugar
2-1/2 c.	half & half
2 tsp.	vanilla
1 c.	flaked coconut
1	(9-inch) pie shell, baked
1 c.	whipping cream
2 Tbsp.	powdered sugar
1/2 c.	flaked coconut

Combine corn starch with flour and 1/2 cup half & half; stir until corn starch and flour dissolve. In separate bowl beat eggs, egg yolks and sugar together until light and fluffy. Heat 2-1/2 cups half & half to boiling. Add corn starch mixture to hot half & half and gradually pour over egg mixture, beating constantly. Cook over medium heat, stirring constantly, until thick. Remove from heat. Add vanilla and 1 cup coconut. Cool filling completely. When filling is cold, spoon into baked pie shell.

Whip 1 cup whipping cream until stiff; add powdered sugar. Spread sweetened whipping cream over filling. Sprinkle 1/2 cup coconut over top. Refrigerate overnight.

9-INCH PIE SHELL

1 c.	all-purpose flour
1/4 tsp.	salt
1/2 tsp.	sugar
1/4 c.	vegetable shortening
2 Tbsp.	lard
3 Tbsp.	ice water

Preheat oven to 425 degrees. Lightly oil 9-inch pie pan. Combine flour, salt and sugar; mix well. Cut in shortening and lard with pastry blender until mixture is mealy. Stir ice water into flour mixture and mix well. Wrap dough in waxed paper and refrigerate 30 minutes.

On lightly floured board, roll out dough to 1/8-inch thickness. Press dough firmly into prepared 9-inch pan. Prick dough well with a fork. Bake at 425 degrees 12 to 15 minutes or until golden brown. Cool pie shell completely before filling.

Yield: 1 (9-Inch) Pie Shell

TEA TIME

To make a proper cup of tea, add a little boiling water to the teapot to warm it. Pour it out. Add a good quality tea to pot, one teaspoon for each cup to be served and one teaspoon for the pot. Bring water in kettle to rapid boil and add to pot; let tea steep for five minutes before serving. Stir before pouring.

English-style tea is served with milk and sugar.

Today, the majestic 350-foot S.S. *Keewatin* is permanently docked at Harbour Village in Douglas, Michigan where she proudly serves as a museum in all of her original grandeur. Visitors are transported back in time as they view first-class passenger staterooms, crew quarters, plant filled Flower Well Lounge with its Italian hand-etched and painted skylight windows, forward Lady's Drawing Room with Victorian writing desk, 120 seat walnut-lined Edwardian Dining Saloon, galley with its 11-1/2-foot cast iron coal stove and the hand-carved oak panels of the original Men's Lounge. The guided tour also includes the Captain's Suite, which is preserved as it was left by the *Keewatin's* last master, and a visit to the Wheel House, which contains the main wheel, and all of the navigational equipment in use when the boat was retired in 1965.

S.S. *KEEWATIN* MARITIME MUSEUM
Docked at Harbour Village
Blue Star Highway and Union Street
P.O. Box 638, Douglas, Michigan 49406
In Season: (616) 857-2464   Off Season: (616) 857-2107

Open 7 Days a Week – Memorial Day Weekend Through Labor Day
10:00 a.m. to 4:30 a.m.
Guided Tours Daily – First Tour Begins at 10:30 a.m.

Michigan State Car Ferries

Straits of Mackinac, City of Cheboygan, City of Munising, City of Petoskey, and Vacationland

(The five ferries in service when operations ceased in 1957)

ARIEL

The Michigan State Car Ferry Service began with the Ariel, a vessel built in 1881 for the Wakerville Ferry Line at Detroit. It was purchased for use transporting cars across the Straits of Mackinac in 1923.
In her first year of service, with just a 20-car capacity, the Ariel transported 10,351 vehicles across the Straits.
The Ariel was sold a year later, proving unsuitable for the tumultuous Straits. She was not among the five ferries in operation when service ceased in 1957.

The opening of the majestic Mackinac Bridge on November 1, 1957, brought an abrupt end to a colorful era and way of life in the history of northern Michigan. Since 1923 the *Michigan State Car Ferries* had served as a floating highway covering the over six miles of water that lay between Mackinaw City in Michigan's lower peninsula and St. Ignace in the state's upper peninsula. For 35 years this fleet of shiny white car ferries provided dependable year-round passage across the Straits of Mackinac, carrying over 12 million vehicles in its lifetime. The cost to cross on a ferry was $1.25 for a car and driver; each additional passenger in the car was charged 25 cents. The fleet was upgraded and enlarged several times over the years to keep up with the ever-growing traffic, but eventually progress demanded a quicker, more efficient way to get vehicles across the Straits.

STRAITS OF MACKINAC
Year Acquired: 1928 • **Vehicle Capacity:** 56

During the peak months of July and August, and especially during hunting season in the fall, cars would sometimes be lined up over 16 miles, back to Cheboygan, awaiting passage on one of the ferries. Over the years that the ferries operated, more than 30 million passengers had enjoyed the fresh crisp air of the Straits of Mackinac from their decks.

When the *Michigan State Car Ferries* ceased operation more than 400 employees said good-bye to the merchant seaman way of life, the co-workers they considered family and the ships they had grown to love. As Michigan launched a year-long celebration to commemorate the opening of the Straits of Mackinac Bridge, which was a wonderful achievement and the longest bridge of its kind in the world when it was built, the 400 displaced seamen began relocating to other state jobs throughout the region.

The crews responsible for the daily safe and timely operation of the *Michigan State Car Ferries* put in long hard hours. They depended on their fellow crewmembers for their own well being, as well as that of the passengers. This closeness and their shared lifestyle developed a bond and loyalty between these merchant seamen, as it does in the crews of today's Great Lakes vessels. Frank Kelley, Michigan's beloved Attorney General from 1961 until his retirement from office in 1999, worked on the ferries during the late 1930s and early 1940s while earning his money for college. His fond, and sometimes humorously honest, memories of the era bring alive the daily life these dedicated seamen shared. The variety and amount of food served to the crews of the ferries also left a lasting impression on the teenaged Frank Kelley.

CITY OF CHEBOYGAN
Year Acquired: 1937 • **Vehicle Capacity:** 85

He recalls:

"Working on the *Michigan State Car Ferries* was a great job for college students. They needed extra crew for July and August; the regular crew could handle the rest of the year, except for hunting season. All you needed were seaman's papers, which required being 18 years of age.

I was 14 years old, 5'8" tall and weighed a mere 139 pounds when I fibbed about my age and acquired my papers. My dad said it was all right to fib since I was trying to get ahead in life and become a man. My father was a friend of the head of the Department of Transportation and made an application for me to work on the boats. It seems a connection or being a local high school football player helped in landing a job on the ferries.
For my first year, 1939, I was assigned to work on the dock at Mackinaw City tying up boats. As a dock man you got $97 a month and had to pay rent out of that. Seamen got the same pay, but also got room and board on the boat. I was disappointed about not being assigned to one of the boats, but I tried to make up the difference by mastering the art of tying up the boats quickly so I could get to the mess hall. I would give the cooks cigarettes and they would give me food. I was called the "seagull" because every time the boat would dock, I would go to the mess hall to scavenge food. At the age of 14, I easily consumed 9,000 calories a day.

The real fun started in 1940 when I was assigned to the *City of Cheboygan*. My father, I think, had put in a specification 'please put my son on a boat.' I worked all summer until Labor Day. If you were on a morning ship

CITY OF MUNISING
Year Acquired: 1938 • **Vehicle Capacity:** 105

you got up at 4:30 am and were on deck with your boots on shortly thereafter. We had to squeegee the whole deck with warm water, soap powder and lye. Six of us would do the entire deck. Once in a while, when we were at the dock, we would take four hours off and do the side of the ship, the block and tackle.

It took a good 40 minutes for our ship to cross the Straits if we were lucky, depending upon the weather and the load. Once we got it tied up, we could unload in 9 minutes, reload in 14 to 15 minutes and be off again. So in an hour and ten minutes you could come in and be out again. We had to load the ship with a certain number of cars and we had to be quick, because long lines made unhappy citizens.

When the boats were in dock and the men could leave, either I or one of the college students would act as designated driver and make sure 'Old Louis' made it back to the ship. Many a night I would scrounge the bars in St. Ignace, Mackinaw City or Cheboygan looking for shipmates, because that was one thing they didn't tolerate. If you missed a boat because you had been drinking, you were fired.

I must say, in order to be honest, we did act wild once in a while. We'd get off the ship on payday and some of the older seamen would get roaring drunk. I was in the unique position of weighing only 149 pounds. One night we were in the Dixie Tavern, now a McDonald's Hamburger Store, in Mackinaw City and a fight started. The local boys had an ongoing jealousy against the seamen, thinking they were stealing all their girls. My buddies

CITY OF PETOSKEY
Year Acquired: 1940 • **Vehicle Capacity:** 105

picked me up and sat me atop a piano, telling me not to hit anyone until they sent them over to me. One big husky guy would hit someone in my direction and then I would take a punch at him. I'm ashamed to even talk about it, but it was part of being a merchant seaman…if your buddies got in a fight you had to fight too. One for all and all for one!

When I was 15 years old I got my first automobile, a six year old Ford that cost $90. Imagine that! My dad sent the car up for me and it made me very popular with the captain. He would say, 'Frank, put your car on the last ship.' My job was to take the captain to town to buy cigarettes, razor blades and other things he needed. As a matter of fact, I must confess since the Statute of Limitations has run, I had girlfriends in towns on both sides of the Straits and kept both relationships going. It was nothing serious, I was 15 and it was puppy love, but I thought it was great fun!

I often look back on those days before the war and the unsophisticated equipment we had on the ships. We didn't have radar, so the deckhand and watchman had to do the technical work. At night, I would be lookout for the *City of Cheboygan*. I had to watch and hear everything. I would stand with my nose over the bow listening and watching. When the weather was bad the captain would take charge. He was a good captain,

VACATIONLAND
Year Acquired: 1952 • **Vehicle Capacity:** 150

Captain Coleman. I would be at the bow and he would be behind me about thirty feet in the cabin with the glass open. That's how we worked the fog.

One night in July in St. Ignace, Captain Coleman had me up in the bow. I could only see about 12-inches in front of me it seemed. He told me, 'I'm going to go as slow as I can go and if you see anything just say: stop.' He told me not to waste words. There would be no time. I thought to myself, 'I wonder if he knows I'm only 15!' I watched and listened. Finally I saw a POST?? in front of me. I said 'Stop.' The captain stopped immediately, pulled the ship around and we made a perfect landing. The next time I took him to town he bought me a triple dip ice cream cone.

When you are one of 30 or 40 people on a ship, you develop a feeling of closeness with those people more than any other place, other than the bosom of your own family. If you're a decent person, you can't help feeling that way. You become very close. Later when I became a lawyer, I remembered that closeness, and I represented seamen for nothing. They knew I understood their habits and their problems. I understood that they got drunk and got into fights. I would put them in my car and take them back to their captain who would tell them if they ever did it again they would be gone. I later received my just desserts for my service to seamen when the *Bradley* went down. It was a ship out of Rogers City. I represented several widows in their cases. I was to make the biggest fee of my life. But, before the cases were done I became Attorney General. I didn't want to be accused of conflict so I gave the cases to my partner, John Mack. With the fee he got from those cases he bought himself a cottage with a pool!

The passengers on the *Michigan State Car Ferries* never stayed in their cars, unless they were sick. The passengers would come up on deck and walk around. They were jovial and had a sense of expectancy. I think moving away from land and being on the water gives a feeling of emancipation. I think that's why cruise ships are so popular now. Going across the Straits on a ferry was quite an experience; you had to have an hour of leisure in your trip. Traversing the Straits in your own car is just not the same. There is a tranquil aspect and it gives a person a sense of freedom to be on the water. It seems for people now, cars are their own little ships. At the turn of the century people had to rely on other forms of transportation, but now you can get into your own car and go wherever you like. It is your independence and freedom. Anyone who has had an experience on ships, like me, is a very lucky human being. The people I knew on the ships took me in, and they were friends for the rest of my life."

Frank Kelley also has very fond memories of the food on the *Michigan State Car Ferries…*

"We had wonderful, wonderful meals and I had an appetite that wouldn't quit. Taxpayers knew we didn't make much money, but probably would have rebelled if they knew how good we were fed. We were eating better than the taxpayers! I remember one cook who prepared several pies on Sundays. Every Sunday he prepared a pear pie as a special treat for me. Steak was a common item on the menu. Homemade chicken with dumplings and several pies was typical Sunday fare."

Former Michigan State Attorney General, Frank J. Kelley, worked on the ferries during the late 1930s and early 1940s, earning his money for college.

PEAR PIE

1	unbaked pie crust, for double crust pie
3 Tbsp.	flour
1 tsp.	apple pie spice
1/4 tsp.	ground cinnamon
1/4 tsp.	salt
4	pears, peeled, sliced
6 Tbsp.	brown sugar
1-1/2 tsp.	vanilla
1 Tbsp.	butter
1 Tbsp.	milk
	Brown sugar

Combine flour, apple pie spice, cinnamon and salt. Toss pear slices in flour mixture and place in unbaked pie crust. Combine vanilla, butter and 6 tablespoons brown sugar; spread over pear slices. Cover with top crust and seal edges. Brush milk and a little brown sugar over top crust. Bake at 425 degrees 15 minutes. Reduce oven temperature to 350 degrees and bake an additional 25 to 30 minutes, until crust is browned.

Automobiles are systematically loaded onto the *City of Petoskey* for the 45-minute trip across the Straits (left).

Visitors wait in line for their turn to board a ferry. During peak months the line of cars could stretch over 16 miles (bottom).

(Ferry Schedules courtesy of Charles H. Truscott Collection).

1950 MICHIGAN STATE FERRY SCHEDULES 1951

SPRING SCHEDULE
April 16 through May 31

Leave Mackinaw City		Leave St. Ignace	
6:00 a.m.	4:30 p.m.	6:00 a.m.	4:30 p.m.
7:30 a.m.	6:00 p.m.	7:30 a.m.	6:00 p.m.
9:00 a.m.	7:30 p.m.	9:00 a.m.	7:30 p.m.
10:30 a.m.	9:00 p.m.	10:30 a.m.	9:00 p.m.
12:00 noon	10:30 p.m.	12:00 noon	10:30 p.m.
1:30 p.m.	1:30 a.m.	1:30 p.m.	12 midnight
3:00 p.m.	4:30 a.m.	3:00 p.m.	3:00 a.m.

(Start of Spring Schedule depends on ice conditions in the Straits of Mackinac.)

SUMMER SCHEDULE
June 1 through Sept. 18

Leave Mackinaw City		Leave St. Ignace	
6:30 a.m.	4:30 p.m.	6:00 a.m.	4:00 p.m.
7:30 a.m.	5:30 p.m.	7:00 a.m.	5:00 p.m.
8:30 a.m.	6:30 p.m.	8:00 a.m.	6:00 p.m.
9:30 a.m.	7:30 p.m.	9:00 a.m.	7:00 p.m.
10:30 a.m.	8:30 p.m.	10:00 a.m.	8:00 p.m.
11:30 a.m.	9:30 p.m.	11:00 a.m.	9:00 p.m.
12:30 p.m.	10:30 p.m.	12:00 noon	10:00 p.m.
1:30 p.m.	11:30 p.m.	1:00 p.m.	11:00 p.m.
2:30 p.m.	1:30 a.m.	2:00 p.m.	12 midnight
3:30 p.m.	4:30 a.m.	3:00 p.m.	3:00 a.m.

FALL SCHEDULE
Sept. 19 through Nov. 6

Leave Mackinaw City		Leave St. Ignace	
6:00 a.m.	4:30 p.m.	6:00 a.m.	4:30 p.m.
7:30 a.m.	6:00 p.m.	7:30 a.m.	6:00 p.m.
9:00 a.m.	7:30 p.m.	9:00 a.m.	7:30 p.m.
10:30 a.m.	9:00 p.m.	10:30 a.m.	9:00 p.m.
12:00 noon	10:30 p.m.	12:00 noon	10:30 p.m.
1:30 p.m.	1:30 a.m.	1:30 p.m.	12 midnight
3:00 p.m.	4:30 a.m.	3:00 p.m.	3:00 a.m.

HUNTING SEASON SCHEDULE

Effective November 7 through November 30 service night and day as often as required to accommodate hunter traffic.

EARLY WINTER SCHEDULE
Dec. 1 through Dec. 15

Leave Mackinaw City		Leave St. Ignace	
6:00 a.m.	3:00 p.m.	6:00 a.m.	3:00 p.m.
7:30 a.m.	4:30 p.m.	7:30 a.m.	4:30 p.m.
9:00 a.m.	6:00 p.m.	9:00 a.m.	6:00 p.m.
10:30 a.m.	7:30 p.m.	10:30 a.m.	7:30 p.m.
12:00 noon	9:00 p.m.	12:00 noon	9:00 p.m.
1:30 p.m.	10:30 p.m.	1:30 p.m.	10:30 p.m.

WINTER SCHEDULE
Dec. 16, 1950 through April 15, 1951

Leave Mackinaw City	Leave St. Ignace
7:30 a.m.	6:00 a.m.
10:30 a.m.	9:00 a.m.
1:30 p.m.	12:00 noon
4:30 p.m.	3:00 p.m.
7:30 p.m.	6:00 p.m.
10:30 p.m.	9:00 p.m.

For better service in peak traffic periods, such as summer holidays and deer season, the State Ferries will run off regular schedule, departing as fast as they can unload and reload, making possible departures as often as every 35 minutes.

ALL SCHEDULES EASTERN STANDARD TIME

RATES

PASSENGERS—Adults .... $.25
    Children under 6 free. Under 12 .... .10

PASSENGER AUTOMOBILES—(Based on wheelbase)
    Under 105 inches 1.00
    105 inches and under 115 inches 1.25
    115 inches and over 1.50

PASSENGER BUSSES—(Based on passenger capacity)
    16 passenger capacity and under 2.00
    Over 16 and including 24 passenger capacity .. 2.50
    Over 24 passenger capacity 3.00

TRUCKS—(Based on rated capacity)
    Under 2 tons 2.00
    2 tons and under 3 tons 2.50
    3 tons and over 3.00

TRAILERS—(Based on extreme overall added length) Truck and trailer must not exceed 48 ft. overall length
    Under 10 feet of added length 1.00
    10 feet and under 15 feet of added length 1.25
    15 feet and under 20 feet of added length 1.50
    20 feet and over, of added length—Base rate ..$1.50
    plus .05 for each additional foot or major fraction thereof
    over 20 feet. Horses and cows, $1.00; Wagons, $1.00;
    Motorcycles, $.50.

Passenger rates shall apply to all persons except vehicle drivers. No package freight other than that carried in or on vehicles will be handled. The Ferries are operated as a governmental function of the State Highway Department and, therefore, damage claims cannot be paid. Service complaints shall be reported immediately to superintendent or ship's captain. SCHEDULE SUBJECT TO CHANGE WITHOUT NOTICE. During the open navigation season passenger service by boat is available between Mackinaw City and Mackinac Island and between St. Ignace and Mackinac Island. These boats are owned and operated by independent companies.

The Michigan State Highway Department ferry fleet which operates the year 'round between St. Ignace and Mackinaw City forms a highway on water linking the Upper and Lower Peninsulas of Michigan.

As the traveler takes this restful, 50-minute trip across the Straits of Mackinac aboard comfortable steamers, a scene of rare beauty unfolds before him. The Straits area, the passing steamers and an excellent view of historic and beautiful Mackinac Island make the trip by state ferry one long to be remembered.

MICHIGAN STATE FERRY SCHEDULE
THROUGH APRIL 15, 1951

MICHIGAN
STATE HIGHWAY DEPARTMENT
CHARLES M. ZIEGLER
STATE HIGHWAY COMMISSION

Richard Therrian also has first-hand memories from his days working aboard the *Michigan State Car Ferries*. He worked as 2nd cook on the ferries from 1947 until they closed in 1957. He started on the ferry *Straits of Mackinac*, working the 6:00 pm to 2:00 am shift, seven days a week. It was a good job but did have a few drawbacks. Working seven days, spring through fall, left little time to spend with his wife Darlene and their four children. He was luckier than some though, as his home was in the area so his family was nearby. His schedule soon changed to a better shift and he went on to enjoy ten years on the ferries. After a decade in the galleys of the ships, he is very familiar with what the day-to-day operation was like. "You name it, we had it!" is his response when asked what was on the menu. "Steaks, roast beef, oyster stew, fresh hot breads and rolls, homemade cakes and pies, the whole shot…anything you can imagine. We were fed well!" Preparing the food on days when the water was rough could be a little tricky, but it was always hot and ready when his crewmates filed into the mess room.

With an average crew of 42 hungry seamen to be fed at least three times a day, every day in the galley was busy and every meal was complete. Organization and planning were very important. Menus were prepared weekly. The fresh meats, vegetables and other supplies were picked up weekly too, from their warehouse in St. Ignace. The porter on the afternoon shift would peel 20 to 25 pounds of potatoes for the next noon meal. On the rare occasion there were any potatoes left, they were fried with some onions for the afternoon meal. The 1st cook kept his eye on the costs to feed the large crew. He also did most of the baking, which helped keep costs down.

Richard had an opportunity to work on all of the ferries during the ten years he was with the operation. "The employees were a great bunch of people, all were enthusiastic and did a good job." He remembers one night when he was working on the *City of Petoskey*. "We were crossing to Mackinaw City in heavy fog when our ship blasted three short whistles, the signal for danger. My partner and I ran to the crew's mess to see what was going on. The freighter *Ireland* was headed right at us. Our captain immediately turned hard left and we escaped only rubbing the *Ireland* full length. It was a close call, but luckily for both ships there was no damage!"

As 2nd cook, Richard served the officers who dined in the Officer's Dining Room at a large table covered with white linen. The porter took care of the crew's mess room, which had two tables, colored tablecloths and stools. The crew's mess was always a favorite gathering spot for the seamen. The large galley on the *City of Munising* was Richard's favorite because of the layout of the galley itself, and the captain and crew on board. Cooking gear including large kettles, roasters, frying pans, a big French fryer and coffee pots were used constantly and always left clean and waiting for the next shift. When the water got rough the coffee pot was hung on a hook over the stove and rolling bars were put on the stove to hold pans in place. Nothing changed, not the menu or the time of a meal, you just went on with your work. The seamen were family and gathering for meals was the highlight of their long days. He was working on the *City of Munising* when the bridge opened and the ferry operation was shut down. "The ferry boat operation is something I was in love with, I enjoyed my job. I was sorry to see them go, but the bridge was the solution to the traffic problem."

Richard and his wife still live in the St. Ignace area. Darlene does most of the cooking at home, but does get a little help from "2nd Cook Richard" on the holidays. His home crew's favorite…turkey, dressing and gravy!

RICHARD'S FRIED CHICKEN

Chicken pieces
Soda crackers, ground
Eggs, as needed
Milk, as needed

*M*ix eggs and milk together well. Dip chicken pieces into milk mixture and then into cracker crumbs. Brown chicken pieces in frying pan. Place a cup cake pan upside down in a large roaster; add small layer of water. Lay browned chicken pieces on cup cake pan and bake in oven until done. Serve with mashed potatoes, vegetable and biscuits.

BREAD BUNS

1	yeast cake
1/3 c.	sugar
1 tsp.	salt
1 qt.	milk
3 big mixing spoons	shortening, melted
3	eggs
	Flour

*P*ut yeast in large mixing bowl; add salt and let stand until soft or liquid. Add sugar, milk, melted shortening and eggs. Add flour until dough in somewhat stiff. Let dough rise 1-1/2 to 2 hours. Punch dough down. Shape dough into buns, place on baking sheet and let rise approximately 20 minutes. Bake at 350 degrees until done.

BAKED BEANS

4 lbs.	Great Northern beans
1 tsp.	baking soda
14 oz.	ketchup
1 lb.	brown sugar
8 Tbsp.	molasses
1/2 tsp.	black pepper
2 tsp.	salt
1 lb.	bacon, raw, cut into pieces

Soak beans in water overnight. Parboil beans 20 minutes. Transfer kettle to sink and add baking soda; it will foam up and can boil over into sink. Rinse beans through a colander and put in roaster. Mix in ketchup, brown sugar, molasses, black pepper, salt and bacon pieces. Cover bean mixture with water; add water while baking as needed. Bake at 325 degrees until beans are soft.

RICE PUDDING

1-1/2 c.	sugar
10 c.	milk
4 Tbsp.	butter
3/4 c.	rice
3	whole eggs
1-1/2 tsp.	corn starch
1/2 tsp.	vanilla
1 pinch	cinnamon

In saucepan mix together sugar, milk and butter; bring to boil, stirring often. Add rice and simmer. In bowl beat eggs with corn starch and vanilla until smooth. While stirring, slowly pour a little of the hot mixture into egg mixture to temper the egg mixture and prevent curdling. Stir rice and milk mixture slowly. Add tempered egg mixture, stirring constantly until pudding thickens. Sprinkle with cinnamon.

CHOCOLATE CAKE

1-1/2 c.	shortening
3 c.	sugar
6	eggs
2 c.	milk
4 c.	flour
3 Tbsp.	cocoa
4 tsp.	baking soda
1/2 tsp.	salt

Mix shortening and sugar together well. Add eggs, 1 at a time, mixing well after each addition. Add milk, flour, cocoa, baking soda and salt; whip together well. Transfer to baking pan and bake at 350 degrees until done.

Yield: 1 Large Cake

WHITE CAKE

1-1/2 c.	shortening
3 c.	sugar
6	eggs
2 c.	milk
4 c.	flour
4 tsp.	baking powder
1/2 tsp.	salt

Mix shortening and sugar together well. Add eggs, 1 at a time, mixing well after each addition until thoroughly combined. Add milk, flour, baking powder and salt; mix again thoroughly. Transfer to baking pan and bake at 350 degrees until done.

Yield: 1 large Cake

Marble Cake Variation: Reserve some of the batter before transferring to baking pan. Add approximately 2 teaspoons chocolate or cocoa and 1/2 teaspoon baking soda to reserved batter. Drop chocolate batter by spoon onto white batter in baking pan, weaving it in. Bake at 350 degrees until done.

WHERE ARE THE FERRIES NOW?

When the *Michigan State Car Ferries* ceased operation in 1957 the five ships met various fates.

The *Straits of Mackinac* was sold to a group of crewmembers for $25,000. They used the ship to provide passenger service between Mackinaw City and Mackinac Island for over ten years, until 1968. It was later bought by Peterson Builders of Wisconsin and converted into a floating dormitory for Navy men sent to their area for training and shakedown cruises aboard other ships built by the company. It was later used as a storage barge.

The *City of Munising* and *City of Cheboygan* both served as floating warehouses for Edward H. Anderson, a major potato grower and dealer on Washington Island in Lake Michigan. They were later towed to Italy and sold for scrap.

The *City of Petoskey* was sold for scrap in 1961.

The 350-foot *Vacationland,* pride of the fleet, led a somewhat more glamorous life for the next three decades. It hauled truck trailers between Detroit and Cleveland for a few years and then carried vehicles and passengers across the Gulf of St. Lawrence. In 1967 it was bought by the Province of British Columbia, renamed the *Sunshine Coast Queen* and towed to the Pacific coast for ferry service there. Over $600,000 was spent altering the ship and increasing its capacity to 220 cars. There was talk of bringing the *Vacationland* back home for daily service on Lake Michigan by a private company, but unfortunately nothing ever came of it. In December of 1987, while enroute to a scrap yard in Shanghai, the *Vacationland* sank in the Pacific Ocean approximately 100 miles off the coast of Washington.

S.S. Milwaukee Clipper

Year Built:	1905, as the *S.S. Juniata* American Ship Building Company
Length:	361'
Beadm:	45'
Decks:	6
Rebuilt:	1941, as the *S.S. Milwaukee Clipper* Wisconsin and Michigan Steamship Company
Passengers:	900
Automobiles:	120, (225 automobiles during winter months)
Crew:	108

Captain Hoxie joins a guest in one of *Milwaukee Clipper's* dining areas.

*S*even years before the S.S. *Titanic* set sail on her fateful voyage, the Great Lakes welcomed first class travel to their waters aboard the *S.S. Juniata*. Launched in 1905, the 361-foot passenger and package freight steamer *Juniata* carried passengers in utter elegance from Buffalo, New York to Duluth, Minnesota, with stops along the way at Mackinac Island and other favorite ports. It was an eight or nine day voyage for the 350 passengers on board, during a glorious era of shipping on the Great Lakes. Finding the captain on deck, mingling with guests and pointing out the northern lights, was not an uncommon sight as the steamer steadily forged ahead towards the new frontier. A great oak staircase, highly varnished mahogany woodwork and stylish wicker furniture provided elegance and comfort, while music provided merriment on board. Below deck, *Juniata's* highly advanced 3,000 horsepower Quadruple Expansion steam engine, one of only seven such engines built for Great Lakes passenger service, provided the power as pioneers and vacationers enjoyed the adventure of traveling to a new land.

When our ancestors arrived at the east coast of the United States they traveled by rail to reach Buffalo, New York. From there, it was much easier to travel west across the Great Lakes than through the heavily forested regions of the midwest. The S.S. *Juniata* was one of three ships built at the time — sister ships S.S. *Tionesta* and S.S. *Octorara* — for Erie and Western Transportation, a division of Pennsylvania Railroad, to accommodate this travel and haul badly needed building materials west. On return trips she brought back raw materials needed to feed the booming industrial expansion. *Juniata* was designed by Naval Architect Frank Kirby and built at a cost of 500 thousand dollars. Historians help put that figure into perspective for us by explaining that a man mining three tons of coal a day (which very few men could do) earned $11 for his day of work.

The *Juniata* was elegant in design and appointments. Guests entered her dining room through beautiful beveled glass doors with highly polished brass fixtures. Inside the dining room plush carpet covered the floor and rich velvet curtains adorned the portholes. A barrel-vaulted ceiling formed a shrine over tables covered with white linen cloths and china, where passengers dined in complete comfort. It was an elegant setting for the unrivaled cuisine served aboard *Juniata*.

Almost half of the Steward's Department aboard the *Milwaukee Clipper*, including chefs, cafeteria staff and servers, devoted their time to serving homemade meals to 900 passengers on each sailing.

In 1916 new anti-trust laws deemed it inappropriate for railroad companies to own shipping lines, fearing it gave one entity too much control over transportation. As a result, Pennsylvania Railroad sold Erie and Western, better known as Anchor Lines, to Great Lakes Transit Corporation. Otherwise unaffected by the controversy, the *Juniata* and her sister ships continued to thrive for another two decades, hauling passengers and freight for their new owners. *Juniata* went on to carry millions of passengers in luxury, becoming the pride of her fleet.

Well trained in passenger service, a happy group of servers (left) show off their soda fountain skills and crisply pressed uniforms at the Soda Bowl on the second deck.

Guests aboard the *Milwaukee Clipper* enjoyed a variety of meals prepared by top-notch chefs.

By the mid-1930s many modern innovations of the twentieth century were already being enjoyed by Americans. Automobiles were more affordable and the cost of gasoline was reasonable. Passenger ships on the Great Lakes began to fall on hard times. Complicating matters, a series of catastrophic shipboard fires in the 1920s and 1930s, most famously the destruction of the *S.S. Morro Castle* off the shores of New Jersey where 134 lives were lost, prompted the U.S. Coast Guard to take action. All passenger ships with wooden superstructures were required to be equipped with automatic sprinkler systems, fireproof doors and sails in lifeboats, among other things. Because of the fact that passenger service on the Great Lakes had taken a downturn, the company felt reconditioning the ship to conform to the new requirements was an invitation to economic disaster. The *S.S. Juniata* was retired in 1937, taking with her three decades of legendary Great Lakes voyages.

Fortunately, the majestic steamer did not sit idle long. In 1940 she was purchased by Max and Mark McKee of the Wisconsin and Michigan Steamship Company. The McKee brothers retained the services of honored Naval Architect George Sharpe (famous for his design of the nuclear ship *Savannah*) and renovations on *Juniata* began immediately. Sharpe's design called for the most extensive reconstruction attempted on a ship, and his results were magnificent. At the Manitowoc Shipbuilding Company in Wisconsin her wooden superstructure was removed and replaced with a new, all steel, streamlined, art deco superstructure; the first design of its type in the world. Warren McArthur, once a student and later a co-worker of Frank Lloyd Wright, designed the art deco furniture placed on board during the renovation. State-of-the-art Pullman Berths, complete with bedding from Simmons Bedding Company, were installed, providing the best in passenger comfort and privacy.

Completely fireproof, the new ship featured air-conditioned staterooms, a children's playroom, movie theatre and live entertainment complete with dance floor. Four short years after facing an uncertain future at retirement, she was back on the lakes in full glory.

Re-named the S.S. *Milwaukee Clipper*, the newly remodeled ship made her maiden voyage in June of 1941. For the next three decades her ports-of-call were Milwaukee, Chicago and Muskegon. Round trip fare for the six-hour trip each way incredibly cost only $3.33 per person. An extra $8.00 was charged to bring an automobile. It is estimated that half of the passengers on board used the voyage as part of their cross-country journey; the other half was on board simply for enjoyment. The "Queen of the Lakes" as she was officially voted by the Michigan Legislature and affectionately known by the public, was a favorite means of travel on Lake Michigan, ferrying both passengers and automobiles to their destinations. Nine hundred passengers and 120 automobiles sailed across Lake Michigan on her graceful shoulders twice a day. Their trips were elegant, carefree, and more than once featured Liberace at the piano in the Marine Lounge. During the winter months she was used to ferry new automobiles from Muskegon to Milwaukee, transporting 225 vehicles per trip. Finally, in 1970, once again because of economics and the need for extensive repairs, her work on the lakes was done and she was laid up for the last time.

The *Milwaukee Clipper* found two temporary homes over the next few years as she made her long voyage back to her original port of Muskegon. James Gillon purchased the steamer in 1977 and had her towed to Sturgeon Bay, Wisconsin for repairs. Unable to gain Coast Guard Certification for a planned excursion service, in 1980 he moved her to Navy Pier in Chicago. Her art deco interior was restored to perfection before opening as a floating maritime museum and banquet center in Chicago. In 1983 the S.S. *Milwaukee Clipper* was designated a National Historic Landmark "worthy of the most careful preservation." In 1990 she sailed on to the Hammond, Indiana Marina where she served as a centerpiece for that community until her dock space was needed for a gaming boat in 1996.

Today the proud S.S. *Milwaukee Clipper* sits along Muskegon's waterfront where hundreds of dedicated volunteers have painstakingly restored the "Queen of the Lakes" to her original grandeur. Every detail has been addressed. Original art deco furniture, designed by Warren McArthur in the early 1940s, survived the *Clipper's* many moves and are just a few of the many original appointments restored on board. She will soon be open to the public for tours, banquets and as a learning center for the history of passenger trade in the region.

One of the ship's most dedicated volunteers, Bob Priefer, has ties to the *Milwaukee Clipper* dating back decades before he stood on her bridge as she was proudly brought home to Muskegon. As Captain Robert Priefer, he stood at the ship's helm for eight years, masterfully maneuvering her in and out of port, and across the open water of Lake Michigan. Captain Priefer's first contact with the *Milwaukee Clipper* came in the early 1940s, when his father was supplying choice cuts of meat and provisions to the meticulous McKee brothers for use aboard ship. Years later, after serving in the Merchant Marines and acquiring his certification as Master Seaman, he returned home to his family and the *Milwaukee Clipper*. Starting as a "Pearl Diver," his affectionate name for a dishwasher on board, he worked his way up through the ranks to deckhand and eventually captain. Captain Priefer knows the ship well, and has been very instrumental in reconstructing daily life on board. As with most retired Great Lakes Captains, he has vivid and fond memories of dining on his ship.

Dining aboard the S.S. *Milwaukee Clipper* was an event, featuring food as legendary as the steamer herself. As the S.S. *Juniata* she welcomed passengers into a huge dining room, seating 250 guests at a time. Meal selections were made from menus in the shape of the ship, featuring a variety of homemade goodness. Steak and eggs were commonly served at breakfast along with other early morning favorites including ham, lamb chops, bacon, and griddlecakes with maple syrup, honey and preserves. In the evening, passengers dined on Lake Trout Cooked in Sizzling Butter and other *Juniata* specialties.

In later years, as the S.S. *Milwaukee Clipper*, meals were served cafeteria style with the same, if not higher, standards of superb service and quality. Working closely with a local meat supplier the McKee brothers offered nothing but choice cuts of meat on their menus. Their chefs came from top-notch backgrounds and their waiters were well trained in passenger service. The fully appointed galley below deck housed all food preparation, which was then sent through large dumb-waiters to the shiny, well-appointed, cafeteria on the upper deck. Meals were served on specially created *Milwaukee Clipper* china, and carried to tables for diners by busboys. Inferior brands of liquor were banned from ever being carried on board; they wanted their passengers treated right. Of the 108 officers and crew on board for every sailing, 72 worked in the Steward's Department, devoting their time to food preparation, service and the overall comfort of passengers. Prime rib became a *Milwaukee Clipper* specialty and a favorite of guests. Entertainment on the Dance Floor Deck followed dinner and the second deck Soda Bowl was always open with sandwiches, sundaes and between-meal snacks.

A *Milwaukee Clipper* guest is assisted with her dinner selection during the 1940s.

SOCIAL HALL

MUSIC ROOM, LOOKING AFT

DINING ROOM

DINNER CALL

GALLEY

A 1911 Anchor Line brochure showing the luxurious grand staircase, highly polished mahogany woodwork, and elegant dining area on board.

(Courtesy of *S.S. Milwaukee Clipper* Preservation, Inc. – Charles H. Truscott Collection)

GREAT LAKES TRANSIT CORPORATION

One of the Favorite Haunts on the Ship

THE DINING SALOON OF THE TIONESTA—JUNIATA—OCTORARA
WHERE THE CUISINE IS UNPARALLELED

SEATING CAPACITY, TWO HUNDRED FIFTY

LOCATED ON SALOON DECK

TABLES ARRANGED TO ACCOMMODATE TWO AND FOUR PERSONS

EVERY SEAT PROVIDES AN UNOBSTRUCTED VIEW

[10]

A 1930 Great Lakes Transit Corporation brochure highlights the elegant dining on board.

(Courtesy of *S.S. Milwaukee Clipper* Preservation, Inc. – Charles H. Truscott Collection)

THE ERIE AND WESTERN
TRANSPORTATION CO.

ANCHOR LINE.

PENNSYLVANIA RAILROAD STEAMERS

Luncheon

SOUP

HOT ROAST HAM, JELLY SAUCE   POTATOE

COLD

ROAST MUTTON   VEAL LOAF   SARDI

GIRKINS   MIXED PICKLES   OLIVES

SALAD

CHEESE   CRACKERS

PIES   FRUIT   PRESERVES

HOT TEA AND COFFEE   MILK   ICED TEA

STEAMSHIP JUNIATA   Monday, A

An additional charge of 25 cents each will be made for meals serve

GREAT LAKES TRANSIT CORPORATION

STEAMSHIP JUNIATA
CAPTAIN ANGUS MCKENZIE

LUNCHEON

SOUP

ROAST VEAL WITH DRESSING

BOILED AND HASHED BROWN POTATOES

BOSTON BAKED PORK AND BEANS

COLD

ROAST LAMB   BOILED TONGUE

CHOW CHOW   SLICED CUCUMBERS

OLIVES

SALAD

CHEESE

ICE CREAM   CRACKERS

FRUIT   PIES   CAKE

TEA

COFFEE   MILK

SATURDAY, JULY 15, 1916

An additional charge of 25 cents will be made for meals served in rooms.

Menus from the early 1900s (above) that were
presented to guests in the elegant dining room
when the vessel sailed as *S.S. Juniata.* Sister ship,
S.S. Tionesta, offered similar menus (facing page).

(Courtesy of *S.S. Milwaukee Clipper* Preservation, Inc. -
Charles H. Truscott Collection)

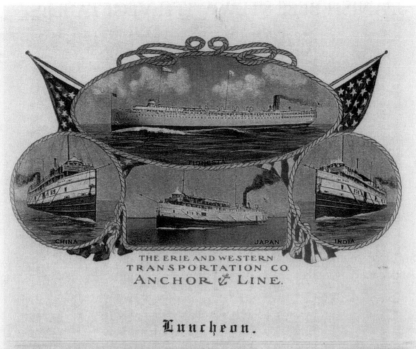

THE ERIE AND WESTERN
TRANSPORTATION CO.
ANCHOR & LINE.

Luncheon.

SOUP.

LAMB POT PIE.　　POTATOES, BOILED.

COLD.

ROAST BEEF.　　HAM.

SLICED CUCUMBERS.　　BEETS.

SALAD.

CHEESE.　　CRACKERS.

PIES.　FRUIT.　PRESERVES.　CAKE.

HOT TEA AND COFFEE.　　ICED TEA AND COFFEE.

MILK.

STEAMER TIONESTA.　　Thursday, August 6, 1903.

Research on the *Milwaukee Clipper* did not uncover authentic recipes known to be used on board, but similar recipes representing the menus and era were found, and help bring the tastes of the retired steamer alive.

SPANISH BEEF STEW WITH VEGETABLES

1 (1-1/2 lb.)	chuck roast, *or* stew meat
4	potatoes, peeled, cut into chunks
1	onion, chopped
1	green pepper, chopped
4	tomatoes, peeled, chopped
3	garlic cloves, minced
1	bay leaf
1 Tbsp.	parsley, chopped
1 c.	beef stock
6 Tbsp.	olive oil
	Salt and pepper, to taste

Cut meat into bite-sized chunks. Heat oil in large kettle; sauté onions and garlic. Add meat and cook until lightly brown. Add remaining ingredients, cover and simmer 45 minutes. Stir stew occasionally while cooking.

BROILED WHITEFISH WITH LEMON BUTTER

3 lbs.	whitefish fillets
	Olive oil
	Salt and pepper, to taste

Sauce

1 c.	butter
2 to 3 Tbsp.	freshly squeezed lemon juice
1/2 tsp.	pepper
1/4 c.	parsley, chopped
1 tsp.	dried tarragon leaves
1	dash tabasco sauce
	Flour
	Water

Season fillets with salt and pepper; rub oil over both sides. Place on broiler rack 5-inches below heat source and broil 5 minutes on each side. To prepare sauce let butter soften at room temperature. Melt butter in small saucepan. Stir in lemon juice, pepper, parsley, tarragon and tabasco sauce. Whisk together until blended. Mix small amount of flour with water until smooth; stir into sauce to thicken.

LAMB POT PIE

Pastry for Double-Crust Pie

2 c.	flour
1 tsp.	salt
2/3 c.	shortening
6 to 7 Tbsp.	cold water

Lamb Filling

2 lbs.	stewing lamb
2 sm.	onions, sliced
2 lg.	potatoes, peeled, thinly sliced
2	carrots, shredded
1/2 lb.	fresh mushrooms, thinly sliced
1-1/2 c.	vegetable broth
2 Tbsp.	vegetable oil
2 Tbsp.	butter
1/2 tsp.	pepper
1/2 tsp.	salt
1 tsp.	ground coriander
1 Tbsp.	prepared mustard
1/4 c.	flour
1/2 c.	vegetable broth *or* water

Egg Wash

1	egg
4 Tbsp.	milk

To prepare pastry stir together flour and salt in large bowl; cut in shortening. Sprinkle 1 tablespoon of cold water into pastry mixture and gently toss with fork. Repeat with remaining cold water until entire pastry mixture is moistened. Divide dough into 2 balls. Roll out 1 ball and line bottom of pie plate. Reserve remaining crust for top.

To prepare filling, combine vegetable oil and butter in large kettle; heat together to melt butter. Cut lamb into bite-sized pieces and add to kettle. Cook until lamb is lightly browned. Add onions, potatoes, carrots, mushrooms, vegetable broth, salt, pepper, coriander and mustard. Stir to combine and simmer, covered, 20 minutes. Uncover and cook an additional 15 minutes, stirring occasionally. Place filling over bottom crust in pie plate. Roll out remaining crust and place over filling. Crimp edges to seal and cut 3 small slits in top crust to vent. Combine egg wash ingredients and lightly brush over top crust. Bake at 375 degrees 20 to 30 minutes.

BROILED LAMB CHOPS WITH HONEY MUSTARD

4	lamb chops
1/2 c.	mustard
1/2 c.	honey
2	garlic cloves, minced
1/4 tsp.	ground ginger
	Salt and pepper, to taste

Combine mustard, honey, garlic and ginger; mix together well. Season lamb chops with salt and pepper, to taste. Place lamb chops on broiling pan and baste with mustard mixture. Place pan 4 to 5-inches from heat source and broil 5 to 6 minutes. Turn chops over, baste with mustard mixture and broil an additional 5 to 6 minutes, to desired doneness.

ITALIAN SPAGHETTI WITH CHEESE

1/2 c.	olive oil
4	garlic cloves, coarsely chopped
6 c.	tomatoes, peeled
1 tsp.	basil
1 tsp.	parsley, chopped
1 tsp.	oregano
2 tsp.	salt
5 Tbsp.	tomato paste
	Spaghetti
	Cheese, grated

Heat oil in large pan over medium heat. Add garlic and sauté until golden. Remove pan from heat and allow to cool slightly. If desired, garlic may be removed. Return pan to heat. Crush tomatoes and add to pan. Add seasonings and simmer 30 minutes. Add tomato paste and bring to boil. Reduce heat and simmer until thickened, approximately 20 minutes. Cook spaghetti according to package directions; drain. Serve sauce over cooked spaghetti. Top with grated cheese.

S.S. MILWAUKEE CLIPPER FAVORITE CUSTARD PIE

1 (8-inch)	pie shell, unbaked
4 eggs	slightly beaten
1/2 c.	sugar
1/2 tsp.	nutmeg
1/4 tsp.	salt
1-1/3 c.	milk, scalded
3/4 c.	cream, scalded
1 tsp.	vanilla

Preheat oven to 450 degrees. Add sugar, nutmeg and salt to eggs; beat just until blended. Gradually add scalded milk and cream to egg mixture, stirring constantly. Stir in vanilla. Strain filling into unbaked pie shell and bake at 450 degrees 10 minutes.

Reduce oven temperature to 350 degrees and bake an additional 15 to 20 minutes, until knife inserted between center and edge of pie comes out clean. Cool on wire rack and then place in refrigerator until serving.

The S.S. *Milwaukee Clipper* has been designated a National Historical Landmark, "Worthy of the Most Careful Preservation." Tours lead guests up the grand staircase, across floors of restored dining areas and through lounges complete with original deco-style furnishings. Below deck, visitors may view the engine room that powered the graceful passenger ship across the lakes. Guests may visit the legendary *Milwaukee Clipper* along the waterfront in Muskegon, Michigan. Information on tours and special events is available through S.S. *Milwaukee Clipper* Preservation, Inc.

S.S. MILWAUKEE CLIPPER
S.S. *Milwaukee Clipper* Preservation, Inc.
P.O. Box 1370, Muskegon, MI 49443
(231) 755-0990
Email: SSMilwkClipper@webtv.net
Website: www.milwaukeeclipper.org

S.S. Valley Camp

Producers Steamship Co. – Wilson Transit Co.
Republic Steel Corp.

Built:	1917, American Ship Building Company, Lorain, Ohio
Built For:	Producers Steamship Company
Former Name:	*Louis W. Hill* (until 1955)
Length:	550'
Beam:	58'
Depth:	31'
Cargo:	Iron Ore, Coal, Stone, Grain
Crew:	32
Passenger Capacity:	2
Retired:	1966
Current Name:	Historic Museum Ship *Valley Camp*
Home Port:	Sault Ste. Marie, Michigan

The bright and cheerful Crew's Dining Room features overhead portholes.

The S.S. *Valley Camp* began its life of service on the Great Lakes in 1917 with the distinction of being "as modern as the genius of man can make her." She was originally christened the *Louis W. Hill*, in honor of then-president of the Great Northern Railroad Company and son of James J. Hill, the railroad pioneer. The *Louis*

W. Hill was the first of three Great Lakes freighters built by the American Ship Building Company for Producers Steamship Company. The building of this ship, along with her sister ships the *Carmi A. Thompson* and the *William A. Amerg*, coincided with the outbreak of World War I, which threatened the destination of their maiden voyages. Their fate was in question for a while, as the U.S. Government began to requisition all steel-hulled ships over 2500 tons being built in American shipyards at the time for use in the war effort. However, they were among several ships later released to their owners, and were launched from the docks at the American Ship Building Company three months apart.

The Pilot House aboard the *Valley Camp* appears today as it did when the ship was retired in 1966.

In 1955 the ore carrier was traded to Wilson Transit Company and renamed to honor the Valley Camp Coal Company in Pennsylvania. As the newly named *Valley Camp*, it was the first ship to pass through the Soo Locks on its 100th Anniversary, June 18, 1955. In 1957 the *Valley Camp* was one of six ships purchased by Republic Steel Corporation. She sailed with this fleet until taken out of service in 1966. The ten years during which Republic Steel owned the *Valley Camp* were among the company's best in terms of production and profit.

The S.S. *Valley Camp* logged over three million miles on the Great Lakes and is estimated to have carried 16 million tons of iron ore, coal, stone and grain during her 50 years of service. By the mid 1960s the ship could no longer compete economically with the larger, more modern ships of the Great Lakes, so the decision was made to retire her. She delivered her final cargo during the fall of 1966 under Captain Gerard Bebeau, carrying coal from Milwaukee to Superior, Wisconsin.

While the *Valley Camp* was sitting inactive in Superior, Wisconsin, the Le Sault de Sainte Marie Historical Sites, Inc. was being formed to recover and restore Sault Ste. Marie's historic past. This non-profit firm's first goal was to acquire a Great Lakes freighter that could be used as a visitor attraction; the second was to create a Great Lakes Maritime Museum in its cargo hold. Great Lakes Historian John O. Greenwood connected the group with Robert Carpenter of Republic Steel. A deal was made offering the *Valley Camp* on a "as is, where is" basis for $10,000 (a figure much less than her actual worth) and the ship was prepared for a final voyage to her new home in Sault Ste. Marie, Michigan.

Two coal-fired boilers powered the *Valley Camp's* original 1800 horsepower steam engine.

Thomas Manse, later to become the museum ship's manager, was selected as "skipper" for the voyage to Sault Ste. Marie. Since the *Valley Camp* was being towed to her new home by the tug *John Purves*, only two experienced sailors were hired to accompany "skipper" Manse and two others. Provisions were loaded aboard for the three-day, 350-mile trip, including lots of milk, eggs, bacon and bread. They were ready to start their voyage and eager to get their ship to her new home. The *Valley Camp* pulled out of Superior Harbor early on June 30, 1968. The weather was stormy and Lake Superior was in full furry, causing some tense moments and slight delays, but the sun was shining when the *Valley Camp* pulled into the Soo Locks on July 3, 1968. Cars had lined the pier to greet "their ship" and welcome her home. With only a few weeks of painting and modifications, the *Valley Camp* was transformed from an ore carrier to a museum ship. She welcomed her first visitors on July 18, 1968.

During its 50 years of service the *Valley Camp* and her crew of 32 sailed the region through both the calm and perilous weather the Great Lakes are known for. The galley and most of the crew quarters were at the stern.

Overhead porthole type skylights above the table made the dining area a bright a cheerful spot for the crew to enjoy their favorite meals. During their off hours on the lonely lakes, the men of the *Valley Camp* passed time by playing cards, storytelling and letter writing. Many had hobbies such as wood carving and photography. Current newspapers and magazines were not always available, nor were the conveniences of today such as radio, television and VCRs. So, the homey dining area became a favorite spot on board for socializing as well as meals.

The Steward's Department, which included a steward, 2nd cook and three porters, was always ready with three fresh hot and hearty meals a day for the crew, and plenty of extras to satisfy hunger pains between meals. Holiday menus on board the *Valley Camp* offered all the favorites from home, plus much, much more.

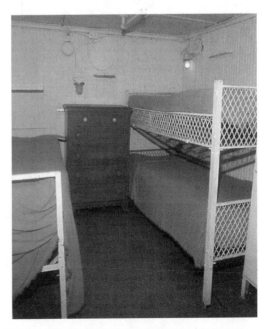

Located at the ship's stearn, crew quarters were small rooms with bunk beds bolted to the floor.

THANKSGIVING DAY 1983

Shrimp Cocktail
Fresh Fruit Salad

Chicken Dumpling Soup

Roast Tom Turkey with Sage Dressing
Stuffed Chicken Breast
Roast Prime Rib – Au Jus
Boiled Lobster with Lemon Butter

Whipped Potatoes
Candied Sweet Potatoes
Baked Hubbard Squash
French Style Green Beans with Mushrooms
Gravy

Stuffed Celery
Radishes, Carrot Sticks, Green Onions
Stuffed Olives, Ripe Olives
Cranberry Sauce

Hot Rolls and Butter

Pumpkin Pie with Whipped Cream
Mince Meat Pie
Apple Pie
Fruit Cake
After Dinner Mints

Salted Nuts
Hard Candy
Peanuts
Chocolates
Apple Cider
Beverages
Cigars
Cigarettes

Thanksgiving

Menu

THURSDAY, NOVEMBER 24, 1983

HAPPY

M-V. Burn's Harbor

Menu

Shrimp Cocktail
Fresh Fruit Salad
Chicken Dumpling Soup

Roast Tom Turkey   Sage Dressing
Stuffed Chicken Breast
Roast Prime Rib - Au Jus
Boiled Lobster   Lemon Butter

Whipped Potatoes   Candied Sweet Potatoes
Baked Hubbard Squash
French Style Green Beans with Mushrooms
Gravy

Stuffed Celery   Radishes   Carrot Sticks   Green Onions
Stuffed Olives   Ripe Olives
Cranberry Sauce

Hot Rolls

Pumpkin Pie with Whipped Cream   Mince Meat Pie
Fruit Cake   Apple Pie
Ice Cream

After Dinner Mints

Salted Nuts   Apple Cider   Hard Candy   Peanuts
Chocolates
Cigars   Beverage   Cigarettes

HAPPY THANKSGIVING

Steward   Asst. Steward   Porter
CARL   PAUL   ART

THANKSGIVING FROM...

CARL, *Steward*
PAUL, *Assistant Steward*
ART, *Porter*

CHICKEN AND LYONNAISE POTATOES

This recipe is easy, no matter how many people you are serving.

Chicken	skin removed (enough for at least 2 pieces per person)
Potatoes	washed, sliced (2 small *or* medium, *or* 1 larger per person)
Onions	quartered (1 medium *or* large per 2 people)
Rosemary	(2 tsp. to 1 Tbsp., depending on how much you like this spice)
	Salt and pepper to taste
	Cooking oil
	Butter *or* margarine

Put 3 tablespoons oil in warmed pan; roll oil around pan to cover pan thoroughly. Crush rosemary in palm of hand to make pieces smaller; add to pan and fry over medium-high heat approximately 1 minute. Stir rosemary to cover pan. Add chicken and 1/2 onions. Brown chicken on both sides; cover and reduce heat to medium-low. In separate frying pan heat 3 tablespoons butter or margarine over medium-high heat. Add potatoes and remaining onions. Stir well to coat potatoes and onions with butter. Add 1 to 1-1/2 cups hot water. Season with salt and pepper. Cover and reduce heat to medium-low. Cook until potatoes are tender. Uncover to cook off any excess liquid. By the time the potatoes are cooked the chicken should be done, approximately 20 to 30 minutes.

SINFUL POTATOES

Virginia Hobaugh

2 lg. pkgs.	Oreida hash brown potatoes
1 qt.	Hellmann's mayonnaise
1 bunch	green onions, stems and all
1 (2 lb.) box	Velveeta cheese, cubed
1 lb.	bacon, fried crisp, crumbled
	Onion flakes

Combine potatoes, mayonnaise, green onions and Velveeta cheese in casserole; stir to mix. Sprinkle onion flakes and crumbled bacon over top. Bake at 325 degrees until bubbly.

LAZY MAN'S CABBAGE ROLLS

2 lbs.	ground beef
2 lbs.	ground pork
1 lg. *or* 2 med.	onions, chopped
3	garlic cloves, chopped
4	celery stalks, chopped
4 c.	Minute rice
2 whole heads	cabbage, coarsely chopped
2 cans	tomato juice
	Salt and pepper, to taste

In large frying pan brown ground beef and pork; add onions, garlic and celery. When meat is browned add rice. Season with salt and pepper, mixing well. Combine meat mixture and cabbage in large roasting pan or casserole dish; mix well. Pour tomato juice over entire mixture. Cover and bake at 375 degrees 1 to 1-1/2 hours or until cabbage is tender.

Note: If you use regular rice, you may have to add more juice or water to insure rice will be tender.

PULLED APPLE STRUDEL

1/4 c.	warm water
1 tsp.	sugar
1/2 tsp.	salt
1	egg
1 Tbsp.	olive oil
1 c.	flour
3/4 lb.	apples
1/3 c.	butter, melted
1 c.	cake crumbs
1/2 c.	sugar mixed with 1 tsp. cinnamon

Combine water, sugar, salt, egg and olive oil; mix well. Add flour to make a smooth dough. Round dough, place on oiled pan and brush with oil; let rest approximately 1 hour. Peel, core and slice apples. Place a clean cloth over a table that covers an area at least 20x40-inches. Dust cloth very lightly with flour. Roll dough out over cloth until relatively thin. Sprinkle dough with butter and cake crumbs. Cover the top 1/6 of dough (lengthwise) with apples and sprinkle with cinnamon/sugar mixture. Using the cloth as an aid, roll dough, apple end first, toward the empty end of the dough, trying to make the roll reasonably tight. Divide dough into 2 equal portions and place on paper-lined pan. Brush with melted butter; sprinkle coarse sugar over top. Bake at 425 to 450 degrees until golden brown and baked through. Dust with powdered sugar or a sugar glaze.

Yield: 2 Strudels

TEXAS BRISKET

Virginia Hobaugh

1 (6 to 8 lb.)	brisket, NOT corned beef
	Salt
	Pepper
	Chili Powder
	Garlic powder
	Accent
	Kitchen Bouquet

Mop Sauce

1 c.	beef consommé
1/3 c.	water
3/4 c.	Worcestershire sauce
1/3 c.	cider vinegar
1/3 c.	salad oil
1/2 tsp.	paprika
1 tsp.	garlic powder
1 tsp.	dry mustard
1 Tbsp.	chili powder
1 Tbsp.	tabasco sauce
1	bay leaf

Prepare Mop Sauce the night before using and let stand at room temperature. To prepare Mop Sauce combine beef consommé and water in saucepan; bring to boil. Add remaining sauce ingredients, stirring to mix. Rub brisket well with all seasonings listed. Bake, uncovered, at 250 degrees 1 hour. Reduce heat to 140 degrees, mop with Mop Sauce and cook 23 hours, covered.

GRECIAN ORANGE CAKE

Virginia Hobaugh

1 box	yellow cake mix
1 (6 serving size) pkg.	instant lemon pudding
4	eggs
3/4 scant c.	oil
3/4 c.	water

Glaze

2 c.	powdered sugar
1/3 c. + 2 Tbsp.	frozen orange juice
2 Tbsp.	butter

To prepare cake combine all ingredients in mixing bowl; beat 2 minutes at medium speed. Pour batter into greased and floured tube or bundt pan. Bake at 350 degrees approximately 45 minutes. Remove from pan and glaze while hot.

Combine all glaze ingredients in saucepan; stir over low heat until dissolved. Poke hot cake with utility fork and pour on glaze.

BILL ESSMAKER'S SECRET SEAGOING RECIPES

Breakfast – Toast

4	slices bread
	Peanut butter
	Milk or fresh juice

SUGGESTION: Toast bread. Spread peanut butter on toasted bread. Serve with milk or fresh juice.

Lunch – Sandwich

2	slices bread
	Peanut butter
	Fresh fruit
	Fresh juice

SUGGESTION: Spread peanut butter on bread. Serve with a piece of fruit and some fresh juice.

Supper

SUGGESTION: Eating too late in the evening is not healthy!

Today, the Historic Museum Ship *Valley Camp* in Sault Ste. Marie, Michigan, offers visitors the opportunity to explore this unique 1917 steam powdered Great Lakes freighter from the captain's quarters to her massive steam engine. The world's largest Great Lakes maritime museum is on board, featuring exhibits from shipbuilding to shipwrecks. Exciting artifacts, exhibits, photography, aquariums, paintings, models and video presentations bring Great Lakes maritime history to life. The Museum Ship *VALLEY CAMP* is listed on the National Register of Historic Places. Nearby is the Tower of History, offering a birds-eye view of the Soo Locks and St. Mary's River ship traffic.

HISTORIC MUSEUM SHIP *VALLEY CAMP*
LeSault de Ste. Marie Historical Sites, Inc.
501 E. Water Street
Sault Ste. Marie, Michigan 49783
(906) 632-3658
Website: www.soohistoricinc.sault.com

Hours
Open 7 days a week – last tickets sold one hour before closing.
July and August: 9:00 am to 9:00 pm daily
May 15 – June 30: 10:00 am to 6:00 pm
September 1 – October 15: 10:00 am to 6:00 pm

The Steamer William A. Irvin

Pittsburgh Steel Company (USS Great Lakes Fleet)

The oak paneled Guest Dining Room aboard the *S.S. William A. Irvin*, where guests of U.S. Steel gathered for meals created by talented Guest Chefs.

Built:	1937-1938, American Ship Building Co., Lorain, Ohio		
Built For:	Pittsburgh Steel Company, Div. of U.S. Steel		
Launched:	November 10, 1937		
Length:	610'9"		
Beam:	60'	**Cargo Capacity:**	14,000 Tons
Depth:	32'6"	**Cargo:**	Iron Ore
Crew:	32	**Passenger Capacity:**	8

Retired:	December 16, 1978
Current Name:	The Steamer *William A. Irvin*
Current Home Port:	Duluth, Minnesota

*I*n 1937, as the nation's economy was beginning to recover from the Great Depression, the Pittsburgh Steel Company, a Division of U.S. Steel, announced plans for the construction of four new ore boats. All four ships sailed on their maiden voyages in 1938; the *William A. Irvin* on June 25, 1938.

The guest's lounge provided an elegant setting for relaxing aboard the *Irvin*. Portraits of the ship's namesake, William A. Irvin and his wife Gertrude, are visible on the wall.

The *William A. Irvin's* namesake was born in 1873. William Irvin dropped out of school at the end of the 8th grade to help support his mother and younger brother after the death of his father. He went on to work his way up through the ranks at Pennsylvania Railroad and then quickly up the ranks in the steel industry. He became the fourth president of U.S. Steel and chairman of the board based completely on self-taught experience in the work world. William Irvin is fondly remembered by friends and family as "the last of the self-taught giants."

The *Irvin* and her sister ships employed a number of innovations for Great Lakes vessels when they entered service. These vessels were the first to be powered with steam turbine engines providing a direct drive to the propeller shaft via reduction gear. This marked the start of a 30-year period which favored the use of turbines in new Great Lakes vessels. They also used electric-hydraulic systems for steering and water tube boilers to produce steam which were fed by automatic coal stokers. On deck, the hatches used the one-piece cover, and an electric hatch crane traveled on deck to remove and replace the covers. Underneath the deck, tunnels enabled crewmembers to move from one end of the ship to the other in relative safety. Finally, the vessels incorporated mostly welded deck plates versus the riveted construction used in previous vessels (the outer hull was still all riveted, though.)

The *Irvin* also had the distinction of four elegant walnut-paneled Guest Staterooms in the forward end and an oak-paneled dining room on deck. Brass rails adorned the Engine Room and Pilot House, and a spacious Guest Lounge provided guests a panoramic view plus featured a bar and refrigerator for refreshments. The accommodations for guests aboard the *Irvin* were highly unusual by Great Lakes standards and are nearly non-existent today. The *Irvin* would typically carry eight guests each trip during the summer months.

Luxurious staterooms provided privacy and comfort to the *Irvin's* special passengers.

The oiler's room, though less elegant, offered quiet and comfortable space for resting.

During her 40 years of service, the *William A. Irvin* was primarily engaged in the iron ore trade. Approximately 90% of her trips were to carry either raw iron ore or the newer taconite pellets (processed iron ore.) Most of the iron ore originated in Duluth or Two Harbors, Minnesota on western Lake Superior and would usually be unloaded at one of four lower lakes ports (South Chicago, IL; Gary, IN; Lorain, OH; or Conneaut, OH.) The *Irvin* could make a trip from western Lake Superior to the lower lakes and back in approximately seven days. She remained in service for U.S. Steel throughout her entire career on the Great Lakes, but the fleet itself changed to the USS Great Lakes Fleet.

The *William A. Irvin* was laid up for the last time on December 16, 1978, and faced an uncertain future until the spring of 1986. The vessel was simply too small to compete in the iron ore trade any longer, and was also considerably slower. She required a larger crew to operate and her unloading time was longer than the unloading time for a vessel twice her size equipped with a self-unloading system. So, she sat quietly idle, waiting in Duluth for several years while many of her fleetmates were being sold for scrap, including her three sister ships.

During the spring of 1986, the *William A. Irvin* was given new life beginning with over $250,000 in refurbishing work. With help from the Marshall family in Duluth, well known for their community efforts, the Duluth State Convention Center Board was able to purchase the vessel from U.S. Steel for $110,000, an amount equal to its scrap value. This was less than one-tenth of the over $1.5 million it cost to build the vessel in 1937-38.

The Officer's Dining Room

The main galley (above) served both officers and crew. The guest's galley (below) where Guest Chefs catered to the appetites of *Irvin's* special passengers.

Today, The Steamer *William A. Irvin* sits proudly in Duluth, no longer idle but open to the public in all its restored grandeur. Since its opening on June 28, 1986 the proud vessel has been offering visitors the opportunity to view first-hand this marvel of Great Lakes shipping that began over 60 years ago.

The crewmembers that worked aboard the *William A. Irvin* while she was in service were separated into the officers and the unlicensed crew for meals, a common practice aboard Great Lakes vessels. Dining for officers was typically more formal, as the 2nd cook would take the orders and return with the food, beverages and condiments brought directly to the officer. In the crew's dining area, beverages and condiments were placed on the center of the table. The two groups were given identical menus written on chalkboards. Several nights offered traditional meals, such as steak on Saturday nights. If a crewmember became hungry during the galley crew's off-hours, the night lunchbox (a refrigerator in the center of the galley) was stocked with leftovers, sandwich makings, milk and juice for their use. Additional leftovers were warmed on a steam table in the galley. Meal times aboard were set up to fall close to the watch changes which ran 12:00-4:00, 4:00-8:00, and 8:00-12:00 around the clock. Crewmen on the watch system worked two 4-hour shifts each day.

The V.I.P. accommodations and Guest Dining Room aboard the *William A. Irvin* look as luxurious and inviting today as they did when they were filled with the pampered guests of U.S. Steel decades ago. It is easy to envision the Guest Chefs and Steward that were brought aboard specifically to cater to the comfort and appetites of these special passengers.

Perhaps the best way to describe the food aboard, particularly for the guests, is to look at the comments that guests themselves made. The late Captain Spencer J. Kidd, who served as the *Irvin's* captain from 1967 through 1971, took meticulous care in making sure each of the guests' trips during his tenure were recorded. He maintained scrapbooks for the guests to complete. Here are some excerpts from those books, which Captain Kidd donated to the *Irvin* in 1986:

From the guest log as written by the Jim and Marion Traa party, guests on board from July 2 through July 9, 1967, describing the Guest Cooks on board, the food and the service…

> "To Dave:
> We tip our hat to mighty Dave
> Whose yummy food rates every rave
> And we're so happy that we met
> Although he changed our silhouette!
>
> To Charles:
> To Charles we give our vote of thanks
> His service was the best!
> At breakfast, lunch and dinner time
> He put us to the test!"

Mrs. John Guba, a guest on the *Irvin* July 16-23, 1967 describes the service provided by Columbus, a Passenger Porter on the vessel…

> "We climbed aboard the William A.
> And started to relax
> Columbus made us right at home
> With instant ice and snacks"

A group of guests nicknamed "The Big 'D' Crowd" from Dallas who sailed July 21-27, 1968 wrote the following about Guest Steward Dave…

> *"Dave, our chef, was really wise*
> *To the ways of Irvin's guests*
> *But even he was signaling 'Help!'*
> *When the Texans dashed to mess*
> *Rare recipes and magic spoons*
> *Meant goodies in his kitchen*
> *But nowhere in the reg book*
> *Is there a cure for snack snitching*
> *Doughnuts vanished like mad*
> *Nothing left but crumbs*
> *Chocolate chips walked out the door*
> *The sea gulls cried 'The Bums'."*

Guests dining aboard the *William A. Irvin* selected from menus featuring a wide variety at every meal. In addition, they were presented with "Guest Chef Specialties," considered by some as memorable as the trip itself. The following menus and recipes show the homemade goodness offered on board.

Breakfast

Club Breakfast Special:

Choice of Cereal, 1 Egg, Potatoes,

Toast and Coffee

⚓

Fresh Fruit and Juices

Ham, Bacon and Sausage

Eggs, Any Style

Hot Cakes, French Toast and Waffles

Sweet Rolls and Doughnuts

Coffee, Tea, Hot Chocolate and Milk

Entrées

T-Bone Steak

Top Sirloin Steak

New York Steak

Chicken Fried Steak

Ground Round Steak

Breaded Veal cutlets

Pork Chops

Lamb Chops

Country Sausage

American Beef Pot Roast

Spanish Meat Loaf

Southern Fried Chicken

Spaghetti with Meat Balls

Liver and Onions

Vegetable Plate

Cold Meat and Potato Salad

Sardines with Potato Salad

Chili and Beans

Chili Straight

Tamale with Chili

"Good Morning!"
Club Breakfast Special

Choice of Cereal
One Egg, Potatoes
Toast and Coffee

PLEASE ORDER BY NUMBER

No. 1 Fruit or Cereal, Toast and Coffee ....
No. 2 Ham, Bacon or Sausage, (1) Egg, (2) Hot Cakes, Coffee ....
No. 3 Hot Cakes with Ham, Bacon or Sausage and Coffee ....
No. 4 Two Eggs, Hot Cakes and Coffee ....
No. 5 Waffles with Ham, Bacon or Sausage and Coffee ....
No. 6 Choice of Juice, Choice of Cereal, Toast and Coffee ....
No. 7 Two Eggs with Ham, Bacon or Sausage, Toast and Coffee ....
No. 8 Choice of Cereal, Two Eggs, Toast and Coffee ....

FRESH, CRISP CEREALS

WITH MILK—
Corn Flakes
Rice Krispies
40% Bran Flakes
Raisin Bran

WITH CREAM
Shredded Wheat
Pep   All-Bran
Cooked Cereal
Corn Soya

FRUIT, and JUICES

Orange Juice ....
Grapefruit Juice ....
Tomato Juice ....

Half Grapefruit
Fruits in Season ....

BREAKFAST a la CARTE

Two Eggs (any style) ....
with Bacon or Sausage ....
with Ham ....
Plain Omelette ....
Sweet Rolls ....
Doughnuts ....

Hot Cakes with Syrup ....
with Bacon or Sausage ....
Waffles ....
Jelly or Cheese Omelet ....
Toast ....
French Toast ....

BEVERAGES

Coffee
Hot Tea ....

Ice Cold Milk
Hot Chocolate ....

Now Serving Food Where Prices Appear

We reserve the right to refuse service to anyone   Not responsible for lost or stolen articles

Vegetables (In Season)

Green Beans

Fresh Beans

Corn

Carrots

Buttered Beets

Lima Beans

French Fried Potatoes

Hash Brown Potatoes

Lyonnaise Potatoes

Asparagus Tips

A la Carte

T-Bone Steak
Top Sirloin Steak
New York Steak
Chicken Fried Steak
Ground Round Steak
Breaded Veal Cutlets
Pork Chops
Lamb Chops
Country Sausage
American Beef Pot Roast

Meat Loaf Spanish
Southern Fried Chicken
Spaghetti with Meat Balls
Liver and Onions
Vegetable Plate
Cold Meat and Potato Salad
Sardines with Potato Salad
Chili and Beans
Chili Straight
Tamale with Chili

VEGETABLES IN SEASON

Green Beans
Fresh Beans
Corn
Carrots
Buttered Beets

Lima Beans
French Fried Potatoes
Hash Brown Potatoes
Lyonnaise Potatoes
Asparagus Tips

SALADS

Potato Salad
Sliced Tomato
Cole Slaw
Fruit Salad
Chicken Salad
Vegetable Salad

Avocado Salad
Hearts of Lettuce
Chef's Mixed Green Salad
Shrimp de Luxe
Cottage Cheese with Fruit

SANDWICHES

Hot Roast Beef
Hot Roast Pork
Ham or Bacon and Egg
Fried Ham
Egg
Hamburger
Corned Beef
Sizzling Club Steak
Bacon, Lettuce and Tomato

Cold Beef
Cold Pork
Cold Ham
Cheese
Peanut Butter
Tuna
Avocado
Sardine
Deviled Egg

PASTRY and DESSERTS

Assorted Pies
Cake
Puddings
Ice Cream
Pie a la Mode

Doughnuts
Fruits in Season
Cup Custard
Fruit Jell-O
French Pastry

Kindly Report Any Inattention or Overcharge

MADE IN U.S.A.

Sandwiches

Hot Roast Beef

Hot Roast Pork

Ham or Bacon and Egg

Fried Ham

Egg

Hamburger

Corned Beef

Sizzling Club Steak

Bacon, Lettuce and Tomato

Cold Beef, Pork or Ham

Cheese

Peanut Butter

Tuna

Avocado

Sardine

Deviled Egg

Salads

Potato Salad

Sliced Tomatoes

Cole Slaw

Fruit Salad

Chicken Salad

Vegetable Salad

Avocado Salad

Hearts of Lettuce

Chef's Mixed Green Salad

Shrimp de Luxe

Cottage Cheese with Fruit

Pastries and Desserts

Assorted Pies

Cakes

Puddings

Ice Cream

Pie a la Mode

Doughnuts

Fruits in Season

Cup Custard

Fruit Jello

French Pastry

APPLE CIDER DOUGHNUTS

1 c.	apple cider
1 c.	sugar
1/4 c.	shortening
2	eggs
1/2 c.	buttermilk
3-1/2 c.	all-purpose flour
2 tsp.	baking powder
1 tsp.	baking soda
1/2 tsp.	cinnamon
1/2 tsp.	salt
1/4 tsp.	nutmeg
	Vegetable oil or shortening, for deep frying

Glaze

2 c.	powdered sugar
1/4 c.	apple cider

Boil apple cider in saucepan until reduced to 1/4 cup; set aside to cool. In large bowl beat sugar and shortening together until smooth. Add eggs 1 at a time, beating well after each addition. Add buttermilk and cooled cider. In separate bowl combine flour, baking powder, baking soda, cinnamon, salt and nutmeg. Add dry ingredients to apple cider mixture, stirring just to combine. Transfer dough to lightly floured board and pat to 1/2-inch thickness. Cut dough with doughnut cutter.

Place 3-inches of oil or shortening in deep pan and heat to 375 degrees. Fry doughnuts, several at a time, until browned and cooked through; approximately 4 minutes. Using a slotted spoon transfer doughnuts to paper towels to drain.

To prepare glaze mix apple cider with powdered sugar until smooth. Dip warm doughnuts into glaze.

Yield: Approximately 2 Dozen

BUTTERMILK DOUGHNUTS

1-1/2 c.	buttermilk
3 Tbsp.	vegetable oil
3	eggs
1-1/2 c.	sugar
1 tsp.	ground ginger
1 tsp.	ground nutmeg
1 tsp.	vanilla
1/2 tsp.	baking powder
1 tsp.	baking soda
1 tsp.	salt
5-1/2 c.	flour, not sifted
	Oil, for deep frying

Preheat approximately 1-inch of oil in deep fryer to 350 degrees. Mix together buttermilk, vegetable oil, eggs and sugar with wire whisk until completely blended. Add spices, vanilla, baking powder, baking soda and salt; mix well. Fold in flour just until ingredients are mixed. Let batter sit 5 to 10 minutes to thicken. Do not add additional flour. Divide dough in half. Drop one-half dough onto floured board and knead into ball. Knead remaining dough into ball. Roll each ball into circle approximately 1/2-inch thick and cut with doughnut cutter. Deep fry doughnuts in preheated oil 1-1/2 minutes on each side, until done. Drain on paper towels and dust with cinnamon sugar, if desired.

Yield: 2-1/2 Dozen

FILLED PASTRY

4 c.	flour
1 lb.	margarine
4	egg yolks
8 oz.	sour cream
	Fillings of choice, (poppy seed, preserves, fruit, etc.)

Mix flour with margarine as for pie dough. In separate bowl combine egg yolks and sour cream, beating well. Pour sour cream into flour mixture and blend with hands. Carefully wrap dough in waxed paper that has been coated with margarine. Cover again and refrigerate overnight. Divide dough into workable portions; roll each portion into large square. Cut into 4-inch squares. Place filling of choice in center of each square. Bring two opposite squares of pastry together, meeting in center over filling; pinch to seal using a little water. Bake at 350 degrees 10 to 15 minutes.

CHOCOLATE PASTRY ROLLS

Cream Cheese Pastry

1 (8 oz.) pkg.	cream cheese
1 c.	butter
1	egg yolk
2 c.	all-purpose flour

Chocolate Filling

16 Tbsp.	Nestles Chocolate Quik mix
1 (8 oz.) pkg.	chocolate chips
2 Tbsp.	butter
1 c.	nuts, chopped, (optional)

To prepare pastry cream together butter and cream cheese until completely blended. Beat in egg yolk. Add flour and beat until blended; do not over beat. Turn dough out onto floured waxed paper. Shape dough into circle, wrap in waxed paper and refrigerate several hours or overnight.

To prepare filling melt chocolate chips with butter and chocolate mix in saucepan. Stir in chopped nuts, if desired. Divide dough into fourths. Roll out one part at a time into 10-inch square. Spread 1/4 filling over dough and roll up. Repeat with remaining dough and filling. Place rolls on coated baking pan, seam-side down. Bake at 350 degrees 30 minutes or until lightly browned. Let pastry rolls cool in pan. To serve cut into slices and sprinkle with powdered sugar.

ASPARAGUS WITH HOLLANDAISE SAUCE

1 lb.	asparagus
1 c.	butter
4	egg yolks
2 Tbsp.	lemon juice
1/4 tsp.	salt
1/4 tsp.	tabasco sauce

Remove ends from asparagus and discard; wash asparagus. In large kettle bring 4-quarts water to boil; add asparagus. When water boils again, reduce heat and boil slowly 15 minutes; do not over cook. Drain asparagus.

To prepare Hollandaise Sauce heat butter until very hot, but not brown, in small saucepan. Whisk together egg yolks, lemon juice, salt and tabasco sauce until well blended. Pour hot butter into egg yolk mixture, whisking to mix well. Serve sauce immediately over drained asparagus.

ASPARAGUS WITH CASHEWS

1-1/2 lbs.	asparagus
2 Tbsp.	sesame oil
2 Tbsp.	olive oil
1 Tbsp.	ginger root, finely chopped
1/2 c.	cashews, coarsely chopped
1 Tbsp.	soy sauce

Remove ends from asparagus and discard; wash asparagus. Cut each stalk diagonally into 3 or 4 pieces. Heat oils together in wok over high heat. Add chopped ginger and stir-fry 1 minute. Add asparagus and stir-fry until tender-crisp, 4 to 5 minutes. Stir in cashews and soy sauce. Serve immediately.

POTATO SALAD

8 c.	red skin potatoes, unpeeled
1 c.	red onion, diced
1 c.	celery, diced
3 Tbsp.	sweet pickle relish
4	eggs, hard boiled, chopped
1 c.	mayonnaise
1 Tbsp.	parsley, minced
1-1/2 tsp.	salt
1/4 tsp.	pepper

Steam potatoes over boiling water until tender, approximately 30 to 40 minutes; cool. Peel potatoes and cut into 1/2-inch cubes. In large bowl stir together potatoes, celery, onion, salt and pepper. Add relish, eggs and mayonnaise; stir to combine. Adjust seasonings and sprinkle with parsley.

CREAMED PEAS AND POTATOES

	New potatoes
	Frozen peas
3 Tbsp.	butter *or* margarine
1/4 c.	flour
1/4 tsp.	salt
1 c.	milk
	White pepper, to taste

Boil potatoes and peas until done; drain. To prepare white sauce, melt butter in saucepan over low heat. Blend in flour, salt and white pepper. Add milk all at once and cook, stirring constantly, until thickened. Remove sauce from heat when it bubbles. Pour white sauce over peas and potatoes, stirring to mix.

CREAMED LIMA BEANS AND CORN PARMESAN

3 Tbsp.	butter
1/4 c.	onion, chopped
3 Tbsp.	flour
1/2 tsp.	salt
1 c.	milk
1 (16 oz.) can	lima beans, drained, liquid reserved
1 (16 oz.) can	whole kernel corn, drained
1/3 c.	Parmesan cheese, grated
	Pepper, to taste

Heat butter in saucepan. Sauté onion in butter approximately 5 minutes, until tender. Stir in flour and salt until blended. Gradually stir in milk and reserved liquid from lima beans; cook and stir until thickened. Combine lima beans with corn and place in 9x13-inch baking dish. Sprinkle Parmesan cheese and pepper over vegetables. Pour sauce over top. Bake at 375 degrees 30 minutes or until hot and bubbly. Let stand a few minutes before serving.

GRILLED LAMB CHOPS

1 c.	red current jelly
1 c.	Grey Poupon mustard
1	rack of lamb
1 c.	white wine
1/2 c.	butter
1/2 c.	shallots, minced
2 Tbsp.	rosemary, crushed

Combine jelly and mustard in saucepan; simmer over low heat to melt jelly. Remove lamb chops from rack, being careful not to remove fat. Marinate lamb chops in jelly mixture overnight. Grill lamb chops 2 to 3 minutes per side for medium to medium rare, basting with sauce occasionally. Turn chops and grill an additional 2 to 3 minutes. To prepare sauce, brown shallots in butter. Stir in white wine and rosemary. Serve lamb chops with sauce.

COUNTRY FRIED STEAK

1 lb.	round steak
1/2 c.	flour
1/2 tsp.	salt
1/2 tsp.	pepper
2 Tbsp.	canola oil
2 Tbsp.	flour
2 c.	milk

Trim fat from steak and cut into 4 equal serving pieces. Mix together flour, salt and pepper. Dredge each piece of meat in flour mixture, coating well on both sides. Heat oil in pan until hot. Brown coated meat pieces on both sides. Reduce heat, cover and fry 15 to 20 minutes, until done. Remove cover and cook an additional 5 minutes. Remove cooked steak from pan and drain.

To prepare gravy leave approximately 2 tablespoons of drippings in pan. Sprinkle flour into drippings and stir. Slowly add milk, stirring constantly. Cook 3 to 5 minutes, until thickened. Season to taste.

BANANA PINEAPPLE PECAN CAKE

3 c.	all-purpose flour
2 c.	sugar
1 Tbsp.	baking soda
1 Tbsp.	salt
1 Tbsp.	cinnamon
1 (14 oz.) can	crushed pineapple, undrained
3	eggs
1-1/2 c.	oil
2 c.	ripe bananas, mashed
1-1/2 c.	pecans, chopped
2 Tbsp.	vanilla

Frosting

1/3 c.	crushed pineapple, drained, juice reserved
1/4 c.	butter *or* margarine, softened
3 c.	powdered sugar, sifted
2 to 3 Tbsp.	pineapple juice

To prepare cake combine flour, sugar, baking soda, salt and cinnamon in large bowl. Measure and add 1-cup undrained crushed pineapple to dry ingredients; reserve rest for frosting. Add eggs, oil, bananas, pecans and vanilla; mix just until thoroughly combined. Transfer batter into 10-inch greased and floured cake pan. Bake at 350 degrees 50 to 70 minutes, until cake tester comes out clean. Cool on rack 15 minutes, then remove from pan and cool completely.

To prepare frosting drain reserved pineapple well. Combine butter, powdered sugar and pineapple juice; mix together well. Fold in pineapple and spread over cooled cake.

PINEAPPLE UPSIDE DOWN CAKE

3/4 c.	butter
1-1/2 c.	brown sugar
1 (20 oz.) can	pineapple rings
1 c.	walnuts, chopped
1-1/2 c.	flour
1 tsp.	baking powder
1/4 tsp.	salt
5	eggs, separated
1-1/2 c.	sugar
8 Tbsp.	pineapple juice

Preheat oven to 375 degrees. Melt butter and brown sugar in 9x13-inch pan. Arrange pineapple rings in pan and cover with walnuts; set aside. Beat eggs yolks; add sugar and pineapple juice. Add flour, baking powder and salt. Fold in beaten egg whites and pour over pineapple mixture in pan. Bake 40 to 45 minutes. Cool 5 minutes and invert onto serving plate.

Visitors can tour the proud flagship of U.S. Steel's Great Lakes Fleet, The Steamer *William A. Irvin*, along the waterfront in Duluth, Minnesota. Tours take guests through the elegant lounges, staterooms and dining areas reserved for V.I.P.'s in the past, and on through the Pilot House and Engine Room. A visit is educational and entertaining, with a glimpse inside a Great Lakes vessel and plenty of history to fill in the gaps. "She was the Queen of the Lakes and so shall she remain for the rest of her days" was the final entry in the ship's log, penned by Captain John J. McDonough in 1986, when he brought the *Irvin* into Minnesota Slip.

There are many other attractions along Duluth's waterfront, including Canal Park, the Tug *Lake Superior* and Duluth's Omnimax Theater.

THE STEAMER *WILLIAM A. IRVIN*
Duluth and Area Convention Center
Port of Duluth, Minnesota
350 Harbor Drive, Duluth, Minnesota 55802
Phone (218) 722-7876   Fax (218) 722-4247
Email: decc@decc.org

Website: www/decc.org/attractions/Irvin.htm

Open Memorial Day Through Labor Day
Sunday – Thursday 9:00 am to 6:00 pm
Friday and Saturday 9:00 am to 8:00 pm

Labor Day Through Mid-October
Sunday – Thursday 10:00 am to 4:00 pm
Friday and Saturday 10:00 am to 6:00 pm

Famous Annual "Haunted Tours" presented late in October featuring "Ship of Ghouls"

The Steamship William G. Mather

Cleveland-Cliffs Steamship Company

Built:	1925, Great Lakes Engineering Works, Ecorse, Michigan
Built For:	Cleveland-Cliffs Steamship Company
Launched:	May 23, 1925
Length:	618'
Beam:	62'
Draft:	22'
Cargo:	Iron Ore, Coal, Grain
Cargo Capacity:	14,000 Tons
Crew:	37 (1925-1964); 29 (1965-1980)
Retired:	1980
Current Name:	The Steamship *William G. Mather* Museum
Current Home Port:	Cleveland, Ohio

The Steamer *William G. Mather* dockside.

The Steamship *William G. Mather* was built during the golden years of the Great Lakes steamboat. When her 618' long riveted steel hull was launched in 1925 she was among the largest vessels afloat. Named in honor of then-president of Cleveland-Cliffs Iron Company, William Gwinn Mather, she proudly carried her name throughout 55 years of distinguished service on the lakes. William Mather was the son of Samuel L. Mather, descended from the famous Mathers of New England. William, himself, was a

The *William G. Mather* in 1997, outlined from stem to stern with over 1,500 lights, maintains the Great Lakes tradition of "bedecking" lake vessels at the end of the shipping season to ensure a prosperous New Year.

leader in the mining and shipping circles for over six decades and was known in Cleveland for his philanthropic work. "Gwinn," his lakefront home in Bratenahl, Ohio has been preserved as a meeting place for non-profit groups.

As flagship for Cleveland-Cliffs Iron Company, the Steamship *William G. Mather* was state-of-the-art with respect to capacity, power and accommodations. During her 55-year career, this grand lady of the Great Lakes carried millions of tons of iron ore, coal and grain, and hundreds of distinguished guests. She was nicknamed "The Ship That Built Cleveland" because Cleveland's steel mills were a frequent destination.

In early 1941, to aid the war effort and supply the Allied need for steel, the *Mather* led a convoy of 13 freighters through the ice-choked upper Great Lakes to Duluth, Minnesota, setting a record for the earliest arrival in a northern port. This heroic effort was featured in the April 28, 1941 issue of *Life Magazine*. A few years later, in 1946, the *Mather* became one of the first commercial Great Lakes vessels to be equipped with radar. In 1964, she

Mather's Engine Room circa 1954.

became the very first American vessel to have an automated boiler system, manufactured by Bailey Controls of Cleveland. And then, in 1980, after 55 years of hauling freight from port to port, the *William G. Mather* was laid up in Toledo, Ohio for the last time. She was the last ship owned by Cleveland-Cliffs Inc. as it divested itself of its Great Lakes shipping interests.

During her career the *Mather* and her crew were also known as heroes, when Lake Huron was in the middle of one of her notorious fall storms at midnight on October 30, 1967. As they were steaming up Lake Huron off Harbor Beach the *Mather's* 2nd Mate, W.H. Pollard, intercepted a radio conversation between the

The elegant Dining Room aboard the *William G. Mather*, carefully prepared for a group of her frequent distinguished guests.

Steamer *Bethlehem* and the Tawas Coast Guard. The *Bethlehem* was disabled and caught in the heavy sea. *Mather* Master Captain Harry A. Anderson called the *Bethlehem* directly and learned she had engine failure. He immediately arranged to meet the *Bethlehem* and take her in tow. Within two hours the disabled ship was secured by cable to the *Mather* and on her way to safety. After weathering the storm for over 13 hours, both ships arrived safely at the Detour Lighthouse, some 150 miles from where the *Mather* had first met *Bethlehem's* grateful crew.

Captain Anderson was quick to praise the officers and crew of the *Mather* for their splendid work under the adverse conditions. "Without their efforts and cooperation, this operation would have been a failure. Also, I must give praise to the ship's bow thruster, which not only helped me immensely, but also gave me confidence. I feel very proud to be part of a company that believes in maintaining and equipping its ships with many extra aids and equipment so as to make operations such as this not only possible, but successful." In turn, the company commended Captain Anderson and his crew for serving "beyond the call of duty" and demonstrating skilled seamanship.

In 1987, Cleveland-Cliffs Inc. donated the *William G. Mather* to the Great Lakes Historical Society to be restored and preserved as a museum ship and floating maritime museum. On May 23, 1991, after three years of intensive restoration, the Steamship *William G. Mather* Museum opened to the public as northeast Ohio's only floating maritime museum. To date, over $2,000,000 and 250,000 volunteer hours have been invested in the project. Dedicated volunteers carry out almost all restoration and maintenance, and 30% of her educational programs.

The *Mather* is listed in the International Register of Historic Ships. She is also referenced in Delgato and Clifford's "Great American Ships," published by the National Trust for Historic Preservation. In 1995, the American Society of Mechanical Engineers conferred National Landmark status on the *Mather* for the following technological Great Lakes firsts: single marine boiler system, boiler automation and dual bow thruster system.

For 55 years, the Steamship *William G. Mather* made some 30 trips per shipping season, transporting the iron ore and coal that made Cleveland a major steel producing center in the twentieth century. The busy daily life aboard worked up hearty appetites in her crew. The steward, and those that worked closely with him, worked sun up to sun down, making sure those appetites were always satisfied in a delicious way! Fresh baked goods, homemade soups and several hot entrees were served daily in the crew dining areas.

Elegant staterooms and dining rooms welcomed the *William G. Mather's* frequent distinguished guests. They graciously sailed the Great Lakes and leisurely dined in the style this era is famous for. Special china was created featuring the Cleveland-Cliffs Iron Company initials in patterns of white, gold and green. Delicate intertwined leaves circled the border of the plates and saucers, all adding to the elegance of the food served aboard the *Mather*. Wonderful, full menus were offered three times a day. The memorable food presented on holidays, such as the 1962 and 1973 Thanksgiving Menus, offered more freshly prepared dishes than anyone could dream of eating, but no doubt they tried and enjoyed every delicious minute of it.

Bob Roeder and Jack Schwarzwalder, standing in the galley (right), are always ready to lend Bill a helping hand.

Bill Kress, current steward aboard the *Mather*, comes down to the steamer on Saturdays to cook lunch for his fellow volunteers (left).

"Guest China" used aboard the *William G. Mather* was designed with a delicate gold pinstripe and intertwined leaves as a border. The initials of Cleveland-Cliffs Iron Company (CCIC) were set in the center of each plate, cup and saucer.

Menus
THANKSGIVING DAY
November 22, 1973

Appetizer
Shrimp Cocktail

Soups
Cream of Tomato Soup
Turkey Noodle Soup

Salads
Waldorf Salad
Cranberry Sauce
Tomato and Lettuce Wedges
Assorted Dressings
Pickles and Olives

Entrées
Roast Turkey with Apple or Sage Dressing
and Giblet Gravy
Orange duck with Celery Rice Dressing
and Orange Sauce
Baked Ham with Pineapple and Raisin Sauce
Prime Rib Au Jus

Vegetables
Mashed Irish Potatoes
Candied Sweet Potatoes
Buttered Asparagus
Buttered Whole Kernel Corn

Desserts
Apple Pie
Pumpkin Pie with Whipped Cream
Mincemeat Pie
Fruit Cake
Ice Cream
Mixed Nuts, Assorted Candies, Gum

Other Offerings
Assorted Breads and Rolls
Chilled Friska, Coke and Wines
Cigars
Cigarettes

THE
CLEVELAND CLIFFS
IRON COMPANY

THANKSGIVING DAY --- NOVEMBER 22, 1973
aboard
STEAMER WM. G. MATHER
Menu

APPETIZERS
Shrimp Cocktail
SOUP
Cream of Tomato   Turkey Noodle
SALAD
Waldorf Salad   Cranberry Sauce   Tomato and Lettuce Wedges
Assorted Dressing
Pickles   Olives
ENTREES
Roast Turkey   Apple or Sage Dressing   Giblet Gravy
Orange Duck   Celery Rice Dressing   Orange Sauce
Baked Ham   Pineapple and Raisin Sauce
Prime Rib Au Jus
VEGETABLES
Mashed Irish Potatoes   Candied Sweet Potatoes
Buttered Asparagus   Buttered Whole Kernel Corn

DESSERTS
Apple Pie   Pumpkin Pie w Whipped Cream   Mince Meat Pie
Fruit Cake   Ice Cream
Mixed Nuts   Assorted Candies   Gum
Assorted Bread and Rolls
Chilled Friska, Coke and Wines
Cigars   Cigarettes

A
HOLIDAY
WISH
from
CLEVELAND
CLIFFS
IRON CO.

Bill Kress currently serves as steward on the *William G. Mather*, putting to use what he learned during the 11 years he sailed the Great Lakes for Interlakes Shipping Company. Bill comes down to the *Mather* on Saturdays to cook lunch for his fellow volunteers with a little help from his friends Bob Roeder, Jack Schwarzwalder and Rose Ginley. Many of his recipes are favorites with today's volunteer crew on board.

COLE SLAW

1 lb.	green cabbage
1-1/2	carrots
4 tsp.	green pepper
8 (scant) tsp.	vinegar
2 tsp.	salt
1-2/3 c.	mayonnaise
10 tsp.	sugar
1-3/4 c.	celery seed

Shred all vegetables. Combine remaining ingredients and pour over shredded vegetables. Chill and serve.

Yield: 6 Servings

CHICKEN A LA KING

1 (2-1/2 lb.)	fryer chicken
1/3	green pepper
1	celery stalk
1 sm.	onion
2 oz.	mushrooms
4 tsp.	pimiento
1/2 c.	chicken fat, oil *or* other shortening
2/3 c.	flour
2 c.	chicken broth
1-1/2 c.	milk
	Salt and pepper, to taste

Cook chicken; skin, debone and chops into chunks. Reserve broth for later use. Chop green pepper, celery and onion. Slice mushrooms and pimiento. Combine fat with flour in large skillet. Slowly add broth and milk. Bring to slow boil, stirring bottom constantly. When done add remaining ingredients. Cook over low heat, or in oven, until celery is done. Serve over biscuits or toast.

Yield: 6 Servings

SPAGHETTI

1 lb.	ground beef
2	celery stalks
1/3	green pepper
1 lg.	onion
1 (32 oz.) can	tomato purée
1 dash	thyme
1	bay leaf
1 tsp.	garlic salt
1/2 tsp.	basil
1 lb.	pasta

*B*rown ground beef; pour off grease and water twice. Chop vegetables to desired size. Add vegetables with remaining ingredients (except pasta) to ground beef. Simmer 2 hours. Remove bay leaf and serve over cooked pasta.

Yield: 6 Servings

GROUND BEEF STROGANOFF

1 lb.	ground beef
1 med.	onion
1/3 c.	green pepper
1	celery stalk
3 oz.	mushrooms
1-1/3 oz.	tomato puree
1 tsp.	Worcestershire sauce
1-1/3 c.	milk
1 can	cream of mushroom soup
1/2 c.	sour cream
	Salt and pepper, to taste
	Noodles

*B*rown ground beef; discard fat and water. Chop onion, green pepper and celery to desired size; add to beef. Combine all ingredients (except noodles) and cook slow or in oven. Serve over noodles of choice.

Yield: 6 Servings

STEAMBOAT CHILI

1 lb.	Italian sausage, (hot, mild *or* mixed)
1/2	green pepper, chopped
1 sm.	onion, chopped
8 oz.	tomato sauce
1/2 can	green beans, drained
1/2 can	wax beans, drained
1/2 can	chili beans, NOT drained
1/2 can	kidney beans, NOT drained
1/3 c.	barbeque sauce
1/2 can	pork and beans

Brown sausage; drain fat and water. Add green pepper and onion. Simmer until tender. Add remaining ingredients and heat to serve.

Yield: 6 Servings

COLD CHICKEN SALAD

1 lb.	dry pasta shells
1 can	pineapple chunks, drained, 1/2 juice reserved
1 c.	mayonnaise
1 c.	sour cream
7-1/3 Tbsp.	white vinegar
5-1/3 tsp.	mustard
1-1/3 tsp.	basil
1 tsp.	celery seed
2/3	red pepper, chopped
2/3	green pepper, chopped
1/3 c.	black olives, sliced
2/3 c.	sweet *or* green onions, chopped
1/3 c.	celery, chopped
4 c.	chicken, cooked, chopped
2 oz.	pimiento, chopped, (optional)
2/3 c.	Cheddar cheese, shredded, (optional)

Cook pasta shells; drain. Mix together mayonnaise, sour cream, white vinegar, mustard, basil and celery seed. Toss all ingredients together, including reserved pineapple juice. Chill and serve.

Yield: 8 Servings

HOT CHICKEN SALAD

4 c.	chicken, cooked, chopped
1-1/3 c.	celery, chopped
1 can	pineapple chunks, drained
2/3 c.	almond slices, toasted
2/3 tsp.	salt
2/3 tsp.	pepper
1-1/3 Tbsp.	onion, chopped
1-1/4 c.	mayonnaise
2/3 c.	American *or* Cheddar cheese, shredded
1-1/3 c.	potato chips, finely crushed
2-2/3 Tbsp.	lemon juice
2/3 c.	sour cream, (optional)
2 oz.	pimiento, chopped, (optional)

Mix all ingredients together, except shredded cheese and potato chips. Transfer chicken mixture to 9x13-inch pan. Sprinkle shredded cheese and potato chips over top. Bake at 375 degrees for up to 30 minutes, until brown.

BANANA-PINEAPPLE DESSERT

1 stick	margarine, melted
2 c.	graham cracker crumbs, (30 to 32 sqs.)
2 sticks	margarine
2	eggs
1 lb.	powdered sugar
2 tsp.	vanilla
4	bananas, cut in thirds
1 (2 lb.) can	crushed pineapple, drained
12 oz.	Cool Whip
	Nuts, chopped
	Maraschino cherries

Combine melted margarine with graham cracker crumbs; spread in bottom of 9x13-inch pan. Beat together remaining 2 sticks margarine with eggs, powdered sugar and vanilla. Spread mixture over graham cracker crust. Place banana slices over powdered sugar mixture and cover with crushed pineapple. Spread Cool Whip over top. Garnish with chopped nuts and/or maraschino cherries. Refrigerate overnight and serve.

FRENCH SILK PIE

1 c.	sugar
3	eggs
3/4 c.	butter, (DO NOT substitute with margarine)
3 sqs.	baking chocolate, melted with 1/4 stick margarine
1 Tbsp.	vanilla
1 c.	Cool Whip
1	pre-made pie shell of choice, baked if necessary

Beat together sugar, eggs, butter, chocolate mixture and vanilla at high speed until very fluffy. Fold in Cool Whip. Pour mixture into pie shell. Decorate with additional Cool Whip or shaved chocolate.

Yield: 1 Pie

DEATH BY CHOCOLATE

1 (19 *or* 20 oz.) box	fudge brownie mix
1/4 to 1/2 c.	Kahlua
2 (3.5 oz.) pkgs.	instant chocolate mousse
4 (1-1/2 oz.)	Heath bars
16 oz.	Cool Whip

Prepare and bake brownies according to package directions; cool. Prick top with fork and pour Kahlua over top. Prepare mousse according to package directions. Break Heath bars into pieces. Cover brownies with 1/2 of mouse, then 1/2 candy pieces and 1/2 Cool Whip. Repeat layers. Chill and serve.

CREAM CHEESE BANANA-PINEAPPLE DESSERT

1-1/2 c.	graham cracker crumbs, (approx. 24 crackers)
1/4 c.	sugar
1/3 c.	margarine, melted
3	bananas, sliced
8 oz.	cream cheese
3-1/2 c.	milk
2 pkgs.	instant vanilla pudding mix
1 can	crushed pineapple, drained
8 oz.	Cool Whip

Mix graham cracker crumbs with sugar and melted margarine; press into bottom of 9x13-inch pan. Arrange banana slices over crust. Beat cream cheese with milk; add vanilla pudding mixes. Spread pudding mixture over bananas. Spoon pineapple over pudding layer. Spread Cool Whip on top. Chill and serve.

CHOCOLATE BANANA PIE

4 sqs.	semi-sweet chocolate
2 Tbsp.	milk
1 Tbsp.	margarine
1	pre-made graham cracker pie crust
1	banana, sliced
2-3/4 c.	milk
2 pkgs.	instant vanilla *or* banana pudding mix
	Whipped topping

Melt chocolate with 2 tablespoons milk and margarine; spread into graham cracker crust. Chill until chocolate is firm. Arrange banana slices over chocolate. Mix milk with pudding mixes and whisk together 1 minute; let stand 5 minutes. Pour pudding mixture into shell. Cover with whipped topping and refrigerate 4 hours.

BREAD PUDDING

	Margarine, melted
24	slices bread
3-1/2 c.	sugar, divided
3 to 4 tsp.	cinnamon
16	eggs
8 c.	milk
	Raisins

Cut crusts off bread. Brush bread with melted margarine. Combine 1-1/2 cups sugar with cinnamon and sprinkle on bread. Cut each slice into quarters and place in greased 9x13-inch pan. Sprinkle each layer with raisins. Beat eggs with milk and remaining 2 cups sugar; pour over bread. Bake at 350 degrees 1 hour.

Visitors can tour the Steamship *William G. Mather* Museum at her permanent home port in Cleveland, Ohio. The Museum is located on the East 9th Street Pier at North Coast Harbor Park. Tours include the *Mather's* cavernous cargo holds, spit-and-polish pilot house and four-story engine room. Her elegant state and dining rooms appear as they did decades ago, recalling yesteryear's gracious living. In addition, the forward cargo hold has been transformed into an exhibit hall that chronicles the history of Great Lakes shipping. A variety of on-board tours, programs and activities are available that emphasize the role of Great Lakes shipping in the building of the American industrial midwest. Regular tours average an hour, but adults can arrange an extended, more technical tour on Saturday at 1:00 pm, lasting approximately 2-1/2 hours. Other attractions on North Coast Harbor include the USS *Cod*, a World War II vintage submarine (now a museum vessel), the Great Lakes Science Center and the Rock-and-Roll Hall of Fame Museum.

May 2000 marked the 75th Anniversary of this proud ship's launching and the beginning of her invaluable career on the lakes. Still ship-shape, still welcoming guests aboard, and still serving Cleveland.

THE STEAMSHIP *WILLIAM G. MATHER* MUSEUM
1001 East 9th Street Pier, Cleveland, Ohio 44114-1003
Telephone: (216) 574-6262   Fax: (216) 574-2536

Email: admather@aol.com
Website: http:/little.nhlink./wgm/wghhome.html

Open 7 Days a Week – Memorial Day Through Labor Day
Monday-Saturday 10:00 am to 5:00 pm
Sundays Noon to 5:00 pm

May, September and October
Fridays and Saturdays 10:00 am to 5:00 pm
Sundays Noon to 5:00 pm

Special
Faces
of the
Great
Lakes

Special Faces of the Great Lakes

It's hard to imagine a person living in the Great Lakes region whose life is not somehow enriched by the lakes themselves. Their natural beauty inspires paintings and novels. Their fresh waters are an endless arena for fishing and recreation, and their mere size supports an entire shipping industry.

The following pages feature Arlene Earl, Lawrence Hayes and George Yaworski...three individuals whose lives were not only enriched, but shaped, by the Great Lakes. To the best of our knowledge they never met, yet their lives are as intertwined as three waves that become one on the open waters of the lakes. There is even a chance that they "passed on ships in the night."

Lawrence Hayes and George Yaworski were both stewards aboard Great Lakes freighters; Lawrence for the Tomlinson Shipping Line and George aboard the *S.S. Edmund Fitzgerald*. Arlene Earl had an uncle in the profession, and has gone on to become a legend in her own right as "Flower Lady of the Great Lakes." Lawrence Hayes passed away in 1967, leaving his family with many fond memories of his steamship days, and his sailor-tested recipes, which they still use. Arlene and George are practiced in the art of feeding hungry sailors, and plan to continue doing so for many years to come. Their recipes from the Great Lakes are sure to enrich our appetites!

Arlene Earl
Legendary *"Flower Lady"* of the Great Lakes

Flower Lady Arlene Earl with Norman LaCroix
(Uncle Norman), retired Chief Engineer.

*"Your reputation as the Flower Lady will long live as
part of the lore of the Great Lakes shipping industry.
You are our navigational star.
Someone who brings a rare bright light
to our often remote and isolated life out here."*

Dale K. Mason
M.V. Saturn

*Thank you so much for thinking of us.
The flowers you send are rare and beautiful.
They soften the cold, hard steel somehow."*

Joseph Ruch
S.S. Charles Beeghley

They work long hard days, they're tough, they've weathered some of the most ferocious storms the Great Lakes can dish out....**AND THEY LIKE FLOWERS!** They are the men and women who serve aboard the magnificent freighters that sail the Great Lakes. The same men and women whose thoughtfulness and caring earned them an eternal spot in the grateful heart of Arlene Earl, also known as the *"Flower Lady."*

The legend of the *Flower Lady* dates back to 1984, when Arlene and her husband Dick invited their beloved Uncle Norman to live with them on Harsen's Island. The legend of Arlene herself dates back over a century, to 1883, when her great-grandfather Christopher immigrated to America from Germany. His first order of business upon arrival was to build a house for his family in the Detroit area, and then to open a flower shop. Christopher grew fresh flowers and vegetables in a garden beside the house. Word of his services spread quickly and he was soon busy supplying fresh flowers and vegetables to area hotels. Arlene's grandfather, Albert, eventually took over and in turn handed the business down to her father, Chris Engle. A greenhouse was built in 1910 and a truck eventually replaced the horse and buggy used for deliveries, but the family tradition of supplying fresh flowers remained unchanged.

Chief Engineer Norman LaCroix, "a dedicated company man," spent 47 years sailing the Great Lakes on the ships he loved.

Arlene learned the flower business from her father, who in addition to passing down the family business, passed along a wealth of knowledge on plant care and flower design. She became the fourth generation to run her great-grandfather's dream (The Chris Engle Greenhouse in Detroit, Michigan) and carries on the tradition with pride. Arlene's son, Chris, still lives in the house his great-great-grandfather built over a century ago.

The *Flower Lady,* as Arlene if affectionately known by the sailors whose lives she has touched, became an immediate legend on the Great Lakes in 1984. She didn't intend to become a legend; in fact she didn't expect any recognition at all. Arlene simply wanted to thank the passing sailors for their thoughtfulness towards her Uncle

Norman. Norman LaCroix (Uncle Norman) was born on Harsen's Island in 1905. When he was 23 years old he began sailing the Great Lakes with the Oglebay Norton Fleet as an oiler. He quickly worked his way up to Chief Engineer and went on to spend 47 years on the ships he loved. "He was a dedicated company man and absolutely loved his time on the ships," Arlene remembers of the uncle that always made time to come back and visit his family on the island.

Uncle Norman in later years, as one of his beloved ships passes by his new home with Dick and Arlene on Harson's Island.

Arlene Earl, legendary *Flower Lady* of the Great Lakes, aboard the *J.W. Westcott* boat to deliver flowers to a passing freighter.

"He made some wonderful friends during his 47 years on the lakes." The depth of those friendships is still felt by Arlene today.

Norman retired from Oglebay Norton as Chief Engineer of the *Reserve* in 1967. Several years later, in 1984, it became apparent he was afflicted with Alzheimer Disease. Arlene and Dick invited Uncle Norman to stay with them on Harsen's Island, knowing he would enjoy the sight of freighters passing by everyday. As suspected, he spent most of his days outside, waving to passing ships. Arlene sent a few simple notes to the shipping companies, informing them of Norman's whereabouts, and that's all it took. His waves from shore were soon greeted with salutes from the passing ships (1 long whistle and 2 short whistles) and he came to believe that each ship passing was his. Norman's tears of joy at the thoughtful gesture did not go unnoticed by Arlene. In fact, the salutes brightened both of their days.

Arlene set out to thank the thoughtful crews of the passing ships the best way she knew how…she sent them beautiful flowers. Using the services of the mail boat at J.W. Westcott Company (the Detroit boat that services passing freighters) fresh flowers were delivered to the ships with a note of thanks from Arlene. Little did she know her flowers would mean as much to the sailors as their thoughtfulness meant to her and Uncle Norman. Her heartfelt bouquets of thanks sparked thoughtful expressions of gratitude from men and women Arlene thought may be too busy to even notice her flowers. Cards and letters addressed to the *Flower Lady* started arriving at Arlene's door and an unsuspected legend took root. Notes and flowers blossomed into friendships and, much to Arlene's delight, a lasting tribute to Uncle Norman.

Arlene receives greetings of frienship as the *J.W. Westcott* boat pulls alongside a slowed freighter to deliver her bouquets of thankfulness.

Dear Flower Lady:

All of us sailors want to thank you very much. We sure do appreciate the flowers that you send to us. It makes the holiday seem more like home.

Many, Many Thanks!
M.V. Joseph H. Frantz Sailors

Dear Flower Lady:

On behalf of the officers and crew of the M.V. Saturn, we'd like to thank you again for your thoughtful flowers at Sweetest Day and all the other holidays.

You are our navigational star – someone who brings a rare bright light to our often remote and isolated life out here. Thanks for caring.

All the best,
Dale K. Mason
1st Engineering Officer

Dear Flower Lady:

Many thanks from all the dads on the M.V. Gemini for the great flowers and balloons for Father's Day. Much Appreciated!

A Thankful Crew

Dear Flower Lady:

The crew of the M.V. George A. Sloan would like to wish you a very happy Mother's Day. We appreciate very much your sending us the flower arrangements. They are very beautiful and they fit the many different occasions.

Everyone is glad that the long winter is over. When we started out this spring Lake Superior was covered from shore to shore with ice. Actually, it was quite a beautiful sight. Now the ice is gone and the temperature is on the rise. Trees are budding and flowers all over are in bloom. The Good Lord sure does make things wonderful.

Thanks Again and God Bless You and Yours
Frank E. Cicero
2nd Mate

Dear Arlene:

This will be my last note of appreciation to you, as the re-flagging of the M.V. Gemini to Canada will put me out of work with Cleveland Tankers. I've taken a shore job near home and will be able to spend more time with my family.

The dictionary defines a "heroine" as the central figure in any important event honored for outstanding qualities." And so, you will remain one in your own right for doing something no one else ever did to help raise the morale of so many in a thankless job, forgotten by the world, except you!

So if you no longer hear from the M.V. Gemini you will know why. On behalf of the ships and crews that never said thanks for being an important event, your reputation as the "Flower Lady" will long live as part of the lore of the Great Lakes shipping industry.

Wishing you all the best and I hope to be able to meet you at your shop sometime.

Yours in the faith,
Dale K. Mason

Mrs. Earl:

Just have to take a little time out to thank you. The flowers that were sent to Captain Ralph Yanich were really beautiful. I've been sailing 20 years now and there have been many trips by your house. It is so nice to wave at your place. I don't know if we will ever get the chance to meet but in many ways some of us feel we already know you a little!

Thanks so much for the beautiful flowers you have sent to us over the years. The "Flower Lady" will always be in this sailor's heart and prayers.

Your Friend,
John B. Poluth
M.V. Fred R. White, Jr.

Dear Arlene and Dick:

Thank you so much for thinking of us. The flowers you send are rare and beautiful; they soften the cold hard steel somehow. We look forward to passing your house and waving. When you're not home we look and look and speculate on the cause …"must be grocery shopping."

Again, thank you for thinking of us. Please know that we think of you often and fondly.

Sincerely,
Joseph C. Ruch
Master, S.S. Elton Hoyt 2nd

To The Flower Lady:

We were guests on M.V. Roger Blough June 22nd through June 28th. Each afternoon our passenger porter would deliver wonderful appetizers and each mid-morning we were served delicious pastries. One day he delivered a lovely bouquet of fresh flowers. It was truly one of the memorable moments of our trip! How special you made us feel! Thank you for your thoughtful touch, it was enjoyed by all aboard.

Sincerely,
Lori and David
Duluth, Minnesota

For 10 years, until his death in 1994, Norman waited patiently for "his" ships to sail by, blowing their whistles in salute. He was never disappointed and Arlene never stopped expressing their gratitude to the thoughtful crews. Uncle Norman is gone now, but the legendary *Flower Lady* is far from finished in expressing her thanks to the crews who brightened his final days. "They brought so much joy into his life, and into mine," she remembers. At least four times a year (Easter, Father's Day, Thanksgiving and Christmas) the *Flower Lady* creates and sends fresh flower arrangements to over 60 freighters as they pass by. She surprises the crews with flowers on other days too. Special guests aboard, a special crewmember's birthday or just the passing of a ship that hasn't been by in a while are reasons enough for a bouquet of gratitude and friendship from the *Flower Lady*. Cost has never been a consideration to Arlene. "Yes, it's expensive, but when you make a flower arrangement and put it aboard a ship, you make 30 sailors happy. You can't put a price on that…the joy is in the giving."

Arlene treasures the letters and cards she receives from sailors thanking her for the flowers, for brightening an otherwise dreary day and for making them feel a little closer to home. The whistle salutes from passing ships continue, now in honor and recognition of the *Flower Lady* and she lights up every time she hears the familiar sound. When Arlene is busy running the greenhouse back on the mainland, Dick mans the helm at Harsen's Island, waving to passing freighters and signaling with Uncle Norman's cannon. "We have been more than

Dear Arlene and Dick:

Words cannot express the thoughtfulness in the bouquet of flowers we received from you. Without realizing it, it has become the best morale builder I've ever seen. When the crew sees the flowers on the table it seems to bring them together again. Thank you from the bottom of our hearts. We will continue to wake you up in the morning, providing it is after 6:00 a.m.

Captain R. Sobuck and Crew of the M.V. Calute II

Arlene,

You are always making us feel better. There are a lot of fathers out here wishing they were home. Thanks again.

Joseph C. Ruch, Master, and Crew of the S.S. Charles M. Beeghly

thanked," they both readily insist. "Our lives have been enriched and blessed by the special friendships that have come into them through Uncle Norman. We honor his memory with flowers and at the same time thank the thoughtful sailors of the Great Lakes for remembering one of their own.

Crewmembers often visit Arlene and Dick at their home on Harsen's Island, taking in the view of a passing freighter or two themselves as they enjoy a homemade lakeside lunch. The *Flower Lady* can cook too, and has plenty of food on hand for always-welcome friends from the Great Lakes.

The *Flower Lady's* Favorite Lakeside Lunch

Lakeside Sangria · Fruit Kabobs · Cauliflower Salad
Fresh Asparagus Quiche
Herbed Crescent Rolls
Sailor's Favorite Cookies · Old-Fashion Apple Cake

LAKESIDE SANGRIA

1 (20 oz.) can	pineapple chunks
2 (11 oz.) cans	mandarin oranges
1/3 c.	frozen lemonade concentrate, thawed, undiluted
1 c.	club soda
2 c.	red wine
	Orange rind curls, for garnish
	Pineapple chunks, for garnish

Drain pineapple chunks and mandarin oranges. Reserve several pineapple chunks for garnish. Spread remaining pineapple chunks and mandarin oranges on tray; freeze until firm. Place frozen fruit in food processor or blender and mix 30 seconds. Add lemonade concentrate and 1 cup wine; mix until smooth. Pour mixture into serving pitcher. Stir in remaining wine and club soda. To serve pour into individual glasses garnished with pineapple chunks and orange rind curls.

Yield: 6 Servings

FRUIT KABOBS

Strawberries
Kiwi, sliced
Pineapple, cut into chunks
Grapes, green *or* purple
Orange sections

Thread fresh fruit onto skewers. May substitute ingredients with fresh fruit of choice, in season. If desired, serve with fruit dip.

Fruit Dip

2 (8 oz.) tubs	soft cream cheese
1 (8 oz.) jar	marshmallow crème

Mix ingredients together well and chill. If desired, add 2 teaspoons grated orange peel or use strawberry flavored cream cheese instead of regular.

CAULIFLOWER SALAD

1 head	lettuce
1 lb.	bacon
1 lg. or 2 sm.	onions
1 head	cauliflower
2 c.	mayonnaise
3/4 to 1 c.	sugar
1-1/2 c.	Parmesan cheese, grated

Break lettuce into pieces and place in bottom of glass serving bowl. Cut bacon into small pieces, fry and drain. Spread bacon pieces over lettuce. Chop onion small and layer over bacon. Cut cauliflower into very small pieces and layer over onion. Mix mayonnaise with sugar and spread over cauliflower. Sprinkle cheese over top. Cover salad and refrigerate. Stir before serving.

FRESH ASPARAGUS QUICHE

1 (9-inch)	deep dish pie shell, unbaked
1 lb.	fresh asparagus
3	eggs
1-1/2 c.	half & half
8 oz.	Swiss cheese, cubed
4 oz.	Cheddar cheese, cubed
3 Tbsp.	Parmesan cheese, grated
1 Tbsp.	flour
3/4 tsp.	salt
1 dash	nutmeg
1 dash	pepper

Place 1/2 cubed cheese, Parmesan cheese and flour in blender; grate until smooth. Add remaining cheese and continue to grate. Place cheese mixture in bottom of pie shell. Wash asparagus and chop into 1-inch pieces. Blanch approximately 3 to 4 minutes in boiling water; drain. In bowl combine eggs, half & half, salt, pepper and nutmeg. Stir asparagus into egg mixture. Pour egg mixture over cheese. Bake at 350 degrees 45 to 60 minutes. Remove from oven and let stand 10 minutes before cutting.

Yield: 6 Servings

HERBED CRESCENT ROLLS

2 (8 oz.) pkgs.	refrigerated crescent rolls
1 stick	butter, melted
2 Tbsp.	onion, grated
1 tsp.	beau monde
2 Tbsp.	Parmesan cheese

Separate crescent roll dough into triangles and spread flat. Mix together melted butter, onion, beau monde and Parmesan cheese. Brush butter mixture over each triangle. Roll coated dough to form crescent rolls and bake according to package directions.

Yield: 16 Rolls

SAILOR'S FAVORITE COOKIES

2 c.	sugar
2 c.	brown sugar, firmly packed
1/4 c.	butter
1 c.	Crisco
4 lg.	eggs
2 tsp.	vanilla
3 c.	all-purpose flour
2 tsp.	salt
2 tsp.	baking soda
3 c.	oatmeal
2 c.	soft raisins
1 c.	chocolate chips
1 c.	nuts, chopped
2 c.	coconut

Cream together sugar, brown sugar, butter, Crisco, eggs and vanilla. In separate bowl mix flour with salt and baking soda. Mix dry ingredients into creamed mixture. Stir in remaining ingredients by hand. Chill dough. Using a small scoop, place dough on ungreased cookie sheets. Bake at 350 degrees 8 to 10 minutes.

OLD-FASHION APPLE CAKE

4 c.	apples, peeled, diced
2 c.	sugar
2 c.	flour
1 c.	nuts, chopped
2	eggs
1/2 c.	oil
2 tsp.	baking soda
2 tsp.	vanilla
2 tsp.	cinnamon
1 tsp.	salt

Cream Cheese Frosting

1/2 c.	butter
1 (3 oz.) pkg.	cream cheese
1 c.	powdered sugar
1 tsp.	vanilla

To prepare cake combine apples with flour; toss to coat. Add remaining ingredients and stir to combine. Batter will be very stiff. Bake in greased 9x13-inch pan at 350 degrees 45 to 60 minutes.

Combine frosting ingredients and beat until smooth. Spread frosting over cooled cake.

In 1996 Arlene Earl, *Flower Lady of the Great Lakes*, received a high and cherished honor from the maritime community in being appointed one of 29 Bell Ringers at the Annual Memorial for the *Edmund Fitzgerald* held at Mariner's Church in Detroit. The service is held every November to honor the 29 crewmembers lost with their ship that tragic day in 1975. Arlene's Uncle Norman had been acquainted with most of the 29 men lost, making her appointment not only a great honor, but also a time of personal tribute to all of the men and women that sail the Great Lakes.

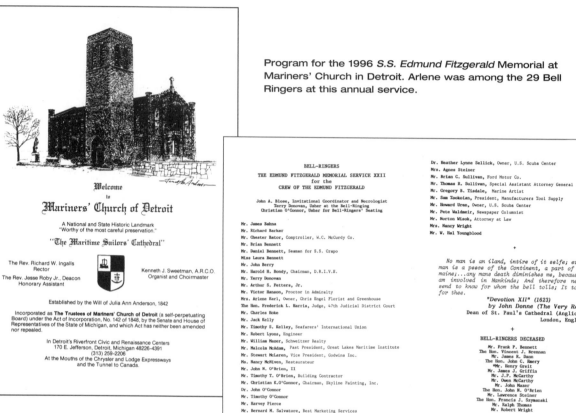

Welcome
to
Mariners' Church of Detroit

A National and State Historic Landmark
"Worthy of the most careful preservation."

"The Maritime Sailors' Cathedral"

The Rev. Richard W. Ingalls
Rector

The Rev. Jesse Roby Jr., Deacon
Honorary Assistant

Kenneth J. Sweetman, A.R.C.O.
Organist and Choirmaster

Established by the Will of Julia Ann Anderson, 1842

Incorporated as **The Trustees of Mariners' Church of Detroit** (a self-perpetuating Board) under the Act of Incorporation, No. 142 of 1848, by the Senate and House of Representatives of the State of Michigan, and which Act has neither been amended nor repealed.

In Detroit's Riverfront Civic and Renaissance Centers
170 E. Jefferson, Detroit, Michigan 48226-4391
(313) 259-2206
At the Mouths of the Chrysler and Lodge Expressways
and the Tunnel to Canada.

Program for the 1996 *S.S. Edmund Fitzgerald* Memorial at Mariners' Church in Detroit. Arlene was among the 29 Bell Ringers at this annual service.

BELL-RINGERS

THE EDMUND FITZGERALD MEMORIAL SERVICE XXII
for the
CREW OF THE EDMUND FITZGERALD

John A. Blose, Invitational Coordinator and Necrologist
Terry Donovan, Usher at the Bell-Ringing
Christian O'Connor, Usher for Bell-Ringers' Seating

Mr. James Bahna
Mr. Richard Barker
Mr. Chester Bator, Comptroller, W.C. McCurdy Co.
Mr. Brian Bennett
Mr. Daniel Bennett, Seaman for S.S. Crapo
Miss Laura Bennett
Mr. John Berry
Mr. Harold H. Bondy, Chairman, D.R.I.V.E.
Mr. Terry Donovan
Mr. Arthur S. Fetters, Jr.
Mr. Victor Hanson, Proctor in Admiralty
Mrs. Arlene Earl, Owner, Chris Engel Florist and Greenhouse
The Hon. Frederick L. Harris, Judge, 47th Judicial District Court
Mr. Charles Hoke
Mr. Jack Kelly
Mr. Timothy S. Kelley, Seafarers' International Union
Mr. Robert Lyons, Engineer
Mr. William Mazer, Schweitzer Realty
Mr. Malcolm McAdam, Past President, Great Lakes Maritime Institute
Mr. Stewart McLaren, Vice President, Godwins Inc.
Ms. Nancy McNiven, Restaurateur
Mr. John N. O'Brien, II
Mr. Timothy T. O'Brien, Building Contractor
Mr. Christian K.O'Connor, Chairman, Skyline Painting, Inc.
Dr. John O'Connor
Mr. Timothy O'Connor
Mr. Harvey Pierce
Mr. Bernard M. Salvatore, Best Marketing Services

Dr. Heather Lynne Sellick, Owner, U.S. Scuba Center
Mrs. Agnes Steiner
Mr. Brian C. Sullivan, Ford Motor Co.
Mr. Thomas R. Sullivan, Special Assistant Attorney General
Mr. Gregory B. Tisdale, Marine Artist
Mr. Sam Zookoian, President, Manufacturers Tool Supply
Mr. Howard Uren, Owner, U.S. Scuba Center
Mr. Pete Waldmeir, Newspaper Columnist
Mr. Norton Wisok, Attorney at Law
Mrs. Nancy Wright
Mr. W. Hal Youngblood

+

No man is an iland, intire of it selfe; every man is a peece of the Continent, a part of the maine;...any mans death diminishes me, because I am involved in Mankinde; And therefore never send to know for whom the bell tolls; It tolls for thee.

"Devotion XII" (1623)
by John Donne (The Very Rev.)
Dean of St. Paul's Cathedral (Anglican)
London, England

+

BELL-RINGERS DECEASED

Mr. Frank P. Bennett
The Hon. Vincent J. Brennan
Mr. James R. Dann
The Hon. John C. Emery
*Mr. Henry Greit
Mr. James J. Griffin
Mr. J.P. McCarthy
Mr. Owen McCarthy
Mr. John Mazer
The Hon. John N. O'Brien
Mr. Lawrence Steiner
The Hon. Francis J. Szymanski
Mr. Ralph Thomas
Mr. Robert Wright

*Deceased 1996

A beautiful wreath of tribute prepared by Arlene for the 1996 memorial service in honor of the *Fitzgerald.*

Lawrence Hayes
Steward
1912–1967

They were "Steamboat People" and they loved the life they lived. For two decades Larry Hayes sailed the Great Lakes as a steward for the Tomlinson Fleet, while at the same time raising seven children with his wife Gert. Shipping season was a time of constant travel and excitement for all of them. When Larry was on a freighter bound for Duluth, his family was in a car bound for the same port, with their watches synchronized. Home was where the ship was, where they could all be together, and life was full of the joys and heartaches the Great Lakes are known to churn out.

Youngest son, Michael, was at his dad's side whenever possible. In 1961 he is seen helping dad with the Christmas baking. Michael is credited with inheriting Larry's skills in the kitchen, and also — according to family members — his talent for leaving a messy kitchen behind him.

Larry started his career in cooking at the tender age of nine. His father served as cook at a lumber camp and Larry's favorite place was right beside him. Propped up on crates to reach the counter, he learned his first recipe for biscuits. The biscuit recipe came in handy as he went on to serve as cook at the lumber camp himself, and then as cook with the Civilian Conservation Corps. After five years with the CCC Larry signed on as cook aboard a construction boat bound for Greenland. He improved his culinary skills while cooking in the U.S. Army, where he once received an award for feeding 1,000 unexpected soldiers in less than two hours. Larry joined the Tomlinson Fleet after the war, and from 1948 until his death in 1967, Larry put his talents to work on the Great Lakes, preparing three hot meals a day for the shipmates he considered family.

The *Merton E. Farr*

When Larry started with the Tomlinson Line in 1948 he was assigned to the flagship of their fleet, the *Merton E. Farr*. Throughout his 20 years on the Great Lakes he worked on four other ships in the fleet, (*Big Davidson, Little Davidson, G.A. Tomlinson and Sylvania*) but the *Merton E. Farr* always held a special place in his heart.

During this era of shipping, before unions became involved in the industry, it was quite common for the majority of a ship's crew to come from the same community. Brothers, sons, and even neighbors, were hired for the desirable jobs based simply on the trusted recommendation of a crewmember. In turn, families of crewmembers became a close-knit group bound by their shared concern for the ship's crew, each other and their community. As a group they were known as "Steamboat People" and as a group they took care of each other.

It was also quite common for family members to be allowed aboard ship. As the wife of an officer, Gert was on the ship often, for up to two weeks at a time, mingling with the captain's guests and dining in the elegant Officer's Dining Room. Their children were allowed on board for two or three days at a time. They spent these memorable days visiting with dad when his work was done, wandering around the ship with other crewmembers they considered family and even enjoying the luxury of staying in the elegant guest rooms once in a while. Larry and Gert's two youngest sons, Michael and Peter, were Larry's constant companions. All of their children enjoyed the time with dad aboard ship. It was a time that allowed Larry and Gert to raise their family together, even though he sailed the Great Lakes and she ran their home in northern Michigan.

Idealistic and carefree as it may sound, the captains ran tight ships and crews worked long, hard hours. At 6:00 am every morning Larry was in the galley and breakfast was being prepared. Cooked cereals, cold cereals, eggs made to order, pancakes and breakfast meats were common fare. As steward, Larry had four additional crewmembers in his department, (2nd cook, 1st porter, 2nd porter and dishwasher) and all hands were busy preparing the noon meal as soon as breakfast was cleared away. The meal served at noon was the largest of the day and the crew's favorite.

Captain Ed Cohours, pictured with his wife Grace, hired Larry in 1947 for his first job on the Great Lakes.

416

Fried chicken, pot roast, turkey, stroganoff or stew were accompanied by freshly baked breads and rolls, salads, vegetables and desserts all prepared that morning in the galley. The evening meal usually offered creatively prepared leftovers from the day before. In addition, the galley staff was always happy to make a fresh sandwich for the crewmember that decided later on he just hadn't had enough. The crew enjoyed as much as they wanted of anything they wanted.

While the *Merton E. Farr* was tied up for the winter months one year, a fire swept through the galley. Larry helped design the brand new stainless steel galley that was installed.

Larry did all of the baking on board, which helped tremendously in keeping costs down and never drew a complaint from the crew. Because of this, he consistently won the annual bonus awarded by the Tomlinson Fleet to the steward who prepared the best food at the best (most economical) price.

Officers and guests of the captain dined in the elegant Officer's Dining Room. Tables covered with white linen and fresh flowers complimented the meals prepared by Larry and his crew in the galley. When in port for a few days, Larry would put together picnic lunches for the captain and his guests to enjoy on shore. These meals, too, were prepared from scratch on board and featured full menus including fried chicken, homemade biscuits, jars of good fruit and a salad. Larry often received hundreds of dollars in tips from these guests, in recognition of his culinary skills and the extra work he put in while they were on board.

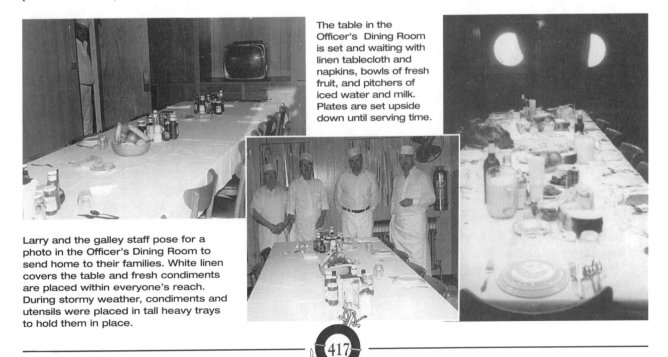

The table in the Officer's Dining Room is set and waiting with linen tablecloth and napkins, bowls of fresh fruit, and pitchers of iced water and milk. Plates are set upside down until serving time.

Larry and the galley staff pose for a photo in the Officer's Dining Room to send home to their families. White linen covers the table and fresh condiments are placed within everyone's reach. During stormy weather, condiments and utensils were placed in tall heavy trays to hold them in place.

Since the shipping season ran well into December, the crew celebrated Thanksgiving together on board with a full turkey dinner and all the trimmings. These menus always included a few of Larry's specialties that had quickly become crew favorites. Tables in the Crew's Mess Room were covered with special checkered tablecloths for the occasion and the galley staff started extra early with all the holiday baking.

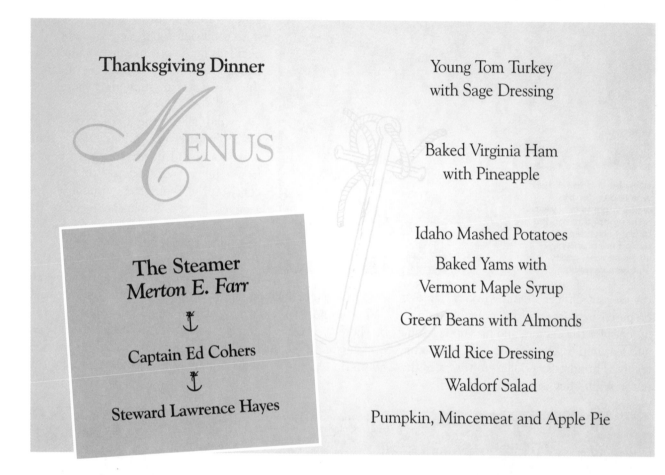

Thanksgiving Dinner

MENUS

The Steamer
Merton E. Farr

⚓

Captain Ed Cohers

⚓

Steward Lawrence Hayes

Young Tom Turkey
with Sage Dressing

Baked Virginia Ham
with Pineapple

Idaho Mashed Potatoes

Baked Yams with
Vermont Maple Syrup

Green Beans with Almonds

Wild Rice Dressing

Waldorf Salad

Pumpkin, Mincemeat and Apple Pie

And, of course, Larry did a little cooking for his "crew" at home during the off-season. This is where he received his only complaint and it stemmed from his lack of practice in cutting down recipes. After a day in town, Gert and the children returned home to find Larry had baked fresh rolls (for a crew of 35 no less!) and had them scattered throughout the house, even on beds, to cool. The neighbors didn't complain though, they got the extras!

Off-season also allowed Larry time to teach his children a few tricks in the kitchen. His youngest son, Michael, and middle son, Peter, were always at his side and proved to be quick studies. Michael is credited with inheriting his dad's culinary talents and also, according to family members, one of his dad's few bad habits…leaving a messy kitchen behind him! Larry would be proud to know Michael is a doctor today, with two children of his own, both showing promise in the kitchen. Peter went on to become a school principal with four sons of his own. It has been said Peter and his boys find their kitchen talents in the "consumption end" of the culinary process. Larry's favorite recipes from his days on the Great Lakes have stood the test of time and are still frequently prepared for family gatherings.

Larry (in brown hat at right) prepared picnic lunches for the captain and his guests to enjoy on shore. Their picnics were complete meals freshly prepared on board.

Second youngest son, Peter (right), was also dad's constant companion. Together they enjoyed the carefree summer days of shipping season.

Steward Lawrence Hayes enjoyed over 20 years in the galleys of the ships he loved.

Larry's wife, Gert, wandered through the ships freely, even taking a supervised turn at the helm.

Daughters Phyllis and Maggie pose on deck in 1952. With their brothers and sisters, they were often on board for two or three days at a time.

Some of those 20 years were spent aboard the "Big" *James Davidson.*

WILD RICE DRESSING

Make a broth from the giblets and neck.
Add seasoning (salt, pepper, etc.) to taste, or use a commercial broth.

1/2 lb.	wild rice
1 c.	celery, finely diced
1/4 c.	pimiento, drained
1/2 c.	onion, finely diced
	Salt and pepper, to taste

Add all ingredients to broth and bring to boil. Reduce heat to slow rolling boil and watch carefully, wild rice takes a long time to cook. It is done when it appears to break open revealing a white interior. You may add additional broth if the cooking process removes the liquid. Rice should be moist, not watery, when served.

CHINESE STYLE FISH BATTER

2	eggs, well beaten
1 c.	cold water
3/4 c.	flour
1 Tbsp.	corn starch
1/2 tsp.	baking soda
1/2 tsp.	salt

Mix beaten eggs and cold water together well. In separate bowl mix dry ingredients together. Using a fork, mix dry ingredients into egg mixture. Mixture should be thin and lumpy. Coat fish with batter and deep fry.

PEPPER STEAK

1-1/2 lb.	round steak, cut in thin strips
3/4 tsp.	unseasoned instant meat tenderizer
3 Tbsp.	salad oil
3 lg.	green peppers, cut in 1-inch squares
3	scallions, with tops, thinly sliced
1/2 c.	celery, diagonally sliced
1-1/2 c.	beef consommé *or* bouillon
1 Tbsp.	corn starch
1/3 c.	light molasses
3 Tbsp.	soy sauce
1 tsp.	garlic powder
1-1/2 tsp.	MSG
1-1/2 tsp.	ginger
2 tsp.	lemon juice
4 c.	hot cooked rice

Slice beef thin and sprinkle with tenderizer; set aside. Heat oil in large skillet over high heat. Add beef slices and cook briefly until lightly browned. Add green pepper, scallions and celery. Cook 3 to 4 minutes, stirring frequently. In a bowl blend corn starch into beef consommé. Stir molasses, soy sauce, garlic powder, MSG, ginger and lemon juice into corn starch mixture; add to meat and vegetables. Stir well and cook an additional minute or two. Serve over rice, chow mein noodles or regular cooked egg noodles.

Yield: 6 Servings

BEEF STROGANOFF

1 lb.	round steak, cut into 1-1/2-inch cubes
1/2 c.	onion, chopped
1	garlic clove, minced
1 (6 oz.) can	mushrooms, drained, juice reserved
1 c.	sour cream
1 (10 oz.) can	tomato soup
1 Tbsp.	Worcestershire sauce
4 to 6 drops	tabasco sauce
1/2 tsp.	salt
1 dash	pepper

Dust meat cubes with flour and brown in large frying pan. Add onion, garlic and mushrooms to meat; stir fry a few minutes. Combine reserved mushroom juice with remaining ingredients and add to meat mixture. Cook together slowly until meat is tender. Serve over egg noodles or spaghetti.

MIRACLE WHIP DEVILS FOOD CAKE

1 c.	sugar
4 Tbsp.	cocoa
1 c.	Miracle Whip
1 c.	luke warm water
2 c.	cake flour
2 tsp.	baking soda

Combine all ingredients and mix together well. Bake at 350 degrees until cake tests done.

Frosting for Miracle Whip Devils Food Cake

1 c.	sugar
1 sq.	chocolate
1/4 c.	shortening, butter like
1 dash	salt
1/3 c.	milk

Mix all ingredients together in saucepan and boil 1 minute. Spread frosting over cooled cake.

APPLE CRISP

2 c.	quick cook oatmeal
1-1/2 c.	flour
1-1/2 c.	brown sugar
1 c.	margarine
1/2 tsp.	salt
1/4 c.	brown sugar
1 Tbsp.	cinnamon
4-1/2 to 5 c.	apple sauce

Combine oatmeal with flour, 1-1/2 cups brown sugar, margarine and salt. Mix with hands until crumbly like pie dough. Place 1/2 oatmeal mixture in bottom of well greased rectangle cake pan; pour apple sauce over top. Combine 1/4 cup brown sugar and 1 tablespoon cinnamon. Sprinkle over apple sauce. Cover apple sauce with remaining oatmeal mixture. Bake at 350 degrees 45 minutes or until light brown. Serve with whipped cream or ice cream.

Larry enjoyed his life on the Great Lakes and was always thankful for the secure lifestyle it offered his family. Being in port for a few days and having his family join him on board were Larry's happiest times. Other days, after the galley was clean and shut down for the night, he enjoyed playing cards with shipmates, writing a letter home and listening to his short wave radio. The short wave was a favorite hobby of Larry's and he always had the best one money could buy. One night in mid-November of 1958, he was lying on his bunk, half asleep, listening to his radio when he heard: "May Day! May Day! This is the *Carl D. Bradley*. We're breaking up! We're breaking up!" At first he thought he hadn't heard it right but jumped up, grabbed the galley phone that connected him to the wheelhouse and told them he had just heard a "May Day" from the *Bradley*. He heard several shipmates run into the wheelhouse reporting the same message. They never heard from the *Bradley* again. Larry's ship proceeded immediately to the area the *Bradley* had radioed from and upon arriving found several ships already there, a German freighter among them. They stayed in the area several hours, but there was nothing they could do. The 640-foot *Carl D. Bradley* had gone down in Lake Michigan during a fierce storm. Larry later learned that 33 of the *Bradley's* 35 crewmen had lost their lives.

Eight years later, in 1966, Larry was working aboard the G.A. *Tomlinson* looking forward to the end of the shipping season and getting home to his family. They had just left a sheltered area where they had spent a few days at anchor waiting out a storm. Larry was in bed when they headed out, but was soon awakened by the rolling of the ship. When he went up on deck he learned the watchman had just spotted a body floating in a life preserver. He later learned they had been the first ship on the scene where the *Daniel J. Morrell* had gone down in Lake Huron on November 29, 1966. Larry wrote the letter on the following page, sharing the tragic news with his family.

December 1, 1966
Detroit, Michigan

My Dearest Gert:

Just a line to say we are all okay and I am fine. But we all saw something yesterday that we won't forget for a long time. We were the first boat on the scene where the *Daniel Morrell* went down. In fact, they hadn't found any bodies or anything as yet. I had been in bed about one hour when all of a sudden the ship rolled and I heard the rudder groan. Gert, you know that noise…when we turn around. Well, we had been going towards Port Huron and Don Beam was on watch and he spotted a body in a life preserver. So the captain stopped and turned around. It was quite frightening and sad. We saw three bodies floating by. Then the little Coast Guard boat came along and picked them up. We watched them, it wasn't very nice. The Coast Guard had planes and a helicopter, so we only stayed there about an hour and we left. All we saw of the boat, and it was a little bigger than ours, was a couple of buoy cans, two ores and a piece of painted board. We left Rogers City last Sunday night at midnight and went right across to Detour and anchored in the river until 1:00 a.m. Wednesday morning.

I sure give Joe (Captain) credit. If it looks bad and the weather reports are bad he starts for shelter and stays there until he is sure its safe. The captain on the *Morrell* sure made a bad, bad mistake. But, it's over now. God help them. I think there will be the one survivor and the rest are gone.

I will be calling you from Rogers City before you get this, if we are not delayed on account of weather. Oh yes, why don't you order that pool table from Sears. It's pretty nice I think and the boys would enjoy it lots this winter. Well honey, I am going to say good-bye for this time. I love you lots and the boys I miss lots.

I send my love to all of you.

Larry

They were "Steamboat People" and they experienced both the joy and sorrow of the Great Lakes. Lawrence Hayes passed away at home on February 1st, 1967, just a few short weeks after returning home to his family at the end of the 1966 shipping season. He was only 55 years old, but lived a life fuller than most. He lives on in the hearts of his family, in the galleys of the freighters that pass by and in the minds of his grandchildren, who never knew him, but know the "Grandpa Larry" stories as if they had been there.

George Yaworski
Steward
S.S. Edmund Fitzgerald

Built:	Great Lakes Engineering River Rouge, Michigan (for Northwestern Mutual Insurance)
Launched:	June, 1958
Length:	729'
Beam:	75'
Draft:	26'6"
Cargo:	Taconite (Iron Ore Pellets)
Crew:	29
Passengers:	Luxurious Accommodations for Four
Lifesaving Equipment:	Two 50-Man Lifeboats Two 25-Man Inflatable Life Rafts 83 Life Preservers

George Yaworski worked as a steward with the Oglebay Norton Company for many years. He worked aboard the *Edmund Fitzgerald* during the 1973 and 1974 shipping seasons.

It has been over a quarter of a century since the 729-foot *S.S. Edmund Fitzgerald* set out on what would be her final voyage across the unpredictable waters of the Great Lakes. When launched in 1958, the *Fitzgerald* was the longest ship to sail the Great Lakes, a record she held for over 11 years. During her 17 years of distinguished service the *Edmund Fitzgerald* achieved several other shipping firsts, including setting records for speed, most tons of iron ore hauled in one season, most iron ore carried in one trip and most tons of iron ore carried through the Soo Locks. Records that no other ship surpassed for years, except the *Fitzgerald* herself. She was the flagship of the Oglebay Norton fleet and pride of the Great Lakes. Duty aboard was considered a privilege. Her crew took such pride in the magnificent ship, they were known to chase seagulls away to keep the decks and hatch covers clean.

On November 9, 1975 the *Edmund Fitzgerald* began loading a cargo of taconite in Superior, Wisconsin bound for the Detroit area. It would be the 40th voyage of her 17th season on the Great Lakes. At 2:20 pm that afternoon she left Superior with 26,116 tons of cargo. A few hours later gale warnings were issued for all of Lake Superior and the region braced for yet another of the lake's legendary fierce early winter storms. The *Edmund Fitzgerald* and her crew gallantly weathered the storm for over 24 hours, holding their own against unrelenting rain and snow, wind gusts over 85 miles per hour and 25-foot waves beating across the decks.

On November 10, 1975 at 7:10 pm the *Edmund Fitzgerald* radioed they were "holding their own." That was the last communication received from the magnificent ship and her proud crew of 29 sons, fathers, husbands, brothers, uncles, grandfathers and friends. Shortly thereafter she disappeared from radar to the bottom of Lake Superior. Unfortunately, time did not allow the ample lifesaving equipment to be used that cold November night and all 29 crewmembers perished with their ship. As she set shipping records throughout her 17 years on the Great Lakes, no one dreamed the *Edmund Fitzgerald* would also set the record as the largest ship to rest at the bottom of Lake Superior.

The *S.S. Edmund Fitzgerald*

Annual services, permanent exhibits and many publications have come forth to honor the 29 brave seamen that joined the *Edmund Fitzgerald* in her final resting place on November 10, 1975. (see page 440.) In 1995 surviving family members agreed to allow a dive down to the *Edmund Fitzgerald* for retrieval of the ship's bell, which is now permanently displayed at the Great Lakes Shipwreck Museum at Whitefish Point, Michigan. (A ship's bell is considered the "heart of the ship" because, traditionally, the bell was used to sound the time every half hour, to change the watch (every four hours), to summon sailors to meals and to serve as a warning signal whenever the ship was in fog or other foul weather.) A replica brass bell, inscribed with the name of each lost crewmember, was carefully left in its place as a permanent memorial. The Tug *Anglian Lady* proudly carried the necessary equipment out to the dive site and assisted in raising the ship's bell. (See page 95.)

Personal tributes to the *Edmund Fitzgerald* and her crew are shared less publicly with memories and stories of those who once walked her decks, knew the men that were lost or just witnessed the beauty of her passing by.

George Yaworski is among the men who knew the *Edmund Fitzgerald* well. He worked aboard the ship and treasures his memories of serving in her galley during the 1973 and 1974 shipping seasons. "I thought she was the most beautiful thing I'd ever seen," George recalls of taking his first steps aboard. He knew all but four of the 29 men lost, and had the honor of cooking many meals for them while he shared their ship. He prepared and served the crew what would end up being their last Thanksgiving Dinner aboard the ship in 1974. Fate alone is the only explanation for why George was not on the *Fitzgerald* when it went down in November 1975. A relief steward was needed for the fateful voyage due to health problems of the assigned steward, and George was not selected. "If I'd been on it, I'd had been in the galley," he said. "That's upside down now in over 500 feet of water." George went on to spend over 15 years in the galleys of Great Lakes freighters, combining his love of the Great Lakes with his talent for cooking. The *Edmund Fitzgerald* was his first assignment and he helped assure those sailors were fed well!

George knows his way around a kitchen, whether his feet are firmly planted on dry ground or deep in the galley of a Great Lakes freighter. His career began in the 1940s, when he joined the Civilian Conservation Corps in the Rocky Mountains as a cook. It was here, as a teenager, that he learned to prepare 20 gallons of hearty soup over the uneven heat of a wood-burning camp stove. A few years later, eager to answer Uncle Sam's call for help in the war effort, George enlisted in the Merchant Marines. Being only 17-1/2 years of age, he was too young to help there, so he immediately signed on with U.S. Coast Guard. As Ship's Cook Third Class, George served his country and the hungry Coast Guard crews in the Pacific four years.

In 1947 George returned to civilian life as 2nd cook for the Hotel Chippewa in Manistee, Michigan. He quickly worked his way up to Chef and spent over 20 years at the Chippewa ordering supplies, holding down costs, creating menus and preparing food that kept the customers coming back. Hotel Chippewa was just a few miles from Lake Michigan, keeping George close to his love of the sailor's life and the freighters that docked in Manistee with loads of coal, stone and wood.

After the death of his wife, George decided to follow his heart back to the Great Lakes and signed on with Oglebay Norton Company in 1973. He was assigned as a porter aboard the pride of their fleet, the 729-foot *Edmund Fitzgerald*. After being quickly promoted to 2nd cook, he spent the rest of the winter studying for a steward's position. With the required training completed, George spent the next shipping season with Oglebay Norton as a relief steward. Stewards worked 60 days on/30 days off, so Relief Steward Yaworski always had an assignment waiting for him on one of the fleet's 18 ships.

George remained a sailor from 1973 through 1988, working on the *Edmund Fitzgerald* during the 1973 and 1974 shipping seasons. He found the steward's position similar to that of chef at the Chippewa Hotel; his two decades of training came in handy. Aboard ship he was responsible for ordering supplies, creating menus, cooking the main dishes and keeping costs in line with other ships in the fleet. The latter proved his biggest challenge…Great Lakes sailors are notorious for their "great big appetites!" "The more you ate, the more you earned," explains George, noting that free food is part of a sailor's compensation package. He fondly remembers what it was like to be a steward on the Great Lakes, the bond of friendship shared by sailors and the food:

The Food, as brought to life by Steward George Yaworski…

The reputation of stewards on Great Lakes carriers is legendary. Ship's crews are treated to New York strip steaks every Saturday; if you can eat more than one steak, order it! (Some stewards prepare the steaks over charcoal grills in the summertime. They have the grills strategically placed out on deck.) Steak…mushrooms…baked potatoes…corn on the cob…garlic bread! Hey! It's Saturday!

Thanksgiving Day is the biggest day of the year for crews on the Great Lakes. The galley crews go "all out" to make Thanksgiving away from home a pleasurable experience, and hope the ship is underway, so crewmembers aren't torn between eating on board and going home to their respective families. "My wife didn't serve lobster tail on Thanksgiving Day…did the steward have any left over?" is a common rejoinder by a crewmember who went ashore that day. "The lobster is all gone, but there are a few slices of mince and pumpkin pie out there."

The stewards and their 2nd cooks take pride in feeding the men who man the ships. Breakfast, dinner and supper. The breakfast menu consists of eggs, pancakes, French toast, bacon, sausage, ham, hot or dry cereal and fried potatoes. Bowls of apples, oranges and bananas are standard fare. At the ten o'clock coffee break the 2nd cook brings out freshly made doughnuts, sticky buns, Danish rolls, coffee cakes and cookies…cookies…cookies.

Dinner menus feature hearty soup and sandwich fare, along with omelets, casseroles, sometimes huge sheet pans of pizza and other similar items. The two o'clock coffee break may have cupcakes, brownies, date bars, etc., because supper is less than two hours away.

At suppertime time, they feature roasts, chops, (steaks on Saturday), fish, poultry, Cornish hens, veal patties, etc. For anyone who still suffers hunger pangs, the night lunch refrigerator is stocked with half a dozen different types of cold cuts and several kinds of cheese, along with supper leftovers.

If a merchant sailor ever drops by your home for a visit and declines your offer of doughnuts, cupcakes, cookies, pies or cake don't feel badly. He reached his saturation point a long time ago!

The Steward and the Galley, as a firsthand account from George...

Walk through the pantry of any cargo carrier and see the shelves loaded with canned goods, cereals, coffees and teas. Step into the refrigerators and see the various meats, poultry, eggs, fresh fruits and vegetables. Go through the bakeshop and check the flour and sugar bins, or smell the freshly made breads, cakes, cookies and sticky buns. You may even get a glimpse of the steward, the man in charge of the galley department.

The steward's job is to prepare the menus, order the food, cook and serve it, and see to it that the men get clean bed linens and bath towels every week. He also prepares and sends food reports to the front office regularly. Most ships on the Great Lakes have "short runs." Two and a half days from Toledo to Duluth and two and a half days back.

During "spring fit out," the steward orders enough staples and perishables to last about a week. Each time a 2nd cook or porter takes the last can from the pantry shelf, he writes it on a list so the steward can re-order. During hot summer months, the deckhands drink lots of Kool-Aid, which they call "Bug-Juice," along with iced tea, hot coffee and milk. The consumption of 100 quarts of milk every two and a half days is not usual.

The steward writes requisitions for food every time the ship leaves the dock. Approximately 12 hours before the ship is due to dock, he phones the order to the ship's Chandler by "ship-to-shore" telephone. The moment the ship reaches the dock, the groceries are there, waiting. The average food order amounts to $1,200 to $1,500. Food costs are monitored and controlled. If most ships in the fleet have approximately the same food cost, and your ship is consistently higher, you can be sure the company executives will send a representative to learn why.

Officers and deckhands have exactly the same menu. Deckhands, wipers and watchmen eat in the crew's mess. A porter waits on the deckhands. The captain, mates, engineers and wheelsmen eat in the officer's dining room and are waited on by the 2nd cook. The steward dishes up the portions and garnishes the plates.

Advice From George...

If you long to visit ports along Lake Michigan, Lake Huron, Lake Superior, Lake Erie or Canada, you love good food and the lure of the sea, join the Great Lakes Merchant Marines!

George Yaworski sailed until the end of the 1988 shipping season. He was 65 years old and ready to return to life on land. During his 15 years on the Great Lakes he cooked everything from steaks, lobster and turkey to breads, rolls and pastries, with several soups thrown in for good measure. On the following pages he shares some of the crew's favorite recipes.

KNICKERBOCKER BEAN SOUP

1-1/4 lbs.	Navy beans
2 gal.	boiling water
4 oz.	salt pork, cubed
2 oz.	carrots, diced
6 oz.	onions, chopped, divided in half
1-1/2 gal.	beef stock
3 lbs.	potatoes, diced
4 oz.	bacon, diced
3 lbs., 3 oz.	tomatoes
2 Tbsp.	salt
1/2 tsp.	pepper

Cover beans with cold water and soak 2 to 3 hours; do not drain. Combine beans with boiling water, salt pork, carrots and half of onions; cook until beans are tender. Add beef stock and potatoes; cook approximately 5 minutes until potatoes are tender. Fry bacon and remaining onions. Add bacon mixture to soup. Add tomatoes, salt and pepper. Adjust seasonings to taste.

This is a hearty, rich flavored soup that will keep them asking for more!

Yield: 50 (1-Cup) Servings

YELLOW SPLIT PEA SOUP

2-1/2 lbs.	yellow split peas
3 gal.	ham stock
3 lbs.	onions, chopped
1/2 tsp.	whole cloves
1 c.	flour
2 c.	cold water

Pick over, wash and soak peas in ham stock 3 hours; do not drain. Add onions and cloves. Simmer approximately 2 hours, until tender. Do not scorch. Blend flour with cold water and stir into boiling soup. Simmer 5 minutes to kill the taste of the flour. Adjust seasoning and serve.

FRENCH ONION SOUP

10 lbs.	onions, thinly sliced
1 lb.	fat
3 gal.	beef stock
1/4 c.	Worcestershire sauce
4 oz.	flour
	Cold water

Fry onions in fat until slightly browned. Add beef stock and simmer approximately 10 minutes. Add Worcestershire sauce. Blend flour with cold water and stir into soup while simmering. Stir vigorously to avoid lumps. Some people like to sprinkle grated cheese on a slice of trimmed rye bread, place it into the soup bowl and add the hot soup.

CORN CHOWDER

8 oz.	onions, diced
4 oz.	celery, diced
2 oz.	green peppers, diced
4 oz.	salt pork, diced
2-1/2 qts.	chicken stock
1 tsp.	thyme
1 Tbsp.	salt
1/2 tsp.	white pepper
2 lbs.	potatoes, diced
4 oz.	butter
1/2 c.	flour
1 qt.	milk
1 can	evaporated milk
3 sm. cans	whole kernel corn

Combine onions, celery, green peppers and salt pork; brown slightly. Add chick stock, thyme, salt and white pepper; simmer approximately 15 minutes. Add diced potatoes and simmer 5 minutes or until potatoes are tender. In separate stock pot melt butter; add flour. Blend into paste and let simmer approximately 5 minutes without letting it get brown. Heat milk and stir into butter-flour paste, stirring until thickened and smooth. Add to chicken stock mixture and blend well. Prior to serving add evaporated milk for extra-rich flavor. Stir in corn and heat.

CREAM OF CORN SOUP

1 qt.	beef stock
4 oz.	onions, chopped
3 oz.	pimientos, chopped
1-1/4 c.	butter
1-1/4 c.	flour
2 qts.	milk
1/2 tsp.	white pepper
2 Tbsp.	sugar
5 (16 oz.) cans	whole kernel corn

Add onions and pimientos to beef stock; cook 5 minutes. In separate pot combine butter and flour, cooking over low heat without browning. Heat milk and add to roux; mix until thickened and smooth. Add to beef stock mixture with white pepper and sugar. Add corn and transfer to double boiler to prevent scorching.

CREAM OF CHICKEN SOUP

3-1/2 qts.	chicken stock
8 oz.	celery, finely chopped
8 oz.	onions, finely chopped
1-1/4 c.	butter
1-1/4 c.	flour
2 qts.	milk, hot
8 to 10 oz.	chicken, diced, cooked
1 can	evaporated milk

Add chopped celery and onions to chicken stock; simmer approximately 20 minutes. In separate stock pot melt butter; add flour and make a paste. Cook 5 minutes over low heat without letting it turn brown. Add hot milk and stir until smooth. Add to chicken stock and blend. Add chicken. Add evaporated milk for extra rich flavor.

CHICKEN PAPRIKASH

8	frying chickens, cut in quarters
2 c.	flour
2 Tbsp.	seasoning salt
2	green peppers, diced
1 lb.	onions, diced
2 c.	chicken stock
4 Tbsp.	paprika
4 oz.	tomato paste
2 c.	sour cream

Thoroughly mix together flour and seasoning salt. Dredge cut up chickens in flour mixture and place in roasting pan. Sprinkle diced green peppers and onions over chicken and bake at 350 degrees 30 minutes. Mix together chicken stock, paprika, tomato paste and sour cream; pour over baked chicken. Cover pan tightly with aluminum foil and bake an additional 30 minutes.

Note: I prefer to make two batches of the sauce (chicken stock mixture) because it looks neater when poured over the chicken prior to serving.

BEEF STEW

6 lbs.	beef, cut into cubes
1 lb.	onions, diced
10 oz.	celery, diced
2 qts.	beef stock
1 (2-1/2 lb.) can	crushed tomatoes
1/2 tsp.	allspice
2	garlic cloves, minced
1/2 tsp.	rosemary
1 sm.	bay leaf
2 lbs.	potatoes, diced
1-3/4 lbs.	carrots, thickly sliced
3/4 c.	flour
	Water

Brown beef cubes in oven. Brown onions and celery in skillet; add to beef after browned. Cover with beef stock, crushed tomatoes, allspice, garlic, rosemary and bay leaf; simmer approximately 2-1/2 hours. Cook potatoes and carrots separately until tender. Mix flour with water and add to stock after it has simmered 2-1/2 hours, stirring until smooth. Add potatoes and carrots. Adjust seasonings and serve.

CHICKEN A LA KING ON TOAST

8 oz.	green pepper, diced
1 c.	chicken stock
2 c.	butter
2 c.	flour
2 qts.	milk
2 qts.	chicken stock
3 lbs.	chicken, cooked, neatly diced
2 oz.	pimientos, diced, (optional)

Simmer diced green pepper in 1-cup chicken stock 5 minutes. Make a roux from butter and flour; fry over low heat 5 minutes without letting it brown. While preparing roux, heat milk with 2 quarts of chicken stock. Pour milk mixture into roux and mix until smooth. Add neatly diced chicken. Add green pepper. Add pimiento, if desired, for color. Serve over toast.

CORN RELISH

1 (20 oz.) pkg.	frozen corn kernels
2 oz.	green pepper, chopped
2 oz.	red pepper, chopped
2 oz.	onions, chopped
2 oz.	celery, chopped
1 Tbsp.	prepared mustard
1 Tbsp.	mustard seed
2 tsp.	celery seed
1/4 tsp.	ground turmeric
1/2 c.	sugar
1 pt.	vinegar
2 tsp.	salt

Combine all ingredients and simmer 30 minutes. Cool; chill.

PICKLED BEETS

1 (approx. 72 oz.) can	cooked beets, drained, sliced
3 c.	vinegar
4	(half dollar sized) bay leaves
1 c.	sugar
1 Tbsp.	salt
8 oz.	onions, sliced

Combine all ingredients in crock and let set overnight. Juice can be saved for a second batch.

MACARONI SALAD

1 lb.	elbow macaroni
8 oz.	green pepper, diced
1 lb.	celery, diced
8 oz.	American cheese, grated or diced
1 pt.	relish
3 c.	mayonnaise
1 Tbsp.	salt
1/2 tsp.	white pepper

Cook macaroni 12 to 15 minutes; drain. Add remaining ingredients and mix. Refrigerate until ready to use.

QUICK 'N EASY CHEESE CAKE

1 (8 oz.) pkg.	cream cheese
1/3 c.	lemon juice
1 tsp.	vanilla
1 can	sweetened condensed milk, (not evaporated)
1	graham cracker crust
	Small cans fruit pie fillings, (optional)

Combine cream cheese with lemon juice, vanilla and sweetened condensed milk; blend until smooth. Scrape mixture into graham crack crust and chill 2 hours. Cut and serve. Small cans of fruit pie fillings can be used to add extra flavor to the cheese cake, although it has an excellent flavor by itself.

CARROT CAKE WITH CREAM CHEESE FROSTING

"I entered this cake in the Lake County Fair and it won a Blue Ribbon!"

3 c.	carrots, grated
2 c.	sugar
2 c.	flour
2 tsp.	cinnamon
2 tsp.	baking powder
1 tsp.	baking soda
1-1/4 c.	cooking oil
1 tsp.	salt
4	eggs

Combine all ingredients and mix. Transfer batter to greased 10x14-inch baking pan. Bake at 325 degrees 35 to 38 minutes.

Cream Cheese Frosting

1-1/2 sticks	butter or margarine
4 oz.	cream cheese
1 lb.	powdered sugar
1 tsp.	vanilla

Combine all ingredients in blender and mix until smooth. Frost cooled cake.

COOKIE RECIPES

Most cookie recipes begin with…cream shortening and sugar to a creamy paste. No need to cream the shortening and sugar in these cookie recipes. Just measure and mix. Test one cookie in a pie tin before baking off the whole batch. Adjust the recipe by adding a little more flour or more liquid.

FUDGE COOKIES

2 lbs., 4 oz.	flour
2-1/2 Tbsp.	baking powder
1 Tbsp.	salt
3/4 tsp.	baking soda
6 oz.	cocoa
1 lb., 2 oz.	shortening
1-1/2 lbs.	sugar
6	eggs
1 Tbsp.	vanilla
3 c.	(variable) milk

Measure all ingredients into mixing bowl and mix at medium speed to a smooth dough. Drop on greased baking sheets. Bake at 375 degrees 10 to 12 minutes. Remove from baking sheet while still warm.

GINGER COOKIES

1-1/2 lbs.	sugar
1 c.	shortening
3-1/2 Tbsp.	ginger
1 Tbsp.	cinnamon
1-1/4 Tbsp.	salt
4	whole eggs
1-1/2 Tbsp.	baking soda
2 c.	molasses
3 oz. (variable)	water
2-1/2 lbs.	flour

Measure ingredients into mixing bowl and mix at medium speed to a smooth dough. Roll dough to 1/4-inch thickness. Cut with floured cookie cutter and place on well-greased baking sheet. Bake at 375 degrees 10 to 12 minutes. Remove from baking sheet while still warm.

SOFT MOLASSES COOKIES

3 lbs.	flour
1-1/2 tsp.	baking powder
2-1/2 tsp.	baking soda
2 tsp.	salt
3 tsp.	ginger
1-1/2 Tbsp.	cinnamon
2-1/4 c.	shortening
2-1/4 c.	sugar
8	whole eggs
1-1/8 pts.	molasses
1 pt. + 1/2 c.	milk

Measure ingredients into mixing bowl and mix at medium speed to a smooth dough. Drop on greased baking sheet and bake at 375 degrees 10 to 12 minutes. Remove from baking sheet while still warm.

SOFT SUGAR COOKIES

3 lbs.	flour
2-1/2 Tbsp.	baking powder
1 Tbsp.	salt
3-1/2 Tbsp.	nutmeg
1-1/2 lbs.	shortening
2 lbs., 4 oz.	sugar
6	whole eggs
1 Tbsp.	vanilla
1 qt. + 1-1/2 c.	milk

Measure ingredients into mixing bowl and mix at medium speed to a smooth dough. Drop on greased baking sheet and bake at 375 degrees 8 to 10 minutes. Remove from baking sheet while still warm.

RICH SUGAR COOKIES

2 lbs.	sugar
1-1/2 lbs.	shortening
1-1/2 Tbsp.	salt
1-1/2 tsp.	mace
2 lbs., 12 oz.	flour
4-1/2 Tbsp.	baking powder
5	whole eggs
1 c.	milk

Measure ingredients into mixing bowl and mix at medium speed to a smooth dough. Roll dough out to 1/4-inch thickness. Cut out with cookie cutter and place on greased baking sheets. Bake at 375 degrees approximately 10 minutes.

MEMORIALS

The S.S. *Edmund Fitzgerald* and her crew of 29 are memorialized, and the tragic loss of life solemnly remembered, every November at Mariners' Church of Detroit (known to many as "The Maritime Sailors' Cathedral.")

The annual service follows the tradition set forth by Reverend Richard W. Ingalls, Rector of Mariners' Church, the morning after the *Fitzgerald* was lost in Lake Superior in 1975. After tolling the church bell 29 times, once for each man lost, Reverend Ingalls entered the sanctuary to remember the lost souls in his private prayers. Reverend Ingalls' private tribute is repeated and the bell at Mariners' Church has been rung 29 times every year since that fateful day of November 10, 1975, at the Annual *Edmund Fitzgerald* Memorial Service.

An Annual Memorial Service for the lost crew of the *Edmund Fitzgerald* is also held at the Great Lakes Shipwreck Museum, Whitefish Point, Lake Superior in Michigan's Upper Peninsula. With support from surviving relatives of the lost seamen, the original ship's bell was recovered from the wreckage in 1995 and replaced with a replica brass bell inscribed with each lost crewman's name. The original bell from the *Fitzgerald* is now part of the S.S. *Edmund Fitzgerald* memorial and display at the Great Lakes Shipwreck Museum.

Appetizers & Snacks

Appetizers

Bar Desserts

Beverages

Breads, Rolls, and Muffins

Breads

Pies

Salads

Fruit Salads

Sandwiches

Sauces and Seasonings

Soups & Chili

Chili

Vegetables and Side Dishes

Miscellaneous

Also available... *"Ships of the Great Lakes Keepsake Cookbook,"* the perfect keepsake gift from the Great Lakes. This unique 3-3/4x4-1/4-inch keepsake cookbook shares excerpts from the original book on a smaller scale. Hand-tied ribbons of blue, green and gold compliment the laminated cover, while inside readers find 100 pages of recipes, ship sketches and information on touring each vessel. Makes a unique kitchen accent, holiday ornament, or simply the perfect gift of remembrance from the magnificent ships that sail the great lakes.

Name: _____

Address: _____

City: _____

State: _____ Zip: _____

Phone: _____

E-mail: _____

Mail completed order form with payment payable to:

Creative Characters Publishing Group
P.O. Box 699 · Central Lake, MI 49622

Credit card orders, call **1-800-947-4136** *or fill in below*

☐ Visa   ☐ MasterCard   ☐ American Express

Card No.: _____ Expires: _____

Signature: _____

Please Send

_____ copies of Ships of the Great Lakes Cookbook @ $24.95 each (US Funds)

Amount . . . .$_____

Shipping . . . .$_____
(First copy ships for $5.95, additional copies to same address ship for $1.00 each - Note: shipping charges may be higher after February 2002. Please call).

_____ copies of Great Lakes Keepsake Cookbook @ $9.95 each (US Funds)

Amount . . . .$_____

Shipping . . . .$_____
(First copy ships for $4.95, additional copies or when ordered with Ships of the Great Lakes Cookbook add $1.00 per copy)

Michigan Residents
add 6% tax . . . .$_____

Total Enclosed: . . . .$══════════

Also available... *"Ships of the Great Lakes Keepsake Cookbook,"* the perfect keepsake gift from the Great Lakes. This unique 3-3/4x4-1/4-inch keepsake cookbook shares excerpts from the original book on a smaller scale. Hand-tied ribbons of blue, green and gold compliment the laminated cover, while inside readers find 100 pages of recipes, ship sketches and information on touring each vessel. Makes a unique kitchen accent, holiday ornament, or simply the perfect gift of remembrance from the magnificent ships that sail the great lakes.

Name: _____

Address: _____

City: _____

State: _____ Zip: _____

Phone: _____

E-mail: _____

Mail completed order form with payment payable to:

Creative Characters Publishing Group
P.O. Box 699 · Central Lake, MI 49622

Credit card orders, call **1-800-947-4136** *or fill in below*

☐ Visa   ☐ MasterCard   ☐ American Express

Card No.: _____ Expires: _____

Signature: _____

Please Send

_____ copies of Ships of the Great Lakes Cookbook @ $24.95 each (US Funds)

Amount . . . .$_____

Shipping . . . .$_____
(First copy ships for $5.95, additional copies to same address ship for $1.00 each)

_____ copies of Great Lakes Keepsake Cookbook @ $9.95 each (US Funds)

Amount . . . .$_____

Shipping . . . .$_____
(First copy ships for $4.95, additional copies or when ordered with Ships of the Great Lakes Cookbook add $1.00 per copy)

Michigan Residents
add 6% tax . . . .$_____

Total Enclosed: . . . .$_____